The Art of M&A Due Diligence

Other books in the McGraw-Hill Art of M&A series

The Art of M&A
The Art of M&A Integration
The Art of M&A Financing and Refinancing

The Art of M&A Due Diligence

Navigating Critical Steps & Uncovering Crucial Data

Alexandra Reed Lajoux

Charles Elson

With a Foreword by Philip J. Clements

McGraw-Hill

New York San Francisco Washington, D.C. Auckland Bogotá
Caracas Lisbon London Madrid Mexico City Milan
Montreal New Delhi San Juan Singapore
Sydney Tokyo Toronto

Library of Congress Cataloging-in-Publication Data

Lajoux, Alexandra Reed.
    The art of M&A due diligence : navigating critical steps & uncovering crucial data / by
Alexandra Reed Lajoux and Charles Elson
      p.   cm.
    ISBN 0-7863-1150-9
    1. Consolidation and merger of corporations—United States.   2. Liability (Law)—United
States.   3. Risk assessment—United States. I. Title: Art of M & A due diligence. II. Title:
Art of M and A due diligence. III. Elson, Charles (Charles M.), 1959- IV. Title.

KF1477 L35 2000
346.73'06626—dc21

00-029950
      CIP

McGraw-Hill

A Division of The **McGraw·Hill** Companies

1 2 3 4 5 6 7 8 9 0 AGM/AGM 0 9 8 7 6 5 4 3 2 1 0

ISBN 0-7863-1150-9

The sponsoring editor for this book was *Kelli Christiansen,* the editing supervisor was *Janice
Race,* and the production supervisor was *Tina Cameron.* It was set in Palatino by *Judy Brown.*

Printed and bound by Quebecor World/Martinsburg.

McGraw-Hill books are available at special quantity discounts to use as premiums and sales
promotions, or for use in corporate training programs. For more information, please write to
the Director of Special Sales, Professional Publishing, McGraw-Hill, Two Penn Plaza, New
York, NY 10121-2298. Or contact your local bookstore.

This publication is designed to provide accurate and authoritative information in regard to the
subject matter covered. It is sold with the understanding that neither the author nor the publisher is engaged in rendering legal, accounting, or other professional service. If legal advice or
other expert assistance is required, the services of a competent professional person should be
sought.

*—From a Declaration of Principles jointly adopted by a Committee of the American Bar Association
and a Committee of Publishers.*

 This book is printed on recycled, acid-free paper containing a minimum of 50%
recycled de-inked fiber.

This book is dedicated to our spouses

Bernard Lajoux

Aimee Elson

CONTENTS

PART ONE

THE DUE DILIGENCE PROCESS   1

Chapter 1

Conducting Due Diligence: An Overview   3

Introduction. Legal Foundations. The Scope of Due Diligence.
The Duration of Due Diligence. The Key Participants in Due
Diligence. Due Diligence and the Law. Securities Exchange Act of
1934. Verification and Risk Prevention. Concluding Comments.
Appendix 1A: Sample Confidentiality Agreement for Acquisition of a
Private Company. Appendix 1B: Sample Confidentiality Agreement
for Acquisition of a Publicly Held Company. Appendix 1C: Sample
Engagement Letter for a Consultant. Appendix 1D: Transaction
Timetable for Fast-Track Due Diligence. Appendix 1E: Sample
Preliminary Request List. Appendix 1F: Annotated Sample Initial
Document Request List. Endnotes.

Chapter 2

The Financial Statements Review   69

Introduction. Financial Statements. Key Ratios. Special Industry
Considerations. Red Flags. Assessing Internal Controls. The Role of
The Audit Committee. Concluding Comments. Appendix 2A: AICPA
Statement on Auditing Standards 82, "Consideration of Fraud in a
Financial Statement" (1997)—Excerpts. Endnotes.

Due Diligence: A Safety Net for Shareholder Value

Philip J. Clements, Partner
PricewaterhouseCoopers LLP
New York, New York

Throughout the world, business is being challenged to create shareholder value. Mergers and acquisitions have become a core part of creating such value. In 1999, reports Securities Data Publishing of Newark, New Jersey, nearly 33,000 companies worldwide announced $3.4 trillion worth of transactions—an all-time record that continues apace. In the first four months of 2000 alone, more than 11,653 companies worldwide announced M&A deals worth over $1.32 trillion. Yet despite the considerable interest and experience in M&A worldwide, many acquisitions fail to create value—and some actually diminish it. In a recent PricewaterhouseCoopers survey, up to 80 percent of M&A transactions destroyed or failed to create value. Why the shortfall?

While there is no single reason for the high failure rate, many transactions are unsuccessful because *the acquirer cut corners on due diligence*—downsizing or delegating important due diligence work. Mistakenly believing that they can gain time, save money, or spare feelings by shortening this deal phase, acquirers miss out on this valuable one-time chance to explore the risks inherent in buying another company before signing on the dotted line. Other contributing causes include lack of strategic clarity and failure to execute in line with the corporate strategic plan.

Exploring acquisition risks is more important today than ever, as the new e-business economy leads to so much merger activity that it becomes an end in itself. Companies are being created for the sole purpose of being acquired. For example, Lycos recently bought Valent Software Corporation, a virtual company, for $45 million. J. Scott Benson, former chief of Valent, has said that his goal from day one was to get acquired. He is not alone. As Mario Morino of the Morino Institute told a crowd of 300 at a February 2000 Netpreneur conference in Washington, D.C.: "You will *always* sell your business." The question for sellers and buyers alike is: At what price—and, more important, at what risk?

SAFETY NET

Due diligence is important in the New Economy for sellers and buyers alike, whether they are involved in traditional businesses or the dot-com world. It makes little difference whether the value of a company stems from tangible assets such as manufacturing plants or from intangible assets such as patents, trademarks, know-how, and even Internet domain names. *Every transaction requires due diligence.*

Simply put, in the transaction process, *due diligence is the safety net*. It reduces the potential of being caught by surprise when a transaction ends in lost shareholder value. With due diligence, validation of whether the deal will create value can occur in the transaction cycle rather than in the execution cycle. This affirmation takes into consideration four actions in the due diligence process: (1) confirming the strategy and the transaction's corresponding fit, (2) verifying that operations and assets are as represented, (3) determining whether the business plan has feasibility, and (4) evaluating opportunities to improve the strategy's execution. Thorough due diligence involves far more than analyzing financial statements.

Too often acquirers of public companies rely extensively on public disclosure documents, in effect letting the Securities and Exchange Commission do their work for them. But this is unwise. Certain laws limiting the exchange of information govern public companies and render a thorough evaluation difficult. The directors of public companies have the responsibility of overseeing their shareholders' interest in management's actions and ensuring that the transactions create value. They fulfill this obligation by evaluating due diligence and fairness opinions. Nevertheless, acquiring a public company is the ultimate "caveat emptor" transaction. After the closing, the acquirer is alone. Given the widely dispersed ownership of many public companies, there is no "seller" to go after.

The acquirer of a privately held company faces a different situation. Such an acquirer will by definition have access to a seller before and after the transaction. The question for such an acquirer, however, is this: How good are these numbers? Private companies do not have the same rigorous disclosure standards required of public companies. At times a buyer may have to "kick the tires" or "look under the hood" in a number of areas.

As this book explains in detail, an acquirer must look at a candidate company's potential exposure to a broad variety of risks—financial, operational, and legal, as well as transactional. Before plunging into a detailed examination of these areas, readers may want to consider these brief examples based on my own knowledge and experience.

HIGHLIGHTS

In the *financial* area, due diligence must not only evaluate past operating results, but also incorporate those results into the acquisition business case, taking competitive threats into account. This applies whether the focus is on revenues, operating margins, cash flow, or any other financial category. Consider revenues, for example. Projected revenue growth may be based on market positioning, new product introduction, or market expansion. All these need to be checked out. In "kicking the tires," companies need to take advantage of the information age, which can allow for intensive market position analysis—including analysis of competitive threats. Take the case of the large pharmaceutical company that purchased a new medical device company on the basis of limited competitive market positioning with anticipated high unit pricing. Shortly after closing, two competitors entered the market, driving prices down. Bad luck? The product was an extension into a new area. Due diligence in the form of competitive threat analysis may well have prevented this problem.

In the *operational* area, acquirers have a multitude of issues to consider. These include not only the quality of management systems they have put in place, but also the quality of the people running those systems. Sellers and buyers alike can benefit from discreet background checks on their new partners. More generally, there is the issue of postacquisition culture and merger integration. Pan American World Airways acquired National Airways decades ago to create feeder routes for PanAm's international flights. The culture clash between the two employee groups kept the companies from integrating for years and contributed to PanAm's eventual demise. Cultural due diligence could have helped the company plan its integration of human resources.

In the *legal* arena, it is imperative to take into account intellectual property law. The following example shows why. Recently, a public company represented itself, to a group of investors, as the holder of a patent on new medical technology that would "revolutionize" long-term care. The investors agreed to form a company to bring the product to the U.S. market. The product was well received until the shocking revelation that the patent was in a foreign country, not the United States. Preinvestment due diligence could have saved the investors millions, and spared the resulting litigation.

Transactional due diligence is a grand summary of all the above, as contained in the acquisition agreement. The buyer should seize due diligence as the opportunity to thoroughly evaluate the seller's representations, including representations claiming ownership of assets. Confirmation of asset ownership may seem too basic for deliberation. Yet as the previous example shows, for companies with a global presence, this simple step is critical to avoiding loss. Also important is an analysis of the proposed transaction structure with respect to tax, accounting, and securities law issues. The fairness opinion itself can benefit from "due diligence" scrutiny. Is it truly independent? In the United States, the investment banker advising management generally renders the opinion. A far more rigorous approach to this important aspect of due diligence would be to require an independent expert—one unaffiliated with the transaction—to render the fairness opinion.

MINDSET

All four of these areas are crucial, and reading this book can help buyers and sellers master them. But due diligence, ultimately, cannot be done "by the book." It must become a mindset—a mentality that asks questions constantly. Every acquisitive company has flushed out classic postacquisition projection errors through due diligence—or wished they had. One classic example is the growth in unit sales that far outstrips the existing plant's capacity. Another is cost savings through staff reductions in warehouses that will leave no one to load the trucks. Or take the case of projected margin reversals that cannot be supported by current trends. The list is quite extensive. As an acquirer, you need to start making your own list now—before you buy. As a seller, you need to anticipate and correct such problems before you sell.

While the variables related to acquisition success are numerous, the message from a long line of mergers and acquisitions is quite clear. Due diligence is one of the cornerstones of acquisition success. All companies, large or small, public or private, should build acquisition oversight on a firm foundation of clear business strategy, thorough due diligence, and effective integration plans. Having an in-depth understanding of the shareholder value creation expectation of the acquisition, validated by due diligence and subsequently tracked for achievement, can ensure success for any transaction.

Philip J. Clements, a Partner with PricewaterhouseCoopers LLP, New York, is the firm's Global Leader of Corporate Value Consulting (CVC). CVC's 1,000 professionals help companies around the globe address business issues surrounding the definition, creation, and enhancement of shareholder value. Mr. Clements has worked with leading companies in the defense, financial services, retail, pharmaceuticals, telecommunications, and utilities industries, among others. Prior to heading up CVC, he led the investment banking practice at PricewaterhouseCoopers Securities LLC, and the corporate finance practice at the predecessor firm Coopers & Lybrand LLP. Mr. Clements serves on the PricewaterhouseCoopers Global Oversight Board and the U.S. Board of Partners.

PREFACE AND ACKNOWLEDGMENTS

How diligent must an acquirer be during the "due diligence" phase of an acquisition? Judging from some of the books now available on the subject, acquirers cannot be too careful. Some buyers spend millions of dollars identifying every possible risk before signing on the dotted line.

This thoroughness is encouraged by the existing guides to due diligence, which feature long lists of applicable laws and legal precedents—depicting the typical selling company as a vast field of land mines just waiting to explode. The message of these guides is clear: "Watch out! After acquiring a company, you can become insolvent or get sued, and insurance may not cover you—so beware!" Hearing this, prudent deal makers have only one choice: to walk away from the deal table and go back to their day jobs.

Our book aims higher. We will urge not just *diligence*, but *due* diligence—the care that is *commensurate* with the deal at hand—a process of verification tempered with a sensible level of *trust*. That is, rather than presenting you, the reader, with a barrage of risks to sort out on your own, we intend to show how to *predict* and—more important—*limit* the risks inherent in acquisitions.

- To help you *predict* postmerger risk, Part One discusses risk in three categories: *financial statement risk, operational risk,* and *liability risk.* Part Two examines *transactional risk,* relating to the transaction itself. Part Three presents a closer look at legal compliance, describing the various statutes and agencies with authority in key areas ranging from antitrust law to employment law.
- To help you *limit* risk, we explain throughout this book how the U.S. legal system can work to protect your decisions as an acquirer, as long as you make those decisions in good faith and with due care.

In covering these topics, we aim to be comprehensive, but no book can cover all the topics of interest to every acquirer. We urge readers to seek the expert opinions of practicing attorneys and accountants—just as we have done.

Throughout this book, we use the question-and-answer format adopted since the beginning of the Art of M&A series, starting the with first edition of *The Art of M&A* in 1989.

ACKNOWLEDGMENTS

The basic concept of this book began over a decade ago, in 1987, at Lane & Edson, P.C., Washington, D.C. The firm's founders, Bruce Lane and Charles Edson, joining with Stanley Foster Reed, founder of *Mergers & Acquisitions* magazine, asked Alexandra Lajoux to interview them and the firms' mergers and acquisitions specialists on the work they were doing in due diligence and other areas. The transcripts of those interviews formed the foundation for *The Art of M&A: A Merger/Buyout/Acquisition Guide* (now in its third edition with McGraw-Hill) as well as a series of "spin-off" books published by McGraw-Hill.

The spin-off books build on existing sections in the basic *Art of M&A* guide (sometimes excerpting sections verbatim), but each book goes into greater depth. The first two titles in the series covered integration and financing; this book covers due diligence. Dr. Lajoux is honored to have Professor Charles M. Elson, attorney, scholar, and corporate director, join her in this endeavor.

The authors of this book in turn are pleased to draw on the wisdom of others. Former Lane & Edson Partner Eugene M. Propper (now with the law firm of Holland & Knight in Washington, D.C.) contributed substantially to the due diligence chapter in the original (1989) edition of *The Art of M&A*. Thomas Weill (now with Skadden Arps in Houston, Texas) was the lead contributor to that book's chapter on closing. Richard L. Perkal (now a partner with Kirkland & Ellis, Washington, D.C.) wrote that book's original materials on acquisition agreements, and has reviewed relevant portions in the pages ahead. Mr. Perkal has worked on financings, refinancings, debt and equity issues, workouts, venture capital, and a variety of minority investments.

In addition, we would like to extend thanks to the following individuals, chapter by chapter:

Chapter 1: Conducting Due Diligence: An Overview. This book benefits from the wisdom of speakers at the 1999 Conferences on Conducting Due Diligence, held by the Practicing Law Institute, chaired by L. Markus Wiltshire, Brown & Wood LLP, New York, and Katherine Hudson Zrike, Merrill Lynch & Co., Inc., New York. These contributors are cited in the end-of-chapter notes. Special thanks go to Mark Schonberger, Partner, Battle & Fowler LLP, New York, who generously provided many of the forms in this book, including the forms at the end of Chapter 1. The forms reflect Mr. Schonberger's extensive experience working in a variety of transactions, including acquisitions, joint ventures, and public and private securities offerings.

Chapter 2: The Financial Statements Review. This chapter owes a debt to the many sources cited in its notes. In particular, we acknowledge the expertise of John Flaherty, Chairman, Committee of Sponsoring Organizations of the Treadway Commission, Longboat, Florida; and John C. Fletcher, Managing Director, Delta Control Group, Geneva, Switzerland. We also acknowledge the collective wisdom of the members of the National Association of Corporate Directors (NACD) Blue Ribbon Commission on Audit Committees. This group, which included coauthor Charles Elson, was chaired by A. A. Sommer, Jr., of Counsel, Morgan Lewis & Bockius, Washington, D.C.

Chapter 3: The Operations and Management Review. A major contributor to this chapter was Jonny Frank, Partner, PricewaterhouseCoopers, New York. PwC is the first of the Big Five professional services firms to become fully licensed for investigation. We owe John Verna, Senior Vice President, Kroll Associates, Washington, D.C., a great debt for sharing his expertise in the investigation and management of risk. Other contributors included Bobby Vick, Partner, Vick & Co., LLP, and Cochair, Kennesaw State University Corporate Governance Center, Atlanta, Georgia; and Michael J. Riley, CEO and Director, Cutler Manufacturing Co., Lakeland, Florida.

Chapter 4: The Legal Compliance Review. Expertise on director and officer liability insurance came from Ty R. Salalow, Chief Underwriting Officer, National Union, New York, New York.

Chapter 5: The Documentation and Transaction Review. Richard Perkal, mentioned above, was the original author of the basic text of this chapter, updated for the present edition.

Chapter 6: Detecting Exposure Under Securities Law. Daniel A. MacMullan, Partner, PricewaterhouseCoopers, Philadelphia, answered our questions on fairness opinions.

Chapter 7: Detecting Exposure Under Tax Law and Accounting Regulations. This chapter still contains wisdom provided by attorney Michael J. Kliegman, formerly with Lane and Edson, PC. Mr. Kliegman is now a partner with PricewaterhouseCoopers LLP, New York.

Chapter 9: Detecting Exposure Under Intellectual Property Laws. Sincere thanks go to Carl Davis, Partner, Kennedy, Davis & Hodge, Atlanta, Georgia; David Ashby, Flehr Hohbach Test Albritton & Herbert LLP, Palo Alto, California, and Julie L. Davis, Partner, Arthur Andersen, Chicago, for materials on intellectual property due diligence.

Chapter 12: Detecting Exposure Under Employment Laws. We acknowledge gratefully the contributions of Christine A. Amalfe, Gibbons, Del Deo, Dolan,

Griffinger & Vecchione, Newark, New Jersey. Ms. Amalfe sent us many of the background materials cited in this chapter, and provided expert commentary as the lead reviewer of this chapter.

In addition, we extend thanks to the individuals who helped us with the following items:

Master Due Diligence Checklist. This list is an expanded version of a checklist originally prepared by Dan Goldwasser, Esq., New York. Denis C. Picard, Partner, PricewaterhouseCoopers, advised the authors on checklist elements. Based in New York and Florham Park, New Jersey, Mr. Picard heads the firm's Merger and Acquisition Risk Services practice. Kaoru Usami, Senior Manager, Orion Power Holdings, Inc., Baltimore, Maryland, also provided considerable expertise for this checklist.

Sample Acquisition Agreement. The authors extend their appreciation to Richard L. Perkal, Partner, Kirkland & Ellis, Washington, D.C., mentioned above, and to Jack M. Feder, an independent M&A consultant based in Washington, D.C. When Mssrs. Perkal and Feder were attorneys with Lane & Edson, they provided the first version of this annotated agreement.

Landmark Due Diligence Cases. The authors have compiled these cases on the basis of their own research, with the help of FindLaw.com, law.cornell.edu, and various experts. The cases in Part One were based in part on writings of Michael P. Marsalese, an attorney in private practice in Troy, Michigan (published in Reed and Lajoux, op. cit.). In researching cases decided conclusively before 1981, we also delved into *The Corporate Directors' Legal Casebook: Landmark Cases* (Philadelphia, Pa.: Directors and Boards, 1981). The cases in Part Two came from Reed and Lajoux, op. cit., plus a variety of sources. Cases in environmental law came from Sean Monagan, Shanley & Fisher PC, Morristown, New Jersey; and cases in patent law came form Carol Anne Been, Sonnenschein, Nath & Rosenthal, Chicago. The environmental and patent cases appeared in *Conducting Due Diligence 1999* (Minneapolis, Minn.: Practising Law Institute, 1999), pp. 907–912 and 1028–1030.

The Federal Circuit Courts. This list was adapted with permission from the *1999 Judicial Staff Directory* (Mount Vernon, Va.: Staff Directories, Ltd., 1999).

In closing, we wish to thank the knowledgeable, talented, and industrious crew at McGraw-Hill. First acknowledgments go to our sponsoring editor Kelli Christiansen, who offered a thorough and candid critique of each chapter as we journeyed through the first draft. Also on our thank-you list: copy editor Louise Marinis, typesetter Judy Brown, proofreader Michael Ryder, and indexer Kay Schlembach. The McGraw-Hill name is known worldwide for excellence, thanks to superbly competent employees and subcontractors such as these. Finally, we wish to thank Mary Graham and Braulio Agnese, independent editors, for proofreading this and all books in the *Art of M&A* series.

The Due Diligence Process

Conducting due diligence in a merger or acquisition requires a sense of the whole as well as of all key parts. Thus in Chapter 1 we provide broad coverage of the M&A due diligence process: what it is, who conducts it, and when it begins and ends. Then, in the following chapters, we go into greater depth on how due diligence is conducted in various areas: financial, operational, and legal.

In Chapter 2, after a discussion of financial reporting, we introduce the important topic of internal controls. Citing the Committee of Sponsoring Organizations of the Treadway Commission (COSO), leading standard setter for this area, we define controls as the interplay of financial reporting with operations and compliance. In Chapters 3 and 4 we cover these two subjects in greater depth.

Chapter 3 shows acquirers how to study a candidate company's operations and management. Although we emphasize a traditional due diligence approach, we also cover conflict resolution and culture—two new entrants into M&A due diligence work.

Chapter 4 shows acquirers how to assess the litigation risks that may lie ahead. We call for caution in dealing with each and every constituency—including customers, employees, shareholders, and suppliers—and, of course, with federal and state governments, which may sue on behalf of any of these constituencies or the broader public. (In Part Three, we follow through on the compliance theme, presenting overviews of the major statutes and agencies in these areas.)

Throughout Part One, we cite the securities laws. We do this not merely to encourage securities law compliance, although this is certainly important. Rather, we quote these laws to help acquirers and sellers meet their own informational needs.

Conducting Due Diligence: An Overview

Risk and opportunity—they are opposite sides of the same coin.

J. Michael Cook
Chairman and CEO, Retired
Deloitte & Touche LLP

INTRODUCTION

The due diligence phase of any acquisition—the study of the risks that the deal poses—can make the difference between success and failure. Yet despite its importance, the due diligence phase need not dominate the acquisition process. Rather, it must be considered in conjunction with other acquisition activities and goals, including strategic plans, valuation, financing, and—most important—the future of the combined company, with all its *new* risks and opportunities.

To put due diligence in its proper perspective, we begin this chapter with the legal foundations of due diligence. Then we discuss the "what, when, and who" of due diligence—that is, *scope, duration,* and *key participants.* We then give some further background on the legal aspects of due diligence (focusing on the "due diligence" in the *securities law* context). Finally, we close with suggestions for *verification* and *risk prevention.*

Our goal: to build a strong platform of understanding for the more detailed work ahead.

LEGAL FOUNDATIONS

What are the legal origins of due diligence?

The term *due diligence* originated in so-called *common law,* also known as the case law—the law that develops through decisions of judges in settling actual

3

disputes. The common law system arose in medieval England after the Norman Conquest, and is still in use there as well as in the United States, among other countries. In adopting this approach to legal regulation, judges resolve disputes by using the precedents of previous case decisions, rather than following legislatively enacted rules. Much of U.S. common law, however, has been codified into the legislatively enacted statutes of individual states as well as in a widely used guide to commercial transactions called the Uniform Commercial Code. (For more about the U.S. legal system, see Chapter 4.)

The precise origins of due diligence are lost in the mists of time. *Black's Legal Dictionary* defines due diligence as "the diligence reasonably expected from, and ordinarily exercised by, a person who seeks to satisfy a legal requirement or to discharge an obligation."[1]

The concept of diligence clearly goes back to the Roman law concept of *diligentia*. Roman law distinguished two main types of diligence: *diligentia quam suis rebus*, the care that an ordinary person exercises in managing his or her affairs, versus *diligentia exactissima* or *diligentia boni patrisfamilia*, a more exacting care, exercised by the head of a family.[2] English law spoke of diligence as early as the seventeenth century, and by the eighteenth century had developed three kinds:

> 1) Common or ordinary . . . 2) High or great, which is extraordinary diligence . . .
> 3) Low or slight, which is that which persons of less than common prudence, or indeed of any prudence at all, take of their own concerns.[3]

The question obviously arises: What order of diligence is "due" diligence? Is it ordinary, extraordinary, or slight? In the United States, the term *due diligence* describes a general duty to exercise care in any transaction. For example, in securities law, the term refers to the duty of care and review exercised by officers, directors, underwriters, and others in connection with public offerings of securities. What level of diligence should be expected of them?

Case law in the United States suggests an ordinary standard—as explained later in this chapter and in Chapter 4. Clearly, however, the more diligence expended on a transaction, the lower the risk of problems afterward. To be safe, one might well revert to a strict "high Roman" standard. According to one early source, "If the interests of the parties are not identical, the Roman law, at least, requires extraordinary diligence."[4]

The most commonly cited "due diligence" case is *Escott v. BarChris Construction Corp.* (1968). In this case, holders of debt (5½ percent 15-year convertible subordinated debentures) sued certain directors and officers of BarChris, a bowling alley builder, as well as the company's advisers. The plaintiffs accused BarChris of securities fraud after the company went bankrupt. Although this was a securities offering case, not a merger case, it is considered instructive to acquirers. A summary of this case and other illustrative cases appears at the end of this book. All these cases—even those not directly pertaining to M&A due diligence—can help in the conduct of such an activity.

What exactly is M&A due diligence?

In mergers and acquisitions (M&A), due diligence refers primarily to an acquirer's review of an acquisition candidate[5] to make sure that its purchase would pose no unnecessary risks to the acquirer's shareholders. The term also refers to the mutual review undertaken by the two parties to a merger. Finally, the phrase can apply to a candidate company's review of the acquirer to ensure that relinquishing control will not bring unreasonable risks to the company's owners or employees.

The basic function of M&A due diligence, then, is to assess the benefits and the liabilities of a proposed acquisition by inquiring into all relevant aspects of the past, present, and predictable future of the business to be purchased. Those making this assessment should focus on risk.

Acquirers generally do this by creating a checklist of needed information (see Appendix 1A for a sample), and then obtaining that information by:

- Examining financial statements (see Chapter 2).
- Assessing management and operations (see Chapter 3).
- Reviewing legal liability (see Chapter 4).

In this process, acquirers may conduct interviews and visit sites, maintaining records of all this information. Chapter 3 contains guidance on setting up a due diligence filing system.

Caveat: An acquirer cannot, and should not be expected to, discover every possible risk. The sheer effort required to do so could surely bankrupt the acquirer and certainly alienate the seller.[6] Companies are complex entities operating in a complex world; no investigation can uncover all potential risks. Due diligence conducted "must be reasonable, not perfect." Even if an expert can later find fault, its "ability to poke holes in the diligence conducted is not dispositive."[7]

THE SCOPE OF DUE DILIGENCE

What general areas should the due diligence review cover?

At a minimum, the due diligence effort should include:

- Financial statements *review* (to confirm the existence of assets, liabilities, and equity in the balance sheet, and to determine the financial health of the company based on the income statement).
- *Management and operations review* (to determine the quality and reliability of financial statements, and to gain a sense of contingencies beyond the financial statements).
- *Legal compliance review* (to check for potential future legal problems stemming from the candidate company's past).
- *Document and transaction review* (to ensure that the paperwork of the deal is in order, and that the structure of the transaction is appropriate).

These parts of due diligence are listed in a typical sequence, in which the most accessible information is reviewed first, with the least accessible (or transaction-dependent) information reviewed last. But note: These phases may or may not be sequential, and may or may not be in this order. For example, if an acquisition candidate is known to be close to resolving a major lawsuit, then the legal compliance review might occur very early on.

The first three areas are covered in separate chapters in Part One. Transactional review is examined in Part Two. Legal compliance is covered in more depth in Part Three.

How extensive should due diligence be?

How far a buyer wishes to go in the due diligence process depends in part on how much time the buyer has and how much money it has to investigate the company it wishes to buy. This will depend to some extent on the status of the company in the community, the years it has been in business, whether it has been audited by a major firm for some years, whether executive turnover is low, and any other factor that helps establish the basic stability of the firm, such as long-term customer retention. If a broker is involved in the transaction, the broker may wish to require some basic level of acquirer due diligence. In fact, it is not unusual for brokers to include a contractual requirement that the purchaser undertake due diligence.[8]

Furthermore, due diligence can vary by type of company. The due diligence work in the acquisition of a large, diversified, global manufacturer listed on several stock exchanges is obviously far more extensive than the work involved for a small, single-product, domestic service firm that is privately owned. Due diligence in public companies can be more complex than due diligence in private companies. Manufacturers have greater legal exposure than many service companies. Finally, transaction type can limit the due diligence effort, since stock purchases trigger more due diligence responsibilities than do asset purchases.

- In any sale of *stock*, no matter how accounted for, the resulting entity will bear all the liabilities of both parties to the transactions, so the level of due diligence obviously has to be as extensive as possible.[9]
- In sales of *assets*, by contrast, the structure of the transaction can make a significant difference. In general (with some exceptions), when a company sells or otherwise transfers all its assets to another company via *acquisition*, the successor is *not liable for the debts and legal liabilities of the predecessor* unless it expressly assumes them. In classic asset sales, therefore, the due diligence effort need not include a study of debts and legal liability exposure. On the other hand, acquirers that are used to the protections of securities laws should realize that these laws do not apply to any transaction structured as an asset sale. Note also: If the asset sale is structured as a *merger*, then the acquirer *does* assume debts and legal liabilities unless the seller expressly retains them.[10]

Source of financing is another determining factor. In acquisitions financed through equity, all parties are interested in uncovering problems early, because postdeal problems that *could* or *should* have been uncovered can be very expensive to solve, and can result in lawsuits against all parties involved. As one due diligence expert states, "Risk disclosure is cheap. Defending litigation is not."[11] So it is useful for a company conducting due diligence to continually ask itself (as well as those interviewed during the due diligence process) what could possibly go wrong, and to disclose all *material* risks that have any likelihood at all of occurring.

We emphasize the term *material*, because it is crucial to due diligence—and a staple of U.S. disclosure rules. (In the case of a public company, "material" contracts, debt, litigation, and risks are often identified in the 10-K, 10-Q, registration statement, and proxy statement.) In a word, material means important, and the point of due diligence is to identify potential risks that could be important later on.

Over time, a number of specific definitions for materiality have evolved—"more than 5 percent," "more than $1 million," and so forth. Many of these are contained in U.S. securities and tax laws themselves. (Consider the 5 percent ownership disclosure triggers of Section 13B or the $1 million pay cap for compensation deductions under Section 162(m) of the tax code.) Setting numerical benchmarks is helpful, and such benchmarks usefully appear in due diligence documents. But these thresholds, while useful, may not be enough.

According to the August 1999 Staff Accounting Memorandum 99 (SAM 99) of the Securities and Exchange Commission (SEC), materiality is not merely a matter of percentage or amount. Rather, it is a highly relative term. It refers to a level that would be considered significant by the average prudent investor.[12]

How is due diligence different for public versus private companies?

Any company that has issued securities has already been the subject of a due diligence study by underwriters and their counsel in preparing the company's original prospectus. Acquirers, then, can use the company's prospectus as a guide, and can rely to some extent on the due diligence that the prospectus required. The extent of this due diligence will depend on the size of the offering and the history of the company's previous security registrations, as explained further below in the section on securities laws.

If the candidate company has issued stock any time in the last several months, the acquirer can rely on the due diligence conducted by the underwriter at that time, with "bringdown" updates as necessary. Underwriter due diligence conducted a year or more ago, however, leaves a cold trail that acquirers will need to retrace—and perhaps even reconstruct in detail.

If the candidate has been a public company for some time, it will have 10Ks and 10Qs on file with the SEC. The buyer should obtain copies of these, and examine closely the agreements, contracts, and other significant company documents that may be filed with them as exhibits.

In private companies, due diligence becomes a much more intensive process. The acquirer will have to do more investigation of the seller, and will ask the seller to provide assurances via *representations* (statements) and *warranties* (promises) in the acquisition agreement. Although representations and warranties are seen in contracts with both public and privately owned candidates, they are more extensive in private company deals.

Thus the scope of a private company investigation depends in part on what information the seller is willing to give in the form of the representations and warranties to be included in the purchase agreement. Beware the seller that resists making any representations or warranties. Such deals are high-risk transactions and are rarely the bargains they appear to be. If stockholders wind up losing money, the law may not necessarily protect the hasty wheeler-dealer on either side despite the shelter of the famed business judgment rule, explained in Chapter 4. Many sellers discourage thorough due diligence. In negotiating reductions in the representations and warranties, they will insist that buyers "see for themselves" by visiting a key plant or office. By all means, buyers should do so, but without letting such "eyeballing" and "tire kicking" relieve the seller of any possibility of misrepresentation.

Even if the buyer decides to rely on the seller's representations and warranties, it must nevertheless still conduct at least enough due diligence to be assured that there will be a solvent company and/or seller to back the representations and warranties. If there is any doubt, the acquirer must establish cash reserves.

How can the buyer conduct proper due diligence without harming its relationship with the seller?

Communication is key. This process begins with the letter of intent and is reinforced in the acquisition agreement. Negotiated by both buyer and seller, these documents should lay down the ground rules for due diligence. For example, they should:

- State the time available for due diligence.
- Promise the buyer access to the selling company's personnel, sites, and files.

With respect to site examination, here is some sample language from a typical acquisition agreement (which appears at the end of this book).

> Section 6.6. Investigation by Buyer. The Seller and Company shall, and the Company shall cause its Subsidiaries to, afford to the officers and authorized representatives of the Buyer free and full access, during normal business hours and upon reasonable prior notice, to the offices, plants, properties, books, and records of the Company and its Subsidiaries in order that the Buyer may have full opportunity to make such **investigations** of the business, operations, assets, properties, and legal and financial condition of the Company and its Subsidiaries as the Buyer deems reasonably necessary or desirable; and the officers of the Seller, the Company, and its Subsidiaries shall furnish the Buyer with such additional financial and operating data and other information relating to the business operations, assets, properties, and legal and financial condition of the Company and its Subsidiaries as the Buyer shall from time to time reasonably request.
>
> Prior to the Closing Date, or at all times if this Agreement shall be terminated, the Buyer shall, except as may be otherwise required by applicable law, hold confidential all information obtained pursuant to this Section 6.6 with respect to the Company and its Subsidiaries and, if this Agreement shall be terminated, shall return to the Company and its Subsidiaries all such information as shall be in documentary form and shall not use any information obtained pursuant to this Section 6.6 in any manner that would have a material adverse consequence to the Company or its Subsidiaries.

The representations, warranties, and agreements of the Seller, the Company, and its Subsidiaries set forth in this Agreement shall be effective regardless of any investigation that the Buyer has undertaken or failed to undertake.

A few notes about this language (as stated in the annotations to this agreement in the back of the book):

- The first paragraph of this clause is called an *investigation covenant*. It ensures that the seller will cooperate with the buyer by granting access and logistical support for the buyer's due diligence review of the seller and its subsidiaries. This is one of the most valuable parts of any acquisition agreement.
- The second paragraph, sometimes nicknamed a *burn or return* provision, may help allay seller fears about confidentiality. Note, however, that the seller will often require the prospective buyer to enter into a separate confidentiality agreement. Sample confidentiality agreements are found in Appendices 1A and 1B at the end of this chapter.
- The third paragraph might be called an *off-the-hook* clause. It makes a statement that removes the burden of perfect investigation from the acquirer. Without such a statement, the seller can avoid liability following a breach of contract. It can argue that since the buyer could have discovered the breach during its investigation of the seller's company, the seller should be relieved of any responsibility for such misrepresentations.

How can the buyer ensure seller cooperation in a due diligence investigation of broad scope?

The seller is more likely to cooperate when the buyer (or the buyer's counsel) conveys the important message that full exploration of facts and risks benefits everyone. At the very least, it can help protect against the risk of an even more adversarial process via cross-examination in court, if either the seller or buyer is sued after the transaction is closed.[13] For example, just as a buyer can be sued for paying too much money for an acquisition, a seller may be sued for accepting too little money. Also, a seller's reputation may be damaged if—even inadvertently—it provides false information. The buyer's investigation of the seller's representations can thus be a boon to the seller.

Buyers can invite sellers to conduct their own due diligence. All sellers need to conduct some kind of due diligence in connection with the legal opinions to be given. And the seller will need to conduct due diligence of the buyer when the buyer is paying for the acquisition with its stock. Finally, it is in the interests of the seller to investigate the buyer if the seller's ownership and/or employment will continue after the sale of the business.

Also, by conducting its own due diligence, the seller is more likely to develop an appreciation for what the acquirer is doing in a due diligence investigation.

Throughout the process, the buyer should be sensitive to the stress on its own personnel and on its relationship with the seller. The due diligence effort is a disruption of the ordinary business routine and may be viewed by the seller as a sign of unwarranted suspicion by the buyer and disregard for the seller's interests. The seller may fear adverse consequences for the conduct of its business and its future sale to others if the contemplated deal does not close. Indeed, many potential transactions do fall through because of the rigors of the due diligence process, which can alienate and inconvenience the seller, the buyer, or both.

Thorough due diligence can lessen the feelings of mutual trust between buyer and seller. It can also substantially increase pretransaction costs and can absorb the attention of key employees who have other jobs to do. Nonetheless, it is unavoidable. The key is to make the process thorough, yet reasonable.

Suppose the seller refuses to produce the requested documentation but offers access to its files?

If the buyer is faced with a do-it-yourself due diligence process, it must organize an on-site document review effort. This will typically entail traveling to the entity's corporate headquarters and, depending on the number of sites involved and the nature of the business conducted at each site, other sites as well.

As mentioned before, the acquisition agreement will form the basis for a checklist, which the acquirer may expand as necessary. The seller should be willing to direct the buyer to employees with knowledge of each subject of inquiry detailed on the checklist or, at least, to the relevant files.

The acquisition agreement should include the seller's representation to the buyer that the buyer will have access to all relevant files for requested information. The buyer should also ask the seller to provide sufficient personnel and photocopying facilities to make copies of all significant documents produced by the review effort. Copying of documents may also be specified in the acquisition agreement. If the seller refuses to cooperate, the buyer may have to rent photocopying machines and hire temporary help. This is not of grave consequence, but the seller should be urged to cooperate. A refusal to support appropriate due diligence will not look good for the seller should the acquisition ever undergo judicial review for any reason.

As a courtesy to the seller and to avoid confusion over documents, which can vary in format from company to company, the buyer should make two copies of each document—one for itself and one for the seller. In any event, some identification system involving numbering should be devised to keep track of the documents produced, especially of those that are copied. For a sample numbering system, see the Index of Data Room Documents at the end of Chapter 3 (Appendix 3A).

What forms can an acquirer use to keep the due diligence review on track?

All important financial, operational, legal, and transactional elements should appear in the two key documents driving the due diligence process:

- Due diligence "checklist"
- Acquisition agreement

The checklist should be drafted first, and should undergo constant revision as the acquirer discovers important points. The acquisition agreement will express the most important elements on the checklist. In fact, the two documents should parallel each other. Examples of a checklist and an agreement appear at the end of this book.[14]

The checklist reminds buyers of the types of issues they should investigate. As mentioned, the list will often parallel the structure of the representations and warranties that the seller makes in the acquisition agreement. It is important to note, however, that in its early stages, the list cannot be considered final. As one expert notes, it is helpful to avoid a rigid "checklist mentality" when conducting due diligence. Instead, the investigators should focus on the particular issues that arise. They should "view the effort as a series of independent mini-investigations with respect to the key issues."[15]

In drafting a workable checklist, acquirers should concentrate on areas of particular relevance to the transaction at hand. For example, inquiries regarding the frequency of returned goods are more relevant to a consumer goods retail business than to a management consulting business. Similarly, questions regarding environmental violations are obviously more critical in acquiring a manufacturing operation than in buying a department store chain.

In the acquisition of a large company, the checklist may reflect a threshold of materiality. For example, it may include only capital expenditures above $50,000, or it may set a limit of five years back for certain documents. These limits are obviously practical when an all-inclusive checklist would impose high cost and little benefit. Nonetheless, such limits should be used with caution. As noted above, materiality transcends simple numbers: the acquirer should search for what is truly material, even if it lies beyond a threshold.

Also, the seller may try to apply the same threshold to its representations and warranties—an action clearly not in the interests of the acquirer, which will want the representations and warranties to be as extensive as possible.

The checklist should be broad, but not overly ambitious. The seller will not welcome any request for information that requires the creation of new documentation. Therefore, whenever possible, the checklist should require the seller to produce only documents already in existence. The purchaser should attempt to obtain other data through interviews with the seller's officers or by other appropriate investigative means.

What other forms are useful in conducting due diligence?

In addition to the checklist and agreement, it is very important to have these forms:

- Transaction timetable
- Document request lists

Samples of these documents appear at the end of this chapter (Appendixes 1D through 1F).

Also, in collecting and managing information about the selling company, the acquirer will find the following forms useful:[16]

- "Closing memorandum" including:
  - Abstract for review of minute books
  - Index of documents

Copies of these forms appear at the end of Chapter 5, which goes into more detail about "transactional due diligence"—that is, making sure the documentation of the deal is in order.

What agreements should the acquirer sign before engaging in due diligence?

Initial forms include:

- Confidentiality agreement
- Engagement letter for consultant

See the end of this chapter for samples. (Appendixes 1A through 1C).

THE DURATION OF DUE DILIGENCE

When does the due diligence process begin?

The initial stages of due diligence unfold during the search and screen, valuation, and financing processes. During these phases, the acquirer asks and answers three opening questions:

- Is it in our stockholders' long-term interests to own and operate this company?
- How much is it worth?
- Can we afford it?

More thorough due diligence goes beyond these questions and asks:

- Do the firm's financial statements reveal any signs of insolvency or fraud?
- Do the firm's operations show any signs of weak internal controls?
- Does the firm run the risk of any major postmerger litigation by the government or others?

The next three chapters of this book are devoted to these questions.

How long should the due diligence process take?

Due diligence occurs throughout the acquisition process, which lasts from a few weeks to a year or more. A rule of thumb is "as long as it takes—but no longer." If the parties are eager to deal, they may substitute extensive warranties for the due diligence process.

When buyers do initiate a formal, organized due diligence investigation, they should put it on a fast track. Speedy due diligence ensures minimal disruption to ongoing business activities and lower out-of-pocket costs to both parties. Another benefit can be smoother relations between the parties. The most valuable result of fast-track due diligence is timely information so the buyer can quickly determine whether the acquisition is of interest and, if so, on what terms and conditions. The buyer can then focus attention on determining the appropriate structure for the transaction; the basis for calculation of the purchase price; what representations, warranties, and covenants should be negotiated into the final acquisition agreement; and what conditions to closing need to be imposed.

The earlier the acquirer can draw up its list of "conditions to closing," the better. Once that document is "on the table" and under constant revision as

due diligence proceeds, all parties seem to feel more optimistic about the likelihood that the deal will close. Although there may—and usually should—be
"bringdown" due diligence at the very end, this need not extend the deal indefinitely.

What is bringdown due diligence?

Bringdown due diligence is the performance of due diligence right up until
the closing date. Deal makers speak of "bringing down" the due diligence
through additional meetings, conference calls, reexamination of disclosure
items, and updating of seller warranties and representations. Bringdown due
diligence can protect a buyer against a claim that it should have uncovered
some eleventh-hour development not included in representations and warranties. The term is also used in underwritings for the due diligence conducted just prior to the effective date of a registration statement.[17]

    For more about bringdown due diligence, see Chapter 5.

When does the due diligence process properly end?

As important as it is for due diligence to be completed rapidly, the due diligence effort really should extend beyond closing. The discipline imposed by
the process—dealing with the realities of the complications of business—should never be abandoned, and it is a rare deal that does not have, on
closing day, a revision to the acquisition agreement covering unfinished items
of due diligence inquiry. This bringdown list can be extensive, and may require extension of the effective closing date—or in effect two closings. Many
prefer to wait until everything is completed and the purchase agreement can
be executed simultaneously with closing the deal. (For more about
transactional matters, see Chapter 5.)

THE KEY PARTICIPANTS IN DUE DILIGENCE

Who conducts due diligence?

To conduct due diligence, the acquirer typically draws from in-house sources
of expertise and from retained consultants and advisers. At a minimum, the
due diligence team will include accounting personnel for the financial statement review and legal personnel for the liability exposure review. The two
have separate and distinct responsibilities, although they may communicate
with each other.[18] The acquirer may also bring in economic consultants, engineers, environmental experts, and a host of other professional talent.

Typically, outside counsel to the acquirer directs the review, with help from a variety of other agents of the acquirer. These agents might include senior management (especially the chief financial officer), internal legal and accounting staff, external accountants, and investment bankers. The party directing the review should be clear from any conflict of interest.

What are some working definitions of "conflict of interest" for the purpose of due diligence investigations?

If a firm has a consulting engagement with the company it is studying, it may have a conflict of interest with respect to the transaction. One example of a person with a conflict of interest is an auditor who works for a professional services firm that provides consulting work. Another example is a professional who owns stock in a client company.[19]

Sometimes advisors are paid a contingency for the completion of the transaction. Although this is a common practice for many professionals, it can jeopardize objectivity. Therefore, advisors paid on contingency normally should not direct the due diligence review, although they may participate in it.

In sum, the independence of advisers is very important in the conduct of due diligence. This is a key topic under U.S. federal securities laws, as explained below.

DUE DILIGENCE AND THE LAW

What laws require due diligence?

There are two basic sources of responsibility for due diligence: common law, including the law of contracts; and statutory law, especially state and federal securities statutes. (In Chapter 4, we explain how these types of laws fit into a broader liability scheme.)

- If a company (whether the acquirer or the company to be acquired) has issued a private placement for stock pursuant to a purchase agreement, then it is responsible to the other party to the contract for some level of due diligence (lack of negligence) in the transaction.
- If a company (acquirer or acquired) has issued a public offering of stock, then it is responsible for some level of due diligence (lack of negligence) under state and federal statutory law.

Is due diligence required by federal securities laws?

Not exactly. Neither of the two most significant statutes—the Securities Act of 1933 and the Securities Exchange Act of 1934—employs the term *due diligence*. But although the term is not used in federal securities laws, securities lawyers do use a "due diligence defense" to protect their clients from lawsuits alleging violation of securities laws. Diligence and negligence are opposite qualities; the presence of one suggests the absence of the other. Due diligence activities, by their very name, imply the absence of negligence; conversely, the absence of due diligence activities suggests some degree of negligence.

The latter was a finding in *Escott v. BarChris Construction Corp.* (1968), which established that it is not reasonable to rely on exclusively management for key data. Data must be double-checked through an independent investigation. Even outside directors must ask for reasonable assurances that facts are correct.

On the positive side, consider the court's finding in *Glassman v. Computervision* (1996), which puts it succinctly: "Due diligence is equivalent to non-negligence." Thus due diligence, well conducted and documented, can be a defense against charges of negligence during the transaction.

How can an acquirer show due diligence (avoid negligence charges) under the Securities Act of 1933?

First, a general comment about the 1933 Act. Although it applies to the issuance of securities (not always a part of a merger transaction), it has broader implications. Some of the concepts in the 1933 Act, and in rules promulgated under this law, have had far-reaching influence in court decisions. Therefore, mastering the disclosure principles in the 1933 Act can help companies, both public and private, maintain good business practices. The following summary of the key sections of the 1933 Act may prove useful to acquirers interested in conducting due diligence studies of acquisition candidates.[20]

Section 11

Section 11 forbids "material" misrepresentations and omissions in registration statements. To defend themselves against such charges, the accused can state (or, better yet, show) that they exercised due diligence. The so-called due diligence defense arises under Section 11(b)(3) and 11(c).

Under Section 11(b)(3), there is a dual standard for due diligence: expert versus nonexpert.

- If the accused parties are *experts* advising or testifying about a transaction (e.g., expert witnesses), their due diligence means that they made a reasonable investigation into the facts; and they had reason to believe, and did believe, that their statements made were true and complete at the time.
- Nonexperts (e.g., directors and officers) may rely on experts. As such, nonexperts are not automatically liable for misrepresentations or omissions made by experts. To avoid liability, they merely have to show that they had no reason to believe that the information they approved was false or misleading. Nonexperts, however, must show that they took reasonable steps to ensure that the statements were truthful. One such reasonable step would be to ascertain the independence of the expert.

For example, federal securities laws recognize the importance of independent audits by requiring, or allowing the SEC to require, that financial statements filed with the commission by public companies, investment companies, broker/dealers, public utilities, investment advisers, and others, be certified (or audited) by independent public accountants. Federal securities laws also grant the SEC the authority to define the term *independent*.

The SEC may consider that an auditor lacks independence if the auditor provides additional client services that create one or more of the following conflicts for the auditor:

- The auditor is dependent on fees from nonaudit services.
- The auditor supplants the role of management in making decisions about a particular problem.
- The auditor conducts a self-review, auditing the product of systems designed or modified by the auditor.

Going beyond the subject of expert versus nonexpert diligence and related concerns about independence, Section 11(c) addresses the subject of reasonableness. It sets an important limit on the extent to which a person must go in ensuring the accuracy and completeness of a statement. In defining "reasonableness," Section 11 draws on the famed "prudent man" theory—a time-honored image of the due care taken by a "prudent man in the management of his own property." The SEC has issued Rule 176 to clarify this approach.

Rule 176

Rule 176 of the Securities Act of 1933 succinctly describes "circumstances affecting the determination of what constitutes reasonable investigation and reasonable grounds for belief under Section 11 of the Securities Act."

In defining a "reasonable" amount of attention, Rule 176 says that it depends on a number of factors, including:

- The type of issuer [entity].
- The type of security.
- The type of person.
- The office held when the person is an officer.
- The presence or absence of another relationship to the issuer when the person is a director or proposed director [conflict of interest].
- Reasonable reliance on officers, employees, and others whose duties should have given them knowledge of the particular facts [in light of the functions and the responsibilities of the particular person . . .][21]

Although Rule 176 originated as an SEC guide to what constitutes a reasonable investigation under Section 11, it is a ready-made summary of the vast wisdom of case law on the subject of due diligence in any transaction. As such, it can help acquirers prepare well ahead of time to show that they exercised due diligence in a transaction, as follows:

- *Type of issuer.* The due diligence conducted for a diversified multinational will obviously be more extensive than the due diligence conducted for a single-product, domestic concern.
- *Type of security.* Some transactions do not involve securities: an acquirer may pay cash for assets. But many transactions do involve securities—whether purchased from the seller, paid by the buyer, or both. The more complex the security, the more extensive the due diligence.
- *Type of person.* The level of due diligence expected by individuals will rise in accordance with the person's role in the transaction and the person's status. Clearly, a chief financial officer, as a knowledgeable and accountable insider, is expected to exercise more diligence in a transaction than an outsider of lesser rank—such as an advisory board member.
- *Level of reliance.* If an acquirer's senior managers do the due diligence work themselves, then they can control its level of diligence. If they delegate this work to others, then they lose direct control over it, thus potentially (but not necessarily) lowering its level of diligence. In determining the quality of diligence, courts will accept delegation or reliance, but only if it is appropriate and well monitored. Relying on independent sources is considered better than relying on sources that are not independent, and relying on experienced individuals is considered better than relying on inexperienced

ones. If a due diligence effort uses junior people, then those people should undergo special training, and they should document their work for senior review.[22]

SECURITIES EXCHANGE ACT OF 1934

What does the Securities Exchange Act of 1934 have to say about due diligence?

This law is literally the sequel to the Securities Act of 1933, discussed above: the 1933 Act covers the initial registration and sale of securities, while the 1934 Act effectively covers their exchange. Since mergers more often involve the exchange of securities (rather than registration), the so-called due diligence portions of this law are even more important for acquirers to master.

Like the 1933 Act, the 1934 Act does not use the term *due diligence* anywhere, but due diligence may be used as a defense in a suit alleging a violation of the act. In particular, such a defense may sometimes be useful in defending against charges under Rule 10b-5, promulgated under Section 10(b) of the 1934 Act.

Many deal makers involved in stock-based transactions have been surprised when they are targeted in suits under Rule 10b-5. Yet its reach is broad.

What does Rule 10b-5 say?

Rule 10b-5 forbids certain practices deemed to be fraudulent in connection with the purchase or sale of a security. This applies to both public and private sales of securities, although application to private sales may be narrower in some situations.[23] The fraudulent acts must be committed intentionally, with *scienter*, a Latin term meaning "with knowledge," and (in legal tradition) with implied malicious intent. Legal complaints can come from any buyer or seller of a security who claims to be harmed by such a fraud—not just from the government.

The text of Rule 10b-5 reads as follows:

> It shall be unlawful for any person, directly or indirectly, by the use of any means or instrumentality of interstate commerce, or of the mails, or of any facility of any national securities exchange:
>
> **(a)** To employ any device, scheme, or artifice to defraud,
> **(b)** To make any untrue statement of a material fact or to omit to state a material fact necessary in order to make the statements made, in the light of the circumstances under which they were made, not misleading, or

(c) To engage in any act, practice, or course of business which operates or
would operate as a fraud or deceit upon any person, in connection with
the purchase or sale of any security.

Can the due diligence defense be used in all 10b-5 cases?

No. The defense can be used only in the 10b-5 cases where the plaintiff alleges
that the fraud in question stemmed from extreme negligence, or recklessness,
as opposed to a conscious intent to deceive. As mentioned earlier, diligence
suggests the absence of negligence.

Recent court decisions indicate that recklessness may meet the *scienter*
requirements of Rule 10b-5, making 10b-5 suits a threat to acquirers that have
done insufficient due diligence in the conduct of acquisitions involving public
companies. Unless and until the courts reject recklessness as a type of *scienter*
requirement, plaintiffs will be able to cite a "breakdown in due diligence" as
evidence in suing under Rule 10b-5 or other private securities litigation suits.[24]

VERIFICATION AND RISK PREVENTION

To what extent is an acquirer expected to verify representations made by the seller?

A classic case in this regard is *In re Software Toolworks Inc. Sec. Litig.* (1994). In
this Ninth Circuit case, the court stated, "It would be unreasonable . . . to rely
on management representations when said representations could have been
reasonably verified." On the other hand, the court also stated, "It is not unreasonable, however, to rely on management representations with regard to information that is solely in the possession of the issuer and cannot be reasonably verified by third parties." In other words, *some kinds of information can be
verified independently, and others cannot.* In conducting a due diligence investigation, attorneys (or others) need to obtain independent verification of facts
wherever *reasonable.*

Can you give an example of reasonable, independent verification of facts?

Reasonable, independent verification, based on accepted wisdom concerning
due diligence in securities offerings, usually means referencing information
sources outside the company as well as inside the company.

For example, if a company is the subject of a tender offer, the board of that company might wish to obtain a *fairness opinion* as to the appropriateness of the offering price. The opinion must be from a qualified, independent source, such as an investment banking firm, a commercial banker, an appraiser, or a consultant specializing in valuation.

It is important to verify the basis for the fairness opinion. The court in the above-mentioned case of *Escott v. BarChris Construction Corp.* (1968) stated that it is not "sufficient to ask questions, to obtain which, if true, would be thought satisfactory, and to let it go at that, without seeking to ascertain from the records whether the answers in fact are true and complete."

In reviewing the actions of underwriters asserting a due diligence defense in specific transactions, courts have suggested that certain practices help satisfy the requirements of such a defense. These practices, in effect, show diligence.[25] (Clearly, all these due diligence practices are applicable to M&A transactions, when an acquirer is looking to buy the shares or the assets of another company.)

- Courts have been impressed with underwriters' direct contacts with the issuing firm's:

  Accountants

  Bankers

  Customers

  Distributors

  Lenders

  Licensees

  Suppliers

- Courts are also impressed by efforts to cross-check statements made by insiders of the firm—for example, speaking with lower-level employees to verify statements of upper-level management.

- On-site visits to the facilities of a company can prove diligence.

- Diligence can also be shown by examining documents that provide the factual basis for officers' statements.

- Further verification can be accomplished by reviewing press and analyst reports about the company and its industry.

- One's *own economic models* can be used to test those offered by the company.

Says one expert in the due diligence defense, "The courts are favorably impressed by such palpable efforts to 'cross-check' . . . representations."[26] As the above-cited *Software* case found, cross-checking is particularly important when negative or questionable information arises.

What kinds of "negative" or "questionable" information might an acquirer look for?

Throughout this book, we will identify many examples of such information. The following are warning signs that need to be investigated to some degree:

- *Financial red flags* (covered in Chapter 2) include resignation of external or internal auditors, change in accounting methods, sales of stock by insiders, and unusual ratios. These may indicate fraud and/or potential insolvency.
- *Operational red flags* (covered in Chapter 3) include very high or very low turnover and sketchy reporting from important nonfinancial programs (for example, quality, compliance). These may indicate unstable operations.
- *Liability red flags* (summarized in Chapter 4 and explored more fully in later chapters) include potential exposure to litigation from regulators, consumers, and employees.
- *Transactional red flags* (covered in Chapters 5 through 7) include potential securities law violations stemming from the transaction, and conflicting accounting and tax goals for the deal.

In addition to identifying such risks, the acquirer can take steps to limit them. There are many ways to do so. The first and most obvious is to consult with a broker of *liability insurance* that protects directors and officers (D&O) of the acquiring company against acquisition-related risks, and to enter into an agreement with an insurance provider. Since D&O liability insurance providers employ actuaries who specialize in predicting risk, acquirers can learn a lot from talking to them. Insurance brokers and vendors are natural allies of those who seek to limit risk.[27]

In seeking acquisition candidates in the first place, the acquirer can favor companies that have in place strong *programs for financial reporting, risk management, and legal compliance*. If suspicions arise during standard due diligence, acquirers can employ the services of *private investigators*. (See Chapters 2 through 4.)

In addition, the acquirer can make sure that the various deal-related *agreements* include adequate protections against postacquisition losses stemming from preacquisition conditions. In documenting and structuring the transaction, the acquirer can minimize risks through various technical devices. (See Chapters 5 through 7.)

Above all, the acquirer needs to make sure that its own *due diligence process* includes all the steps generally considered to show "due care" under relevant law.

CONCLUDING COMMENTS

Due diligence provides two distinct benefits to any acquirer.

First, individuals who had hands-on involvement in the due diligence process will gain good insight into the financial, operational, and legal areas they studied. They may be called upon during the postacquisition "re-startup" period under new ownership to answer questions or provide guidance. (There are *always* items of unfinished business growing out of the due diligence process that must be resolved after closing. They should be listed and assigned to people to solve with completion dates attached, and someone should be assigned to follow up.)

Second, in the event of a claim by the buyer or the seller against the other, the resolution of the claim may go back to a due diligence issue—that is, whether or not one party disclosed certain facts or made available certain documents. Insofar as the acquisition agreement fails to identify the information that the defendant was supposed to know or learn, the due diligence process must be examined to determine where liability lies. Acquirers that have conducted a thorough due diligence process, and have kept records of their efforts, will be prepared to meet this challenge—as well as the more important challenge of meeting the combined company's future risks and opportunities.

A P P E N D I X   1A

Sample Confidentiality Agreement for Acquisition of a Private Company[*]

STRICTLY PRIVATE AND CONFIDENTIAL

[Date]

Acquisition, Inc.
Corporate Office Towers
New York, New York

To the Board of Directors:

In connection with your consideration of a possible transaction with Seller, Inc. (the "Company") or its stockholders, you have requested information concerning the Company so that you may make an evaluation of the Company to undertake negotiations for the purchase of the Company. As a condition to your being furnished such information, you agree to treat any information (including all data, reports, interpretations, forecasts and records) concerning the Company which is furnished to you by or on behalf of the Company and analyses, compilations, studies or other documents, whether prepared by you or others, which contain or reflect such information (herein collectively referred to as the "Evaluation Material") in accordance with the provisions of this letter. The term "Evaluation Material" does not include information which (i) was or becomes generally available to the public other than as a result of a disclosure by you or your directors, officers, employees, agents or advisers, or (ii) was or becomes available to you on a nonconfidential basis from a source other than the Company or its advisers provided that such source is not bound by a confidentiality agreement with the Company, or (iii)

---

[*] This confidentiality agreement is adapted with permission from an agreement appearing in Stanley Foster Reed and Alexandra Reed Lajoux, *The Art of M&A: A Merger/Acquisition/Buyout Guide, Third Edition* (New York: McGraw-Hill, 1999), pp. 382–385.

was within your possession prior to its being furnished to you by or on behalf of the Company, provided that the source of such information was not bound by a confidentiality agreement with the Company in respect thereof, or (iv) was independently acquired by you as a result of work carried out by an employee of yours to whom no disclosure of such information has been made directly or indirectly.

You hereby agree that the Evaluation Material will not be used by you in any way detrimental to the Company. You also agree that the Evaluation Material will be used solely for the purpose set forth above, and that such information will be kept confidential by you and your advisers for five (5) years provided, however, that (i) any such information may be disclosed to your directors, officers and employees, and representatives of your advisers who need to know such information for the purpose of evaluating any such possible transactions between the Company and you (it being understood that such directors, officers, employees and representatives shall be informed by you of the confidential nature of such information and shall be directed by you to treat such information confidentially and shall assume the same obligations as you under this agreement), and (ii) any disclosure of such information may be made to which the Company consents in writing. You shall be responsible for any breach of this agreement by your agents or employees.

In addition, without the prior written consent of the Company, you will not, and will direct such directors, officers, employees and representatives not to disclose to any person either the fact that discussions or negotiations are taking place concerning one or more possible transactions between either the Company or its stockholders, on the one hand, and you, on the other hand, or any of the terms, conditions, or other facts with respect to any such possible transactions, including the status thereof. The term "person" as used in this letter shall be broadly interpreted to include without limitation any corporation, company, group, partnership or individual.

In addition, you hereby acknowledge that you are aware, and that you will advise your directors, officers, employees, agents and advisers who are informed as to the matters which are the subject of this letter, that the United States securities laws prohibit any person who has material, nonpublic information concerning the matters which are the subject of this letter from purchasing or selling securities of a company which may be a party to a transaction of a type contemplated by this letter or from communicating such information to any other person under circumstances in which it is reasonably foreseeable that such person is likely to purchase or sell such securities. You consent that you will not, and you will cause each of the aforementioned persons to not, violate any provisions of the aforementioned laws or the analogous laws of any State.

You hereby acknowledge that the Evaluation Material is being furnished to you in consideration of your agreement (i) that neither you nor any of your affiliates nor related persons under your control will for a period of three (3) years from the date of this letter make any public announcement with respect to or submit any proposal for a transaction between you (or any of your affiliates) and the Company or any of its securityholders unless the Company shall have consented in writing in advance to the submission of such proposal, nor will you, directly or indirectly, by purchase or otherwise, through your affiliates or otherwise, alone or with others, acquire, offer to acquire or agree to acquire any voting securities or direct or indirect rights or options to acquire any voting securities of the Company, for a period of three (3) years from the date of this letter without such permission, and (ii) that you will indemnify any director, officer, employee or agent of the Company and any "controlling person" thereof as such term is defined in the Securities Act of 1933, for any liability, damage or expense arising under federal and state securities laws from an actual or alleged breach of this agreement by you or your directors, officers, employees, representatives or affiliates. You also agree that the Company shall be entitled to equitable relief, including an injunction, in the event of any breach of the provisions of this paragraph.

In the event that you do not proceed with the transaction which is the subject of this letter within a reasonable time, you shall promptly redeliver to the Company all written material containing or reflecting any information contained in the Evaluation Material (whether prepared by the Company or otherwise) and will not retain any copies, extracts or other reproductions in whole or in part of such written material. All documents, memoranda, notes and other writings whatsoever, prepared by you or your advisers based on the information contained in the Evaluation Material, shall be destroyed, and such destruction shall be certified in writing to the companies by an authorized officer supervising such destruction.

Although we have endeavored to include in the Evaluation Material information known to us which we believe to be relevant for the purpose of your investigation, you understand that we do not make any representation or warranty as to the accuracy or completeness of the Evaluation Material. You agree that you shall assume full responsibility for all conclusions you derive from the Evaluation Material and that neither the Company nor its representatives shall have any liability to you or any of your representatives resulting from the use of the Evaluation Material supplied by us or our representatives.

In the event you are required by legal process to disclose any of the Evaluation Material, you shall provide us with prompt notice of such requirement so that we may seek a protective order or other appropriate remedy or waive compliance with the provisions of this agreement. In the event that a protective order or other remedy is obtained, you shall use all reasonable efforts to ensure that all Evaluation Material disclosed will be covered by such order or other remedy. Whether such protective order or other remedy is obtained or we waive compliance with the provisions of this agreement, you will disclose only that portion of the Evaluation Material which you are legally required to disclose.

This agreement shall be governed by and construed and enforced in accordance with the laws of the State of New York, U.S.A.

Any assignment of this agreement by you without our prior written consent shall be void.

It is further understood and agreed that no failure or delay by the Company in exercising any right, power or privilege hereunder shall operate as a waiver thereof nor shall any single or partial exercise thereof preclude any other or further exercise of any right, power or privilege.

If you are in agreement with the foregoing, please so indicate by signing and returning one copy of this letter, whereupon this letter will constitute our agreement with respect to the subject matter hereof.

Very truly yours,

SELLER, INC.

By: Its:

Confirmed and Agreed to:

ACQUISITION, INC.

By: Its:

Date:

A P P E N D I X 1B

Sample Confidentiality Agreement for Acquisition of a Publicly Held Company[*]

PERSONAL AND CONFIDENTIAL

Gentlemen:

The purpose of this letter agreement is to set forth our understanding with regard to disclosures of information relating to your consideration of any future transactions between you and/or your affiliates and _____, a California corporation, and/or _____, a California general partnership (collectively, and/or the affiliates of either of them) with regard to the possible acquisition (the "Proposed Acquisition") by you and/or your affiliates of the voting securities of, or other interests in, one or more of the entities listed on Schedule A hereto (collectively, the "Subsidiaries"), each of which is directly or indirectly owned or controlled by _____ and has ownership interests in and/or contractual arrangements with one or more of the limited partnerships listed on Schedule B hereto (collectively, the "Programs").[**]

In order to determine the viability of any future transaction, _____ may need to disclose to you and/or your Permitted Persons (as such term is defined below) certain information relating to its operations and the operations of the Subsidiaries and/or one or more of the Programs. _____ may also need to disclose the nature of assets, including intellectual property such as trade secrets, not generally known to the public. As a condition to your and/or your Permitted Persons being furnished such information, you hereby agree to treat any information relating to _____, any of the Subsidiaries and/or any of the Programs

---

[*] This document was provided by Mark Schonberger, Partner, Battle Fowler LLP, New York, and is reprinted courtesy of Battle Fowler LLP.

[**] Schedule A and Schedule B are not included with this sample agreement.

(whether prepared by _____, its advisors or otherwise) which is furnished to you and/or your Permitted Persons (whether orally or in writing) in connection with your evaluation of the Proposed Acquisition (herein collectively referred to as the "Evaluation Material") in accordance with the provisions of this letter agreement and to take or abstain from taking certain of the actions herein set forth. The term "Evaluation Material" shall also be deemed to include all notes, analyses, compilations, studies, interpretations or other documents or materials prepared by you or any of your Permitted Persons which contain, reflect or are based upon, in whole or in part, any information furnished to you or your Permitted Persons pursuant hereto. The term "Evaluation Material" does not include information which (i) was in your possession prior to the date first set forth above, provided that such information is not known by you to be subject to another confidentiality agreement with or other obligation of secrecy to _____, one of the Subsidiaries or Programs or another party, (ii) is or becomes generally available to the public other than as a result of a disclosure by you or your directors, officers, partners, affiliates, employees, agents or advisors, or (iii) becomes available to you on a nonconfidential basis from a source other than _____, one of the Subsidiaries or Programs or any of their respective advisors, agents or affiliates, provided that such source is not known by you to be bound by a confidentiality agreement with or other obligation of secrecy to _____ or another party.

You hereby agree that you will use, and you will direct your Permitted Persons to use, the Evaluation Material solely for the purpose of evaluating and/or effecting the Proposed Acquisition and that such information will be kept confidential by you and your Permitted Persons (it being understood and agreed that the efforts you use to keep such information confidential shall not be less than the efforts you currently use to keep nonpublic information about yourself confidential); provided, however, that (i) any of such information may be disclosed to your directors, officers, partners in _____, affiliates, employees, advisors, lenders and representatives of your advisors and lenders (collectively, the "Permitted Persons") who need to know such information for the purpose of evaluating any such possible transaction between _____ and you (it being understood that such Permitted Persons shall be informed by you of the confidential nature of such information and the Permitted Persons shall agree, which agreement shall not require a writing, to treat such information confidentially in the manner provided in this letter agreement) and (ii) any disclosure of such information may be made to which _____ consents in writing. You hereby agree, at your sole expense, to take all reasonable measures (including but not limited to court proceedings) to restrain your Permitted Persons from disclosing, using or otherwise dealing with any of the Evaluation Material in a manner which is inconsistent with, or prohibited by, this letter agreement.

You hereby acknowledge that you are aware, and that you will advise the Permitted Persons, that the federal securities laws prohibit certain persons who have material, nonpublic information concerning an issuer from purchasing or selling securities of such issuer or from communicating such information to any other person under circumstances in which it is reasonably foreseeable that such person is likely to purchase or sell such securities.

You agree that without the prior written consent of _____, you will not, and will direct any Permitted Persons not to, hold any discussions or otherwise communicate in any way, with any person who is not otherwise a Permitted Person (a "Prohibited Person") concerning any proposal for any transaction between or among you and _____, the Subsidiaries or the Programs, you and any Prohibited Person, any Prohibited Person and _____, the Subsidiaries or the Programs, or between or among any Prohibited Person with regard to the possible acquisition by any person of the voting securities of, or other interests in, one or more of the Subsidiaries and/or any of the Programs (it being understood and agreed that the efforts you use not to hold, or allow a Permitted Person to hold, discussions with a Prohibited Person shall not be less than the efforts you currently use to keep nonpublic information about yourself from being communicated to persons outside your organization). In addition, without the prior written consent of _____ you will not, and will direct the Permitted Persons not to, disclose to any Prohibited Person either the fact that you are considering, or that discussions or negotiations are taking place concerning, a possible transaction between _____ and/or any of its affiliates and you and/or any of your affiliates or any of the terms, conditions or other facts with respect to any such possible transaction, including the status thereof (it being understood and agreed that the efforts you use not to disclose, or allow a Permitted Person to disclose, such discussions or negotiations shall not be less than the efforts you currently would use to keep nonpublic information about a possible transaction involving yourself confidential).

You agree that until the date which is three (3) years from the date of this Agreement, neither you nor any person who is an Affiliate (as that term is defined under Rule 405 of the Securities Act of 1933, as amended) will, without the written consent of _____ (which consent can be withheld by _____ in its sole discretion for any reason or for no reason), (i) in any manner, acquire, attempt to acquire or make a proposal to acquire, directly or indirectly, any securities, partnership interests or other equity interests or property of any of the Subsidiaries and/or any of the Programs, (ii) propose to enter into, directly or indirectly, any merger or business combination involving any of the Subsidiaries and/or any of the Programs or to purchase, directly or indirectly, any of the assets of any of the Subsidiaries and/or any of the Programs, (iii) make, or in any way participate, directly or indirectly, in any "solicitation" of "proxies" (as such terms are used in the proxy rules of the Securities and Exchange Commission) to vote, or seek to advise or influence any person with respect to the voting of any voting securities of any of the Subsidiaries and/or any of the Programs, (iv) form, join or otherwise participate in a "group" (within the meaning of Section 13(d)(3) of the Securities Exchange Act of 1934) with respect to any Voting Securities of any of the Subsidiaries and/or any of the Programs, (v) otherwise act, alone or in concert with others, to seek to control or influence the management, Board of Directors, general partners, or policies of any of the Subsidiaries and/or any of the Programs or take any action to prevent or challenge _____'s sale of any of the Subsidiaries or any direct or indirect interests therein (including, without limitation, proposing to alter in any way the provisions of the partnership agreements or other similar agreements relating to the management of any of the Programs or asserting a claim that _____'s sale of any of the Subsidiaries represents the violation of a duty or is unauthorized), (vi) disclose any intention, plan or arrangement inconsistent with the foregoing, or (vii) advise, assist or encourage any person in connection with any of the actions described in this sentence (collectively, the "Standstill Restrictions"). You also agree during any period in which you are prohibited from taking certain actions pursuant to this paragraph to take commercially reasonable precautions to avoid taking any action, unless required by law, which might reasonably be expected to require _____, any of the Subsidiaries, and/or any of the Programs, to make a public announcement regarding the possibility of a business combination, merger, acquisition or other transaction of any nature.

Although _____, the Subsidiaries and the Programs, as the case may be, will endeavor to include in the Evaluation Material information known to each of them which each of them believes to be relevant for the purpose of your consideration of the Proposed Acquisition, you understand that none of _____, the Subsidiaries, the Programs, nor any of their respective affiliates, representatives or advisors have made or make any representation or warranty as to the accuracy or completeness of the Evaluation Material. You understand that any estimates or projections with respect to future performance included in the Evaluation Material are provided to assist you in your evaluation but should not be relied upon as an accurate representation or assurance of future results. You agree that none of

_____, the Subsidiaries, the Programs or their respective affiliates, representatives or advisors shall have any liability to you or any of your affiliates, representatives or advisors resulting from the use of the Evaluation Material.

In the event that you or your Permitted Persons are requested or required (by oral questions, interrogatories, requests for information or documents, subpoena or similar process) to disclose any information supplied to you or your Permitted Persons in the course of your dealings with _____, the Subsidiaries and/or the Programs or their respective affiliates, representatives or advisors, it is agreed that you will provide _____ with prompt notice of such request or requirements so that _____ and/or its affiliates may seek an appropriate protective order and/or by mutual agreements waive your compliance with the provisions of this letter agreement. It is further agreed that, if in the absence of a protective order or the receipt of a waiver hereunder you or any of your Permitted Persons are nonetheless, in the opinion of your counsel, compelled to disclose any Evaluation Material to any tribunal or else stand liable for contempt or suffer other censure or penalty, you or such Permitted Persons may disclose that portion of the Evaluation Material which such counsel advises you is legally required to be disclosed to such tribunal without liability hereunder, unless such disclosure to such tribunal was caused by or resulted from a previous disclosure by you or any of your Permitted Persons which constituted a breach of this letter agreement.

If you determine that you do not wish to proceed with the Proposed Acquisition, you will promptly advise us of that decision.

In the event the Proposed Acquisition is not consummated by you or, if a Definitive Agreement (as such term is defined below) relating to the Proposed Acquisition is not otherwise in effect, at any other time prior to such consummation as _____ may determine and specify in a written notice to you, you shall, and you shall direct your Permitted Persons to, promptly deliver to _____ all written Evaluation Material and any other written material containing or reflecting any information in the Evaluation Material (whether prepared by _____, its advisors or otherwise), and will not retain any copies, extracts or other reproductions in whole or in part of such written material. All documents, memoranda, notes and other writings whatsoever prepared by you or your Permitted Persons based on the information in the Evaluation Material shall be destroyed, and such destruction shall be certified in writing to _____ by an authorized officer supervising such destruction.

You also understand and agree that no contract or agreement providing for any transaction involving _____, any of the Subsidiaries and/or any of the Programs shall be deemed to exist unless and until a Definitive Agreement (as hereinafter described) has been executed and delivered, and you hereby waive, except as provided herein, in advance, any claims (including, without limitation, breach of contract) in connection with the Proposed Transaction unless and until you shall have entered into a Definitive Agreement. You also agree that unless and until a Definitive Agreement between _____ and you with respect to any transaction involving _____, any of the Subsidiaries and/or any of the Programs has been executed and delivered, none of _____, the Subsidiaries nor the Programs has any legal obligation of any kind whatsoever with respect to any such transaction by virtue of this letter agreement or any other written or oral expression with respect to such transaction except, in the case of this letter agreement, for the matters specifically agreed to herein. For purposes of this paragraph, the term "Definitive Agreement" does not include an executed letter of intent or any other preliminary written agreement, nor does it include any written or verbal agreement in principle or acceptance of an offer or bid on your part. Neither this paragraph nor any other provision in this letter agreement can be waived or amended except by written consent of _____, which consent (i) can be withheld by _____ in its sole discretion for any reason or for no reason and (ii) shall specifically refer to this paragraph (or such other provision) and explicitly make such waiver or amendment.

You agree that _____ and/or its Subsidiaries and/or the Programs, or the affiliates of any of them, as the case may be, shall be entitled to equitable relief, including injunction and specific performance, in the event of any breach of the provisions of this letter agreement, in addition to all other remedies available at law or in equity.

It is further understood and agreed that no failure or delay by _____ and/or its Subsidiaries and/or the Programs, or the affiliates of any of them, as the case may be, in exercising any right, power or privilege hereunder will operate as a waiver thereof, nor will any single or partial exercise thereof preclude any other or further exercise thereof or the exercise of any right, power or privilege hereunder.

This letter agreement is for the benefit of _____ the Subsidiaries, the Programs and each of their respective directors, officers, stockholders, owners, affiliates, agents, successors and assigns and will be binding upon your successors and assigns. This letter agreement will be governed by and construed in accordance with the laws of the State of California, without regard to the conflicts of law principles thereof. You also agree to cause your Affiliates to comply with the provisions hereof.

You hereby irrevocably and unconditionally consent to submit to the exclusive jurisdiction of the courts of the State of California for any actions, suits or proceedings arising out of or relating to this letter agreement (and you agree not to commence any action, suit or proceeding relating thereto except in such courts), and further agree that service of any process, summons, notice or document by U.S. Registered Mail to your address set forth above (or any other address which you provide to us in writing) shall be effective service of process for any action, suit or proceeding brought against you in any such court. You hereby irrevocably and unconditionally waive any objection to the lack of venue of any action, suit or proceedings arising out of this letter agreement, in the courts of the State of California or the United States of America located in the State of California, and hereby further irrevocably and unconditionally waive and agree not to plead or claim in any such court that any such action, suit or proceeding brought in any such court has been brought in an inconvenient forum.

Notwithstanding anything to the contrary herein, if _____ discloses to any third party, prior to entering into a definitive agreement with such third party for the acquisition of the voting securities or assets of, or other interests in, one or more of the Subsidiaries and/or the Programs, any nonpublic information relating to the operations of the Subsidiaries and/or one or more of the Programs in connection with a possible acquisition by such third party and/or its affiliates of the voting securities or assets of, or other interests in, one or more of the Subsidiaries and/or the Programs and such disclosure is made without the recipient of such information and its Affiliates agreeing (in writing) to restrictions (as they relate to both term and scope) which are similar in all material respects to the restrictions included in the Standstill Restrictions as set forth in this letter agreement, then (a) you shall automatically receive the benefit of such reduced or eliminated restrictions by reducing and/or eliminating the term and/or scope of the Standstill Restrictions as though the Standstill Restrictions as set forth herein included only those restrictions, if any, which were agreed to in writing by such third party in connection with its receipt of nonpublic information from _____ and (b) _____ shall notify you promptly of the reduction (in term and/or scope) or elimination of the Standstill Restrictions; provided that nothing contained in any agreement between _____ and any third party shall reduce or eliminate any right or power granted to you hereunder.

If you agree with the foregoing, please sign and return two copies of this letter agreement, which will constitute our agreement with respect to the subject matter of this letter agreement.

This letter agreement may be executed in two or more counterparts, each of which shall be deemed an original, but all of which together constitute one and the same instrument.

Very truly yours,

By:

Name:

Title:

By:

Name:

Title:

CONFIRMED AND AGREED TO AS OF THE DATE FIRST ABOVE WRITTEN:

By: _____ its

general partner

By: _____

Name:

Title:

A P P E N D I X   1C

Sample Engagement Letter
for a Consultant[*]

PRIVILEGED AND CONFIDENTIAL ATTORNEY'S WORK PRODUCT

[Date]

Re: Consulting Agreement with DEF Law Firm
        Regarding XYZ, Inc. Transaction

Dear _____:

The purpose of this letter is to confirm our discussion that, effective _____, Consultant has been retained by DEF Law Firm ("DEF") to provide professional consultation in connection with the XYZ transaction.

As we discussed, the details of the consulting agreement are set forth below:

1. Consultant will bill at the rate of _____ per hour for the time of other Consultant professionals assigned to this matter, plus expenses, including travel. Consultant invoices shall be provided on a monthly basis to the following address:

DEF
1122 Main Street
Anytown, USA

DEF will forward the monthly invoices to XYZ for payment. You agree to look solely to XYZ, and not to DEF, for the payments of amounts due.

2. During the course of this engagement you agree to accept no work from _____ in the anticipated transaction and you agree not to accept any other engagement which would require an evaluation of the environmental conditions present at the Site or surrounding area. In the event that this engagement terminates prior to the conclusion of the anticipated transaction,

---

[*] This document was provided by Mark Schonberger, Partner, Battle Fowler LLP, New York, and is reprinted courtesy of Battle Fowler LLP.

you agree that you will not accept any engagement at any time from _____ in the anticipated transaction relating in any way to the anticipated transaction.

    3. The scope of your engagement shall include, but may not be limited to, the following:

    a. Consult with DEF and provide expert advice as may be necessary regarding issues in the anticipated transaction; and

    b. Consult with DEF and provide expert advice as may be necessary in analyzing the findings of other consultants regarding issues in the anticipated transaction.

    4. In Consultant's capacity as a provider of consulting services, Consultant may receive or generate materials subject to the attorney-client and attorney work product privileges. Any such materials you may receive from DEF are to be regarded as confidential and privileged and should not be disclosed to any third party without our consent. Since it will be necessary as part of this engagement for us to share our mental impressions, opinions, conclusions and legal theories, your work and work product are to be regarded as confidential and privileged. Any communications, reports and related documents that you generate therefore must be disclosed only to our firm and should bear the legend "Subject to Attorney-Client and Work Product Privileges."

    5. During the course of this engagement Consultant agrees to perform only such work as Consultant is directed by DEF.

    If these terms meet with your approval, please sign, date and return one copy of this letter to us by fax and first class mail, retaining one copy for your files. We appreciate Consultant's assistance and look forward to working with DEF.

Sincerely,

Agreed to and Accepted:

_____
Consultant

Dated: _____

A p p e n d i x   1D

Transaction Timetable for Fast-Track Due Diligence[*]

Working Group Key[**]

B   = Buyer officer

C   = Candidate company officer (in some transactions, this may be a representative of the seller of the company, if the company is a corporate division or unit)

Lb = Lawyer for the buyer (internal, external, or both)

Lc = Lawyer for the candidate (internal, external, or both)

Eb = Expert consultant retained by buyer (optional)

Ab = Accountant for the buyer (internal, external, or both)

Ac = Accountant for the candidate

More than one individual may represent the buyer, the candidate, or their advisers. In the initial meeting and final meetings, the most senior people should attend, accompanied by junior associates. During the actual conduct of due diligence, more junior representatives may be involved, given proper guidance and supervision.

Week of March 6

B,C, Lb, Lc, Ab, E
Buyer's due diligence team meets with candidate company and the company's lawyer in buyer's offices.

Group agrees on:

- Terms of due diligence investigation
- Items on due diligence checklist
- Timetable for due diligence

Lawyer for buyer drafts memo for buyer's board of directors advising board of progress.

---

[*] This document was provided by Mark Schonberger, Partner, Battle Fowler LLP, New York, and is reprinted (and adapted) with permission.

[**] This key has been adapted to apply for an acquisition. The basic form is used for due diligence in securities offerings.

Week of March 13

Lb, C
Lawyer for buyer works with candidate representative to implement due diligence. Together they prepare and distribute:

- First draft of checklist [see sample checklist at end of book].
- Director and officer questionnaire (D&O) and other questionnaires to candidate company (Form S-1).

Lb, C
Lawyers for buyer and candidate make sure that due diligence items are reflected in acquisition agreement representations and warranties.

Lb
Lawyer for buyer sets up folders for due diligence document room.

Lawyer for buyer gives its own team initial document request list and explains purpose [see Appendix 1F].

B, Lb, Ab, Eb
Buyer and all buyer advisers hold telephone conference to check progress.

Weeks of March 20 and March 27

Lb,Ab and/or Eb, plus C, Lc, Ac
Representatives of buyer contact and/or visit the candidate company to obtain financial, operational, and legal information needed from the checklist.

As they work, buyer's representatives send documents to due diligence document room for storage and copying.

Week of April 3

Lb
Staff of buyer's lawyer prepares master set of due diligence documents, with cover memorandum identifying areas of risk for resolution.

Week of April 10

B,C, Lb,Lc, Ab, Ac, Eb
Entire due diligence group attends closing, conducting bringdown due diligence then or later as necessary.

A P P E N D I X 1E

Sample Preliminary Request List[*]

PRELIMINARY DOCUMENT AND INFORMATION REQUEST LIST FOR [NAME OF COMPANY]

PRIVILEGED AND CONFIDENTIAL

Draft [Date]

All references in the following list to the "Company" include [Name of Company] and each of its subsidiaries or divisions.

I. Corporate Records

  1. Charter documents and bylaws of the Company, as amended to date.

  2. Minute books of the Company for the last five years (including copies of reports to members not set forth in the minutes).

  3. Stock books, stock ledgers and other records of the issuance of stock by the Company.

  4. A copy of the most current organizational chart available for the Company, including all entities or investments in which the Company owns less than a 100% interest.

  5. Schedule showing for the Company and each of its subsidiaries: name, jurisdictions where qualified to do business and jurisdictions where it owns or leases real property.

II. Public Filings and Financial Information

  1. Audited consolidated financial statements and the notes thereto for the past five years (or the earliest date available) for the Company.

---

[*] This document was provided by Mark Schonberger, Partner, Battle Fowler LLP, New York, and is reprinted courtesy of Battle Fowler LLP.

2. Interim financial statements for quarters since the last audit for the Company.
3. Most recent internal financial statements for the Company, i.e., for the period since the last quarterly statements.
4. Audited financial statements for any enterprises merged with, or acquired by, the Company in the last five years.
5. Current internal budget, operating and financial plans and projections and any reports or papers relating to any long-term budget, capital development, restructuring program or strategic plan, including any plans regarding systems and operations, of the Company.
6. Any private placement memoranda or offering circulars prepared and used by the Company in the last five years.
7. All annual or other letters or reports from the Company's independent public accountants or internal auditors to management during the last five years regarding accounting control systems, methods of accounting and other procedures. Any other reports prepared by the Company, its internal auditors, counsel or others regarding similar accounting matters.
8. List of tax returns of the Company and the years thereof which have been audited by state or federal tax authorities, and copies of the determination letters related thereto. List of tax years open. Specify whether the Internal Revenue Service or similar authorities have indicated that there may be a claim relating to open tax years.

III. Corporate Agreements

1. All agreements or documents evidencing borrowings (including bank lines of credit) or guarantees by the Company or any partnership in which the Company holds interests, or security related to borrowings or guarantees of the Company.
2. All documents and agreements evidencing other financial arrangements of the Company, including sale and repurchase or leaseback arrangements, capitalized leases, real estate and other installment purchases, equipment leases, etc.
3. Any agreement to loan funds or provide working capital to non-wholly-owned subsidiaries or partnerships in which the Company owns an interest or to other third parties.
4. Material correspondence of the Company with lenders during the past five years, including any compliance reports prepared

by the Company or its auditors and any waivers provided by the lenders.

5. Any agreements (other than those described above) that restrict additional indebtedness or the sale, lease or transfer (by dividend or otherwise) of the assets or capital stock of the Company.

6. All contracts relating to the Company's securities to which the Company is a party, or among shareholders of the Company, or between shareholders and the Company, including (i) any agreements relating to the purchase, issuance, transfer or voting of securities of the Company (e.g., stock option plans, forms of stock option agreements, private placement agreements, registration rights agreements or subscription agreements), (ii) all stockholders' agreements, voting trusts or other restrictive agreements relating to the sale or voting of shares of the Company, and (iii) any agreements under which any person has any rights concerning issued or unissued securities of the Company (e.g., rights of purchase or sale, preemptive rights, rights of first refusal, registration rights, options, warrants or convertible securities).

7. Any joint venture, shareholders', partnership or other management, operating or consulting agreements to which the Company is a party.

8. All divestiture or acquisition agreements and related documents entered into by the Company in the last five years (or earlier if the Company has any material ongoing commitments in respect of any divestiture or acquisition), including all documents relating to any proposed material divestiture or acquisition by the Company.

9. List of material customers of the Company, giving annual dollar amounts purchased during the last three years, and copies of contracts with such persons.

10. List of all distribution agreements and copies of material distribution contracts (or any form contracts) to which the Company is a party.

11. List of material suppliers and volume of purchases made from each listed source in the last two fiscal years. Copies of material supply contracts of the Company and any correspondence with material suppliers, including the agreements and correspondence with sole-source suppliers. Copies of any reports or internal memoranda relating to potential supply or inventory problems.

12. List of all principal properties owned or leased by the Company. Copies of all material leases of real property and personal property to which the Company is a party either as lessee or lessor. Copies of all mortgages and related agreements or other security agreements concerning properties owned or leased by the Company.

13. List of all patents, trademarks, trade names, copyrights, etc. ("Intellectual Property") owned or used in the business of the Company, giving brief descriptions of the use, registration numbers and dates of issuance of registration, names of any persons to or from whom such Intellectual Property is licensed, and brief descriptions of such arrangements. Description of any claims asserted or threatened by any third party with respect to any Intellectual Property.

14. Copies of all material agreements relating to competition, noncompetition, nonsolicitation, licensing, territorial arrangements, distributorships or franchises to which the Company is a party, and any Hart-Scott-Rodino filings.[*]

15. Copies of tax sharing agreements among the Company and any of its affiliates or subsidiaries.

16. Schedule of material insurance policies of the Company.

17. Form of product warranties of the Company.

18. Records relating to customer complaints during the last two years.

19. Material research and development reports prepared by the Company in the last three years.

20. Any material contracts and agreements, not otherwise described above, to which the Company is a party.

IV. Employees

1. All material employment agreements, consulting agreements, retention agreements, agency agreements, noncompete agreements, collective bargaining agreements and similar agreements to which the Company is a party, including employment contracts of executive officers.

2. All bonus, retirement, profit sharing, stock option, incentive compensation, pension and other employee benefit plans or agreements of the Company. Provide a schedule of all outstanding options and warrants, identifying the holders

---

* Note: For an explanation of Hart-Scott-Rodino filings, see Chapter 8.

thereof; issue dates, exercise price, expiration date, price of underlying shares at time of issue and other material terms.

3. List of any strikes, unusual labor relationships, work stoppages or employment-related proceedings during the last five years.

4. All contracts or agreements with or pertaining to the Company and to which directors, officers or beneficial owners of more than 5% of the common shares of the Company are parties. All documents relating to any other transaction between the Company and any director, officer or beneficial owner of more than 5% of the common shares of the Company.

5. Indemnification arrangements with officers and directors of the Company, including a description of any pertinent insurance policies.

V. Governmental Regulation and Environmental Compliance

1. List of all material government permits, licenses, etc., of the Company (obtained or pending).

2. Any correspondence with, reports filed with or other communications between the Company and regulatory authorities within the last five years with respect to significant regulatory matters, including any correspondence, memoranda or other communications relating to (specific regulatory authority).

3. Any correspondence, memoranda or other communications relating to existing or pending governmental regulations affecting the Company's businesses, including any correspondence, memoranda or other communications relating to any proposed legislation.

4. Any information concerning environmental matters and compliance with environmental laws and governmental regulations, including descriptions of any contaminated properties, spills, liabilities to third parties, current or prospective environmental remediation efforts, "potentially responsible party" letters and administrative orders.

5. Copies of waste generation records, including generation registration, hazardous waste manifests and any correspondence, directions or orders relating to waste disposal sites, including PCB waste disposal sites.

6. Copies of all environmental audits, inspections, surveys, questionnaires and similar reports (internal or external) relating to the Company, including any commissioned by legal counsel to the Company.

VI. <u>Legal Matters</u>

  1. A schedule and status report of any material litigation, administrative proceedings or governmental investigation or inquiry, pending or threatened, affecting the Company or any of its respective officers or directors, including a brief description (amount in controversy and name of attorney handling matter, etc.) of all such pending or threatened matters.
  2. Any memoranda of or correspondence with counsel with respect to pending or threatened litigation or litigation settled or otherwise terminated within the last three years.
  3. Any material consent decrees, judgments, other decrees or orders, settlement agreements or other agreements to which the Company or any of its officers or directors is a party or is presently bound, requiring or prohibiting any future activities.
  4. All letters from the Company or from counsel for the Company to the Company's independent public accountants or to any regulatory authority in the last three years regarding material litigation in which the Company or any of its respective officers or directors may be involved, including updates thereof to the most recent practicable date.

VII. <u>Other Material Information</u>

  1. Any recent analyses of the Company prepared by the Company, investment bankers, commercial bankers, engineers, management consultants, accountants, federal or state regulatory authorities or others, including appraisals, marketing studies, future plans, credit reports and other types of reports, financial or otherwise.
  2. Copies of customer profile studies and any other major research projects conducted, undertaken or completed in the last three years.
  3. Press releases issued during the last three years.
  4. Any reports or communications to shareholders for the last three years.
  5. Responses to the directors and officers questionnaires.
  6. Product brochures and other marketing material.
  7. Backlog and order summary records for the last fiscal year.
  8. Copies of accident reports for the Company for the last three years.

9. Any other documents or information which, in the judgment of the officers of the Company, are significant with respect to the business of the Company or which should be considered and reviewed in making disclosures regarding the business and financial condition of the Company.

Note: Acquirers should add additional specific requests according to the type of company involved in the transaction.

The document request list above can then be used as the text of a closing memorandum stating that all requested documents have been reviewed. The introductory language in such a closing memorandum might be as follows:

FINAL CLOSING MEMORANDUM

PRIVILEGED AND CONFIDENTIAL ATTORNEY'S WORK PRODUCT

[DATE]

TO: Client

FROM: Law Firm

RE: Legal Due Diligence Review of XYZ, Inc.

We have conducted a legal due diligence investigation of XYZ, Inc. (the "Company") and its subsidiaries in connection with the proposed sale to the underwriters, represented by ABC & Co. (the "Underwriters"), of 3 million shares of Common Stock of the Company.

We have reviewed minute books, public filings, corporate documents and agreements and other documents relating to the Company, which were supplied to us by the Company and its counsel, DEF Law Firm, in response to a Document Request List submitted by us to the Company. Our review focused on:

1. The authorization and issuance of all shares of Common Stock of the Company and the authorization of material corporate actions of the Company.
2. The contractual relationships of the Company and its subsidiaries with the Founders.
3. Material events and developments regarding the Company.
4. Material liabilities of the Company.

5. The Company's intellectual property assets, the arrangements entered into with respect to those assets, and the legal protection of such assets.

Our findings are summarized and set forth below. A copy of the Document Request List is attached. (Attach checklist above.)

For more examples of closing memoranda, see Chapter 5.

A P P E N D I X   1 F

Annotated Sample Initial Document Request List*

AN ANNOTATED INITIAL DOCUMENT AND INFORMATION REQUEST LIST

Mark Schonberger with:
Ronni S. Bianco
Mark Fajfar
Stephen I. Glover
Jocelyn M. Sturdivant
Vasiliki B. Tsaganos

Junior associates are often handed a document request list similar to the one that follows and instructed to "begin due diligence." Unfortunately, this is often done without much explanation as to why certain documents are requested, and what the associate should be looking for. In general, the associate should be looking for any information that seems unusual or curious. We refer to these items as "red flags." In addition, associates should review all documents with an eye toward provisions of a burdensome nature which may prohibit or inhibit the deal or the company's future plans. We refer to these items as "obstacles." Red flags and obstacles should be brought to the attention of the other team members and, generally, the client.

Mark Schonberger

---

* This document was provided by Mark Schonberger, Partner, Battle Fowler LLP, New York, and is reprinted courtesy of Battle Fowler LLP.

This is a sample only; it should not be used as an exhaustive guide and should be modified for every transaction as appropriate (e.g., a public offering versus a private acquisition). For example, due diligence into the capitalization of the Company may be less significant in an asset sale than in a stock sale. This document request list does not contain specialized sections dealing with intellectual property, environmental, and employment matters, and so forth. For a checklist including those elements, see the Sample Due Diligence Checklist at the back of this book.

I. CORPORATE DOCUMENTS

A. Certificates of incorporation with all amendments and restatements to date of each of Parent, Inc. (the "Company"), its direct and indirect subsidiaries (the "Subsidiaries") and predecessor companies.

- You should obtain all documents on file with the Secretary of State of the company's state of incorporation (e.g., long-form good standing certificate). You should compare documents received from the Secretary of State with documents received from the Company to check for discrepancies. Obtain a good standing certificate at the beginning of your investigation as well as at the closing.

- Compare the certificate of incorporation to the relevant corporate statute.

- The certificate of incorporation is the first document that should be reviewed, as it will provide important information such as the Company's legal name, the duration of its corporate existence, the Company's powers, the history of the Company's authorized share capital, existence of preemptive rights and restrictions upon stock issuances or business combinations. In addition, the charter serves as an important basis for checking what the Company's minutes show as to dates and amounts of authorized stock.

- For the Company, it will be very important to understand its capital structure, including amount of voting stock, voting rights and preferences, particularly if stockholder approval is required for the transaction. For example, you need to know whether a supermajority vote of stockholders is required for the transaction at hand. You should also check applicable state law regarding shareholder approval requirements.

- With regard to the Subsidiaries, your firm may be asked to opine that the Company owns as much of each Subsidiary as it claims. Knowing the amount of authorized capital stock is the first step in supporting this opinion.

- If your firm has been asked to opine that the target or issuer is duly incorporated, you should compare the charter and bylaws with the law of the state of incorporation in effect at the time the Company was incorporated as well as at the time the charter or bylaws were amended, if amended. You must determine whether these documents were properly adopted and amended under the state law governing at that time and if they are in full force and effect.

- You should check closely provisions concerning preemptive rights and rights of first refusal. If such provisions exist, review each issuance of stock. The preemptive rights of the stockholders must have been duly waived or taken into account.

- Check to make sure that the charter contains no restrictions on corporate actions, for example, upon sales or other transfers of stock, issuance of certain types of securities, incurrence of debt, antitakeover provisions or other obstacles to your transaction. These types of restrictions may also impact any future plans your client may have.

- Depending on the transaction, you may have to amend or eliminate certain provisions in the certificate of incorporation.

B. Bylaws of the Company and the Subsidiaries.

- The bylaws usually contain a significant amount of information about corporate procedure. Read the bylaws of each of the companies closely to make sure that there are no procedural obstacles to your transaction.

- You need to be aware of the procedure for amending the bylaws, the powers of the corporate officers, whether shareholders and directors may act by written consent, and indemnification of directors and officers.

- Check also for vote requirements, the notice required for meetings, whether notice can be waived, whether telephonic meetings are permitted (all for both shareholders and directors), the types of action for which shareholder approval is required and the general mechanics of how the company is governed.

- It will also be important to understand the procedures for electing, removing and replacing directors and officers. You will need to verify that the directors and officers have been duly elected, have approved minutes and resolutions regarding the transaction (in the case of directors) and have signed transaction documents (in the case of officers).

- Compare the bylaws to the relevant corporate statute.
- Depending on the transaction, you may have to amend or eliminate certain provisions in the bylaws.

C. Minute books and all materials distributed in connection with meetings of the Company and each of the Subsidiaries for the last five years.

- You should review the minutes of meetings of the board of directors and any committees as well as meetings of stockholders.
- Prior to reviewing minutes, you should be familiar with any stockholders' agreements or voting agreements that may contain restrictions on corporate actions, vote requirements, etc.
- You are checking to see whether the actions taken by the directors and shareholders were taken in accordance with the charter, bylaws, stockholders' agreements and state law.
- If your firm will be opining as to the Company's due incorporation, examine the minutes from organizational meetings and the state law in effect at the time of incorporation to determine whether the incorporation procedure in effect at the time of incorporation was followed, the certificate of incorporation was properly adopted, the bylaws were properly adopted, the subscription agreement was properly approved and the initial issuance of stock was properly approved.
- Be sure you understand how the company was formed, who the initial stockholders or contributors were and what they contributed. There should be clean receipts, canceled certificates, etc., for everything. Did the company receive the consideration it was supposed to receive?
- Whenever directors have authorized or issued securities (including options and warrants), amended the charter or taken other significant action (such as approvals of material contracts, employment and severance arrangements, pension plans, loans, acquisitions and transactions involving officers, directors and principal stockholders), verify that the

procedures prescribed by applicable securities laws, state law, the charter and bylaws were followed, including that the directors were properly elected, each of the meetings was duly and properly called, a proper quorum was present and a proper percentage of votes favorable to the action was recorded (this applies to both director and stockholder meetings).

- Verify that the current directors and officers have been elected in strict accordance with the charter, bylaws and state law in effect at the time of election.

- If the Company keeps detailed board minutes, the minute books can provide a good overview of the Company's operations, material transactions and agreements, litigation and other business affairs—keep an eye out for red flags. If the Company does not keep detailed board minutes, that fact alone can be a red flag.

- If there are consents in lieu of meetings, check that the requisite vote was met.

- Verify that no action has been taken to dissolve the Company or its Subsidiaries.

- If you find actions that have not been taken properly, "cleanup" work will be necessary through ratification action by directors or stockholders.

D. Stock books, dock ledgers and other records of issuance of the Company and each of the Subsidiaries.

- You are checking to see whether the outstanding stock of the company has been duly authorized, validly issued and fully paid and nonassessable.

- The goal is to track stock issuances, transfers, cancellations and exchanges. Sometimes it is helpful to create a flowchart. Check to see if stock issuances were properly authorized by the board and were in accordance with the charter bylaws and federal and state securities laws.

- Has the stock described in the minute books as having been issued in fact been appropriately recorded?

- Does the total number of shares indicated in the stock books as outstanding conform to the number of shares indicated as outstanding in the Company's financial statements?

- If there is a corporate transfer agent or registrar, obtain a certificate showing the number of outstanding shares and compare it to the numbers in the financial statements.
- Were there any stock repurchases? Were they completed in accordance with the state law?
- Obtain a certificate from the Company's independent public accountant that the stock is fully paid; otherwise, you will have to review the Company's financial statements from past years.

E. List of all jurisdictions in the United States and elsewhere in which the Company is qualified to do business.

- You should obtain good standing certificates from each foreign jurisdiction to check that the Company is duly qualified.
- You should check the state laws for all requirements imposed on the Company by foreign jurisdictions.
- Consider whether you need to withdraw from any state or qualify in a new state as a result of the transaction.
- You may need to check with local counsel in foreign jurisdictions if the Company does business in other countries.

F. A copy of the most current organizational chart available for the Company, including all Subsidiaries and any other entities or investments in which the Company owns less than a 100% interest.

- The organizational chart provides a basic understanding of how the Company and the Subsidiaries [collectively, the Companies] are structured and operated. It will become invaluable during your investigation in figuring out who can provide you with certain documents and who would be helpful to interview regarding certain issues.

G. Any and all agreements among shareholders of the Company, or between shareholders and any of the Companies, relating to the management, ownership or control of the Companies, including voting agreements, rights of first refusal, preemptive rights and registration rights.

- Look for potential obstacles to the contemplated transaction such as voting agreements, rights of first refusal, preemptive rights and registration rights. These agreements may affect the potential change of control of a company or the transferability of its stock. Look to see whether the deal will trigger any of these burdensome provisions. In closely held companies, there may be complex agreements between shareholders, including agreements to buy back shares, issue more shares, etc. Nearly all such agreements have complex registration rights upon a public offering.

- If the contemplated transaction is a sale of stock, determine whether the purchaser will be required to enter into such types of agreements (e.g., voting agreement) or, if appropriate, whether such agreements are assignable.
- Review any shareholder rights plans.

H. Reports or other material communications to shareholders of the Company for the last five years.

- Read these communications to make sure that you and your client are aware of all the material information that has been disclosed to stockholders.
- Look for red flags.

II. FINANCIAL INFORMATION

A. If the company is public: All filings by the Company and Subsidiaries with the Securities and Exchange Commission during the last five years. (If the Company is not public: Audited consolidated financial statements and the notes thereto for the past five years and interim financial statements for quarters since the last audit for the Company and the Subsidiaries.)

- These documents will help you understand the Company's business.
- In the case of public companies, you will review annual reports (a Form 10-K) and quarterly reports (a Form 10-Q). The 10-Ks and 10-Qs will contain a significant amount of disclosure about operations, financials and management's view of these results (the Management's Discussion & Analysis of Financial Condition and Results of Operations (MD&A)). Public companies also file a proxy statement annually. In addition to these periodic filings, public companies must disclose extraordinary events on Form 8-Ks. Review these documents to make sure that you and your client are aware of all the material information that has been disclosed to stockholders and the public. Look for red flags.

- The footnotes to the financial statements will contain information on stock options, debt and capital structure; be sure that you understand all footnotes and that you have reviewed all agreements discussed in the footnotes.
- You should look for and obtain explanations of any significant losses or unusually good years.

B. Any private placement memorandum or offering document prepared and used by the Company or its Subsidiaries in the last five years.

- Again, these documents provide useful information in understanding the Company and should be reviewed, with the most recent documents getting the most attention.
- Pay attention to the risk factors section. Use it as a checklist to be sure you have caught all potential problems.

C. If the Company is public: Any Schedule 13D* or 13G** filed with the Company in the last five years.

- In an acquisition, the buyer will want to know who owns stock in the target and how much stock each Stockholder owns. Such information will assist the buyer in analyzing the probability of obtaining stockholder consent to the transaction.
- Use these filings as a check to understanding the Company's capital structure.

D. Current internal budget, operating and financial plans and projections and any reports or papers relating to any long-term budget, capital development, restructuring program or strategic plan, including any plans regarding systems and operations.

- Internal budgets and forecasts are useful in understanding what management thinks the company's current and future prospects are, and for highlighting areas of concern to management. Look for red flags.

---

* A Schedule 13D is a form that must be filed under the Securities Exchange Act of 1934. Generally, this form must be filed within 10 days after an acquisition that brings a stockholder above the 5 percent ownership threshold. It requires disclosure concerning the identity and background of the acquirer, the purpose and funding of the acquisition and the acquirer's plans, agreements and understandings regarding the issuer.

** A Schedule 13G is a form that must be filed under the Securities Exchange Act of 1934. Generally, this form must be filed and updated annually by every beneficial owner of 5 percent of a registered class of voting securities. This form requires disclosure of the owner's identity and size of holdings.

- Check to see if the internal budget matches what the Company has stated publicly. Are the assumptions overly optimistic? Is the Company ignoring or covering up problems? This review may reveal disclosure issues, such as product backlog.

E. Audited financial statements for any enterprises merged with, or acquired by, the Company or any of its Subsidiaries in the last five years.

- Focus especially on the footnotes—they can provide a checklist for just about everything about the Company, including credit agreements, debt structure, capital structure, compensation, options and leases. This holds true for all reviews of financial statements.

F. All annual or other letters or reports from each of the Companies' independent public accountants or auditors to management during the last five years regarding each of the Companies' accounting control systems, methods of accounting and other procedures.

- Look for red flags, especially in terms of hesitancy, qualified opinions or warnings.

G. Any reports prepared by any of the Companies, their internal auditors, counsel or others regarding material accounting matters (such as memoranda relating to a change in the Companies' accountants, inventory markdowns, increases in reserves for doubtful accounts, or other reports prepared for the board of directors).

- These reports are helpful, as they highlight problems that the Company has had in the past. Look for red flags. As part of your investigation, you will want to note what steps have been taken to resolve the problems and to prevent their reoccurrence.

H. List of returns of the Company and the years thereof which have been audited by state or federal tax authorities, and copies of the determination letters related thereto. List of tax years open. Indicate whether the Internal Revenue Service or similar authority has indicated that there may be a claim relating to open tax years.

- You are looking for significant potential liabilities either in the operations of the Company being investigated or in connection with the specific proposed transaction.

- These documents should be brought to the attention of the tax specialist on your team.
- You should also do a search of tax liens. Several search firms have a service that can provide this type of search.

III. MATERIAL CORPORATE AGREEMENTS

There may be agreements that could materially affect the Company's operations or the proposed transaction. Your goal is to find business and legal risks. In most cases, you want to make sure the material agreements will remain in effect. Some of the items that you should consider are the following: (i) what is the term; (ii) what are the Company's obligations and liabilities under the agreement; (iii) how is corporate action restricted; (iv) what are the events of default; (v) what are the consequences of a material breach (e.g., cross defaults, termination); (vi) is the contract assignable; (vii) how can the agreement be terminated; (viii) are there any changes in control provisions; (ix) are any consents required; (x) are any notice provisions triggered; (xi) what is the total exposure; and (xii) what types of indemnification provisions are there. You should also consider obtaining an officer's certificate certifying that the material agreements are still in effect and have not been amended or modified (otherwise than as set forth in subsequent amendments). Also, if need be, material contracts can be verified with the counterparty. When reviewing minutes, you should double-check that material contracts were approved and authorized by the board of directors. Finally, make sure you have reviewed fully executed copies of the material agreements and that the copies are complete. In the context of a public offering you will have to determine which material agreements should be filed as exhibits to the registration statement.

A. All agreements or documents evidencing borrowings (including bank lines of credit) or guarantees by the Company, each of its Subsidiaries or any partnership of which the Company holds partnership interests.

- First, it is important to determine the amount of money the Company owes or has guaranteed, the terms of the debt and the amount and timing of the payments. What are your client's plans? Will it repay debt? Check the repayment and prepayment provisions. Are there any penalties?

- Second, review these documents to make sure there are no obstacles to the transaction. For example, the contracts may not be assignable, or certain covenants may restrict the transaction. Events of default may be triggered by the transaction. When working on a financing, keep in mind that often the sale of securities is deemed an assignment of the agreement. In these documents, you are looking for obstacles. If there are obstacles, your client may have to renegotiate the terms.
- Identify any consents that may be required and make sure that any such consents or waivers that have been previously obtained are in proper form.
- Debt instruments usually contain affirmative and negative covenants (e.g., restrictions on combinations, offering, asset sales, payment of dividends) that can significantly restrict your client's plans for the Company's operations or the pending transaction itself.

B. Material correspondence of the Company and each of its Subsidiaries with lenders during the past five years, including any compliance reports prepared by the Company or any of its Subsidiaries or their auditors.

- Review this correspondence to verify that the Company is not in default on its loans and that there are no outstanding issues with lenders. Look for red flags.

C. All contracts relating to the Company's securities to which the Company is a party, including stock option plans, forms of stock option agreements, private placement agreements, registration rights agreements, subscription agreements, voting agreements, warrant agreements, etc.

- Review these documents to verify that your client is aware of their existence, as well as the significant provisions thereof. Look for obstacles and red flags.
- You should be familiar with the total outstanding amount of options or other rights to acquire stock of the Company.
- What are the Company's obligations under these documents?

D. Copies of all mortgages or other security agreements that are material to the Company or any of its Subsidiaries.

- Depending upon the target or issuer, there may be a few mortgages or several thousand. If there are many mortgages, before reviewing all these agreements, discuss with the other team members whether there is an efficient way to reduce the number of mortgages examined. For example, you might decide to examine only mortgages involving a certain minimum dollar amount. Another option is to examine a randomly selected percentage of mortgages.

- Summarize the key terms of the mortgages, including location and character of property owned, term of debt, payment amounts, due dates of payments and any covenants or obstacles that may impact the transaction.
- Determine whether there are any disputes under the material mortgages.
- Undertake UCC searches to check for liens in the company's state of incorporation, the state where its executive office is located and the state where major operations are conducted or facilities are located. Note that for certain assets such as aircraft, there are special registries that should be checked.
- Review financing statements. Which are the assets in which your client is most interested? Check for liens against those assets.

E. Any agreement to lend funds or provide working capital to non-wholly-owned Subsidiaries, partnerships in which the Company owns an interest or other third parties.
   - Look for red flags, obstacles—do any agreements involve related parties?
   - What is the total exposure to the Company?

F. All documents and agreements evidencing other financial arrangements, including sale and repurchase or leaseback arrangements, capitalized leases, real estate and other installment purchases, equipment leases, etc.
   - Look for red flags, obstacles—do any agreements involve related parties?
   - Has the Company agreed to perform or not perform certain actions in the future?
   - What is the Company's exposure?

G. Any joint venture, partnership or other material management, operating or consulting agreements to which the Company or any of its Subsidiaries is a party.
   - What are the Company's obligations and liabilities? How will the pending transaction affect these agreements?

H. All divestiture or acquisition agreements entered into by the Company in the last five years.
- Which provisions survive?
- What are the Company's continuing obligations (e.g., indemnification, noncompetition)?

I. List of material customers and vendors of the Company and each of its Subsidiaries, giving annual dollar amounts purchased or sold during the last five years, and copies of contracts with such persons.
- Often material relationships may not be documented and you will need to interview Company officials. Consider whether your client will want to document these relationships.
- Are there possible disruptions to sales or supplies? Are prices expected to increase or decrease?
- Look to see whether any single customer or vendor accounts for a large percentage of the total amount purchased or sold annually. What are the terms of the contracts with such customers or vendors? What would happen if these relationships were terminated? Any such concentration should be brought to the attention of the buyer or disclosed in the prospectus.
- Review the contracts for red flags and obstacles.

J. List of all distribution agreements and copies of material distribution contracts to which the Company or any of its Subsidiaries is a party.
- *See* III.I.
- Review the contracts for red flags and obstacles.

K. List of material suppliers and copies of material supply contracts and any correspondence with material suppliers, including the agreements and correspondence, if any, with sole-source suppliers.
- *See* III.I.
- Are the Company's requirements for the future covered by these contracts?

L. List of all principal properties. Copies of all material leases of real and personal property to which the Company or any of its Subsidiaries is a party, either as lessee or lessor.
- If real estate is a significant asset, a real estate lawyer should review these documents.

- Actual documents should be compared against title insurance. You are checking for encumbrances, rights of third parties, etc.
- With regard to leased properties, summarize the key terms of each lease (e.g., term, rent and square footage of the property). Review whether the proposed transaction triggers any provisions in the leases that would be obstacles to the deal. Are there renewal rights? What happens upon a change of control?

M. Copies of all material agreements relating to competition, noncompetition, licensing, territorial arrangements, distributorships or franchises to which the Company or any of its Subsidiaries is a party.

- Obstacles and red flags—does the Company have burdensome obligations, or is it relying on unenforceable provisions?
- You may wish to consult an antitrust lawyer.
- Will these agreements cover the Company's needs in the future?

N. Copies of tax sharing agreements between the Company and any of its Subsidiaries.

- These documents should be brought to the attention of the tax specialist on your team.

O. Schedule of material insurance policies of the Company and its Subsidiaries currently in effect.

- Are all areas of risk covered (e.g., environmental, product liability, directors and officers)?
- You should review each material insurance policy. What is the deductible? Are there liability limits? What types of exclusions exist?
- Sometimes a firm specializing in risk analysis should be engaged.

P. Form of product warranties of the Company and its principal Subsidiaries.

- Look for red flags, such as material contingent liabilities.
- What are the Company's indemnification obligations?

Q. Company records relating to customer complaints during the last two years.

- Look for red flags, such as patterns of complaints.

R. Any material foreign currency exchange agreements, including, without limitation, any hedging agreements, and a summary of derivative trading.

- Given the times, you must make sure you understand these agreements and the exposure and risks to the Company.

S. All material contracts and agreements, not otherwise described above, to which the Company or any of its Subsidiaries is a party.

- Make sure that you have asked the target or issuer to provide you with copies of any documents that you may have overlooked or any agreements or relationships that are not documented.

T. All contracts or agreements with or pertaining to the Company or the Subsidiaries to which any director or officer of the Company or the Subsidiaries or any beneficial owner of more than 5% of the common stock of the Company and the Subsidiaries is a party.

- The concern with respect to affiliate transactions is that the agreements may be on terms more favorable than an arm's-length agreement. If that is the case, the termination of such agreements may adversely affect the Company's business.

- Review these documents as you would any similar document that does not have an insider or large stockholder as a party.

U. All documents pertaining to any receivables from or payables (including loans) to any director or officer of the Company or its Subsidiaries or any beneficial owner of more than 5% of the common stock of the Company.

V. Indemnification arrangements with officers and directors of the Company or any of the Subsidiaries, including any pertinent insurance policies.

IV. GOVERNMENTAL REGULATION

You must understand the significant regulations affecting the Company's business, operations and the proposed transaction. Are any regulatory approvals or consents required? Are any regulatory issues presented by the transaction and/or the Company's business that must be addressed? Are there any regulatory proceedings pending or threatened that may materially affect the Company's business?

A. Filings with regulatory authorities for the past five years.

- Are any filings or approvals required in connection with the transaction?

B. Any correspondence or other communications with regulatory authorities within the last five years with respect to significant regulatory matters, including any correspondence, memoranda or other communication relating to the applicable regulatory authorities.

  - You should review all material correspondence with regulatory authorities.

C. Any correspondence, memoranda or other communication relating to existing or pending governmental regulations affecting the Company's business, including any correspondence, memoranda or other communication relating to any proposed legislation.

  - What effects may proposed legislation have on the Company's business?
  - What will the cost of compliance with any such new legislation be?

D. A list of all governmental permits, licenses, etc., of the Company and its Subsidiaries.

  - You will usually have to consult with expert counsel—FCC, FDA, environmental, etc.
  - What is the impact of the transaction on the permits, licenses, etc.? Can the permits and licenses be transferred? Must your client reapply for such permits and licenses?

V. LEGAL MATTERS

A. A schedule and status report of any material litigation, administrative proceedings or governmental investigation or inquiry (including, without limitation, tax and customs matters), pending or threatened, affecting the Company or any of its Subsidiaries or any of their officers or directors, including brief descriptions (amount in controversy and name of attorney handling matters, etc.) of all such pending or threatened litigation, proceedings, etc.

  - The primary reason for reviewing litigation documents is to determine the total amount of contingent liability and the likelihood of liability. Also look for any patterns of suits. What types of problems does the Company seem to have?

- You want to understand the scope of any ongoing material lawsuit, investigation or inquiry, and the potential consequences, including monetary damages. You probably will have to consult with the litigation counsel handling the case.
- You may have to review complaints and pleadings and discuss exposure with litigation counsel. If the claims are very specialized, you may have to consult expert counsel in that area (e.g., environmental).
- Many times you cannot rely on the information provided to you, and you also should do an independent search through one of the search services.
- Is the potential liability covered by insurance?

B. Any memoranda of counsel or correspondence with counsel with respect to pending or threatened litigation or litigation settled or otherwise terminated within the past five years.

- If you are told a matter has been resolved, make sure you review *signed* settlement agreements.

C. Any material consent decrees, judgments, other decrees or orders, settlement agreements or other agreements to which any of the Companies or any of their officers or directors is a party or is bound, requiring or prohibiting any future activities, regardless of when issued.

- Look for obstacles to the transaction. In addition, in acquisitions, you need to understand whether there are any activities in which the Company may not engage. This is important, as your client may have plans to the contrary.

D. All letters from the Companies or from the attorneys for any of the Companies to the Companies' accountants or to any federal or state regulatory authority for the last five years regarding material litigation in which the Companies (or any of their officers or directors) may be involved, including any and all updates thereof to the most recent practicable date.

VI. OTHER MATERIAL INFORMATION

A. Any recent analyses of the Company or any of its Subsidiaries prepared by any of the Companies' investment bankers, engineers, management consultants, accountants, federal or state regulatory authorities or others, including appraisals, marketing studies, future plans and projections, credit reports and other types of reports, financial or otherwise, including reports detailing plans for new divisions for the Company or any of the Subsidiaries.

- These documents will give you insight into how others view the company. Review these analyses for red flags.

B. Any other documents or information which, in the judgment of officers of the Company, are significant with respect to the business of the Companies or which should be considered and reviewed in making disclosures regarding the business and financial condition of the Companies.

- Look for red flags and obstacles.

C. Copies of press releases, issues, or significant articles written about the Company or its Subsidiaries during the last five years.

- Look for red flags.

D. Copies of responses to the most recent officers' and directors' questionnaires.

- With regard to public offerings, you generally must include information on the Company's officers and directors, their remuneration and employee benefits, and material transactions which they have had with the Company. Underwriters and issuer's counsel should review the completed questionnaires and compare them with the disclosure in the registration statement.

E. Product brochures and other marketing material.

- Look for any red flags. Try to determine whether anything in these materials seems misleading or inaccurate.

- If applicable, compare more "technical" materials to sales-oriented documents. Engineers can often be more frank about a key product's shortcomings.

- Information about customers may not be in writing; interviews with marketing people may be necessary to make sure of the strength of the Company's customer base.

E N D N O T E S

1. *Black's Law Dictionary* (The West Group, 1999) at "diligence."
2. Ibid.
3. 1622 Malynes. Auc. Law Merch. 407. "The diligences which are requisite to bee done herein are . . . to be obserued accordingly." *Sic* irregular spelling, as cited

in The Compact Edition of the *Oxford English Dictionary* (Oxford: Oxford University Press, 1971), at "diligence." 1781 Sir W. Jones Est. Bailment 16 1848 Wharton Law Lex s.v. , cited in the *Oxford English Dictionary* (Oxford: Oxford University Press, 1973), p. 364.

4. "The opposite of Negligence is Diligence, vigilance, attention, which , like Negligence, admits of an infinite variety of gradations." Ibid., p. 480. "If the interests of the parties are not identical, the Roman law, at least, requires extraordinary diligence." 1845 *Poste Gains* 477, cited in the *Oxford English Dictionary* (Ibid).

5. Throughout this book, we will use the terms *acquisition candidate, candidate company,* or simply *candidate* or *company* to indicate a company being considered for possible purchase by an acquirer. The more usual term is *target* company. The authors, however, believe that this term implies a hostile action, and therefore reserve use of the term for such a context.

6. In this book, we will use the term *seller* to represent the individual or group with the authority to sell the company being sold.

7. From *Intl. Rectifier.* See also *Competitive Associates Inc. v. International Health Sciences, Inc.* For full legal citations and case summaries, see the Landmark Due Diligence Cases in the back of this book.

8. Noted by John E. Mendez and William R. Sawyers, "Due Diligence in Private Placements and Private Acquisitions," *Conducting Due Diligence 1999* (New York: Practising Law Institute, 1999), p. 308.

9. Courts have generally held that the same statutory liability holds whether a sale is for a minority interest in a company or for all the stock of a company. Ibid., p. 309.

10. Asset sales structured as mergers are rare, but they can and do occur. For example, there may be a sale of multiple assets (in which some assets of a business are purchased separately from the stock of the company that owns the rest of the assets) followed by a merger of the seller and buyer. This hybrid form of transaction put debts and legal liabilities squarely in the hands of the acquirer, unless expressly assumed by the seller.

11. William F. Alderman and John Kanberg, "Due Diligence in the Securities Litigation Reform Era: Some Practical Tips from Litigators on the Effective Conduct, Documentation, and Defense of Underwriter Investigation," *Conducting Due Diligence 1999,* op. cit. (note 8), p. 198.

12. See Harvey Goldschmid, "The Board Audit Committee: In the Vanguard of Change," *Director's Monthly,* January 2000, pp. 6–7.

13. Alderman and Kanberg, op. cit. (note 11), p. 191.

14. Note: The acquisition agreement used is a sample, not a model. Acquirers can draft their own forms more suitable to their transactions. One useful source for drafting acquisition agreements and more than 500 types of forms is the five-volume series *Contemporary Corporation Forms,* 2nd ed. (New York: Aspen Law and Business, 1999). This reference work includes a "clause locator" that enables form drafters to find key paragraphs to use in drafting their own forms.

15. Alderman and Kanberg , op. cit. (note 11), p. 194.

16. This list of forms is provided by Mark Schonberger of Battle Fowler LLP, New York. It is based on a paper he coauthored with Vasiliki B. Tsaganos, "Top Twelve Most Frequently Asked Questions by Junior Associates Conducting Due Diligence," *Conducting Due Diligence 1999*, op. cit. (note 8), pp. 32ff.

17. Alderman and Kanberg, op. cit. (note 8), p. 191.

18. Schonberger (op. cit., note 8) advises lawyers that "typically all financials are excluded from lawyer's opinions and you rely on the target's or issuer's accountants for the accuracy of the company's financial statements. You may want to speak to the accountants directly regarding such issues."

19. This latter conflict may be resolved by a new set of guidelines, effective January 1, 2000, from the American Institute of Certified Public Accountants. The new rules require auditing firms to (1) communicate internally a list of client companies as "restricted," (2) set up a database that shows all restricted" investments in auditing clients, and (3) establish independent policies governing financial relationships, such as loans and brokerage accounts, between restricted companies and the auditing firm, its benefit plans, and its staff members, as well as staff members' close relatives.

20. The primary source for this section on due diligence under federal securities laws is based on Joseph McLaughlin, Partner, Brown & Wood LLP, New York, "The Statutory Basis for Due Diligence Under Federal Securities Laws," *Conducting Due Diligence*, op. cit. (note 8). McLaughlin also includes a discussion of Section 12(a)2 (formerly 12(2)), focusing on broker liability in exempt offerings, citing *Gustafson v. Alloyd Co.*, 115 S.Ct. 1061 (1995). He also summarizes Section 15, concerning liability of "controlling persons," and Section 17(a), which bars fraud, misrepresentations, and wrongful ("actionable") omissions in the sale of securities. Note: Section 17(a) has dwindled in importance recently. The court in *Finkel v. Stratton* (1992) said that only the government, not investors, can sue under 17(a).

21. *Securities Act Rules: Rules 100 through 236; General Rules and Regulations Under the Securities Act of 1933* (New York: Bowne Publishing, Nov. 15, 1999), p. 49.

22. "Providing organized in-house or other training to junior bankers or lawyers on appropriate due diligence techniques and documentation can help dispel any future claim that they lacked sufficient experience to perform their assigned roles. In addition, thorough documentation by the junior team member will facilitate review and supervision by the more senior members, thereby not only helping to catch and correct any shortcomings in the work, but also enabling the underwriter to point to the careful nature of the process that was used. Finally, it is a good idea to encourage the junior team members who have performed document review to participate in drafting sessions. This will enhance their ability to spot issues and to bring them to the attention of more senior team members." Alderman and Kanberg, op. cit. (note 8), p. 204.

23. It is clear that Rule 10b-5 has broad applicability to all securities sales, including private placements. But consider a countertrend noted by Mendez and Sawyers in "Due Diligence in Private Placements and Private Acquisitions," *Conducting Due Diligence 1999*, op. cit. (note 8), p. 307: "The trend of late has been to limit the potential statutory avenues through which a seller of securities in a private transaction might be found liable." The authors cite the Private Securities Litigation Reform Act of 1995 and the Supreme Court case of *Gustafson v. Alloyd Co., Inc.* (1995). In this case, plaintiffs purchased securities of a closely held corporation under a negotiated private sale agreement, holding that the term *prospectus* under Section 12(2) does not include a private sale contract; therefore, Section 12(2) does not apply to private placement.

24. McLaughlin, op. cit. (note 20), p. 15.

25. For cases involving the role of underwriters, see the Landmark Due Diligence Cases at the end of this book.

26. Alderman and Kanberg, op. cit. (note 11).

27. For an authoritative guide to D&O insurance, see John F. Olson, Josiah O. Hatch III, and Ty R. Sagalow, *Director & Officer Liability: Indemnification and Insurance* (West Group, 1999).

CHAPTER 2

The Financial
Statements Review

When you can measure what you are speaking about,
and express it in numbers, you know something about it.

William Thomson, Lord Kelvin
Lectures and Addresses, 1891–1894

INTRODUCTION

For many acquirers, the review of financial statements is the single most important aspect of due diligence. Although the due diligence journey begins from the moment an acquirer contemplates a potential acquisition candidate, no acquirer can really "hit the road" before seeing some hard numbers. A good set of numbers is like the dashboard display on a car: it can tell you the essentials about the vehicle you are about to operate.

The financial statements review entails, at a minimum, a thorough reading of the candidate company's filings with the relevant government agencies. For U.S. public companies, this review will include all recent 10K, 10Q, and proxy filings. In particular, the acquirer should pay special attention to the *classic financial statements* contained in these as well as *key ratios* derived from them. This chapter will cover these points, along with special industry considerations, and then list some red flags for attention.

Often an acquirer delegates this job to accountants or investment bankers, but senior managers of the acquiring company should pay close attention to these issues as well. Dialogue between financial and nonfinancial (strategic, operational) experts can be a learning experience for both—and certainly prepare the acquirer for the future. Services such as Value Line—which displays key historical and current financial information for hundreds of public companies, one page per company, updated regularly—can help nonfinancial managers grasp the essential message of a company's numbers. (Even acquirers of nonpublic companies can benefit from services such as Value Line, because they can look at publicly held companies in the same industry as a kind of proxy for their own privately held candidate.)

The effective review of financial statements is not really just about numbers, however. To assess the quality of a company's numbers, an acquirer needs to assess the strength of the company's *internal controls*, adopting the perspective of a state-of-the art *audit committee*. Therefore, this chapter will end with a discussion of these important topics.

FINANCIAL STATEMENTS

What are the "classic" financial statements that the acquirer should study?

The balance sheet and the earning (or income) statement are clearly the two most critical ones,[1] with the cash flow statement close behind in importance. So are any statements the company has made about the quality of these financial statements—for example, in the "Management's Discussion and Analysis" section of the annual report and 10K filing.

What does the balance sheet show an acquirer?

A balance sheet, true to its name, shows two equally balanced items. For a particular date—typically the end of a company's fiscal year—the balance sheet shows:

- What a company owns—its *assets*—on the left-hand side.
- How the company financed its assets—its *equities*—on the right-hand side. Equities are composed of liabilities (debt) and owners' equity (value after subtracting value of debt from value of assets).

The total for each of these two sides, by definition, will always be identical. Here is a list of key assets. (For guidance on analysis, see the red flags section below.)

- Cash (bills, coins, and amounts in demand checking accounts). Considered a current (or liquid) asset.
- Investment securities (temporary investments in stocks and bonds—recorded at book value in the balance sheet, with market value in a footnote). Considered a current asset.

- Trade receivables (money owed to the company from customers). Considered a current asset.
- Inventories (physical goods on hand and available to sell).
- Prepaid expenses (bills paid by the company prior to receipt of item).
- Property, plant, and equipment (buildings, land, factories, machines—recorded at historic cost and adjusted for appreciation).
- Deferred charges and other assets (goodwill, intangibles, long-term receivables, and investments in affiliates[2]).

The key equities of the company might include:

- Liabilities—current (a year or less in term) and long-term (over one-year in term).
- Owners' equity (share capital and retained earnings).

In studying a balance sheet, where should the acquirer focus?

There are different levels of assets to consider.

First, and most important, the acquirer should assess the value of *tangible assets used in the business* that are independently marketable, such as machinery, real property, or inventories. Appraisal of these is most important—and mandatory in any transaction funded heavily by debt (a leveraged transaction). Such appraisals can be key for lenders who base the amount of their loans on the market value of the assets available as security. And remember, these are carried at historic cost, which may be much lower than current market value. Look for "hidden gold" here. Land often has a market value far greater than its book value.

Second, the acquirer should appraise the value of *tangible assets not used in the business*—such as unused real property, marketable securities, excess raw material, investments in nonintegrated subsidiary operations, and reserves in the extracting industries. Here, too, there may be hidden values.

Finally, the acquirer should appraise *intangibles such as patents or trademarks* that support an earnings stream. Again, these may add tremendous value to the acquired company.

As for liabilities, the focus should be on various ratios that include current liabilities, as discussed below. These ratios can be very significant to any acquirer that is planning to finance the deal on borrowed cash. Obviously, if the debt-to-equity ratio and similar ratios are already high, a leveraged transaction may not be wise.

The balance sheet is very sensitive to industry differences, and many key ratios used in particular industries will reflect those differences. See below for a section on the balance sheets of banks and insurance companies.

What does the income statement show an acquirer?

Unlike the balance sheet, which shows as of a particular date what a company owns and how it got it, the income statement shows how a company made and spent money during a particular period—typically a fiscal quarter or a year.

The three main parts of the income statement are in fact part of a formula: *Sales* minus *expenses* equals *earnings*.

- Sales are revenues for the goods and services sold during the period.
- Expenses are often broken into two categories: *operating* expenses (sales, general, and administrative expenses) and *interest expenses* (interest paid on loans outstanding).
- Earnings, also called *net earnings*, are what is left after subtracting expenses. If you subtract only operating expenses, you get *operating earnings*, also called *earnings before interest and taxes (EBIT)*. Many acquirers focus on operating earnings rather than the alternatives.

What does the cash flow statement show an acquirer?

The statement of cash flow shows the amount of cash moving in (sources) and out (uses) during the previous fiscal year. In fact, it used to be called the *sources and uses* statement.

- A major contributor to cash flow is *cash flow from operations*. This number will be similar to net earnings (losses), with adjustments for items not received or not paid in cash.
- Another contributor is *cash flow from investing*. If the company purchases new assets or securities, it will use cash, thus lowering the cash level. On the other hand, if it sells assets or securities, it will receive cash.
- A third major category is *cash flow from financing*. This includes borrowing and repaying debt, selling shares to the public, paying dividends, and purchasing treasury stock on the open market.

Cash flow in each of these categories may be positive (with more in than out) or negative (with more out than in). Acquirers will prefer a company with an overall positive cash flow, with most of the cash coming from operations rather than from investing or financing.

What about the seller's statements about the future of the candidate company—for example, in registration statements, in press releases, or in the Management Discussion and Analysis section of the annual report? Can the acquirer rely on these?

The wise acquirer will take such statements with a grain of salt, and the wise seller will make a disclaimer against its "forward-looking statements." Under the "safe harbor" provisions of the Private Securities Litigation Reform Act of 1995, companies can make forward-looking statements about financial performance, as long as they include an appropriate disclaimer.[3]

KEY RATIOS

What are some valuable ratios to calculate when studying a company's financial statements?

The most popular ratios come from the balance sheet, the income statement, or a combination of the two.

Balance sheet ratios, like the balance sheet, show what a company has.

- Current ratio: Current assets divided by current liabilities (shows liquidity).
- Debt ratio: Total liabilities divided by total assets (shows quality of leverage).
- Debt to equity: Total interest-bearing debt divided by total equity (shows degree of leverage).
- Net working capital: Current assets minus current liabilities (shows available funds).
- Quick ratio, also called acid ratio: Current assets such as cash, securities, and accounts receivable divided by current liabilities such as short-term bank debt and accounts payable (measures liquidity).

Income statement ratios, like the income statement, show how a company is doing.

- Contribution margin: Revenue minus variable costs (shows rate of contribution to profits).

- Contribution margin per unit: Revenue per unit minus variable costs per unit (shows how much a unit is contributing).
- Gross margin: Sales minus cost of goods sold, divided by sales (shows efficiency).
- Interest coverage: Earnings before interest and taxes (EBIT) divided by interest expense (shows strength of earnings).
- Operating margin: EBIT divided by sales (shows efficiency of operations).
- Profit margin, also called return on sales: Earnings divided by sales (shows degree of profitability).

Hybrid ratios (combining items from both the balance sheet and the income statement) relate what a company has to what it does.

- Asset turnover: Sales divided by average assets (shows productivity of assets).
- Debt to sales: Total debt divided by total sales (shows how well the company is employing its borrowed capital).
- Dividend payout ratio: Common stock dividend divided by net income (shows generosity of dividend policy).
- Return on assets: Earnings divided by assets (shows productivity of assets).
- Return on equity: Earnings divided by equity (shows shareholder wealth derived from the ongoing operation of the company).

Market-driven ratios (including the current price of the company's shares) are used in public companies.

- Earnings per share (EPS): Earnings for the previous year divided by number of shares outstanding.
- Market cap to sales: Total market capitalization divided by sales (shows worth of the company in the marketplace).
- Price to earnings (P/E): Current market value of common stock, per share, divided by EPS for the previous year.

Other ratios may use items outside financial statements, such as number of employees or number of a key asset such as beds (for hospitals) or rooms (for hotels). Such ratios include:

- Sales per employee: Sales divided by number of employees (shows market productivity of employees).
- Earnings per employee (shows operational efficiency of employees).

SPECIAL INDUSTRY CONSIDERATIONS

How much does financial analysis vary by industry?

Financial analysis varies greatly by industry.

Whereas in a manufacturing company a checking account is an asset and a loan is a liability, in a bank the situation is just the opposite: the checking accounts managed by the bank are liabilities, while loans are assets. Furthermore, loans are classified as "earning assets," an important category in financial analysis. In a bank, assets (like liabilities) are not generally divided into current and noncurrent accounts. Instead, they are classified as earning assets (such as loans made by the bank) versus nonearning assets (such as real estate used by the bank).

When looking at the assets of an insurance company, one must remember that there is a claim against the key asset—collected premiums. The tail of the payout stream can be long and unpredictable. Also, insurance companies typically invest the money they collect in premiums, and the returns on those investments can be uncertain.[4]

What about high-technology companies? What are some special considerations here?

According to one expert, there are seven key ratios for analysis in any high-tech company.[5] They are ordinary ratios used in the analysis of every business (see above for definitions), but they have special importance in high-technology firms. Here are the ratios, along with benchmarks for high-tech companies.

- Asset turnover: Turnover of 2 times per year is good, 3 times is very good, 4 times is excellent.
- Debt to sales: This should not be significantly high in comparison to peers.
- Gross margin: Over 50 percent is good, over 65 percent is very good, 80 percent or more is excellent.
- Sales to market cap: This should not be significantly lower in comparison to peers.
- Operating margin: Over 20 percent is good, over 25 percent is very good, 30 percent or more is excellent.
- Revenue and profit per employee: Amounts vary greatly. Check the *Inc.* 500 list for the current year to see what the Top 10 report. (One

million dollars per employee is not unheard of in highly successful
companies.)

- Trend in gross margin: Is this going up or down? If it is going down,
  trim expenses.

RED FLAGS

What kinds of red flags should acquirers be able to spot?

Every acquirer should develop its own list, based on the industry it is investigating. Acclaimed "fraud buster" Howard Schilit, in his book *Financial She-
nanigans: How to Detect Accounting Gimmicks and Fraud in Financial Statements*
(New York: McGraw-Hill 1993), lists these questionable practices (we might
call them "seven deadly sins" in accounting) and related behaviors:

1. *Early recognition of revenues* (shipping goods before a sale is
   complete, recording revenue when a transaction is not final,
   recording revenue when future services are still due).
2. *Recording revenues that are not genuine* (recording exchanges of
   similar assets, recording refunds from suppliers as revenue, using
   unfunded estimates for interim reporting purposes).
3. *Increasing income with a one-time gain* (selling undervalued assets,
   retiring debt, failing to distinguish nonrecurring items, recording
   "discontinued operations").
4. *Shifting expenses to a later period* (improperly capitalizing current
   costs, prolonging depreciation or amortization, failing to write off
   doubtful or worthless assets).
5. *Failing to record or disclose all liabilities* (recording revenue on
   unearned cash receipts, failing to show accrual of expected
   liabilities, failing to disclose commitments and contingencies,
   creating transactions intended to keep debt off the balance sheet).
6. *Shifting income to a later period* (creating reserves to shift sales
   revenue).
7. *Shifting future expenses to the current period* (accelerating
   discretionary expenses into the current period, writing off future
   depreciation or amortization, recognizing revenue when no
   inventory is held and no risk is taken).

Another good general list is provided by the American Institute of Certified Public Accountants (AICPA) Statement on Accounting Standards 82, "Consideration of Fraud in a Financial Statement Audit." This document covers:

- Risk factors relating to management characteristics
- Risk factors relating to industry conditions
- Risk factors related to operating conditions

A reprint of SAS 82 appears at the end of this chapter (Appendix 2A). (Chapter 3 examines the subject of fraud in more depth, since it is often uncovered during the review of management and operations, rather than in the financial statements review.)

In addition to these general areas, what are some red flags to look for in a financial statement?

Again, each acquirer must find its own path. The following list may be useful. It was created by a panel of auditing practice experts assembled by the National Association of Corporate Directors in Washington, D.C.[6]

- Complex business arrangements not well understood and appearing to serve little practical purpose.[7]
- Large last-minute transactions that result in significant revenues in quarterly or annual reports.
- Changes in auditors over accounting or auditing disagreements (i.e., the new auditors agree with management and the old auditors do not).
- Overly optimistic news releases or shareholder communications, with the CEO acting as an evangelist to convince investors of future potential growth.
- Financial results that seem "too good to be true" or significantly better than results of competitors—without substantive differences in operations.
- Widely dispersed business locations with decentralized management and a poor internal reporting system.
- Apparent inconsistencies between (1) the facts underlying the financial statements and (2) Management Discussion and Analysis of Financial Condition and Results of Operations (MD&A) and the president's letter—for example, the MD&A and letter present a "rosier" picture than the financial statements warrant.

- Insistence by the CEO or CFO that he or she be present at all meetings between the audit committee and internal or external auditors.
- A consistently close or exact match between reported results and planned results—for example, results that are always exactly on budget or managers who always achieve 100 percent of bonus opportunities.
- Hesitancy, evasiveness, and/or lack of specifics from management or auditors regarding questions about the financial statements.
- Frequent instances of differences in views between management and external auditors.
- A pattern of shipping most of the month's or quarter's sales on the final day or during the final week of the period.
- Internal audit operating under scope restrictions, and lacking a direct line of communication to the audit committee.
- Unusual balance sheet changes, or changes in trends or important financial statement relationships—for example, receivables growing faster than revenues or accounts payable that keep getting delayed.
- Unusual accounting policies, particularly for revenue recognition and cost deferrals—for example deferring items for a later accounting period that normally are expensed immediately.[8]
- Accounting methods that appear to favor form over substance.
- Accounting principles or practices at variance with industry norms.
- Numerous and/or recurring unrecorded or "waived" adjustments raised in connection with the annual audit.
- Use of reserves to smooth out earnings—for example, large additions to reserves that get reversed.
- Frequent and significant changes in estimates for no apparent reasons, increasing or decreasing reported earnings.
- Failure to enforce the company's code of conduct.
- Reluctance to make changes in systems and procedures as recommended by the internal and/or external auditors.

Another item to watch in any public company is insider sales of stock. One expert observes: "If insiders have sold, are selling, and/or want to sell . . . a large amount (relative to their total holdings) of stock, appropriate investigation should be made to provide comfort that such sales do not reflect a pessimistic view of the issuer's future financial results."[9] (The context of this statement was underwriting, but it can apply to M&A as well.)

ASSESSING INTERNAL CONTROLS

Why is it important that an acquisition candidate have strong internal controls?

First, such controls are required by law for publicly held companies in the United States. The Foreign Corrupt Practices Act of 1977 sets forth a requirement of "reasonable" internal controls for every publicly held company. More specifically, Section 13(b)2(A) of the Securities Exchange Act of 1934, as amended, requires public companies to "devise and maintain a system of internal accounting controls sufficient to provide reasonable assurances" in a number of areas.[10] There are also judicially created incentives for good internal controls as an aspect of an overall system for legal compliance, as explained in Chapter 4.

Second, purely from a business perspective, good internal controls are a valuable asset for any acquirer. If internal controls in a company are strong, the risk of postacquisition surprises is relatively low. Thus, determining the strength of internal controls—in the full sense of this term—should be one of the chief aims of due diligence.

What exactly is an internal control system?

According to one authoritative definition, advanced by the Committee of Sponsoring Organizations of the Treadway Commission (COSO), an internal control system is

> a process, effected by an entity's board of directors, management, and other personnel, designed to provide reasonable assurance regarding the achievement of objectives in the following categories:
> - Effectiveness and efficiency of operations.
> - Reliability of financial reporting.
> - Compliance with applicable laws and regulations.[11]

The first category, notes COSO, addresses an entity's basic business objectives, the second relates to published financial statements, and the third deals with compliance. The three categories are overlapping, yet distinct. Internal control, says COSO, can be judged "effective" if a board of directors and management (and, we would add, a potential acquirer) have reasonable assurance concerning:

- Achievement of business goals.
- Reliability of financial reporting.

- Degree of legal compliance (including compliance with financial reporting regulations).[12]

Internal control has five components, says COSO:

- Control environment—including management's philosophy and operating style, and the attention and direction provided by a board of directors.
- Risk assessment—identification, analysis, and monitoring of key risks facing the organization.
- Control activities—policy and procedures to help ensure that management directives are carried out.
- Information and communication—reports to shareholders and others.
- Monitoring—ongoing evaluation of the previous four items, and of the quality of monitoring itself.

Do auditors play a role in this process? That is, can an acquirer glean important information from outside auditors about a company's internal control system?

By all means, yes. The *Codification of Statements on Auditing Standards,* issued by the American Institute of Certified Public Accountants, outlines the procedures that an auditor must carry out in the normal course of an examination of a company's financial statements. The section of the codification entitled "Consideration of Internal Control in a Financial Statement Audit" requires that the auditor obtain a sufficient understanding of each of the elements of an internal control structure in order to plan the procedures necessary to carry out an audit. In obtaining this understanding, the auditor should consider the complexity and sophistication of an entity's operations and systems, including whether the method of controlling data processing is highly dependent on computerized controls. The auditor may then perform tests of controls of the computer program during the audit period to obtain evidence that the controls operated consistently during the period.

The codification asserts that "the auditor's understanding of the internal control structure may sometimes raise doubts about the auditability of an entity's financial statements." In addition, the codification states:

> During the course of an audit, the auditor may become aware of matters relating to the internal control structure that may be of interest to the audit committee. The matters that this section requires for reporting to the audit committee are referred to as *reportable conditions.* Specifically, these are matters coming to the au-

ditor's attention that, in his judgment, should be communicated to the audit committee because they represent significant deficiencies in the design or operation of the internal control structure, which could adversely affect the organization's ability to record, process, summarize, and report financial data consistent with the assertions of management in the financial statements.

A key factor in all of these checkpoints is the audit committee. An acquirer should assess the quality of the audit committee in the company it is acquiring. If the audit committee is weak, then the acquirer (or its audit committee) needs to assume this important role on a temporary basis.

THE ROLE OF THE AUDIT COMMITTEE

What is the role of an audit committee, and how does this role relate to the review of a candidate company's financial statements and internal control?

At a minimum, the audit committee of any company ensures that a company's financial statements are prepared in accordance with the appropriate regulatory guidelines. (In the United States, statements are prepared in accordance with generally accepted accounting principles, or GAAP.) More recently, the role of the audit committee has expanded to include oversight of *risk management* as well as oversight of reporting.

On December 15, 1999, the SEC voted to adopt new disclosure rules intended to strengthen audit committees.[13] Among other requirements, the new rules say that:

- Independent auditors must review quarterly reports before the company files them. (Effective March 15, 2000.)
- Each company must provide a written report from its audit committee in its proxy statement disclosing whether the committee has recommended that the company's audited financial statements be filed with the SEC. (Effective December 15, 2000.)
- Each company must disclose in its proxy statement whether its audit committee has a written charter describing the committee's duties, and, if so, must republish this charter every three years in the proxy statement. (Effective December 15, 2000.)

In addition, the SEC approved new listing standards for the New York Stock Exchange and the NASDAQ stock market (now merged with the American Stock Exchange). For all companies listed on these exchanges:

- Audit committees must have a minimum of three members.
- All audit committee members must be independent.
- All audit committee members must be—or become—financially literate.
- At least one audit committee member must possess accounting/finance expertise.

Let us assume that a candidate company has a strong audit committee. How can such an audit committee help a potential acquirer of the company conduct due diligence?

A Blue Ribbon Commission on Audit Committees, formed by the National Association of Corporate Directors (NACD), describes the role of the audit committee as follows:

- Audit committees, functioning as an organ of the board, focus the attention of the board, top management, and the internal and external auditors on the importance of strong financial reporting and *risk management* (identification and control of key risks).[14]

With respect to the reporting and risk management responsibilities of the board, the NACD Blue Ribbon Commission recommended that:

- Audit committees should define and use timely, focused information that is responsive to important performance measures and to the *key risks* they oversee.[15]

As such, the audit committee of an acquisition candidate that meets the above standard may already be in possession of precisely the information needed by an acquirer. An acquirer can and should ask for this information from the directors of the candidate company.

CONCLUDING COMMENTS

When reviewing financial statements, acquirers need to look for the "positives" of hidden values as well as for the" negatives"—the potential for fraud and insolvency. The financial statements contain many of the clues needed.

In the next chapter, we will see how interviews with managers and others can reveal further clues about the opportunities and risks that lie ahead.

A P P E N D I X 2A

AICPA Statement on Auditing Standards 82, "Consideration of Fraud in a Financial Statement" (1997)—Excerpts[*]

SAS 82 was issued to provide guidance to auditors in fulfilling their responsibility to "plan and perform the audit to obtain reasonable assurance about whether the financial statements are free of material misstatement, whether caused by error or fraud." The list can also help auditors or other reviewers detect pressure points that may trigger undue "earnings management" (that is, undue effort to report earnings at the most favorable time). In both respects, this list should be useful for acquirers and their advisers as they conduct due diligence assessments.

RISK FACTORS RELATING TO MANAGEMENT CHARACTERISTICS

- A failure by management to display and communicate an appropriate attitude regarding internal control and the financial reporting process.
- A significant portion of management's compensation represented by bonuses, stock options, or other incentives, the value of which is contingent upon the entity achieving unduly aggressive targets for operating results or financial position.
- An excessive interest in maintaining or increasing the entity's stock price or earnings trend through unusually aggressive accounting practices.

---

* The authors gratefully acknowledge the National Association of Corporate Directors, Washington, D.C., for allowing us to reprint this list, which appears in *The Report of the NACD Blue Ribbon Commission on Audit Committees* (Washington, D.C.: National Association of Corporate Directors, 1999–2000), pp. 45ff. In particular, we thank commission member Bobby Vick, Partner, Vick & Co. LLP, Atlanta, Georgia, who created the adapted list we quote here.

- Nonfinancial management's excessive participation in, or preoccupation with, the selection of accounting principles or the determination of significant estimates.
- A practice by management of committing to analysts, creditors, and other third parties to achieve what appear to be unduly aggressive or unrealistic forecasts.
- High turnover of senior management, counsel, or board members.
- Known history of securities law violations or claims against the entity or its senior management alleging fraud or violations of securities laws.
- A strained relationship between management and the most recent auditor.

RISK FACTORS RELATING TO INDUSTRY CONDITIONS

- New accounting, statutory, or regulatory requirements that could impair the financial stability or profitability of the entity.
- A high degree of competition or market saturation, accompanied by declining margins.
- A declining industry with increasing business failures.
- Rapid changes in the industry, such as significant declines in customer demand, high vulnerability to rapidly changing technology, or rapid product obsolescence.

RISK FACTORS RELATING TO OPERATING CHARACTERISTICS AND FINANCIAL STABILITY

- Significant pressure to obtain additional capital necessary to stay competitive considering the financial position of the entity—including need for funds to finance major research and development or capital expenditures.
- Assets, liabilities, revenues, or expenses based on significant estimates that involve unusually subjective judgments or uncertainties, or that are subject to potential significant change in the near term in a manner that may have a financially disruptive effect on the entity, such as ultimate collectibility of receivables, timing of revenue recognition, realizability of financial instruments based on the highly subjective valuation of collateral or difficult-to-assess repayment of sources, or significant deferral of costs.

- Significant related-party transactions not in the ordinary course of business or with related entities not audited or audited by another firm.
- Significant bank accountings or subsidiary or branch operations in tax haven jurisdictions for which there appears to be no clear business justification.
- An overly complex organizational structure involving numerous or unusual legal entities, managerial lines of authority, or contractual arrangements without apparent business purpose.
- Difficulty in determining the organization or individual that controls the entity.
- Unusually rapid growth or profitability, especially compared with that of other companies in the same industry.
- Especially high vulnerability to changes in interest rates.
- Unusually high dependence on debt, marginal ability to meet debt repayment requirements, or debt covenants that are difficult to maintain.
- Unrealistically aggressive sales or profitability incentive programs.
- Adverse consequences on significant pending transactions, such as a business combination or contract award, if poor financial results are reported.
- A poor or deteriorating financial position when management has personally guaranteed significant debts of the entity.
- Inability to generate cash flows from operations while reporting earnings and earnings growth.
- Threat of imminent bankruptcy or foreclosure.

E N D N O T E S

1. The SEC has identified these two financial statements as the most important ones for public companies. Section 13(b)1, in describing the SEC's powers to require reports, says that the SEC "may prescribe . . . the items or details to be shown in the *balance sheet* and the *earnings statement*, and the methods to be followed in the preparation of reports, in the appraisal or valuation of assets and liabilities, in the determination of depreciation and depletion, in the differentiation of recurring and nonrecurring income, and in the preparation . . . of separate and/or consolidated balance sheets or income accounts of any person under direct or indirect common control with the issuer." No other financial statements are mentioned in this key section. Source: *Securities Exchange Act of 1934 as Amended* (New York: Bowne & Company, June 15, 2000), p. 49.

2. In regard to investment reporting, if the company being acquired has made significant investments in other companies, the acquirer will want to know how such investment is being accounted for—in consolidation with other results or separately? There are several key documents here: the Financial Accounting Standards Board (FASB) report *Exposure Draft on Consolidation Policies: Accounting for Unconsolidated Investees*, and pronouncements stemming from deliberations of the Emerging Issues Task Force (EITF) on the subject of consolidations. The FASB, based in Norwalk, Connecticut, sets accounting standards for U.S. public companies. (Note: FASB is pronounced *fasby*; it is not spelled out.)

3. Also, under a FASB ruling effective December 25, 1992, companies may report their projections of how current losses may offset future gains, even if it is not certain that the losses will trigger an offsetting tax benefit. (Under a previous rule adopted in 1987, companies could not report such projections on the grounds that they were not certain to materialize.)

4. Source: John C. Fletcher, *Getting Behind the Numbers* (Washington, D.C.: National Association of Corporate Directors, 1996–2000), pp. 21ff.

5. This list of ratios and annotations is provided by F. Michael Hruby, President, Technology Marketing Group, Inc., Acton, Massachusetts. It is summarized from his book *Technoleverage* (New York: Amacom, 1999). See also "Overseeing Technology: A Guide for All Directors," *Director's Monthly*, November 1999, pp. 1–6.

6. *The Report of the NACD Blue Ribbon Commission on Audit Committees: A Practical Guide* (Washington, D.C.: National Association of Corporate Directors, 2000), pp. 44–45.

7. For example, beware *intracompany transactions*—especially subcontracts and transfers of assets, including cash and credits. Such transfer payments might not have been audited internally *or* externally for years.

8. Another example: a high *percentage of purchased parts in the cost of goods sold.* At 85 percent, it calls for lots of attention; at 10 percent, very little.

9. Alderman and Kanberg, op. cit. (Chapter 1, note 11).

10. Section 13(b)(2) states that "every issuer . . . shall (A) Make and keep books, records, and accounts, which, in reasonable detail, accurately and fairly reflect the transactions and disposition of the assets of the issuer; and (B) Devise and maintain a system of internal accounting controls sufficient to provide reasonable assurances that: (i) transactions are executed in accordance with management's general or specific authorization; (ii) transactions are recorded as necessary: (I) to permit preparation of financial statements in conformity with generally accepted financial principles or any other criteria applicable to such statements, and (II) to maintain accountability for such assets; (iii) access to assets is permitted only in accordance with management's general or specific authorization; and (iv) the recorded accountability for assets is compared with the existing assets at reasonable intervals and appropriate action is taken with re-

spect to any differences. Source: *Securities and Exchange Act of 1934, as Amended, Law Text* op.cit. (note 1), pp. 49–50.

11. Committee of Sponsoring Organizations of the Treadway Commission, *Internal Control—Integrated Framework* (Jersey City, N.J.: American Institute of Certified Public Accountants, 1992, 1994).

12. As mentioned above (note 2), the source of most accounting regulations is the FASB. Certified public accountants are generally aware of all new pronouncements, and should be consulted when ASSESSING compliance.

13. See Order Approving NYSE Rule Change, SEC Release NYSE-34-42233; Order Approving AMEX Proposed Rule Change, SEC Release NASDAQ-34-42331; and SEC Final Rules on Audit Committee Disclosure published the week of December 20, 2000.

14. *Report of the NACD Blue Ribbon Commission on Audit Committees*, op. cit. (note 6), p. 1. Emphasis added.

15. Ibid., p. 2. Emphasis added.

CHAPTER 3

The Operations and Management Review

I speak of towers, bridges, tunnels, hangars, wonders, and
disasters . . . the shops that have everything, where we spend
everything, and it all turns to smoke.

> Octavio Paz
> "I Speak of the City"
> *Collected Poems, 1957–1987*

INTRODUCTION

Analyzing a company's financial reports may be the most important part of
due diligence, but no analysis is complete without a sound understanding of a
company's operations and management. Yet achieving such an understanding is not easy, for two reasons.

First, the value and risk of operations and management are not fully reflected on financial statements (balance sheets, income statements, and cash
flow statements) as those statements are currently structured. True, as financial statements evolve, they will reflect more aspects of dynamic operational
reality. The Financial Accounting Standards Board (FASB) itself has a natural
interest in this result, and continues to consider the merits of accounting reform. Also, at least two Big Five accounting firms—Arthur Andersen and
Ernst & Young—have supported research in "complex adaptive systems,"
with a goal of making accounting and management models more reflective of
dynamic business reality.[1] For now, however, financial statements hold up
only a distant mirror to company reality.

Second, the review of operations and management can span a broad
range, from the "hard" science of process engineering to the "soft" science of
cultural environment. The term *operations* describes "a company's basic business objectives, including performance and profitability goals and safeguard-
ing of performance," says COSO, the authoritative accounting group men-

tioned in Chapter 2. The term *management* describes the people setting and reaching those goals. Thus *operations and management* encompasses the essential "what and who" of any company: its activities and the people who direct them.

But although the quick study of operations and management is not easy, it is not impossible. To accomplish such a review—often called "business due diligence" (as opposed to accounting or legal due diligence)—merely requires an effective process for collecting and analyzing key information.

EVALUATING OPERATIONS AND MANAGEMENT: AN OVERVIEW

How can an acquirer gain a good sense of a company's operations and management during a due diligence review?

The key lies in a focus on risk. As mentioned, this area spans a very broad range—encompassing myriad issues that even the most expert manager or professional would be hard-pressed to understand fully in a few weeks or even months. But buying a company does not always entail a time-consuming and expensive management study. In fact, only one aspect of operations and management absolutely must concern the investigator: risk.

If time and money allowed, it would seem ideal to conduct a due diligence investigation of anything and everything in corporate life. Indeed, business publications often carry articles and advertisements urging "due diligence" or an "audit" on the area of the writer's or advertiser's expertise. One common appeal is the need for "cultural due diligence." Others we have seen include "marketing due diligence" and "human capital due diligence." Such nontraditional due diligence endeavors are well and good, but pursuing all of them fully would strain the time frames and budgets of most acquirers.

So the question really is: How can an acquirer gain a good sense of the *risks* contained in a company's operations and management? Once again, we turn to the subject of internal controls, introduced in Chapter 2. In that chapter, quoting COSO, we said that any acquirer should assess the internal controls system of a candidate company, since internal controls can provide *reasonable assurance* about the effectiveness and efficiency of operations, the reliability of financial reporting, and compliance with applicable laws and regulations.[2] We also said that an internal controls system does this through various means, including risk assessment—key to operational effectiveness and efficiency.

How can an acquirer assess the riskiness of operations and management of a company?

The best way is face-to-face interviews, but even before this stage, an acquirer can find out a great deal through a variety of traditional business research sources:

- Annual reports, 10Ks, and proxy statements filed with the SEC (see especially Management's Discussion and Analysis of Financial Condition and Results of Operations,[3] or MD&A, describing key risks of public companies).
- Business Periodicals Index (leading to articles published about the company).
- Credit rating agencies such as Dun & Bradstreet and Moody's.
- Newspapers, including the *Wall Street Journal*.
- Research services such as *Value Line Investment Survey*.
- Stock brokerage and independent research reports (listed in *Nelson's Directory of Investment Research*).
- World Wide Web sources (search under company name).[4]

Of all these sources, for publicly traded companies the information contained in the MD&A may be the most important.

USING THE MD&A AS A CHECKLIST

How can an acquirer use the MD&A as a checklist?

The acquirer should conduct its own study to *confirm* the information contained in the candidate company's MD&A. If the company is nonpublic, the acquirer should endeavor to *discover* such information. In most cases, the acquirer can conduct or insist on the production of such a study, and obtain seller cooperation. (One obvious exception is a hostile takeover bid, when buyers are dependent on publicly available information.)

In brief, the MD&A discusses the following information for a company (and, if appropriate, for its units or divisions):[5]

- Demands, commitments, events, or uncertainties that may decrease the company's liquidity.
- Material commitments for capital expenditures.
- Trends, favorable or unfavorable, in capital resources (equity, debt, off-balance sheet financing).

- Significant economic changes that have affected the amount of reported income from continuing operations.
- Known trends or uncertainties that have had or could have a major impact on net sales or will cause a major change in profits.
- Source of higher profits, if any (increases in prices, increases in volume, or introduction of new products or services).
- Impact of inflation.
- Impact of seasonal factors.
- Overall material changes in results of operations.

All this information, whether required by the SEC or not, is obviously useful to any owner. Also useful (but somewhat less mature and thorough) is the typical information required in any offering memorandum or prospectus. Although the candidate company itself might not have recently filed such a document, filings by competitors of the candidate company can give a good idea of the risks out there for such a company.

This all sounds like a lot to check out—far more than analyzing a few financial statements. What is the cost-benefit payout on all this?

Once again, we emphasize the *due* in due diligence. There is no point for an acquirer to deplete its resources in chasing every single potential risk no matter how small or remote. The risk must be both material and possible.

For example, if you are acquiring a luxury goods chain store, you might want to acknowledge and even analyze the risk of recession (both material and possible), but you need not focus on the risk of petty cash theft (likely but not material) or consumer boycotts (material but not likely).

Some areas are material and likely, but are so pervasive that it is difficult to check them out. For example, an acquirer might be buying a mutual fund family containing 80 diversified funds, and may be concerned about potentially risky investments made by all the funds. To save time and expense, the acquirer can consider random sampling of the funds.[6]

Another way to save time is to use preexisting forms for due diligence, rather than creating special forms. Although forms may need to be customized to the candidate company's industry and stage of growth, having them in hand can save time. One source of such forms is the *Due Diligence Handbook* by William M. Crilly, a consultant and engineer with turnaround experience.[7] The 500 forms and checklists that make up this book can show at a glance what is happening in a business—for example, whether the company's distributor-based revenues are going up or not.[8] Some of the forms, moreover, involve areas of risk, such as pending litigation—obviously of relevance to M&A due diligence, as we have emphasized.

DUE DILIGENCE IN PRIVATE COMPANIES

How can information be obtained if the company is privately held and does not report to the SEC?

First of all, certain public records can and must be checked.

To take a complete look at a company's past and current standing, the due diligence process should check out the present and previous corporate names and all trade names, service marks, and trade dress registrations. Any potential infringements by the acquisition candidate should be noted. (Readers should note that, because of a fluke, the famous Bell Telephone mark was never registered.)

In dealing with a privately owned company, the buyer must confirm that the corporation was legally formed and continues to legally exist. To do so, the buyer will establish the jurisdiction of the company's incorporation and document the company's organization by finding and examining the articles of incorporation, including any amendments such as name changes, as well as corporate bylaws and any amendments to these.

Articles of incorporation are public documents that may be obtained (in the form of certified copies) from the secretary of state of the jurisdiction of incorporation. The acquirer should also obtain, from the same office, evidence of the corporation's continuing status in good standing in the state of incorporation. It is also necessary to review carefully the minute books of the board, executive committee, and any stockholder meetings to establish that the articles and any amendments have been properly adopted in accordance with the company's charter, bylaws, and state statutes, and that no action has been taken to dissolve the corporation. An examination of the minute books should also ascertain that they are up to date and that they reflect the election or appointment of the corporation's directors and officers. Insurance policies, discussed in the next chapter, can provide relevant information.

Having established that the corporation was indeed duly formed, the buyer then examines the company's qualifications to do business in jurisdictions other than its state of incorporation—in other words, in whatever other states or countries it may conduct business. To be thorough in wrapping up this initial due diligence stage, the buyer must seek out good standing certificates and tax certificates from each of the states and foreign jurisdictions in which the company operates.

Once the acquirer satisfies itself with respect to corporate formation, qualification, and good standing, it should confirm that the company actually owns the assets it claims to own by examining evidence of key tangible assets, including titles, title insurance policies, and mortgages.

Having confirmed ownership of property, the acquirer should search for liens, encumbrances, and judgments that may exist against the company or any of its assets. Sources to be searched include the following:

- The offices of the secretary of state of the state where the company's principal office is located and of other relevant states and, sometimes, county clerk offices where filings are made to disclose creditors' interests in assets under the Uniform Commercial Code.
- All relevant recorder of deeds offices.
- All relevant courts, including federal, state, and local.
- Any special filing jurisdictions for:
  - Special industries, such as aviation and maritime assets
  - Bankruptcy (e.g., U.S. Bankruptcy Court)
  - Copyrights (see Chapter g)
  - Patents and trademarks (see Chapter g)

In addition to this check of public records, traditional due diligence investigations of operations and management rely on two very important elements that are dependent on seller relations:

- Access to files
- On-site interviews

The acquirer needs to ask (and convince) the seller to allow such access. As mentioned in Chapter 1, this access ideally will appear as part of the acquisition agreement. If such access is not granted, the acquirer should be able to extract discounts from the price paid for the company, to offset the greater risk of purchase. It is better, however, to conduct due diligence and pay a higher price rather than to skip due diligence.

CONDUCTING INTERVIEWS

Why are interviews important in conducting due diligence?

Interviews are a good way to corroborate written material, or to provide documentation when no written material exists. Courts consider interviews with managers—especially a large number of them—as one indication of appropriate due diligence. In the case of *Weinberger v. Jackson* (1991), involving an underwriting, the court granted summary judgment to the underwriters based in part on the fact that they had held "over 20" meetings with various management personnel.[9]

Interviewing officers and directors comes first. To put these individuals and their roles and responsibilities in context, it is a good idea to request an organization chart showing lines of reporting and areas of responsibility. As one expert team has noted, interviews might expand to include division heads, plant managers, division accountants, sales managers, purchasing agents, and so forth.[10] The choice will depend on risk patterns uncovered as the study proceeds. Interviews may be face to face or by written questionnaire. If the company has recently conducted a public offering, acquirers should refer to Form S-1 (filed by issuers with the SEC) when interviewing directors and officers.

Of all officers and directors, the most important one to interview, if he or she is still living, is the founder. Such an interview can give the acquirer a good sense of the "heart and soul" of the company, and an insight into goodwill value.

What guidelines should a buyer follow when conducting interviews?

In conducting interviews of officers, directors, and key employees, the investigator seeks to:

- Corroborate checklist documents.
- Fill gaps in checklist documents.
- Identify any areas of potential liability (or assets of potential value) not identified in the checklist.

This last point deserves emphasis. As experts before us have so well stated, "The best guide to whether a particular fact is important will be instinct and plain old common sense rather than something set forth in a checklist."[11] Therefore, it is very important:

- To expand the checklist as necessary to any relevant items as an investigation unfolds.
- To document the accomplishment of each item on the checklist, or the reason that accomplishment was deemed unnecessary.

The reason for this is twofold. First, the acquirer will have a better sense of postmerger risks. Second, the acquirer will have a better defense against a charge of negligence.

Acquirers can learn from the underwriting community in this regard. Underwriting due diligence experts have observed:

> Our experience in defending underwriters leads us to conclude that it is usually easier to establish the due diligence defense against a claim that the underwriter should have done more to investigate a perceived risk than against a claim that it failed to anticipate at all the risk which ultimately caused alleged damage. Accordingly, we believe anything that stimulates expansive thinking by members of the underwriting team and stretches their horizons is an aid to effective due diligence and disclosure, and correspondingly an aid in defense of any future litigation that may arise.[12]

In other words, it is not a bad idea to have an extensive checklist, even if you do not actually wind up investigating everything on the checklist. You must, however, document the reasons for not investigating the items not examined.

Anyone conducting an interview is well advised to bring an outline of the areas that he or she plans to cover. In the case of *Picard Chemical Inc. Profit Sharing Plan v. Perrigo Co.* (1998),[13] defendants in a due diligence case had neither good notes nor clear memory of their interviews, but the court found that they had shown due diligence. The judge accepted as evidence of interviews the existence of interview outlines and testimony that the interviews had indeed taken place.

Good interview notes include the following:

- Time and place of the interview
- Name and title of the person interviewed
- Scope of the interview
- Significant disclosures made during the interview
- Status (confidential versus nonconfidential) of interview

What should the acquirer do if new assets are discovered during the interviews?

Depending on the size and structure of the transaction and the importance of the assets, the acquirer may wish to use a real estate appraiser to value any owned real property, an engineer to inspect any plants and equipment, and an accounting team to review any inventory.[14]

Every year, the business world is rocked by at least one major fraud scandal. One recent example is Cendant Corp., the parent company for Days Inn and Ramada hotels, the Avis car rental agency, and real-estate brokerage Century 21. The exposure of accounting irregularities caused the company's stock value to drop by $14 billion in April 1999, and shareholders sued. In December 1999, the company agreed to pay $2.83 billion to settle a lawsuit from a major shareholder accusing it of fraud. The company's woes began after a merger. CUC International, which merged with HFS Inc. to create Cendant in 1997, allegedly used fraudulent accounting practices to inflate earnings by some $500 million over the previous three years.

Highly specialized industries require the use of experts—a geologist to confirm the value of mines, a programmer to inspect the value of software, and so forth. The accountants should also review the seller's financial statements with respect to these items.

Most interviews are conducted on site, but what about off-site interviews?

A proper investigation may include the search of key public records and discussions with parties with whom the acquisition candidate has significant relationships. These include customers and suppliers, private lenders, and former key employees, including directors and officers.

The acquirer should be sure to interview parties to any standing agreements with the candidate company, both suppliers and customers. The interview may function as a negotiation, asking that the agreements be assigned to the buyer when and if it acquires the business. If the supplier or customer refuses, this may be the basis for a cause of action as an "adverse change" in the affairs of the business between the execution of the acquisition agreement and the closing. (For more on adverse change, see Chapter 5.)

Note, however, that acquirers should take special care when discussing the seller's business with third parties. Although these discussions may be the source of valuable information, they may also give rise to tensions between buyer and seller. This is particularly true if the seller believes that the discussions may impair its ability to carry on its business, or that the buyer will use the information when and if it buys a competitor. The letter of confidentiality and the engagement letter may provide some assurance on these points. (See Appendices 1A through 1C in Chapter 1.) Nonetheless, acquirers should be especially sensitive on this point.

To what extent and how should the acquirer keep a record of interviews?

Before starting the interview process, the acquirer should prepare a list of interviews to be conducted as well as a strategy for taking and filing notes. The acquirer's attorney can identify which notes should be kept confidential (invoking the attorney-client privilege) and which notes should remain available for use later to prove due diligence in the event of litigation.[15] For example, a frank description of internal control weaknesses might be classified as confidential, while the details of an internal control policy would be nonconfidential. Confidential and nonconfidential notes should be filed separately.

The decision to keep notes is a double-edged sword. Using the legal "discovery" process, plaintiffs can use a defendant's own documents as evidence against the defendant. On the other hand, if the defendant is using a "due diligence defense," it will need documentation to prove its case.

In general, experts advise erring on the side of inclusion. Contemporaneous documents can be very persuasive to judges and (in the case of criminal trials) juries. Furthermore, documentation can refresh the memories of those on the witness stand.[16]

Clearly some records are worth keeping more than others. What records should be kept?

If time and funding permit, acquirers should strive to keep notes or memos documenting dates, participants, and (unless advised otherwise by counsel) substance of the following:

- Due diligence meetings and interviews, including (as outlined above) dates, attendees, scope, and discoveries made.
- Documents reviewed, including summaries or copies as appropriate.
- Visits to facilities, including dates, attendees, and scope of discussion.
- Discussions and interviews with third-party personnel, including dates, attendees, and topics discussed.
- Outlines or checklists used in interviewing issuers and third-party personnel.
- Director and officer questionnaires and certificates (both for the candidate company and, if issuing shares, the acquiring company).
- Reports by investigators or other independent experts engaged to perform parts of the investigation.[17]

Notes should be written with the idea that they may be reviewed in court later.

Who should keep the files and interview notes gathered in a due diligence investigation?

The files of interviews should be maintained by someone functioning as a "librarian." The ideal candidate is an experienced paralegal secretary with special training for this purpose. The paralegal can manage a "data room" (even if it only involves a shelf in a room) where records are stored, including copies of financial statements, interview notes, and other items covering all checklist points. Appendix 3A shows a sample "data room" managed by the law firm of Battle Fowler in New York.

How can outside professionals help in a due diligence study of operations and management operations?

Delegation to outside professionals can be an effective means of not only conducting but also documenting due diligence. Courts have noted that the use of outside professionals is helpful in establishing due care in an investigation. Examples of such professionals commonly used include:

- An engineer or a certified appraiser to evaluate technology or equipment.
- Industry specialists to evaluate operations.
- A professional investigative firm to investigate the employment and personal backgrounds of key management personnel.

This last item might seem like a luxury, but some experts consider it a necessity. For example, David A. Katz of Wachtell, Lipton, Rosen, and Katz, in his often reprinted article "Due Diligence in Acquisition Transactions," puts this as the very first item in his list of due diligence procedures. Katz writes:

> Where the acquirer and the target do not have an existing business relationship, the due diligence investigation should start with general background checks into the reputation of the company and its management. Information on the company's business ethics should be reviewed by contacting industry experts and competitors in the industry, as well as senior management and key shareholders of the company.[18]

BACKGROUND SEARCHES AND FIELD INVESTIGATIONS

How can an acquirer gain assurance that a proposed business partner is legitimate and trustworthy, and that the business is being operated as presented?

A separate component of due diligence—investigative due diligence—addresses these issues and provides information that can help acquirers make, negotiate, and live with their acquisition decisions.[19]

Through investigative due diligence an acquirer can:

- Obtain in-depth background information about its future partner.
- Learn of vulnerabilities to which it may be exposed after the acquisition.
- Develop a better sense of the subject company's corporate culture.
- Acquire more industry-specific business intelligence.

Who should be involved in conducting a background investigation?

Acquirers may take several different approaches to conducting background investigations. As an example, we will use the approaches adopted by PricewaterhouseCoopers LLC. According to PwC, background investigations require a multidisciplinary team—ideally including fraud specialists and investigative attorneys as well as field operatives and law enforcement contacts. International transactions require a team with global reach. The due diligence process provides the greatest value when the investigative due diligence team operates integrally with the whole transaction team.

Should the candidate company be informed of the background investigation?

The acquirer must decide whether the due diligence should be performed discreetly, or openly with the knowledge of the subject of the investigation. The most common tendency is toward closed investigations motivated by fear of offending the proposed business partner. According to PwC, the best practice is to conduct open investigative due diligence, which allows for the collection of more information (via questionnaires and interviews) and permits open conversation when concerns arise.

As a practical matter, in today's business environment, business partners expect that due diligence will be conducted. According to investigators at PwC, most businesspeople—not only in the United States, but all over the globe—are not offended if the acquirer explains up front that this form of due diligence is its routine method for conducting business. Of course, the due diligence must be conducted by qualified professionals and in a manner that does not suggest that the acquirer is suspicious of its potential business partner.

How does investigative due diligence vary by country?

In the United States, as discussed further below, investigators can find out a great deal of information through commercial databases and the Internet. For example, a U.S. company that has ever been sued, or has ever filed for bankruptcy, generally discloses this information, and the disclosed information becomes available online.

In the international arena, the public availability of company information varies greatly from country to country. In many countries, the information may never be disclosed, much less disseminated electronically. Aside from details that companies themselves may provide through their standard corporate records, available information is generally limited to Dun & Bradstreet reports and varying degrees of media coverage.

Therefore, when companies outside the United States are investigated, it is often necessary to supplement database and Internet searches with live investigations by qualified professionals, such as former intelligence officials. For acquirers based in the United States, then, international investigations can be more expensive and time-consuming than domestic investigations.

How are commercial databases and the Internet used in conducting background investigations?

According to PwC, virtually every business investigation now begins with some form of online research—generally using a combination of commercial databases and the Internet. For certain types of information, the Internet cannot match the offerings of commercial services. For others, the Internet is the best and only place to find information. PwC chooses commercial databases over the Internet for most of its background investigations. However, knowing when to use the commercial databases and when to use the Internet is key to developing a comprehensive and thorough investigative strategy.

The choice between the Internet and commercial databases will depend on the nature and extent of the information that the acquirer is seeking. Before going online, the investigator identifies which databases or Internet sites are most likely to contain information most relevant to the target of the investigation, in terms of both geographic location and subject matter. As more information is made available on the Internet, the best approach is to use these research tools in tandem, and to become familiar with the best sources of information to suit the particular needs of the investigation.

Whether received from commercial databases or the Internet, the most valuable sources of information fall into two main categories: news and media sources, and public records sources.

It is usually best to start the online investigative process with a media search, one of the key sources for historical and background information regarding entities and individuals. These sources include local, national, and international newspapers, magazines, trade publications, and television and radio transcripts. Often, a subject's legal, financial, or business troubles are written about in the news media in well-researched and thoughtful articles. Media can also be helpful in identifying a subject's prior employment and personal history.

After online media sources are exhausted, the next step in the online investigation is to search the vast compilation of abstracted public records information—the fastest-growing source of online information. This resource includes:

- Actions of regulatory agencies
- Corporate and other business filings (state, federal—e.g., SEC)
- Corporate records
- Court judgments (state, federal)
- Federal and state civil court proceedings
- Federal criminal records and bankruptcy court records
- Motor vehicle records
- Professional registration and licensing information
- Property records
- Uniform Commercial Code filings and other asset locators

Is it also necessary to conduct a manual search of public records?

The availability of public records information varies from state to state and covers variable time periods, so the extent of coverage in a particular jurisdiction must be carefully considered. Another word of caution: Online records are often inaccurate and incomplete. While a great source of leads, online research cannot be the sole source of information for the investigator. Instead, such research should be supplemented by a manual search of public records. PwC has encountered situations in which a manual search of the public record revealed significant matters that were not identified online, despite the fact that court records were supposedly online for that particular jurisdiction and time period. PwC also cautions that many of the online records, most of which are abstracted, are likely to contain only a portion of the information available from the original document. A combination of online searching and onsite searching at relevant courthouses or agencies is the best approach.

How about field investigation?

Open due diligence inquiries generally include some measure of internal field investigation. As to individual employees and principals, the internal field investigation will consist of a questionnaire and/or an interview of the subject as well as former and present associates of the subject.

Additional investigation might not be required if the acquirer is interested only in the integrity of management and if no red flags are developed from online and Internet investigations and public record retrieval. Field investigation is necessary if red flags are raised or if the acquirer seeks a better understanding of the corporate entity.

Field investigation falls generally into two categories: information obtained from external sources and information obtained from the subject of the investigation. External sources include information obtained from confidential sources and information obtained openly from interviews of industry experts, competitors, customers, former employees, and government sources. For example, when the subject of the investigation has declared bankruptcy or been involved in civil litigation, field inquiry of the former creditors and party opponents can provide invaluable insight into the core integrity of a potential business partner.

Former employees and business associates are a particularly valuable source of information. Many companies suffer high turnover, including the loss of experienced businesspeople. While these employees generally leave the company quietly, many will provide valuable insight and information if asked. Of course, many former employees are bound by confidentiality agreements. Open due diligence overcomes this obstacle, since the acquirer can seek consent from the company to interview former employees.

Hidden liabilities and other business concerns can also be uncovered through interviews of present employees. These interviews should extend beyond the senior management. Experience teaches that it is middle management and staff employees who are most familiar with the nuts and bolts of the business operations, who have the least incentive to lie, and who welcome the opportunity to disclose misconduct or mismanagement.

Sometimes, during the course of a field investigation, difficult questions must be asked. The acquirer needs to consider whether these questions are better posed by the acquirer or by a third party, one that will not be working with the new company going forward.

REGULAR VERSUS IRREGULAR THREATS

Could you give an example of an approach to operations and management analysis conducted by a professional services firm?

Certainly. As our example, we will use Kroll Associates, a well-known investigations firm. According to Kroll, there are two main steps in identifying risks in any company:

- Identifying key assets, tangible and intangible.
- Identifying threats to these assets.

The effort put forth in identifying threats should be commensurate with the value of the assets at risk. If an asset is not particularly valuable, then identifying threats to the asset may not be important. If an asset is crucial, then it is of utmost importance to identify the threats to the asset.

It is important to state here that the most important assets of an enterprise may not be tangible. They may not even appear on the company's financial statements. Nonetheless, it is vital to protect them before, during, and after due diligence. Here are some examples of key assets. A company may have more than one.

Brand
- Reputation
- Brand name
- Logo
- License
- Trademark
- Service mark

Cash
- Positive cash flow
- Financial surplus (retained earnings)

Culture
- Ethical standards

Global reach
- Ability to operate in multiple time zones (up to 24 zones possible)

Market position
- Market share
- Industry leadership

Operations
- Performance standards
- Process integrity

People
- Intellectual capital
- Key employees

Intellectual property (see Chapter 7), including a proprietary
- Product
- Service
- Method
- Technology

Scale
- Number of offices
- Geographic variety of offices

Each of these assets may face significant risks.

How can an acquirer assess the risks to key assets?

Business threats can come in many different sizes, shapes, and disguises. By their very nature, both routine and nonroutine threats can materialize in unexpected forms or unanticipated directions. The best way to assess operational risks is to begin by identifying two types of potential risks—with emphasis on the first:

- Regular or routine business threats (such as the threat of frost for a citrus grower).
- Irregular or non-routine business threats (such as the threat of fraud).

What are some examples of the routine threats that face a particular company?

Routine business threats generally fall into the following categories:

- Financial threats from events such as normal fluctuations in interest, foreign exchange rates, working capital availability, and financial reporting errors.
- Operational threats from events such as such noncatastrophic accidents, raw material shortages, product design challenges, technology shifts, labor shortages, distribution blockages, and government regulations.

- Competitive threats from pricing and cost shifts, new product introductions, continuous product and process innovations, new market entrants, personnel recruiting, and consolidations.

What are some examples of nonroutine business threats?

Business irregularities are threats that are not encountered during the normal course of business, but arise under the following general circumstances:

- *Intentional illegal and/or hostile action on the part of a company employee, an agent of the company, or a third party such as a competitor.* Examples include breach of confidentiality (leaks), economic espionage, fraud, theft, product diversion, product tampering, hostile competitive action, and violence against staff and/or facilities.

- *Catastrophic accidents involving company property and/or employees.* Examples include industrial accidents and plant explosions.

- *Major, unexpected, catastrophic changes in business environment.* Causes include an unexpected rise in interest rates (or an unexpected drop, if the company is a lender) and major shifts in market preferences.

- *Major lawsuits.* As explained in Chapter 5, lawsuits can come from a variety of sources, including competitors, customers, employees, suppliers, and the government.

- *Gross mismanagement or negligence.* Examples include business process breakdown, deterioration of service, and weak internal controls. (For more about internal controls, see Chapter 2.)

For a case study showing how Kroll Associates analyzed the assets and threats of a testing company, see Appendix 3B.

DUE DILIGENCE IN CONFLICT MANAGEMENT, CULTURE, HUMAN CAPITAL, MARKETING, AND OTHER "SOFT" AREAS

Besides threats to assets, what other management areas should the due diligence process cover?

Classic due diligence for management is somewhat limited. It covers only risks arising from the current state and potential future state of the *company being acquired*. Traditional due diligence does not take into account the many issues that can arise from *both companies being combined*. Some of these issues are in the "soft" or "gray" area of human feelings and/or values.

Consider, for example, interpersonal conflicts between the acquiring and acquired management. These can prevent postmerger progress. As a result, some acquirers engage the services of specialists in conflict management to ensure a smooth due diligence process.

One such consultant writes:

> As a former practicing lawyer who was involved in numerous mergers and acquisitions, as well as international commercial transactions, I have seen many instances where the "classic" due diligence totally ignores the conflict management issue as a general rule. In many instances this is done at the expense of the integrity of the merger or acquisition, although the failure is usually blamed upon something else. [The] assimilation of different corporate cultures and values [can cause] conflict, the proper management of which would result in far more successful and profitable deals, mergers, and acquisitions.[20]

There is a lot of talk about "cultural due diligence." What is this?

Cultural due diligence has been conducted since the beginning of time on an informal basis. When announced deals fail to go through to completion, the failure can often be traced to a sense that the two companies' cultures will not be compatible.

Mitchell Marks, a San Francisco-based consultant who has written extensively on cultural due diligence, notes that approaches to considering due diligence fall into four general categories:

- Integrating cultural criteria in the earliest of merger discussions.
- Staffing and preparing due diligence teams with an eye toward cultural criteria.
- Adding cultural criteria to due diligence data collection.
- Using formal tools to assess culture fit.[21]

In recent years, many corporate leaders and advisers have tried to define corporate culture, and to use this definition in a number of key areas, including due diligence.

Perhaps the most extensive work on this topic has been done by Hay Management Consultants, which has identified 56 distinct parts to corporate culture. All these cultural elements are expressed as ongoing actions through gerunds (the noun form of verbs). Appendix 3C lists these terms.

A shorter list is provided by consultant Ron Ashkenas, Managing Partner, Robert H. Schaffer & Associates, Stamford, Connecticut. His "cultural assessment worksheet" lists 10 traits, including:

- *Innovation*. Using traditional and tested approaches versus looking for and experimenting with innovative ways of getting work done.
- *Communication style*. Formal versus informal.
- *Solution sharing*. Sharing of ideas originating in one department throughout the entire organization versus infrequent sharing with other departments in the company.
- *Work orientation*. Emphasis on defined processes and roles versus simply getting measurable bottom-line results.

Do you have any comments on "human capital due diligence"?

Human capital due diligence is the study of a company's programs for human resources management to determine the effectiveness of the programs. When applied in the merger context, it studies the combination of two such programs. Most professional services firms have some expertise in human capital.[22]

According to one methodology—the Arthur Andersen LLP model called human capital appraisal, or HCA—there are five human capital areas to consider:

- Recruitment, retention, and retirement
- Performance management and rewards
- Organizational structure
- Organizational enablers (legal and accounting)
- Career development, training, and succession planning

Moreover, there are phases of review:

- *Clarification*. How do programs in these areas link to the acquiring company's strategy?
- *Assessment*. How much do the programs cost, and are they delivering a benefit?
- *Design*. If an area is not delivering a benefit, how can it be redesigned?
- *Implementation*. How can the newly designed program be implemented after the acquisition?
- *Monitoring*. How can the organization ensure continual relevance and effectiveness of the newly designed program?

What about "marketing due diligence"?

Marketing due diligence is the study of the marketing efforts of combining firms to ensure that the combination will produce maximum synergies. To the extent that a company's success is driven by sales volume, marketing due diligence is obviously very important.[23]

CONCLUDING COMMENTS

The mathematics of due diligence is not pure; it is applied. Although financial statement analysis—along with red tape and paperwork—form a large part of due diligence, the most important part is conducted "live" through interviews and on-site visits. Such interviews should not neglect "soft" information such as conflict and culture.[24]

A thorough analysis of operations and management leads naturally to the next stage of due diligence—checking for legal compliance, the subject of our next chapter.

A P P E N D I X   3A

Index of Data Room Documents[*]

A.   ACCOUNTING
E.   ENVIRONMENTAL
F.   FACILITIES
H.   HUMAN RESOURCES
I.   INTERNATIONAL
L.   LEGAL
P.   PATENTS
R.   RESEARCH and DEVELOPMENT
T.   TRADEMARKS

---

[*] This document was provided by Mark Schonberger, Partner, Battle Fowler LLP, New York, and is reprinted courtesy of Battle Fowler LLP.

NOTES: Data Room Files have been color-coded as follows:

Green: May be copied freely. Copies will be made by
        Data Room personnel.

Yellow: May be copied at discretion of Data Room personnel.

Red: May not be copied—Confidential.

A. ACCOUNTING

Yellow   A.1   Consolidated Balance Sheet 1995

Yellow   A.2   Consolidating Balance Sheet 1995

Yellow   A.3   Consolidated Balance Sheet 1998

Yellow   A.4   Consolidating Balance Sheet 1998

E. ENVIRONMENTAL

Overview

E.1   Binder—Overview Manual

Green   Facility Overview

Red   Facility Descriptions

Green   Emissions Data

Red   Accident & Injury Data

E.2   Binder

Green   Plant Description

Red   General Information

Yellow   Permits

Red   Audit Report

F. FACILITIES

Plant Facilities

F.1   Binder

Green		Key Facts
Green		Photo
Green		Major Equipment
Green		Production Process
Green		Manufactured Products
Green		Operating Permits Listing

H. HUMAN RESOURCES

Benefits Information

Green	H.1	Long-Term Disability Plan Document
Green	H.2	Medical Reimbursement Plan Document
Green	H.3	Dependent Reimbursement Plan Document
Green	H.4	Retirement Income Plan Document
Green	H.5	Personal Plan Document
Yellow	H.6	Retirement Income Plan for Hourly Employees (in process of being amended)
Green	H.7	Dental Plan Benefit Summary—Comprehensive Medical Plan

I. INTERNATIONAL

France

Debt/Credit Arrangements

Green	I.1	Debt/Credit Arrangement—Loan Documentation (loans to company)
Green	I.2	Debt/Credit Arrangement—Guarantees/Comfort Letters/ Promissory Notes/Pledges/Mortgages/Other Liens

Taxes

Green	I.3	Tax—Taxes Paid/1998

Employment

Green	I.4	Employment Headcount
Green	I.5	Employment Total Compensation—1998 (by division/function)
Green	I.6	Employment Payroll List (showing compensation for management personnel)

L. LEGAL

L.1   Binder: Product Liability Litigation

Red	U.S. Product Liability Overview
Red	U.S. Product Liability History—Legal Fees
Red	U.S. Pending Litigation 1999 Legal Fees
Red	Litigation Expenses 1998 and 1999
Red	Case Summaries
Red	Claim Summaries
Red	Letter of Credit

L.2   Binder: Miscellaneous Litigation/Claims (see also related Trademark Binder)

Red	Bankruptcy Litigation
Green	Workers' Compensation Claims Experience 1994–1999

L.3   Binder: Selected Regulations Affecting Business Operations

Yellow	Fair Packaging and Labeling Act
Yellow	Federal Hazardous Substances Act

Leases

Yellow	L.6	Lease

Personalty

Yellow	L. 7	Personalty Lease Telephone Equipment
Yellow	L. 8	Personalty Lease Copiers

Contracts

Green   L.20   R&D Contract

　　　　　L.21   R&D Contract

Data Processing (including licenses)

Software Licenses

Green   L.24   R&D Contract—List of Confidentiality Agreements

Green   L.25   Software License—Software—Accounts Payable System

Acquisitions/Merger Documentation

Yellow   L.100   Acquisition of XYZ Company (bound volume)

Yellow   L.101   Acquisition of ABC Company (bound volume)

Yellow   L.102   Purchase of Certain Assets of New York Company 1994
　　　　　　　　　　(bound volume)

Yellow   L.103   Purchase of Certain Assets of New Jersey Company 1994
　　　　　　　　　　(bound volume)

Yellow   L.104   Certificates of Merger—Merger of UV, Inc. and X, Inc.

Corporate Records

Yellow   L.105   Corporate Records—(2 volumes, 1 book of stock certificates
　　　　　　　　　　and 1 stock transfer ledger)

Yellow   L.106   Corporate Records (2 volumes)

　　　　　L.107   Not Used

Yellow   L.108   Corporate Records (3 volumes)

　　　　　L.109   Not Used

Yellow   L.110   Corporate Records (2 volumes)

P. PATENTS

Red   P. 1   Listing of Patents

R. RESEARCH AND DEVELOPMENT

R.1   Binder: Research and Development Overview

Green   Overview

Green   Building Facilities

Green   Product Development Process

Green   R&D Capabilities

Green   R&D Organization

T. TRADEMARKS

Red   **T.1   Binder**

1. Printout (and update) of worldwide trademark
    registrations and applications of marks (by marks;
    by owner; updates)

2. Printout of trademarks

Red   **T.2   Binder: Printout of Pending Conflicts**

Selected trademarks pertaining to products with sales
exceeding $5 million

T.3–T.6 Not Used

Red   **T.7   Binder: Encumbrances on Trademarks:
Exclusive Licenses, Consents, and Agreements**

A P P E N D I X 3B

Case Study: Asset/Threat Analysis
of a Testing Company

*Each company has its own set of assets, and its own set of threats to those assets.
Acquirers need to develop an asset/threat mentality when conducting due diligence.
The following case study of asset/threat analysis is provided by Kroll Associates.*

Kroll Associates has had numerous assignments to analyze the risks
faced by professional certification testing organizations with global operations. In these cases, Kroll sought to:

■ Identify the key asset and threats to the asset.

- Evaluate the current exam control environment.
- Recommend ways to strengthen and augment existing controls.

AN EXAMPLE

The following case represents a composite of the work Kroll did with such organizations.

Key Asset/Threats

The key asset in the company was of course the exam itself, which must be both high quality and confidential. The key threats to the exam were:

- Loss of exam integrity during development
- Organized cheating and/or theft

The Current Exam Control Environment

Kroll consultants identified several phases in the continuing life cycle of this business, each one exposed to certain risks. The phases were:

- *Exam development.* Here managers acknowledged that the main risks were threats to the basic integrity of the exam itself. Exam integrity is lost when there is a breach of confidentiality during exam development through inadvertent or intentional discussion of specific questions and/or exam direction.
- *Exam printing and shipping.* Risks here include theft and loss.
- *Exam administration.* Here we identified the parties who could steal the exam:
  - Competitors
  - Test takers
  - Staff
  - Volunteers
  - Technology that could be used to steal the exam and communicate results: scanners, video cameras, cell phones, and laptop computers with Internet access.
- *Exam grading and reporting.* Cheating via changing grades (via hackers, for example) was another identified threat. We also identified security risks—such as destruction of results by flood, fire, or computer software or hardware malfunction.

Kroll also ranked countries by degree of risk, since some countries pose more threats than others due to cultural characteristics, infrastructure differences, and/or the prevalence of violence—from sporadic civil unrest to incidents of terrorism to a sustained state of war.

As a result of its risk assessment, Kroll reengineered significant portions of the examination process. Kroll also developed a worldwide crisis management plan and installed an incident-reporting hotline system with global coverage.

A P P E N D I X 3C

Cultural Due Diligence: A Checklist from Hay Management Consultants

To determine a match of cultures, an acquirer can rate itself and a candidate company on each of the cultural elements below. For testing purposes, these elements should be presented to evaluators in random order. Note, however, that in their original order, the traits range from left-brain qualities (involving reason) to right-brain qualities (involving intuition). All traits are expressed as positive; any negative trait can be expressed as a low degree of a particular positive.

Hay uses numeric ratings from 1 for a small extent, 2 for a moderate extent, and 3 for a great extent. Answers will often form bell curves, with the majority of items receiving a 2, and only a few receiving a 3 or a 1. In the center, one can see the "dominant" culture, often clustering in the same number range.

An asterisk (*) indicates a quality that (in the opinion of authors Lajoux and Elson) is highly desirable from a due diligence perspective, since it minimizes the chances of postmerger exposure to lawsuits. Conversely, absence of these elements, while completely normal in many cultures, should trigger more energetic due diligence in these areas. Also, due diligence investigators should be aware that incompatible cultures can mean postmerger trouble. A culture that leans in one direction may not be compatible with a culture that leans in the other direction—unless management works on it.

1. Being highly organized.
2. Using proven methods to serve existing markets.
3. Maintaining clear lines of accountability.

4. Limiting the downside of risk.*
5. Minimizing unpredictability of business results.*
6. Proving secure employment.
7. Establishing clear, well-documented work processes.
8. Treating employees fairly and consistently.*
9. Establishing clear job descriptions and requirements.
10. Respecting the chain of command.
11. Being precise.
12. Minimizing human error.*
13. Supporting the decisions of one's boss.
14. Maintaining customer satisfaction.
15. Providing employees with resources to satisfy customers.
16. Delivering reliably on commitments to customers.*
17. Using limited resources effectively.
18. Participating in training and continuing education.
19. Quality-checking employees' work.
20. Supporting top management's initiatives.
21. Being loyal and committed to the company.
22. Achieving budgeted objectives.
23. Demonstrating understanding of the customer's point of view.
24. Maintaining existing customer accounts.
25. Accepting strong viewpoints, strongly held.
26. Continuously improving operations.
27. Attracting top talent.
28. Rewarding superior performance.
29. Responding to customer feedback.
30. Encouraging teamwork.
31. Taking initiative.
32. Increasing decision-making span.
33. Gaining the confidence of customers.
34. Acquiring cross-functional knowledge and skills.
35. Significantly decreasing cycle time.
36. Sharing successfully.
37. Maintaining a sense of urgency.
38. Applying innovative technology to new situations.

39. Tolerating well-meaning mistakes.
40. Anticipating changes in the business environment.
41. Encouraging innovation.
42. Adapting quickly to changes in the business environment.
43. Encouraging expression of diverse viewpoints.
44. Developing new products or services.
45. Being flexible and adaptive in thinking and approach.
46. Pioneering new ways of doing things.
47. Capitalizing on creativity and innovation.
48. Organizing jobs around capabilities of individuals.
49. Taking action despite uncertainty.
50. Pushing decision-making to the lowest levels.
51. Finding novel ways to capitalize on employees' assets.
52. Using resources outside the company to get things done.
53. Experimenting with new management techniques.
54. Establishing new ventures or new lines of business.
55. Capitalizing on windows of opportunity.
56. Building strategic alliances with other organizations.

ENDNOTES

1. Arthur Andersen partner Morton Egol, based in New York, has written and worked extensively for this cause. See, for example, *Information Age Accounting: Catalyst and Enabler of the Self-Organizing Enterprise* (New York: Arthur Anderson LLP, 1994). Ernst & Young sponsors an annual summer conference on business applications of complex adaptive systems.

2. Committee of Sponsoring Organizations of the Treadway Commission, *Internal Control—Integrated Framework* (Jersey City, N.J.: American Institute of Certified Public Accountants, 1992, 1994).

3. That is, reports on Form 10-KSB and Form 10-QSB, pursuant to Item 303 of Regulation S-K and S-B under the Securities Exchange Act of 1934. Note also that some companies conduct what is in effect a *continuous due diligence* after a new issuance or shelf registration, according to Joseph McLaughlin, "Due Diligence in the Public Offering Process," *Conducting Due Diligence 1999* (New York: Practising Law Institute, 1999), p. 225. These diligent companies provide their underwriters with a continuous flow of information-updating statements in their

original registration statements. Such information can give acquisition investigators a head start in their own due diligence work.

4. The main search engines are Alta Vista, Excite, Hotbot, Infoseek, Lycos, Opentext, and Webcrawler. In addition to these big seven, there are selective Web databases such as C | Net, Excite Reviews, Magellan, and Yahoo, but they are smaller and/or edited and may not turn up as much information as the first seven. Traditional vendors of databases, such as Dialog (now Knight-Ridder Information Inc.), are also different in that their databases are often commercially developed and professionally edited records of commercially published texts in academic, scientific, and technical areas. While all these other services may be comparable for some queries, they really are different from the major search services in scope and purpose.

5. Public corporations must make such disclosure (as "line of business" reports) for units generating 5 percent or more of corporate revenues. In addition, the MD&A report must include such information if material, with materiality judged case by case. Thus, overall quality of information on company units in any due diligence investigation depends on whether the company is private or public and, if public, on what percentage of its revenues comes from the subsidiary. Private corporations may not have to make any public disclosure of subsidiary or divisional performance, depending on their states of incorporation (some states do require the filing of such data). Some companies, private and public, make voluntary public disclosure of all subsidiary and divisional financials, however, and all well-managed companies report such results on an internal basis.

6. Some academic centers specialize in this kind of analysis. For example, Cornell University has an entire program dedicated to "Computer Assisted Survey Techniques" (CAST).

7. William M. Crilly, *Due Diligence Handbook* (New York: Amacom, 1999).

8. For the acquirer of a publicly owned company, such information is generally in the annual report, 10K, and proxy statement. For analysis of a private company, however—or any public company undergoing rapid change—information of this kind can be very useful.

9. William F. Alderman and John Kanberg, Orrick, Herrington, and Sutcliffe LLP, San Francisco, "Due Diligence in the Securities Litigation Reform Era: Some Practical Tips from Litigators on the Effective Conduct, Documentation, and Defense of Underwriter Investigation," *Conducting Due Diligence 1999* (New York: Practising Law Institute, 1999), p. 193. Similarly, *Software Toolworks* cites interviews with "over a dozen" managers, and *International Rectifier* cites interviews with 11 managers. Acquirers seeking to protect against charges of negligence might consider conducting this degree of interview-based investigation.

10. From due diligence guidelines used at Sullivan and Cromwell PC, New York, when coauthor Charles Elson conducted due diligence investigations for the firm.

11. John E. Mendez and William R. Sawyers, "Due Diligence in Private Placements and Private Placements and Private Acquisitions," *Conducting Due Diligence 1999*, op. cit., p. 313.

12. Alderman and Kanberg, op. cit. (note 6), p. 210.

13. *Picard Chemical Inc. Profit Sharing Plan v. Perrigo company* (1998), 1998 U.S. Dist. LEXIS 11783 (W.D. Mich., June 15, 1998).

14. Source: News Digital Media, Inc. Fox News Online, December 7, 1999. Other famous frauds include Cascade International, Cooper Companies, Crazy Eddie, Leslie Fay, Miniscribe, Sun Systems, and ZZZZBest. Each of these stories involves imaginative techniques—from shipping bricks instead of inventory, to creating fictional storefronts. For a guide to detecting and preventing fraud, see the *Report of the NACD Best Practices Council: Coping with Fraud and Illegal Activity*, sponsored by Grant Thornton ('Washington, D.C.: National Association of Corporate Directors, 1998).

15. Alderman and Kanberg, op. cit. (note 12), p. 207.

16. Ibid., p. 193.

17. Ibid., p. 212. Alderman and Kanberg note that absence of these events or notes does not constitute negligence.

18. David A. Katz, Wachtell, Lipton, Rosen, and Katz, New York, "Due Diligence in Acquisition Transactions," *Conducting Due Diligence 1999*, op. cit., p. 334.

19. The authors extend appreciation to Jonny J. Frank, principal, Preicewaterhouse Investigations, New York, and John Verna, Senior Managing Director, Kroll Associates, Washington, D.C., for providing interviews and material for major portions of this chapter.

20. K. W. Stephen Cheung, in a letter dated September 28, 1998, to Judith Q. Iacuzzi, Editor, *ACG Network*, the newsletter of the Association for Corporate Growth, Glenview, Illinois. Mr. Cheung heads Conflict Management Consultants in Birmingham, Michigan and Windsor, Ontario, Canada.

21. Mitchell Lee Marks, "Adding Cultural Fit to Your Due Diligence Checklist," *Mergers & Acquisitions*, November–December 1999, pp. 14–20.

22. For an explanation of the AA model, see Brian Friedman, James Hatch, and David M. Walker, *Delivering on the Promise: How to Attract, Manage, and Retain Human Capital* (New York: The Free Press, 1998). For particular applications, see Bob Roswski and Jill Carson, "How to Save Time and Money in Corporate Acquisitions," *HR Director 1997–1998* (New York: Profile Pursuit, 1997), pp. 70–78; and Jeffrey J. Brown, "Merging Human Capital: The Role of HR in M&A," *HR Director 1999–2000* (New York: Profile Pursuit, 1999), pp. 268–271. Alexandra Lajoux served as editor of *Delivering on the Promise* and of the 1998–1999 and 1999–2000 editions of *HR Director*. The oldest and largest initiative may be the one undertaken by Arthur Andersen's human capital group. Formed in 1975 as a compensation and benefits practice, the group now has more than 2,300 professionals in 120 offices in 50 countries. For the past four years, it has published

annual almanacs of its work in this area, including guidance on merging human resources following a merger.

23. For further information, see Mark N. Clemente and David S. Greenspan, authors of *Winning at Mergers and Acquisitions: The Guide to Market-Focused Planning and Integration* (New York: John Wiley, 1998). Another individual promoting marketing due diligence is John Coldwell, a senior partner at CDS Corporate Development (www.cdscd.co.uk) and also a managing director at InfoQuest, a company formed to help acquirers conduct due diligence on customers of candidate companies (www.infoquestcrm.co.uk).

24. Joseph McLaughlin, Brown & Wood, LLP, writes: "The SEC has actively encouraged issuers to include 'soft' information in their disclosure documents." *Conducting Due Diligence 1999*, op. cit., p. 222.

CHAPTER 4

The Legal
Compliance Review

Are we disposed to be the number of those who, having eyes, see not, and having ears, hear not . . . ? For my part, whatever anguish of spirit it may cost, I am willing to know the whole truth; to know the worst, and to provide for it.

Patrick Henry
Speech to the Virginia Convention
Richmond, March 23, 1775

INTRODUCTION

Legal compliance begins at home, with a responsible due diligence *process* that uncovers current and potential causes of financial, operational, and legal problems. This process itself can eliminate about a quarter of potential suits against directors and officers. According to Tillinghast-Towers Perrin, a worldwide professional services firm, one out of every four lawsuits filed against officers and directors in any 10-year period stems from a merger gone bad. Plaintiffs allege that the buyer or seller committed errors in the purchase or sale of the company. A responsible due diligence process, well documented, can provide a strong defense against such legal actions.

It is somewhat more difficult, however, to master the other causes of lawsuits against corporate officers and directors. These can come from anyone over any issue—and predicting and managing them can be difficult. This chapter is about that vast terrain of potential litigation—one that expands whenever an acquirer buys another company. Why? Because the purchased company's legal vulnerabilities become the responsibility of the buyer, unless the acquisition agreement says otherwise (which it usually does not, absent a shrewd buyer in a tightly structured asset sale).

That leaves the acquirer—even one with an excellent due diligence process—with much work to be done, no matter what kind of company it is buying. Every decent acquirer tries to select acquisition candidates free from any taint of illegal or otherwise legally problematic activity, but how can a buyer be sure? Certainty is impossible, but some kind of prudent assurance is certainly attainable.

Buyers need first and foremost to understand the basic structure of the U.S. legal system. They also need to become familiar with significant business laws and current litigation trends. With respect to the candidate company in particular, an acquirer, working closely with senior legal counsel (internal and/or external), will need to assess all pending litigation and to determine the strength of the company's legal compliance programs in general.

THE U.S. LEGAL SYSTEM: AN OVERVIEW

In determining the legal profile of a company, it is obviously important to know applicable law. How can an acquirer develop such an understanding?

This is a daunting task, but it is worth some effort. The first step is to develop an understanding of the U.S. legal system in general, which is based on three types of law: *common, statutory,* and *regulatory.*[1]

What is common law?

Common law, also known as *case law,* is a body of law created out of court decisions. As mentioned in Chapter 1, this law dates back to medieval England. The common law covers right and wrong in a number of areas, including but not limited to *contracts.* Wrongs done outside of a contractual setting are called *torts,* and the righting of such wrongs over generations has generated a good deal of the law. Much of the common law has been codified in state law, as well as in the following legal models, which have been adapted in various forms by most states and have a tremendous impact on business:

- Uniform Commercial Code (adopted in all 50 states)
- Uniform Partnership Act
- Model Business Corporation Act

The Uniform Commercial Code comes up often in due diligence work. What exactly does it cover?

The Uniform Commercial Code (UCC) regulates conduct in a vast variety of ordinary business matters. Some of the areas it covers include:

- Sales
- Commercial paper
- Bank deposits and collections
- Warehouse receipts
- Bills of lading
- Investment securities
- Secured transactions

The UCC section most relevant to due diligence work is the one on *sales*, which covers formation of contracts, construction of contracts, terms of sale, titles and creditors, good faith purchases, performance, acceptance and breach, repudiation, and remedies. In Chapter 5 we go into more detail on the UCC.

What is statutory law?

Statutory law is a series of laws passed by legislatures, and then interpreted and enforced by the courts through the judicial process. The statutory law of the nation is passed by the U.S. Congress, which is composed of the House of Representatives and the Senate. The statutory law of states is passed by state legislatures. Finally, counties and cities have governments that may pass laws. Federal law supersedes state law, and they both supersede local law, subject to limits imposed by the U.S. Constitution.

There are two types of statutory law for both the nation and for states: *criminal law* and *civil law*. The plaintiff in criminal cases is the government (federal or state) representing the people, and the cases are generally tried before a jury. The plaintiff in civil cases is a wronged individual, and the cases are generally tried before a judge, but may also be tried before a jury. In recent years, business wrongdoing has been increasingly subject to the criminal process. Both civil and criminal laws may be affected by administrative regulations and executive orders from the executive branch of government.

All U.S. law, including state and local law, must pass muster under the U.S. Constitution. Any law that does not is deemed "unconstitutional" and is completely unenforceable.

You mentioned regulatory law. What is this?

Regulatory law is composed of administrative regulations and executive orders, which are various rules created by the executive branch of government. They are neither directly approved by a legislature nor decided by a court, yet they effectively have the force of law. Administrative regulations are created by federal and state agencies, and executive orders are issued by the head of the executive branch of government—the President in the case of the federal government, and the governor in the case of the state.

Administrative law poses a special challenge to acquirers and all businesses. Not only do agencies have the power to issue regulations that have the force of law; they also have the power to initiate proceedings under those regulations as well as under certain statutes. Furthermore, they have the power to investigate, prosecute, and even decide matters. Not surprisingly, because of their broad scope of power, agencies and their administrative regulations have grown exponentially over the past century.[2]

States are preempted from interfering with federal statutory law or with the guidelines promulgated by agencies established under federal law or by the U.S. Constitution.[3]

How many agencies are there, and how can an acquirer keep up with all their rules?

Today, in addition to the 14 departments that make up the executive branch, there are 86 independent agencies—making 100 executive branch entities. Fortunately, not all 100 of these entities engage in rule making; some are mere advisory bodies. Furthermore, of the rule makers, some are focused on a particular industry—such as communications (Federal Communications Commission) or banking (Federal Deposit Insurance Corporation).

In fact, only about 10 percent of this vast regulatory machinery applies to business generally. Specifically, there are four executive branch departments (one-third of the 12-member Cabinet) and six agencies that generate rules potentially applicable to any company. Acquirers should be particularly well aware of this "Big 10"—both the laws these agencies enforce (statutory law) and the regulations they generate (administrative regulations).

What are the executive branch departments and federal agencies that have the most regulatory effect on business?

- Department of Commerce (intellectual property and export/import)
- Department of Justice (including the Antitrust Division)
- Department of Labor
- Department of the Treasury (including the Internal Revenue Service)
- Consumer Product Safety Commission (consumer safety)
- Environmental Protection Agency (environment)

- Equal Employment Opportunity Commission (employment fairness)
- Federal Trade Commission (commercial transactions—supplementing the Justice Department in antitrust)
- Occupational Safety and Health Administration (worker safety and health)
- Securities and Exchange Commission (securities issues and exchanges)

Going back to the basic sources of law making (common, statutory, and regulatory), how do the U.S. judiciary and the state judiciaries deal with these three different types of law?

The federal judiciary is empowered to hear cases involving both federal and state law. The state judiciary traditionally acts to resolve disputes under state law.

For plaintiffs who wish to continue a legal action, there are appeals courts. Each state has appeals courts, plus one supreme court that is the highest court of appeal. The United States has courts of appeal divided into 11 geographic circuits, plus a federal court of appeals. (See the list at the end of this book.) It also has a high court, the U.S. Supreme Court, which typically restricts its review to cases involving substantive and substantial legal issues.

Clearly, acquirers need to remain current on new legal developments in order to assess liability risks in companies being acquired. How can acquirers accomplish this goal?

This is a tall order. As mentioned, there is federal law emanating from courts, from Congress, and from regulatory agencies, as well as state law to consider. Yet the goal is not impossible. Every acquiring company can benefit from having on staff or retaining qualified attorneys with expertise in business law. The most senior attorney (typically called general counsel) should be familiar with all the laws most important to the company. Such an attorney is likely to have staff members with a solid grounding in the most generally applicable laws.

Furthermore, these attorneys can (and typically do) subscribe to specialized publications that keep them abreast of current developments. For example, many law libraries receive the Federal Register, which lists the full text of all new laws and regulations promulgated under these laws. These laws and regulations create a 50-title series entitled the Code of Federal Regulations (CFR). For a list of the 50 parts of the CFR, see Appendix 4A.

No attorney, much less manager, is expected to master all 50 parts of the CFR. However, attorneys and others can remain cognizant of federal law in a number of ways.

- *Case law.* Attorneys can check regularly with various online sources such as *weslaw.com* to learn about new laws and legal precedents on a daily basis. Furthermore, depending on the area, attorneys and others can consult with a myriad of publications designed to keep them abreast of recent developments (such as *Corporate Counsel Weekly*).

- *Statutory law, federal and state.* For federal law, attorneys and others can obtain a copy of the CFR, and then subscribe to services that focus on parts most relevant to a business. For example, one private publisher (Government Institutes of Rockville, Maryland) sells a 29-volume CFR set for environmental, health, and safety issues—a large component of federal law. For state law, this same publisher sells state legal codes. This information can also be gleaned online by the patient Internet researcher. For example, by typing "Ohio AND Code" into any major search engine, researchers can find the entire legal code of the state of Ohio.

- *Legal developments generally.* Periodicals such as *The Business Lawyer* report regularly on legal developments. Also, attorneys can receive continuing education through organizations such as the American Law Institute, the American Bar Association, and the Practising Law Institute. These organizations have professional practices groups that enable specialists to stay current in various areas of the law. These organizations also hold frequent conferences that are open to members and to the general public. In some states, attorneys are required to provide proof of such education in order to maintain their professional licenses.

SOURCES OF LITIGATION

Clearly, acquirers face exposure to many kinds of lawsuits based on many different sources of law. How can they avoid such lawsuits?

Postacquisition lawsuits typically stem from two causes, which may coexist in any particular case.

First, the acquirer may be *sued for its own negligence in making the acquisition*. For example, the officers and directors of an acquirer may be sued for failure to fulfill their statutory duty of due care in asking questions that could have uncovered an obvious risk. Such a suit is generally filed as a private right of action (meaning nongovernment action) under state law. An acquirer may also be sued under federal securities laws for any faulty disclosures it made to shareholders or the public during the course of the acquisition. Lawsuits may allege a general lack of due diligence, or they may target some technicality that the acquirer missed during due diligence, such as the lack of proper filing.

Alternatively (or sometimes in addition) an acquirer may be sued for *alleged legal violations by the company it is buying*—even if these actions occurred prior to the sale of the company. For example, after buying a restaurant chain, an acquirer might learn of a pattern of racial discrimination evident through internal complaints filed prior to the acquisition. Proper due diligence would have uncovered such a problem and resolved it by settling grievances and instituting appropriate policies prior to the acquisition.

How can an acquirer avoid getting sued for negligence in making the acquisition?

While little can be done to avoid lawsuits, much can be undertaken to prevent their success. As discussed in Chapter 1, both buyer and seller should show due diligence in making the acquisition. The case law offers guidance here. A famous example of alleged lack of seller due diligence is *Smith v. Van Gorkom* (1985). (See the Landmark Due Diligence Cases at the end of the book.) Conversely, if an acquirer can show that it exercised due care in deciding to acquire a company, its acquisition decision should not be vulnerable to a successful lawsuit.

How can an acquirer minimize the liability exposure it inherits from the seller?

First, it can try to build protections into the acquisition agreement it cosigns with the seller. Such an agreement can state that the risk of undisclosed liabilities will fall to the seller. Beyond this, there are two main things an acquirer can do:

- Analyze pending litigation, an activity called *litigation analysis*.
- Assess legal compliance, an activity called *compliance review*.

LITIGATION ANALYSIS

What is litigation analysis, when is it conducted, and who does it?

Litigation analysis is an examination of existing claims against the company to determine their validity and their potential dollar impact. It may also include a study of litigation trends within the industry, to determine points of vulnerability. Litigation analysis of acquisition candidates is ideally conducted by attorneys who specialize in commercial or corporate litigation and who are familiar with the seller's industry.

This analysis is conducted throughout the M&A process, including the following phases:

- *Planning and finding.* Acquirers may use compliance as a criterion for acquisition.
- *Valuation.* Acquirers will want to allocate known liabilities in accounting for a transaction, and will want to adjust pricing accordingly.
- *Financing.* Acquirers will want to satisfy lender requirements with respect to compliance–for example, environmental compliance (see Chapter 8).
- *Structuring.* The extent of legal liabilities in a candidate company can influence the choice to structure a transaction as a stock versus an asset purchase.
- *Negotiation.* As they negotiate the acquisition agreement, acquirers will want to verify the accuracy of representations and warranties with respect to liability issues.
- *Closing.* Liability exposure analysis must be concluded by closing, and can make or break a transaction.

Senior counsel for the acquirer (typically external counsel) should take the lead in this effort. Counsel should shape the due diligence study according to the direction of senior managers, while retaining a strong measure of discretion and autonomy. The senior counsel should remain in regular communication with others involved in the due diligence review—not only the junior legal associates counsel performing review, but also any other professionals involved. For example, if the acquirer hires professional investigators during the analysis of operational risks, these investigators should report to the general counsel. This hierarchy makes sense, because all risks eventually translate into legal liabilities.

How do litigation analysts examine claims for validity and exposure—both current and potential?

The individual primarily responsible for the pending litigation review must go through several steps:

1. Determine the parameters of the review, defining what levels of exposure (dollar amounts) would be considered material.
2. Identify the litigation or administrative actions that warrant particular scrutiny.
3. Obtain a schedule of all litigation, pending and threatened.
4. Arrange to receive copies of all relevant pleadings.
5. Arrange to receive copies of all relevant liability insurance policies, including director and officer (D&O) liability insurance.

How does counsel determine whether particular litigation is material to the acquiring company in the due diligence context?

Before gathering information through a due diligence request, counsel must determine what litigation is "material." The materiality determination for litigation, as for other aspects of due diligence, will be relative. A $5 million lawsuit, even if it has merit, may have little significance in the context of a $1 billion deal. On the other hand, even a case with little financial exposure may jeopardize a $20 million deal if the buyer and seller cannot agree on how to handle that case.

When evaluating litigation pending against a midsize company, a materiality cutoff point of $250,000 might be reasonable. In addition, certain types of cases might merit close attention, whatever the financial exposure. For example, a products liability case that looks like it might be the first of many should receive close attention, even if the financial exposure on that one case is insignificant.

In ASSESSING the potential cost of litigation, companies should consider the option of settling out of court. Lately, more and more companies have discovered that much litigation is wrongly created and stubbornly maintained by their executive staff, internal and external legal advisers, and even some corporate directors. Many firms have set up special groups to reduce litigation costs and are using alternative dispute resolution (ADR), a fast-growing field of law in which minitrials that bypass or "supplement" the courts are held to resolve disputes quickly at a fraction of the usual legal costs. This approach may also yield hidden income since many companies maintain expensive legal actions that can be replaced by inexpensive ADR processes that enable cases to be settled quickly and easily even in the course of an acquisition negotiation. In examining offers of current counsel to undertake ADR work, client companies should determine how committed counsel is to this alternative. Begin by asking about counsel's ADR track record.

What material information should the litigator review?

In the due diligence request, counsel should seek a summary of all pending or threatened actions that satisfy the materiality standard that has been established. The summaries should include the following:

- Names and addresses of all parties
- Nature of the proceedings
- Date of commencement
- Status, relief sought, and settlements offered
- Sunk costs and estimated future costs
- Insurance coverage, if any
- Any legal opinions rendered concerning those actions

A summary should also be provided for the following:

- All civil suits by private individuals or entities
- Suits or investigations by government bodies
- Criminal actions involving the candidate company or its significant employees
- Tax claims (federal, state, and local)
- Administrative actions
- All investigations

In addition, counsel should request copies of all material correspondence during the past five years with any government agency (e.g., any of the Big 10) and any other regulatory agency (city, county, state, or federal) to which the seller is subject. If the company is subject to the rules of quasi-regulatory bodies such as the New York Stock Exchange or any other exchanges, all material correspondence should be gathered. If the candidate company itself has subsidiaries, all relevant information should be requested for the subsidiaries as well.

After all this information has been gathered, how is the litigation analysis conducted?

Before the actual analysis begins, the individual in charge of the review must determine who will analyze which claims. Highly specialized claims should be assigned for review to attorneys with the most knowledge of the area involved.

The individual reviewer must arrange to receive pleadings and documents concerning any additional relevant claims and to have access to the attorneys representing the seller's company in those matters. Even in an acquisition characterized by cooperation, obtaining all the relevant pleadings may be difficult. This is particularly true if the company is represented by more than one law firm.

Finally, each pending material case should be systematically evaluated and some number assigned to the pending liability or recovery; the amount should include the costs of executives' time. For litigation on the seller's behalf by outside law firms, the reviewer should evaluate whether the case is being capably handled. Even a meritless case can create significant exposure if handled by an inexperienced or incompetent practitioner.

What cases should the reviewer consider first?

The reviewer should concentrate only on those cases that, if lost, could have a materially adverse impact on the defendant company's business operations, and thus the business operations of the combined company—the "ripple effect." The investigation should also identify and study other known cases involving companies in the same industry. For example, suppose a court decides that a business practice of one company in the industry constitutes a deceptive trade practice or other violation of law. If the seller's company is in the same industry and engages or might engage in the same practice, this can have a significant impact on the future business of the company, even if it is not a party to the litigation in question.

What general rules govern the acquirer's potential liability for the debts and torts of the company it is buying?

The traditional rule is that when one company sells or otherwise transfers all its assets to another company, the successor is not liable for the debts and tort liabilities of the predecessor. The successor may be liable, however, under the following circumstances:

- If it has expressly or implicitly agreed to assume liability.
- If there is a merger or consolidation.
- If the successor is a "mere continuation" of the predecessor.
- If the transaction was fraudulently designed to escape liability. (If a seller knowingly sells a company bordering on insolvency, the transaction—or "conveyance"—may be deemed fraudulent under the Fraudulent Conveyance Act.)

An additional exception exists for labor contracts. If the successor buys the predecessor's assets and keeps its employees, the successor will probably also be bound to recognize and bargain with unions recognized by the predecessor, and to maintain existing employment terms. Existing contracts may also create successorship problems. State law may vary with respect to assumption of debts and liabilities, so the reviewer must be cognizant of the specific statutory or case law that will govern the transaction.

Courts are increasingly likely to find successor liability, particularly with respect to product liability claims, under the "continuity of product line" or "continuity of enterprise" exceptions to the general rule of nonliability. The first of these exceptions applies where the successor acquires a manufacturer in the same product line. The second exception applies where the successor continues the predecessor's business. Faced with an increasingly aggressive plaintiff's bar in search of ever-deeper pockets, the courts are increasingly looking to corporate successors for product liability damage awards, including in some instances punitive damages.

This trend is particularly notable in the case of manufacturers of substances considered harmful, such as asbestos and tobacco. Accordingly, the due diligence reviewer must be aware of the current state of the law concerning successor liability for both compensatory and punitive damages.

D&O INSURANCE

What about insurance policies and cases being handled by insurance companies?

Each and every insurance policy must be reviewed to ensure that pending claims for compensatory damages will be covered. What is the deductible? What are the liability limits per occurrence and in total? Are punitive damages excluded by the policy or by state law? Does the policy contain "regulatory" or other exclusions? For large companies, there may be overlapping policies; all policies must be reviewed in light of these questions. (The task can be subcontracted to firms specializing in insurance-based "risk analysis," *provided* that they are reviewed for their "deal-killing potential" before being retained.)

Another consideration when reviewing insurance policies is whether the policies are for "claims incurred" or for "claims made." Coverage under a claims-incurred policy continues after the cancellation or termination of the policy and includes claims that arose during the period of insurance coverage, whether or not those claims are reported to the insurance company during that period. Claims-made policies cover only those claims actually made to the insurance company during the term of the policy. In addition, under some policies, coverage will continue only if a "tail" is purchased. A tail is a special policy purchased to continue coverage that would otherwise be terminated. It is important that the reviewer identify the nature of the seller's policies and determine any potential problems that may result from a failure to give the insurance company notice of claims during the policy period or from a failure to purchase a tail.

Also, the reviewer should scrutinize cases being handled by insurance companies to determine the status of the cases.

- Has the insurer undertaken the representation under a "reservation of rights"? (This means that it agrees to pay for or provide legal representation, but does not abandon its power to deny coverage later.)
- Has the insurer preliminarily denied coverage?
- Do the damages claimed include punitive or treble damages, and if so, does the insurance policy cover these?[4]

How can the acquirer be sure about the insurance coverage, and how can it make sure that the coverage will carry over to the new owners?

Before reviewing specific cases, the primary reviewer should ask executives of the selling company which cases they believe are covered by liability insurance, and which cases they believe are not so covered. Then the reviewer should study the insurance policies to determine what cases, if any, are in fact covered.

The individual responsible for the litigation analysis must have a working knowledge of transactional liability, discussed in the following chapter. Important here are the structure of the transaction—for example, whether it is to be a stock or asset purchase—and the corporate and tort law rules concerning successor liability for debts and torts, especially with regard to compensatory and punitive damages. These are then applied case by case.

COMPLIANCE REVIEW

How can an acquirer check a seller's legal compliance profile?

As a first step, it is wise to find out if the seller has an active compliance program. The likelihood of this is fairly high today because of two major developments in D&O liability.

One is the Federal Sentencing Guidelines, enacted in 1987 and amended in 1991. These guidelines contained a formula for sentences and penalties that included mitigating points for companies that have an "effective program to detect and prevent violations of law." Companies with such a program exercise "due diligence in seeking to prevent and detect criminal conduct by its employees and other agents." In effect, the candidate companies that have already established such a program expose potential acquirers to less risk. They have, in effect, conducted part of the acquirers' premerger due diligence for them.

Another development is the landmark Delaware Chancery Court case *In Re Caremark* (September 1996). In this case, Chancellor William T. Allen approved a settlement of a derivative shareholder lawsuit filed against the directors of Caremark, alleging lax conduct in allowing violation of federal Medicare rules by the company. The court based its approval of a settlement on the fact that Caremark had a strong legal compliance program. Chancellor Allen further stated that failure to ensure the existence of such a program can "render a director liable for losses caused by noncompliance with applicable legal standards."

As a result of the "carrot" of the Federal Sentencing Act (offering benefits for compliance programs) and the "stick" of Caremark (threatening liability exposure in the absence of such programs), many companies today have legal compliance programs. In some industries, such as health care, there are a wealth of excellent models to emulate.[5]

Obviously, the acquirer cannot check for seller compliance with every single law in existence. With over 1 million federal laws and regulations on the books,[6] not to mention state laws and regulations, this would be impossible. However, the astute acquirer will want to know the likelihood of different types of lawsuits. These may be brought by private individuals or groups belonging to a particular corporate constituency, or they may be brought by a regulatory body. Anticipating both private and regulatory lawsuits in these and other areas can minimize the chances for problems after the acquisition.

If following the checklist yields some areas of difficulty, the acquirer should ask if the company has conducted or would consider conducting an investigation into the matter. The legal literature has some very good guides to this activity.[7]

What are the main constituencies that might file lawsuits against an acquirer?

Any acquirer should be aware of the latest trends in director and officer (D&O) litigation, as reported by organizations such as Tillinghast-Towers Perrin.[8] Here is a list of groups that commonly sue directors and officers, along with an indication of frequency of such suits.[9] Frequency is indicated by the percentage of companies that have been sued at least once by these groups between 1989 and 1999.

- Customers, suppliers, competitors, and other contractors—18.6 percent
- Employees or unions, current or prospective—55.2 percent
- Government, regulatory, and other third-party claimants—4.6 percent
- Shareholders and other investors—19.9 percent

What are the average payments made in these cases?

The average claim made in 1999 by companies as a result of lawsuits by each of these groups was over $3 million ($3,256,508 to be precise). Here is how these groups compare by average cost:

- Customers—$3,106,376; competitors, suppliers, and other contractors—$1,433,468
- Employees or unions, current or prospective—$305,760
- Government, regulatory, and other third-party claimants—$10,348,500
- Shareholders and other investors—$8,672,576

What might all these groups typically sue over?

Customers might sue over the following issues, with the most common ones indicated, as a percentage of all D&O lawsuits (others comprise less than 1 percent):[10]

Contract disputes (2.8 percent)
Cost/quality of product or service
Debt collection, including foreclosure

Deceptive trade practices
Discrimination (3.5 percent)
Dishonesty/fraud (1.3 percent)
Extension/refusal of credit
Harassment/humiliation
Lender liability
Restraint of trade (antitrust issues)

Competitors, suppliers, and other contractors might sue over:

Antitrust actions (in suits brought by suppliers)
Business interference (1.3 percent)
Contract disputes (1.1 percent)
Copyright/patent/trademark infringement (1 percent)
Deceptive trade practices

Employees—including current, past, or prospective employees or unions—might sue over:

Breach of employment contract (2.8 percent)
Defamation (8 percent)
Discrimination (27.1 percent)
Employment conditions/safety
Failure to hire or promote (2.2 percent)
Harassment/humiliation (3.5 percent)
Pension, welfare, or other employee benefits
Retaliation/whistleblowing (2.1 percent)
Salary, wage, or compensation dispute (1.1 percent)
Wrongful termination (13.9 percent)

Shareholders might sue over:

Breach of duty to minority shareholders
Challenge to takeover defense measures
Contract disputes (with shareholders)
Dishonesty/fraud (1.2 percent)
Divestitures or spin-offs
Dividend declaration or change
Duties to minority shareholders
Executive compensation (such as golden parachutes)

Financial performance/bankruptcy

Financial transactions (such as derivatives)

Fraudulent conveyance

General breach of fiduciary duty (2.3 percent)

Inadequate disclosure (6.1 percent)

Inside information use/trading (1.3 percent)

Investment or loan decisions

Merger/acquisition—when the shareholders' company is the survivor (1.4 percent)

Merger/acquisition—when the other company is the survivor

Proxy contests

Recapitalization

Share repurchase

Stock or other public offering (1.3 percent)

Regulators might sue over alleged violations of laws involving:

Antitrust

Consumer protection

Environment

Worker health, safety, and working conditions

Securities

Taxes

Other (nonregulatory) constituencies also sue over these regulatory areas. As indicated above, competitors sue over violations of antitrust law, consumers over consumer protection laws, communities over environmental law, workers over health and safety laws, and shareholders over securities law. The only area that appears to be an exclusive regulatory domain is tax law.

In Part Two, we go into more detail about all these legal areas, paying special attention to the regulators that govern them.

What are some of the emerging legal issues to be concerned about in a due diligence investigation—ones that a buyer might never think of but that could hurt the company later?

Such issues crop up constantly as courts around the country offer innovative legal theories, set new precedents, and abolish old ones. No list of such new legal theories could be complete, but here are a few to consider:

- To what extent can the chief executive of a company, the board of directors, or the company itself be held accountable for the wrongful acts of subordinates?
- To what extent can advisers rely on the word of management? To what extent can management rely on advisers?
- How many times can a company be sued for the same action? Is there a limit to the number of plaintiffs who can ask for punitive damages?
- What product areas and industries are the trial lawyers targeting?[11]

See Chapters 6 through 12 for other important legal topics in the specific areas covered.

CONCLUDING COMMENTS

Every acquisition brings with it the burden of legal compliance review. This is particularly true in the United States, which lives by the "rule of law"—and boasts a plethora of busy practicing attorneys to support that lifestyle. Given this condition, any acquirer of a U.S. company needs to become familiar with the nation's legal infrastructure, particularly with respect to M&A transactions. Acquirers that gain such an insight, and act on it with a thorough compliance review, will clear the way for financial and management success.

A P P E N D I X   4A

The Code of Federal Regulations: A List of Titles

The CFR can be used as a checklist of federal agencies and their regulations. The following list shows all titles of the CFR. (Note: Many of the titles fill multiple book volumes when printed out.) Asterisks indicate titles and agencies that generate laws applicable to business. One asterisk (*) indicates titles and agencies applicable to a broad range of industries; two asterisks (**) indicate titles and agencies applying to a particular industry, such as financial services or utilities. Agencies beginning with the word "Department" (such as Department of Agriculture) have Cabinet status.

Title 1, 2: General Provisions

Title 3: The President (Executive Orders)

Title 4: Accounts (General Accounting Office)

Title 5, 6: Administrative Personnel (Office of Personnel Management)

Title 7: Agriculture (Department of Agriculture)**

Title 8: Aliens and Nationality (Immigration and Naturalization Service)

Title 9: Animals and Animal Products (Department of Agriculture)

Title 10: Energy (Nuclear Regulatory Commission and the Department of Energy)**

Title 11: Federal Elections (Federal Election Commission)

Title 12: Banks and Banking (Comptroller of the Currency, Federal Reserve System, Federal Deposit Insurance Corporation, Office of Thrift Supervision, National Credit Union Administration, Farm Credit Administration)**

Title 13: Business Credit and Assistance (Small Business Administration)

Title 14: Aeronautics and Space (Federal Aviation Administration)**

Title 15: Commerce and Foreign Trade (Department of Commerce)*

Title 16: Commercial Practices (Federal Trade Commission, Consumer Product Safety Commission)*

Title 17: Commodities and Securities Exchanges (Commodity Futures Trading Commission, Securities and Exchange Commission, Department of the Treasury)*

Title 18: Conservation of Power and Water Resources (Federal Energy Regulatory Commission, Department of Energy, Tennessee Valley Authority)**

Title 19: Customs Duties (U.S. Customs Service, U.S. International Trade Commission)*

Title 20: Employee Benefits (Office of Workers' Compensation Programs, Railroad Retirement Board, Social Security Administration, Department of Health and Human Services, Employment and Training Administration)*

Title 21: Food and Drugs (Food and Drug Administration, Drug Enforcement Administration)*

Title 22: Foreign Relations (Department of State, Peace Corps)

Title 23: Highways (Federal Highway Administration)**

Title 24: Housing and Urban Development

Title 25: Indians (Bureau of Indian Affairs)

Title 26: Internal Revenue (Internal Revenue Service)*

Title 27: Alcohol, Tobacco Products, and Firearms (Bureau of Alcohol, Tobacco, and Firearms)**

Title 28: Judicial Administration (Department of Justice)**

Title 29: Labor/OSHA (Department of Labor, National Labor Relations Board)**

Title 30: Mineral Resources (Mine Safety and Health Administration, Mineral Management Service Bureau, Office of Surface Mining Reclamation and Enforcement)**

Title 31: Money and Finance (Department of the Treasury)

Title 32: National Defense (Department of Defense, Departments of Army, Navy, and Air Force)**

Title 33: Navigation and Navigable Waters (Coast Guard, Army Corps of Engineers)

Title 34: Education (Department of Education)

Title 35: Panama Canal (Panama Canal Commission)

Title 36: Parks, Forests, and Public Property (National Park Service, Forest Service)

Title 37: Patents, Trademarks, and Copyrights (Patent and Trademark Office)*

Title 38: Pensions, Bonuses, and Veterans Relief (Department of Veterans Affairs)

Title 39: Postal Office (U.S. Postal Services, Postal Rate Commission)

Title 40: Environment (Environmental Protection Agency—this title includes 24 parts covering various environmental elements, such as air, water, pesticides, and hazardous wastes)*

Title 41: Public Contracts and Property Management (Government Services Administration)

Title 42: Public Health (Department of Health and Human Services)

Title 43: Public Lands (Department of the Interior, Reclamation Bureau, Land Management Bureau)

Title 44: Emergency Management and Assistance (Federal Emergency Management Agency)

Title 45: Public Welfare (Department of Health and Human Services, Commission on Civil Rights)

Title 46: Shipping (Coast Guard, Federal Maritime Commission)

Title 47: Communications (Federal Communications Commission)**

Title 48: Federal Acquisition Regulations System (U.S. Air Force)

Title 49: Transportation (Department of Transportation, Federal Highway Administration, National Highway Traffic Administration, Interstate Commerce Commission)

Title 50: Wildlife and Fisheries (National Marine Fisheries and National Ocean and Atmospheric Administration in the Department of Commerce)

Most government agencies have websites composed of their acronym, plus .gov—for example, sec.gov for the Securities and Exchange Commission.

E N D N O T E S

1. There is also constitutional law, but it generates no laws. Rather, a constitution asserts fundamental rights and limits the ability of any law to abridge those rights. The U.S. Constitution also describes the U.S. government, with its legislative, judicial, and executive branches, and its relation to state governments. (A second tier of law is composed of the constitutions of each of the 50 states in the United States. Therefore, it is fair to say that the system of U.S. constitutional law has "51 parts.") Constitutional law, then, asserts values, marks boundaries, and describes processes. It does not actually generate laws. That is the function of common law, statutory law, and regulatory law.

2. For commentary on this development, see our affirmation of due diligence as an important component of free markets and federalism in the conclusion to this book.

3. Source: Legal Information Institute, Cornell University (citing the U.S. Constitution, Article VI).

4. For an excellent guide to this subject, see Ty R. Sagalow, *D&O Liability Insurance: A Guide for Directors and Officers* (Washington, D.C.: National Association of Corporate Directors, 2000).

5. The Department of Health and Human Services, Office of the Inspector General, has created the "HHS Model Compliance Plan for Clinical Laboratories," which can be used by a variety of health care organizations. Also, Columbia-HCA, having suffered as a result of a weak compliance function, has created a very strong program, with the help of Alan Yuspeh, an ethics specialist who created classic guidelines for the defense industry. For details on the Columbia program, see John M. Franck II, "Energize Your Organization with a World-Class Compliance Program," *Director's Monthly,* March 1999, pp. 1–4.

The same issue features a roundtable discussion including Mr. Yuspeh (pp. 8–12).

6. The authors base the "over 1 million" estimate based on the following facts. The U.S. Code of Federal Regulations, as shown in Appendix 4A, contains 50 titles. For each of these, sections typically number in the thousands. (For example, Title 15 alone has over 5,500 sections.) Furthermore, each code section empowers at least one agency to promulgate regulations under these thousands of code sections. Any given code section can become the cause of multiple regulations. Multiply the number of codes, times the average number of sections per code, times the average number of regulations per section, yields a sum over 1 million.

7. See the *Corporate Compliance Series* (St. Paul, Minn.: The West Group, 1999) , edited by Joseph E. Murphy, Senior Attorney, Bell Atlantic, Philadelphia, and Paul H. Dawes, Partner, Latham and Watkins, San Francisco. This series, each one written by a specialist, has 11 volumes covering a wide range of legal areas. See also Louis M. Brown, Anne O. Kandel, and Richard S. Gruner, *The Legal Audit* (St. Paul, Minn.: The West Group, 1999). Although this book is written from the perspective of an internal investigation, rather than an investigation of an acquisition candidate, many sections are relevant. It includes chapters on investigation process, the legal status audit, the legal audit in the compliance context, specialized audits, protecting the confidentiality of investigative documents, and collaboration in auditing.

8. The figures in this section are based on Tillinghast-Towers Perrin, *1999 Directors and Officers Liability Survey: U.S. and Canadian Results* (New York: Tillinghast-Towers Perrin, 2000).

9. The authors are grateful to Mr. Larsen of Tillinghast-Towers Perrin for providing the data and analysis in this section of the chapter.

10. This list is based on Tillinghast-Towers Perrin figures (op. cit., note 8), with some consolidation and rearrangement of categories.

11. For more items, see Robert Hughes, ed., *Legal Compliance Checkups: Business Clients* (St. Paul, Minn.: The West Group, 1999). This publication has a "questionnaire" format that lends itself to use in due diligence studies prior to acquisitions. It covers a number of areas that can be traps for liability exposure, ranging from franchising to sexual harassment policies.

Transactional Due Diligence

The popular image of due diligence shows advisers counting beans, kicking tires, and looking for skeletons—that is, conducting the financial, operational, and legal due diligence, as covered broadly in Part One of this book (Chapters 1 through 4). But transactional due diligence—the actual crafting of an acquisition agreement with securities, tax, and accounting issues in mind—is equally important.

Part Two delves into the details of paperwork and red tape—a needed focus. Many due diligence investigators think of risk in terms of the grand sweep of financial, operational, and legal risks, such as those discussed in the other chapters of this book. But an equally important area is transactional risk—structural factors that can jeopardize a deal with even the most solvent and litigation-resistant company.

In this part of the book, we take a closer look at due diligence from the point of view of all-important transactional work. In Chapter 5, we look at the acquisition agreement and closing memoranda. Chapters 6 and 7 cover securities and tax law and related accounting regulations.

This material may seem extremely dry, but we urge you to peruse it with care. The technical knowledge presented here—combined with the even more important ingredient of common sense—will help you practice the art of M&A due diligence with uncommon skill.

CHAPTER 5

The Documentation and Transaction Review

Delay is preferable to error.

Thomas Jefferson
Letter to George Washington
May 16, 1792

INTRODUCTION

In addition to examining financial, operational, and legal risks, managers must focus on risks arising from the transaction itself—risks mitigated through the effective negotiation of the acquisition agreement and through proper closing procedures. We call the work involved here "transactional due diligence," as distinguished from the financial, operational, and legal due diligence discussed in the previous three chapters. Those chapters offered guidance on how to measure risks inherent in the business being acquired, either before or potentially after the acquisition. This chapter discusses the risks inherent in deal making itself—the negotiating and "red tape" aspects, if you will.

Unfortunately, transactional due diligence is all too foreign to many corporate executives. Whereas most executives know how to read a financial statement, evaluate corporate operations, and avoid violations of well-known laws, few are familiar with the paperwork necessary to structure and close an actual transaction. As a result, managers often delegate these matters to professionals. Such delegation is appropriate, but managers should monitor developments closely. This chapter provides guidance in this regard.

KEY POINTS IN THE ACQUISITION AGREEMENT

What is the purpose of the acquisition agreement?

The agreement sets forth legal understandings of the buyer and seller about the transaction. Ideally, it accomplishes five basic goals:

- It sets forth the structure and terms of the transaction.
- It discloses all the important legal, and many of the financial, issues affecting the company being acquired, as well as pertinent information about the buyer and seller.
- It obligates both parties to do their best to complete the transaction.
- It obligates the seller not to change its company in any significant way before the deal closes.
- It governs what happens if, before or after the closing, the parties discover problems that should have been disclosed either in the agreement or before the closing but were not properly disclosed.

Unlike the typical letter of intent, which may or may not be binding depending on how it is written,[1] an acquisition agreement is legally binding. Once it is signed, a party that fails to consummate the transaction without a legally acceptable excuse can be liable for damages.

The negotiation of the agreement is, in large part, an effort by the buyer and seller of a company to allocate the risk of major economic loss attributable to company defects that surface after the signing of the acquisition agreement, both before and after the closing.

Both parties should be aware that the value of the acquisition candidate may improve or deteriorate between the agreement and closing. As such, the acquisition agreement often includes provisions that state the parties' right to cancel the transaction or change the price in the event of "unforeseen events of a material" nature. (For more about materiality, see the discussion below.)

One of the typical conditions to closing for the buyer is that there has been no "material adverse change" in the financial condition of the seller. The buyer naturally wants to protect itself against events that might lower the value of the candidate company. Such conditions may include such occurrences as a new lawsuit against the candidate company or a burdensome new law affecting the candidate's industry. The buyer will want the right to lower or withdraw its offer if such events occur.

In reviewing such provisions in the agreement, the seller may note the lack of parallel. After all, the seller typically has no right to back out of the sale in the case of a positive event that raises the value of the company it is selling. The candidate company may obtain a long-awaited legal decision, or make a valuable new discovery. In this case, the seller would want the right to retain ownership of the company. Yet agreements rarely afford sellers this right.

Sellers may not be able to correct this buyer bias in the agreement. However, they can take other steps to protect their interests.

- A deposit
- A liquidated damages provision
- Transfer of risk to buyer as of the date of signing, not closing.

In what circumstances might a seller ask for a deposit?

The seller should receive a deposit in situations where it would lack recourse to the buyer in a breach of contract by the buyer. Buyers may transact a deal through a shell company with no assets, set up specifically and solely for the purpose of the acquisition. Although the seller will have recourse against the shell company, the seller may have no economically meaningful remedy in the event that the buyer breaches the agreement. The seller may win the lawsuit but will not be able to collect damages.

In such circumstances, sellers often insist upon a cash deposit, much as a seller does in the sale of a home. Alternatives include a cash escrow or a letter of credit that can serve as security for the buyer's obligations. It is hard for most buyers to argue their way out of such a requirement. This is particularly true when the seller has several creditworthy suitors, and when signing with the buyer will cause those potential deal makers to lose interest. However, if the buyer has a proven track record of closing deals, and the price is right, it may be able to talk the seller out of a deposit, or to delay posting the deposit until some period of time after the signing. For example, the buyer may agree to post a deposit only if the deal hasn't closed by a specified date, or if the buyer has not obtained financing commitments.

At the very least, a seller should make a strong effort to get a deposit large enough to cover all its expenses and to limit the time given to close the contract so that the company is not off the market too long.

Also, as mentioned earlier, if the buyer has the flexibility to walk away from the deal because of negative events, the seller should also have this flexibility with regard to positive events—or even better offers. But there should be financial sanctions against parties that "walk" from near-completed deals without substantial cause.

When is a liquidated damages clause appropriate?

A liquidated damages clause promises the payment of damages to the seller if the buyer backs out for a reason beyond the control of the seller. If the seller requests such a clause, the parties must approach the issue by crafting a solution that is carefully tailored to the specific concerns of the parties. Compromise can often be reached by adjusting the time frame for providing financing commitments and/or the consequences of the buyer's failure to finance the transaction.

How does risk transfer work for a seller?

Normally, at closing risk transfers from the seller to the buyer. Some sellers try to shift the date of this transfer to the date that the acquisition agreement is signed. Their theory is that the buyer has to accept a balanced economic deal—as mentioned, it gets both the good and the bad occurring after the signing. The reasoning here is that the buyer is getting what it bargained for, as long as the representations and warranties as of the signing date are accurate on the closing date and the seller does not breach its covenants concerning the conduct of the business pending closing.

What are the buyer and seller really concerned about when negotiating the acquisition document?

Once they agree to the key substantive aspects of the transaction (price and terms), the buyer and seller have two different concerns.

The seller wants to be as certain as possible of at least two things: (1) that the closing will occur as soon as possible after the agreement is signed, and (2) that no postclosing events will require a refund of any of the purchase price.

The buyer's and seller's concerns are mirror opposites. The buyer would like flexibility to abandon the transaction in the event that it discovers any financial, operational, or legal defects in the candidate company. After paying the seller at closing what the buyer feels is a fair price, the buyer would like to know that it will be compensated for any economic loss resulting from legal or financial problems that it did not expect to assume.

This is not to be confused with the business risk of operating the company after the closing. General economic downturns, new competition, and failures of management after the closing are pure business risks that any sensible buyer knows it is assuming when it buys a business. But the buyer will seek to protect itself against hidden flaws in the business—flaws that exist beneath the surface at the time of the closing, and show up later after the company is already purchased.

Ideally, the buyer wants protection against major problems such as profit deterioration leading to losses, poor morale leading to top management turnover, and illegal practices leading to legal exposure—the kinds of risks outlined in later chapters. Unfortunately, the seller is unlikely to agree to provide a blanket guarantee against the occurrence of any of these events. Instead, the seller will more typically guarantee only that it has disclosed all debts incurred, lawsuits filed, and fines payable as of a particular date.

The buyer will typically try to include clauses that enable it to withdraw from the transaction before the closing. However, with such flexibility, the agreement is simply an option to acquire, not a legally binding promise to do so. If the buyer really wants to buy the company, it should be willing to be legally obligated, within reason, to do so.

On the other hand, the seller can never be completely certain that the transaction will close, simply because there are too many conditions beyond the control of both buyer and seller that must be satisfied before any transaction can close.

Who should bear the risk of loss associated with undisclosed legal defects in the company discovered after the closing—the buyer, the seller, or both?

The real issue is: What is a fair price for the company? The answer hinges on the assumptions the buyer and seller made when they first agreed to the transaction.

Any buyer has two choices. It can:

- Determine a price based upon assuming the risk—that is, an "as is" deal, which presumably would be less than the price that would be paid if the seller retained some or all of the risks.

- Determine a higher price premised on the seller's retention of some part of the risk.

Although sellers usually want to sell their company on an "as is" basis, buyers should resist such a deal, since it affords them little or no protection after the closing. This alternative is a gamble, but it may be acceptable to a buyer that knows its candidate, or that is buying in an industry with a low-risk profile.

The vast majority of private companies are not sold "as is." Most buyers rightly insist that the seller absorb some of the risk of undisclosed problems. Without such shared risk, the seller has less of an incentive to cooperate in the due diligence effort. Thus, the seller will typically give the buyer at least some protection in the event that the company is not what the seller represented it to be. In fact, it is the rule in most sales of private companies that the seller will bear a significant portion of the risk of company defects, and the deal will be priced accordingly.

The seller, however, does have legitimate concerns about being pestered incessantly about descriptions that prove inaccurate or incomplete. Everyone knows going into an acquisition that no company is perfect, and that in due course blemishes on its legal and financial record will undoubtedly surface.

Accordingly, the customary practice is that the seller will be accountable, but its accountability is limited to significant problems that occur within a defined time period. (See the discussion of indemnification in the Sample Acquisition Agreement at the end of this book.)

This customary practice makes sense for three reasons.

1. If it is unlikely that a problem will be discovered, then an "as is" transaction with reduced pricing forces the seller to accept less money needlessly.

2. If a problem is discovered before the closing, it probably would result in a lower price anyway, even in an "as is" deal.

3. A sharing of the risk between buyer and seller will provide both with a strong incentive to try to discover problems before the agreement is signed or the deal is closed. Thorough investigation by both parties with a stake in the outcome reduces the likelihood that a claim will arise.

This does not mean that every seller should cave in on the accountability issue. In the case of a deal-hungry buyer, or a buyer that has confidence in its assessment of the risk of loss attributable to breaches of representations and warranties, the seller may get the best of both worlds—a high price with little or no postclosing risk. This is especially true in a competitive bidding situation. In the end, the allocation of risk will depend more on the bargaining power and negotiating skills of the parties than on the niceties of pricing theories.

COMPONENTS OF THE AGREEMENT

How are the general concerns of the buyer and seller reflected in the acquisition agreement?

The major concerns of the parties are expressed in two sections of the agreement: the *conditions to closing* section and the *indemnification* section. The conditions section lists the conditions that must be satisfied before the parties become obligated to close the transaction, and thus controls whether the buyer or seller can "walk" from the deal with impunity. The indemnification section establishes the liability, if any, of each party to the other for problems discovered after the closing.

Both sections are generally keyed to two earlier parts of the agreement: the representations and warranties and the covenants.

In the *representations ("reps") and warranties* section, the parties make statements as of the date of the signing about the legal and financial state of affairs of the candidate company, the seller, and the buyer, including the legal and financial ability of each party to enter into and consummate the transaction. In a typical agreement, a buyer or seller will be able to back out of the agreement if it discovers that the representations or warranties of the other party are untrue to any significant extent. Also, the seller must indemnify the buyer for problems that surface after the closing. The representation must be true at the time made and remain true until closing, or amended at closing to reflect any changes. After that, the representation expires.

The *covenants* section contains the parties' agreement to take no action that would change the state of affairs described in the representations and warranties section. Of course, changes resulting from the ordinary operation of business, actions (such as seeking government approvals and other third-party consents) that are necessary to complete the transaction, and changes (such as certain corporate reorganizations) that are contemplated by the acquisition agreement are permitted under the covenants.

Reps, warranties, and covenants are extremely important. The most significant "conditions to closing" are that the representations and warranties are true on the closing date and that the parties have not breached the covenants. Liabilities under the indemnity section, in turn, arise from breaches of representations, warranties, and covenants. The fewer the items represented to, the lower is the risk of cancellation, and the less the legal liability exposure for the seller.

For these reasons, a great deal of the negotiation of the agreement centers around the scope of the representations and warranties. A typical negotiation process is divided into two parts. In the first part, the parties haggle over how much the seller will say about the candidate company in the reps and warranties section and what the seller will agree to do (or not to do) in the covenants section. This is an important process, because the risk of loss from any areas not covered by the seller's statements or covenants falls on the buyer. In the second stage, the parties agree on the consequences if the representations and warranties the seller agrees to make and the covenants it undertakes turn out to be untrue or breached, before or after the closing.

What are the major parts of the agreement?

The major segments of a typical agreement are as follows:

- Introductory matter
- Price and mechanics of the transfer
- Representations and warranties of the buyer and seller
- Covenants of the buyer and seller
- Conditions to closing
- Indemnification
- Termination procedures and remedies
- Legal miscellany

INTRODUCTORY MATTER

What is covered in the introductory matter?

Introductory matter sets the stage for the deal. Contracts often begin by describing the intentions of each of the parties to the agreement. This practice can clarify the meaning of the agreement in the event of a dispute. Therefore, it has become customary to introduce the agreement with a series of "recitals" that set forth the purpose of, and parties to, the agreement. The legal significance of the introductory matter is usually not great, however.

What is the significance of the section on price and mechanics of a transfer?

The section on price and mechanics identifies the structure of the transaction. It identifies the transaction as a stock disposition, an asset disposition, or a merger. This section also describes the mechanics to be used to transfer the property from seller to buyer. The parties may also provide in this section the requirement for a deposit by the buyer (as mentioned) or other security for the buyer's obligations to close.

In the case of a stock acquisition or a merger, this section contains the per share dollar amount to be received by the shareholders receiving shares, as well as all the other terms of the transaction. Merger terms include the identity of the surviving corporation, the articles of incorporation and bylaws governing the surviving corporation, the composition of its board of directors, and the names of its officers.

In the case of an asset acquisition, the price and mechanics section identifies exactly which assets are to be conveyed to the buyer and which of the seller's liabilities the buyer will assume. For both stock and asset purchases, this section will, of course, also identify the nature of the consideration to be received by the seller as well as the timing of its payment.

Also, this section may contain provisions regarding intercompany liabilities, and how they must be satisfied by the surviving company or forgiven by the seller and capitalized as additional equity in the transaction.

How does due diligence differ for stock versus asset transactions?

As mentioned in Chapter 1, in all stock sales, and in all mergers (including even those rare asset sales structured as mergers), acquirers assume seller debts unless the seller agrees otherwise. By contrast, if a transaction is structured as an asset sale, the acquirer will not assume debts and liabilities unless the acquirer agrees otherwise.

Asset sales are less common than stock sales for two reasons. First of all, sellers prefer stock sales, so they can unload their debts and legal liabilities on the acquirer. Second, acquirers sometimes prefer stock sales because asset sales:

- Require a separate transfer of each asset—an onerous feature in the purchase of companies with numerous contracts, deeds, or licenses.
- Generally impose a higher tax cost than (generally tax-free) exchanges of securities.[2]
- Require third-party consent for some assets, such as certain intangibles and leases.
- Can trigger the need to comply with certain provisions of the Uniform Commercial Code, such as bulk sales law.[3]

If an acquirer purchasing a company through an asset sale overcomes these hurdles, will it then be free of responsibility for seller debts and legal liabilities?

Not necessarily. As mentioned earlier, there are exceptions:

- If an acquirer fails to comply with bulk sales law (mentioned earlier), it may have to assume responsibility for some seller debts.
- If an asset sale is deemed a fraudulent conveyance (defined in Chapter 4), seller liabilities automatically transfer to the acquirer.

- Under the laws of some states, a buyer of a manufacturing businesses, even in asset purchases, automatically assumes legal liabilities for faulty products manufactured by the seller prior to the acquisition. (See Chapter 8.)
- Under federal law, acquirers must honor debts under union contracts, such as pension fund obligations. (See Chapter 10.)
- In some states, if a buyer purchases an entire business, and the shareholders of the seller become the shareholders of the buyer, courts may apply the *de facto merger doctrine*, treating the transaction as a merger rather than as an asset acquisition.

REPRESENTATIONS AND WARRANTIES

What is the purpose of the representations and warranties section of the agreement?

In this section of the agreement, the seller makes detailed statements about the legal and financial condition of the company, the property (assets and/or stock) to be conveyed, and the ability of the seller to consummate the transaction. The representations and warranties reflect the situation as of the date of the signing of the agreement and, together with the exhibits or schedules, are intended to disclose important legal, operational, and financial aspects of the business to the buyer.

The buyer should be aware that lenders providing acquisition financing will require the buyer to make extensive representations and warranties about the company being acquired as a condition to funding. To the extent that the acquisition agreement does not contain comparable representations from the seller, with appropriate recourse in the event of a breach, the buyer will take on the dual risk of a loan default and any direct loss as a result of the seller's breach. In some cases, it may be more difficult to obtain adequate financing if there are insufficient representations and warranties about the business. The buyer should make every effort to anticipate the representations and warranties that the lenders will require and attempt to include language in the acquisition agreement to obtain coverage for these areas.

What is the role of exhibits or disclosure schedules?

The exhibits are an integral part of the representations and warranties. Usually each exhibit is keyed to a specific representation or warranty and sets forth any exceptions to the statements made in the representation. For example, a representation might provide that there are no undisclosed liabilities of the company "except as set forth on Exhibit A," or state that there is no litigation that might have an adverse effect on the company "except as set forth on Exhibit B." Another representation might state that "except as set forth on Schedule C," there are no contracts of a "material nature," or there are no contracts involving amounts in excess of a fixed sum—say, $100,000. Schedule C would contain a list of all the contracts that meet the criteria in the representation, that is, contracts that either are material or involve dollar amounts above the threshold. (For more about materiality, see discussion below.)

By design, then, the exhibits list all the items that the buyer needs to investigate in its due diligence effort in anticipation of pricing and financing the deal. The exhibits are a critical part of that due diligence, because they require the seller to make statements about all pertinent aspects of a company. Thus, they create a succinct financial, operational, and legal synopsis of the company.

The use of exceptions to create exhibits might seem odd, but it is merely a practical drafting device. The alternative is to incorporate each of the candidate company's documents in the acquisition agreement, which would make the agreement unwieldy.

In any event, the exhibits and all the documents or matters they reference must be reviewed carefully by attorneys and managers knowledgeable about the matters covered.

It is a major mistake to delegate review to the most junior person on the project, unless this junior reviewer has been carefully trained and will be closely monitored. In fact, in the classic case of *Escott v. BarChris Construction Corp.* (1968), the court based its finding against one individual in part because he had relied on work by a very junior associate.

Nor should the review be conducted in haste. Each litigation matter, for example, should be checked and each contract reviewed. If necessary, backup documents should be requested and provided. Because the review is time-consuming, it should not be left to the day before signing. The review process can be greatly facilitated if, as suggested above, the due diligence checklist parallels the order and content of the representations and warranties that are to appear in the agreement.

What does the term *material* mean when it appears in representations and warranties?

It is often said that materiality is in the eyes of the beholder. As mentioned in Chapter 1 (at note 12), the SEC has recently issued Staff Accounting Memorandum 99 on materiality. The memorandum makes it clear that under the securities laws generally, *material* information is that which would be important to an average, reasonable investor in determining whether to make a given investment. In many contracts the parties agree that a "material" fact must be significant to the business of the candidate company and any subsidiaries taken as a whole. This definition ensures that the importance of the fact relates to the entire enterprise acquired and not solely to the parent corporation or to a single subsidiary.

In order to reduce the opportunity for disagreement, the parties often set a dollar threshold that defines materiality in particular circumstances. For example, rather than asking for representations about "material contracts," the buyer will substitute a request for disclosure about all contracts involving payments above a specified dollar amount. Similarly, the buyer may request disclosure of all liabilities greater than a certain sum. Use of numbers tends to fine-tune the disclosures and in many ways provides protection for the seller as well. If there is a dollar threshold of, say, $100,000 for liabilities, the seller can be assured that a $95,000 undisclosed liability will not be deemed "material" in a later dispute.

As mentioned in Chapter 1, negotiators should set the numbers with care, and due diligence investigators should go beyond the numbers as evidence dictates. All parties should bear in mind the true meaning of materiality, as suggested by regulators and courts.

How can a seller narrow the scope of its representations and warranties?

The seller can use one of two basic strategies to reduce its exposure attributable to representations and warranties.

It can refuse to make any representation or warranty about specific items—for example, accounts receivable or the financial condition or liabilities of certain subsidiaries.

Alternatively, it can refuse to make representations and warranties about matters not material to the transaction, or may attempt to make representations and warranties only to the "best of its knowledge."

To protect itself further, the seller can seek to insert the word "material," or phrases with the same effect, in every one of its representations. For example, it can state that it is disclosing only "material liabilities," or "material litigation," or that it knows of no violations of law by the company that will have a "material adverse effect" on the company.

How and to what degree can the buyer resist the narrowing of the scope of the representations and warranties?

Generally speaking, it is in the buyer's interest to have the broadest possible representations and warranties. However, unreasonable requests for disclosure can threaten a deal. Pressuring the seller of a large, complex company to make comprehensive disclosures may cause the seller to fear that it will inadvertently fail to disclose minor matters, jeopardizing the transaction or leading to unfair liabilities after the closing.

Moreover, anyone buying a business must recognize that no business is more perfect than the human beings who conduct it. Therefore, there are bound to be a variety of problems in connection with the operation or ownership of the business, including litigation, liabilities, or violations of law, which the buyer must accept as part of the package of owning the business. As a result, in most transactions the buyer will permit the seller to limit the scope of the matters that are being represented to those things that are material, individually or in the aggregate, but when appropriate will negotiate over dollar threshold amounts to require more, rather than less, disclosure.

What different motivations might a seller have for narrowing representations and warranties?

For negotiation purposes, it is important for the buyer to understand the seller's real concerns. The seller may be concerned simply about the time and expense necessary to uncover a lot of detailed information that in its view shouldn't matter to a buyer or that, under the time pressure of the deal, just can't be obtained. Or the seller may be far more concerned about making representations and warranties that will increase the risk that the buyer will be able to back out of the transaction. Alternatively, the seller's most significant concern may be with postclosing liabilities for breaches of representations, warranties, and covenants in the agreement.

How can a buyer address these different motivations?

Concern about time and expense is legitimate only to the extent that the buyer is asking for truly inconsequential or irrelevant representations or warranties. The seller should be assured that extensive disclosures will not necessarily increase the risk of a terminated transaction or postclosing liability. The buyer may provide the requisite assurance by agreeing not to terminate the transaction, and by stating that the seller need not indemnify the buyer, except in the event of material breaches of representations, warranties, or covenants.

To summarize, the buyer must look through the stated position of the seller, determine its real interests, and deal creatively with those concerns, rather than simply viewing negotiations as an argument over whether the word "material" is going to modify a particular representation or warranty.

What is the purpose of the "ordinary course of business" phrase often found in representations and warranties?

The phrase "ordinary course of business" is simply a way for parties to narrow the scope of the seller's representations and warranties. The phrase is usually found in representations and warranties to exclude certain things from the representations. For example, the seller may not be required to disclose supply contracts entered into in the ordinary course of business, or may not be required to disclose liabilities accrued in the ordinary course of business.

The definition of ordinary course of business will depend upon the normal practice of the specific business being acquired and the industry of which it is a part, including the normal character and size of routine transactions. The phrase can be generally defined not to include business activities that the seller does not engage in on a regular and consistent basis. For greater clarification, the parties could enumerate in the acquisition agreement the seller's ordinary practices. An important point is that any transactions that are extraordinary in nature, price, or size will be included in such representations and warranties.

What is the function of the phrase "best of knowledge"?

The phrase "best of knowledge" serves a similar function. A seller may ask that its representation as to litigation be limited to the litigation about which it has knowledge, so that it will not be required to represent and warrant absolutely that there is no material litigation. The seller often argues that the phrase should modify other representations and warranties.

At each juncture the buyer should ask whether the "best of knowledge" modification is appropriate. Usually it is not, but it is often agreed to in respect to the existence of threatened litigation and infringements by third parties of copyrights and patents. Beyond those few customary areas, the buyer should resist efforts to base the representations solely on the knowledge of the seller. Because such a representation and warranty tells the buyer only that the seller is unaware of any problems, it protects the buyer only if problems known to the seller are not disclosed. Thus, "best of knowledge" representations have the effect of allocating to the buyer all the risk of defects that no one knows about.

"Best of knowledge" qualifiers may be presented as a compromise to a seller that adamantly refuses to indemnify the buyer for breaches discovered after closing. At the very least, an indemnity should be forthcoming in respect to problems that the seller knew about but didn't disclose.

There are other issues in connection with the phrase. First, whose knowledge are we talking about? Careful sellers will attempt to limit the knowledge to a narrow group of people (such as senior officers) in the company they are selling. Certainly, a large organization ought to be careful about making representations about what "the corporation" knows. Consequently, a buyer accepting a "best of knowledge" representation will often permit the seller to limit the persons whose knowledge will be tested. The buyer ought to be certain that everyone who has material information about the company is included in the selected group of officers. This will force the seller to quiz the officers whose knowledge will be pertinent for purposes of the agreement.

Another issue is whether "best of knowledge" implies any obligation of the seller to look into the matter. That is, does it assume that the knowledge is based upon a reasonable effort to ascertain the existence of any problems? The general answer is that the seller's inquiry would be limited to information already in the seller's possession. A buyer wishing to impose a duty on the seller to make reasonable investigations into the matters represented to the buyer should augment the "best of knowledge" phrase with the words "after due inquiry."

What if the seller claims to have no knowledge, or ability to get knowledge, about an area that is the subject of a representation or warranty?

In this era of rapidly changing ownership of companies through merger, acquisition, buyout, and restructuring, the seller often has not had a chance to become acquainted with all the details of the business it is selling. This may seem reasonable from the perspective of the seller, but the buyer should not give the argument much weight. As noted above, if the buyer must absorb a loss because of a breach of a rep or warranty, the buyer in effect pays an increased purchase price. One veteran in deal making suggests that the buyer respond as follows:

> The real issue is, Who should absorb the risk in the event that there are undisclosed material defects in the business? We have different views, of course, of who should bear the risk, but let's really talk about what matters, not about what each of us knows about the company right now. The agreement between us ought to be structured to provide incentives for both of us to do the best job pos-

sible to unearth problems, and to increase our knowledge of the company now, before we close, rather than wait for problems to surface afterward. Then, if something does surface later, either after we sign or after we close, we need to decide where the risk should reside.[4]

This response addresses the real interest of the parties and will prevent digressions into who knows or can know the most about the company. Sometimes the seller is leery of making legally significant statements without being absolutely certain of their truth. *It is important for both sides to recognize that the representations and warranties are not a test of the integrity of the parties making them.* A party cannot properly be accused of dishonesty if it makes a representation about which it is not certain (provided, of course, that it has no knowledge that the representation is in fact untrue). In order to reduce legal exposure, it makes sense to try to verify the accuracy of the representations and warranties as much as possible.

There will always be, however, some degree of uncertainty. But if the parties recognize that the representations are not a test of integrity but a legal device for allocating risk, the process becomes more manageable.

Are some representations and warranties more important than others?

Yes. The representations regarding financial statements, litigation, undisclosed liabilities, and taxes are usually the most important. If a buyer is pressed to get indemnities only for what it absolutely needs, it should, at a minimum, argue hard for solid representations and warranties on these points. Protection for breaches of the representations on financials should be the last point the buyer concedes; the buyer should make this concession only if it is fully apprised of, and is committed to taking, the associated risk. In general, the audited financial statements represent the best picture of the company as a whole, and any undisclosed material problems will cause that representation to be violated.

COVENANTS

What is the major purpose of the covenants section of an agreement?

The covenants section of the agreement defines the obligations of the parties with respect to their conduct during the period between the signing and the closing.

For negotiation purposes, the most significant covenant relates to the obligation of the candidate company to continue conducting business as usual between signing and closing, except as noted in the agreement or approved later by the buyer. For example, an agreement involving a multinational manufacturer might state that the company must continue to own and operate all its factories, but has permission to divest one of its factories through a pending sale known to the acquirer.

In the representations and warranties, the seller assures the buyer of the legal characteristics of the company as of the date of the signing of the agreement. In the covenants section, the seller in essence agrees not to do anything to change that picture in any material way, except as necessary in the normal operations of the business.

It is often advisable to limit this restriction by requiring the buyer not to "withhold consent unreasonably." This will protect the seller (and the business) if the seller is required to take certain actions in order to preserve the business—for example, restructure a loan, make a capital investment, or sell an asset. The buyer should not be allowed to prevent such actions unless they have a material impact on the transaction.

CONDITIONS TO CLOSING

What is the "conditions to closing" part of the agreement, and how does it affect the key concerns of the buyer and seller?

The "conditions to closing" section is an important part of the agreement. It lists conditions that must be fulfilled if the transaction is to close. If the conditions are not fulfilled, either party, depending on the circumstances, may avoid completing the transaction.

The most significant condition is the so-called bringdown provision. This typically states that the buyer will not be required to close if:

- The seller has breached any of its covenants, or
- Any of the representations and warranties of the seller and the candidate company were not true when made—or were true when made, but are not true on the closing date.

These events can occur as the result of changes outside the control of the seller and the candidate company. For example, the seller may state that its company is waiting to receive a Food and Drug Administration approval of a new drug, and the buyer may learn that the FDA has declined approval after signing. To bring down the status of the approval to the present day in this way, the acquirer conducts bringdown due diligence as described in Chapter 1.

Could you give an example of how the "conditions to closing" works?

The following example will illustrate the process. On the day both parties sign the acquisition agreement (but on a day prior to closing), the seller states in writing that there is no "material litigation" involving the company being sold. The acquisition agreement contains a "condition to closing" stating that the representations and warranties must be true as of the date that the acquisition agreement was signed. If they were not true (i.e., if the seller failed to disclose pending lawsuits), then the buyer may abandon the transaction upon discovering that material litigation existed on the signing date.

What if a lawsuit arises after the signing? Does the "conditions to closing" clause protect the acquirer for that as well?

No—and that is why it is so important to conduct a liability exposure analysis prior to closing, and to continue bringdown due diligence right up to the last minute.

In our example, the seller guaranteed that no lawsuits existed only *as of the date of the acquisition agreement*. Since the representation was true when made, there is no breach of the litigation representation as a result of events between signing and closing. A bringdown condition will obligate the seller to make the same representation as of the closing date, however. On the basis of such a condition, the buyer will be able to terminate the agreement if interim events such as new litigation, liabilities, or other postsigning occurrences reduce the value or viability of the company.

In a typical representation, the seller warrants that the financial statements of the company being sold represent a true and accurate picture of the company as of the date of the financial statements—for example, at the end of the previous quarter. But this representation does not cover the possibility that a change has occurred between the time of the financial statements and the time of the signing. To cover that possibility, the buyer can ask the seller to state that there has been no material adverse change in the financial condition, operations, or prospects of the company between the two dates. This is called a "bringdown condition."

The effect of this bringdown condition is to assure the buyer that, on the closing date, the company it is acquiring will be the same company, from a financial, operational, and legal perspective, that the buyer bargained for in the contract. Because the buyer is not required to close the transaction if any part of the bringdown condition is not satisfied, the condition allocates to the seller the risk of loss attributable to any adverse change during the period between signing and closing. Interim losses may reduce the value of the company, so the bringdown condition may allow the buyer to renegotiate a lower price that reflects the changes.

Do reps and warranties have to be restated as of the closing date?

No. In fact, the typical bringdown clause states that representations and warranties need not be restated as of the closing date. But be careful! Occasionally a seller will attempt to limit the applicability of a representation—for example, an assurance that it is not "currently" involved in material litigation—by adding language like "As of the date . . ." Such a qualifier may deprive the buyer of the right to claim breach of promise and walk from the deal.

Is there any kind of extra protection to ensure the buyer of legal recourse in the event of a breach of a representation?

Some additional comfort beyond bringdown may be provided by an "officer's certificate." This is a statement (typically required as one of the "conditions to closing") by an officer of the company being sold certifying that the representations and warranties are accurate in all material respects as of the closing date. This certificate is in effect a restatement of all the representations and warranties as of the closing date.

In the absence of an officer's certificate, a buyer might be unprotected against certain adverse events occurring between signing and closing. For example, if a material liability arises and is discovered before closing, a closing condition will be unsatisfied, and the buyer can walk from the deal. But if the liability is not discovered, the parties may close because to their knowledge each closing condition—including the condition that the representation and warranty about undisclosed liabilities is true—was satisfied. If, however, an officers' certificate is obtained and proves later to be inaccurate, the inaccuracy may give rise to liability from buyer to seller.

For the officer's protection, the officer's certificate should be made solely on behalf of the corporation and should not be a personal affidavit. Otherwise, the officer may be personally liable to the buyer if the certificate is proved untrue, irrespective of whether he or she is at fault. (See this section in the Sample Agreement at the back of this book.)

Who bears the risk of a general economic downturn affecting the seller's industry?

In all fairness, both parties should bear this risk, but it is usually the seller that does. Agreements often state that if significant problems arise between signing and closing, the buyer can terminate or renegotiate the acquisition. But, as mentioned, the seller has no right to keep the business if positive developments occur.

Some sellers try to get buyers to "lock in" their promise to buy, even in the face of general or industry-specific economic reversals that may affect the seller. Buyers are usually successful in resisting the attempt, but sellers cannot be blamed for trying. After all, in the typical agreement, as mentioned, the buyer clearly gets the upside of unanticipated *positive* movements (since the seller must close, no matter what). To be fair, an agreement could protect the seller against the downside of unanticipated *negative* movements in the same manner.

The buyer cannot be expected to assume the risk of other postsigning adverse changes, such as new lawsuits, major undisclosed liabilities, or major uninsured casualty losses. In any event, the buyer must resist this attempt by the seller, because the buyer may not be able to close its financing in the face of negative events. It does not seem fair to tag the buyer with damages for failing to close in this situation, particularly if the seller knows it is selling in a highly leveraged transaction and if the buyer has obtained financing commitments in advance.

Many sellers try to shift the date of the transfer of risk from the seller to the buyer to the date the acquisition agreement is signed, rather than waiting until the date of closing. Their theory is that the buyer has to accept a balanced economic deal—it gets both the good and the bad occurring after the signing. The seller says that as long as (1) the representations and warranties it made on the signing date were accurate on the signing date and (2) it has not breached its covenants concerning the conduct of the business, the buyer is getting what it bargained for.

The seller's argument has logical appeal, particularly if there will be a great deal of time between the signing and closing, say, on account of the need for regulatory approvals. If the seller is going to push this point, it must also be willing to give up any earnings during the interim period.

Tradition is on the buyer's side, so the seller can expect to give up something significant to win this point. Where the time span between signing and closing is less than 60 days, it may not be worth the fight.

In order to govern events that occur before closing that will harm the financial condition of the company afterward, the "conditions to closing" section of the acquisition agreement should require that there be no material adverse change in the "prospects" of the company. In the absence of such a provision, the buyer would be obligated to close under these circumstances. The seller often argues that the word *prospects* is too vague. The proper response is to be more specific, but without shifting the entire risk to the buyer.

Do buyers ever close even if they know the seller has breached a representation or warranty—and if so, what happens?

This does happen—usually when the buyer has negotiated an appropriate price reduction, or considers the breach unimportant. If the buyer does close while knowing of the breach, it cannot sue the seller for it later.

DUE DILIGENCE IN CLOSING

What are the main phases of closing?

The main phases of closing are the preclosing, closing, and postclosing.

What is a preclosing?

The *preclosing*, also called a *preclosing drill*, is a dress rehearsal for the closing, preferably held no earlier than three days prior to closing and no later than the night prior to closing. Counsel for the parties conduct the preclosing; their clients and other persons will be present as needed. Each party puts all its closing documents out on the closing room table so that the other appropriate parties can satisfy themselves that the conditions to closing embodied in those documents have been met. To the extent feasible, the parties will execute as many documents as possible in order to save time on the closing day and thereby ensure that all conditions to closing will be satisfied early enough in the day to allow any wire transfer of funds or investment of sale proceeds to be completed on the same day. After review of the closing documents and the closing checklist, the parties will identify tasks that must be completed before, legally and logistically, closing can be effected. However, it is not unusual to generate a schedule of minor uncompleted items and agree that they will be resolved postclosing.

In transactions involving third-party financing, lenders and lenders' counsel may require two or more preclosings; that is, one involving their own financing, one involving review of the corporate side of the transaction, and, if applicable, others involving the other financing pieces of the transaction.

What happens on the closing day itself?

Assuming the parties have conducted a preclosing, three things will happen.

First, the parties and their counsel will review any documents that were revised or newly generated and will execute any previously unexecuted documents. All undated documents will be dated, any required meetings of the board of directors that have not previously been held will be held, and any changed documents or signature pages that must be submitted to local counsel prior to release of their opinions will be transmitted to them.

Second, the parties will recheck all the documents lined up on the closing table against the closing checklists.

Finally, when all members of counsel are satisfied that all conditions to closing have been satisfied or waived, they will instruct their clients' respective agents to wire funds or file or record documents (simultaneously or in such order as they have agreed), as applicable, and will deem all the documents on the closing table to have been delivered in the sequence set forth in the closing checklist and other governing agreements.

In the case of a transaction involving third-party financing, what part of the deal closes first?

Typically, all transactions are deemed to take place simultaneously. Practically speaking, the lenders usually will not release the loan proceeds until they receive confirmation that the corporate portion of the transaction has been completed; that is, stock certificates or bills of sale have been delivered or merger certificates have been filed, and security and title documents have been properly recorded.

What are some of the most common logistical snafus that can derail a closing?

Some of the biggest headaches result from the following:

- Unavailability of key businesspeople.
- Failure to have local counsel on standby to review last-minute document changes.
- Failure to provide local counsel with copies of documents or other items that are conditions to release of their opinions.
- Failure to have precleared articles of merger with appropriate jurisdictions.
- Failure to have persons on standby to file or record documents, including merger documents, UCC-1 forms (required under the Uniform Commercial Code), mortgages, and terminations of UCC-1s required to be removed from the record.
- Failure to have adequate support staff to make last-minute revisions in documents.
- Failure to have conducted the preclosing, including execution of all documents not subject to change.
- Failure to have adequate legal staff at closing headquarters to negotiate final documents, including local counsel legal opinions.
- Failure to obtain proper wiring instructions for funds transfers.
- Failure to ascertain time periods by which wires must be sent or to make arrangements to have banks hold their wires open past normal hours.
- Failure to consummate any preclosing corporate reorganizations (such as mergers of subsidiaries into parent companies, dissolution of defunct subsidiaries, or filing of charter amendments) in a timely fashion.
- Failure to have tax counsel review the final terms and documentation to ensure that tax planning objectives have not been adversely affected by last-minute restructuring or drafting.
- Failure to obtain required bringdown good standing certificates or other certified documents from appropriate jurisdictions.

Proper advance planning can prevent most if not all of these failures.

What are typical postclosing activities?

"Postclosing" tasks typically fall into one of two categories: document distribution and cleanup.

Why is document distribution necessary? Can't all the documents go to everybody?

Document distribution requires planning. Although each of the parties to a closing generally wants to depart from the closing table with a complete stack of original closing documents for its file, this is usually impractical. First, each party has different requirements for closing documents. Some parties should not receive documents that other parties will receive, and some parties need original documents whereas others need only photocopies. Further, some documents held or executed at other locations may be available at the time and place of closing only by telecopy, or not at all. Finally, the sheer number and volume of documents may preclude sorting and photocopying of the executed papers swiftly enough to be delivered to the parties prior to their departure from the premises.

Each participant is entitled to a certain set of documents following closing, depending on its status. Shortly after closing, each should receive a complete set of these documents. In some transactions, the initial distribution of originals and copies is followed by the production of a "closing binder" containing a complete indexed set of documents in one or more volumes. These binders may be velobound or, if the expense is approved by the clients, permanently bound in stitched covers with stamped lettering on the spine. The acquisition documents are usually bound separately from the financing documents.

The final document assembly and distribution effort will be much easier if counsel has prepared a good closing document checklist. When completed and updated, the checklist may be turned into a closing memorandum, which may double as an index to the closing document binders. (See Appendixes 5A and 5B.) The memo may include a brief narrative chronology of the transactions taken prior to, at, and following the closing to complete the transaction. A common closing memorandum can be used even if the acquisition and financing closings occurred at different offices.

What is involved in postclosing cleanup?

In the cleanup phase, participants complete tasks and documents that were not or could not have been completed at or prior to closing. This may include the following actions:

- Corrections or amendments to ancillary documents.
- Receipt of consents and approvals not obtainable by closing.

- Completion and documentation of a closing date audit for balance sheet pricing adjustment purposes.
- Receipt of title insurance commitments or policies as of the closing date from jurisdictions with filing delays.

In addition, when many real estate parcels in multiple jurisdictions are required to be mortgaged, or collateral is located in foreign countries, completion of recordation of mortgages and perfection of security interests are commonly put aside as postclosing matters, with a deadline for completion of several months after the closing date. Other cleanup activities might include urgent changes in compensation arrangements, such as restructuring of pension plans.

In all cases, individuals responsible for postclosing efforts should strive to complete their tasks as soon as possible before the pressure of other matters and the passage of time make the wrapping up of these loose ends more difficult than would otherwise be the case. Acquirers should create a postclosing checklist keyed to their closing memorandum.

CONCLUDING COMMENTS

Transactional due diligence demands energy and attention. As experts have noted:

> In due diligence for the sale of an entire company (as opposed to the sales of stock in a securities offering) the buyer and seller are likely to hold extensive negotiations over a number of issues, including qualifiers to the representations, dollar limits, and thresholds before claims can be made—and even a time limit on how long the representations will survive.[5]

To some executives, this may seem like so much wheeling and dealing—far removed from the loftier concerns of market share and product launches. Yet transactional due diligence plays a vital role in setting the stage for postacquisition success.

A P P E N D I X   5A

Closing Memorandum for the Acquisition of a Limited Partnership[*]

DUE DILIGENCE
VOLUME ___
Prepared for

_____

by

_____

_____ __, 2000

SAMPLE DUE DILIGENCE INDEX

_____,

A LIMITED PARTNERSHIP
DUE DILIGENCE
INDEX
TO
DUE DILIGENCE MATERIALS
PREPARED AND COMPILED BY

_____

<u>Document No.</u>
<u>Volume I</u>

I. Due Diligence Summary   See Annex I

II. Corporate/Partnership
    A. *Organization Chart/Schedules*
    B. _____, *A Limited Partnership*
        1. Partnership Agreement Abstract
    C. _____ *Limited Partnership*
        1. Partnership Agreement Abstract
        2. Settlement Agreement Abstract

---

[*] This document was provided by Mark Schonberger, Partner, Battle Fowler LLP, New York, and is reprinted courtesy of Battle Fowler LLP.

  D. *Affiliated Partnerships* (Indexed by Property Owned)
      1. Schedule of Affiliated Partnerships Ranked in
         Order of Management Fees
      2. Partnership Agreement Abstracts.   See Annex II
  E. *Commitments and Contingencies*
      1. Memorandum (_____ __, 2000)
  F. *Litigation*
      1.
      2.
      3.
      4. Schedule of Employment and other Miscellaneous Litigation
      5. Accountant Response Letters (see Document for summary of
         significant litigation other than litigation analyzed in items F 1,
         2, and 3, above)

III. Real Estate Review   See Annex III

  A. *Title Reviews*
  B. *Summaries of Title Issues*
  C. *Summaries of Loan Agreements*   See Annex IV
  D. *Summaries of Mortgage and Deed of Trust Forms*   See Annex V
  E. *Summaries of Leases*
  F. *Environmental Issues*

IV. Tax/ERISA

  A. *Tax*
  B. *ERISA*

V. Due Diligence Memoranda

ANNEX I

———————————,

A LIMITED PARTNERSHIP

DUE DILIGENCE SUMMARY

GENERAL

    The following is a summary of the legal due diligence we have con-
ducted on _____, A Limited Partnership and certain of its affili-

ates ("_____") on behalf of _____
("_____").

This Summary and the materials in the accompanying volumes are divided into the following three categories:

- Corporate/Partnership
- Real Estate
- Tax/ERISA

The INDEX more fully details the specific areas we reviewed within each major category. In addition, we have also compiled the various due diligence memoranda which were previously delivered to _____ during our review.

The abstracts and other written materials included in the accompanying volumes summarize the results of our due diligence through _____ __, 2000, Throughout the materials we have identified particular areas of concern that may warrant more detailed due diligence. The scope of any additional due diligence should be discussed once _____ has developed an overall strategy for pursuing the acquisition of _____. See "Status of Due Diligence Review; Recommended Actions" below.

CORPORATE/PARTNERSHIP

_____/_____

In connection with our review we have analyzed the major partnership entities which comprise _____, namely, _____ Associates Limited Partnership, the general Partner of _____ ("_____"), and itself _____. Our review included abstracting the partnership agreements of each of the two entities as well as reviewing partnership minute books and correspondence files. In addition, with respect to _____, we also reviewed a representative example of the settlement agreement ("Settlement Agreement") entered into in _____ between _____ and _____ (as defined in the _____ Partnership Agreement).

Significant attention was focused on the distribution priorities for _____. See "Tax/ERISA" below.

Affiliated Partnerships

_____, directly and through its affiliates, acts as the general or limited partner of over _____ partnerships. Our initial review of the Affiliated

Partnerships focused on those partnerships which we were advised by _____ ("_____") generated the greatest fee income to _____. In addition, the partnerships which own _____ were abstracted because we were advised by _____ that _____'s equity interest in such partnerships had significant value. With respect to these Affiliated Partnerships, we also reviewed additional documents noted in the abstract, including, in most cases, recent investor correspondence and financial statements. Any unusual items are noted in the abstracts.

Corporate Structure

Included as Document #___ is a corporate/partnership organizational chart provided by _____ which reflects _____'s corporate structure and a major portion of _____'s partnership structure.

Commitments and Contingencies

We reviewed documentation provided by _____ which purports to represent all of the commitments, contingencies and guarantees affecting _____. Our October 27 memorandum summarizing our review is included as Document #___ in the accompanying volumes.

Litigation

Pursuant to _____'s instructions, we limited our initial litigation review to the following three major actions: _____; _____; and _____. In addition, we obtained recent accountant response letters which summarize additional litigation (see Document #___) and prepared a schedule listing the more significant of such actions (see Document #___). Finally, we have included a schedule of miscellaneous employee and labor litigation which was provided by _____. See Document #___.

REAL ESTATE

Title Review

We reviewed the title policies for the _____ apartment properties owned directly by _____ or its subsidiaries (the "Owned Properties").

Loan Documents

We reviewed the major loan documents on the _____ level: (a) _____, (b) _____, (c) _____, and (d) _____.

We have also reviewed the forms of mortgage and deed of trust used in connection with the _____ Agreement and the mortgage used in connection with the properties.

Office Leases

We have reviewed _____'s lease for its headquarters at _____ in _____. We have not reviewed any of _____'s other office leases.

TAX/ERISA

TAX

Deficit Repayment Obligations

We reviewed the partnership agreement provisions, general partner capital account balances and limited partner capital contributions for certain of the partnerships in order to ascertain the effect of any deficit repayment obligation ("DRO") on _____ and _____. The _____ partnerships reviewed were chosen based upon schedules provided to us by _____ and represent those programs which generated the highest fee income to _____ or had the highest investor capital contributions. The results of our review are set forth in a chart which is included as Document #___.

Deferred Tax Liability

We verified the nature and amount of the $_____ deferred tax liability that appears on _____'s _____ ___, 200_ balance sheet. See Document #___.

Distribution Priorities

We have analyzed the distribution priorities as set forth in _____'s Limited Partnership Agreement. See Documents #___ and #___.

ERISA

Our ERISA review focused on whether _____ or any of its affiliates was a fiduciary or a party in interest to any employee benefit plan subject to the Employee Retirement Income Security Act of 1974. Our preliminary discussions with _____'s representatives and our review of the materials furnished to us by them indicated that it was likely that one or more _____ entities was a fiduciary or party in interest to one or more benefit plans. As a result, ERISA's attribution rules could cause one or more _____ entities to become a party in interest to such plan(s) following the purchase of interests in _____.

STATUS OF DUE DILIGENCE REVIEW; RECOMMENDED ACTIONS

General

The abstracts and other materials included in the accompanying volumes identify particular areas where more detailed due diligence may be warranted. The scope of any additional due diligence will best be defined after _____ has developed its overall strategy for pursuing the acquisition of _____.

In addition to those areas identified in the materials, specific areas where additional due diligence should be considered are noted below.

Additional Due Diligence Items

ANNEX II

DUE DILIGENCE ABSTRACT[*]

Name of Entity:

Type of Entity:

Properties:

Type of Offering:

Organizational Structure:

General Partner

Limited Partners

Organizational Documents:

Offering Documents:

Other Documents Reviewed:

Term of Partnership:

Description of General Interests:

Operating Stage

---

[*]   For use with limited partnership agreements.

Liquidating Stage

Description of Fees Payable to GP and Affiliates:

Operating Stage

Liquidating Stage

Restrictions on Payment of Fees

Description of Relevant Partnership Agreement Restrictions:

Affiliate Transactions

Transfer of GP Interests

GP Voting LP Interests

Amendment of Limited Partnership Agreement Provisions:

Removal of General Partner Provisions:

Indemnification of GP:

Material Litigation:

Miscellaneous:

ANNEX III

Reviewer: _____
Date: _____

TITLE AND SURVEY REVIEW FORM

Title Review

Name of Apartment Project/ Project Location:

Title Commitment/ Report/Insurer:

Insured Estate/Current Holder of Title:

Rights of Reverter:

Rights of First Refusal:

Significant Covenants, Conditions and Restrictions of Record:

Recorded Mortgages, Deeds of Trust, Assignments of Leases or Other Security Documents:

Status of Payment of Taxes and Other Charges:

Judgments, Mechanic's Liens or Other Liens:

Missing Documents:

Standard Title Exceptions:

Notes:

Survey Review

Date of Survey/ Date of Last Revision:

Surveyor:

As-Built Survey:

Certification (Parties/Date):

Legal Description Tracked:

Access to Public Streets/Highways:

Encroachments of any improvements over easements, rights of way or restrictions/violations of any easements, rights of way or other restrictions:

Encroachments of improvements located on subject property over adjacent property:

Encroachments of improvements located on adjacent property over the subject property:

Location of all easements, rights of way, restrictions, etc. on survey:

Parking shown on survey:

Zoning Designation:

Flood Zone:

Notes:

Required Revisions:

ANNEX IV

SUMMARY OF TERM LOAN AGREEMENT[*]
between

_____

and

_____

Date:

Borrowers:

Lender:

Amount:

§_____

Term: a.   Initial Term:

§_____   b.   Extension Term:

Interest Rate:

§_____

Extension Option:

§_____

Equity Contribution:

§_____

Prohibited Transactions:

§_____

Permitted Transactions:

§_____

Permitted Additional Debt:

§_____

Permitted Distributions:

§_____

Restrictions on Investments:

§_____

---

[*] This summary contains a brief outline of some of the principal terms of the Term Loan
     Agreement. The Term Loan Agreement itself should be consulted for a more complete
     description of its terms or before taking any action in connection therewith.

Contracts of Material or Significant Nature:

§_____

Approval of Management and Manager Contract:

§_____

Deposit of Proceeds; Other Bank Accounts:

§_____

Indemnification:

§_____

Leasing Matters:

§_____

Loan to Value Ratio ("LTV") Covenant:

§_____

Principal Reduction:

§_____

Debt Service Covenant:

§_____

Recourse:

§_____

Partial Release:

§_____

Events of Default:

§_____

Setoff and Debit:

§_____

Casualty and Taking:

§_____

Right to Participate:

§_____

ANNEX V

MORTGAGE REVIEW FORM[*]

1. Property (indicate whether fee or leasehold):
2. Reviewed by:
3. Date:
4. Document (title and date):
5. Mortgagor:
6. Mortgagee:
7. Amount Secured:
8. Restrictions Regarding:
   a. Transfer of Interest in:
      i. Mortgagor:
      ii. Property:
   b. Encumbrance of interest in:
      i.   Mortgagor:
      ii. Property:
      iii. Managing Agent:
9. Environmental Provisions:
10. Special Provisions Relating to Bankruptcy:
    a. of Mortgagor:
    b. of a partner in Mortgagor:
11. Exculpation:
12. Priority
13. Cross Default Provisions:
14. Insurance:
15. Use of Insurance Proceeds:
16. Restoration
17. Prepayment:
18. Indemnification:
19. Miscellaneous:

---

[*] (1)   Give section reference for each category of information. (2)   Prepare separate
     summary for each mortgage on the Individual Property Mortgage Review.

A P P E N D I X 5B

Closing Memorandum for a Merger of an Acquisition Fund and a Private Company

MERGER OF TARGET ACQUISITION CORP. INTO TARGET CO. INC.: CLOSING MEMORANDUM

December 31, 1999
9:00 A.M. Eastern Standard Time

I. GENERAL

This memorandum describes the principal transactions that have occurred in connection with the acquisition (the "Acquisition") of Target Co. Inc., a Delaware corporation ("Target"), by Purchaser Holdings, Inc., a Delaware corporation ("Holdings"). Holdings; Target Acquisition Corp., a Delaware corporation and a wholly owned subsidiary of Holdings ("TAC"); and Target and Seller Holdings, Ltd., a Delaware corporation which owns all of the issued and outstanding stock of Target ("Seller"), have entered into an Agreement of Merger, dated as of October 1, 1999 (the "Agreement"), pursuant to which TAC will be merged into Target pursuant to the Certificate of Merger.

In connection with the capitalization of Holdings to accomplish the Acquisition on the Effective Date, affiliates (the "Investor Shareholders") of Investor Corporation, a Delaware corporation ("IC"), purchased 800,000 shares of the common stock of Holdings for an aggregate amount of $4,000,000. Concurrently, IC loaned $1,000,000 on a recourse basis to certain management personnel at Target (the "Management Shareholders"). The Management Shareholders purchased 200,000 shares of the common stock of Holdings for $1,000,000 and pledged such stock to IC to secure repayment of the loan. TAC then merged into Target.

On the Effective Date, Holdings entered into a Credit Agreement with Lender Bank ("Bank") pursuant to which Holdings obtained a term loan of $40,000,000 and revolving credit loans of up to $10,000,000 (the "Credit Agreement"). Concurrently therewith, Holdings entered into a Bridge Funding Agreement with The Investment Bank Group Inc. ("Investment Bank Group") pursuant to which Holdings obtained a bridge loan of $60,000,000 (the "Bridge Agreement"). Holdings sold warrants for 200,000 shares of its common stock (the "Investment Banker Warrants") to Lead Investment Banker Incorporated ("Lead Investment Banker") and its designees for $20,000.

After the Effective Date it is anticipated that Holdings and Lead Investment Banker will enter into a Securities Purchase Agreement (the "Securities Purchase Agreement") pursuant to which Holdings will return the $20,000 to Lead Investment Banker and Lead Investment Banker will return the Investment Banker Warrants to Holdings. Holdings will then sell Warrants for 200,000 shares of its Common Stock to the Purchasers named in the Securities Purchase Agreement (the "Purchasers") for $20,000 (the "Note Purchase Warrants") and deliver to the Purchasers Notes due December 31, 2003, in an aggregate principal amount of $60,000,000 and bearing interest at approximately 14 percent per annum (the "Note") for which Holdings will receive $60,000,000 cash which it will use to pay off the $60,000,000 bridge loan under the Bridge Agreement.

After the Effective Time and concurrently with the funding of the term loan, the initial revolving loans and the bridge loan, Holdings contributed to TAC the amount of $100,000,000 as a capital contribution. Seller received $100,000,000 cash less the amount of the intercompany loan to be paid after Closing, Series A Preferred Stock of Holdings having a redemption value of $10,000,000 and a Warrant entitling it to purchase 40,000 shares of the common stock of Holdings (the "Seller Warrant").

The Closing occurred on December 31, 1999 (the "Effective Date"), at 9:00 A.M. Eastern Standard Time. The merger was effective on the Effective Date at the time the Certificate of Merger was filed with the Secretary of State of Delaware (the "Effective Time").

All capitalized terms used herein which are not defined herein and which are defined in the Agreement, the Credit Agreement, the Bridge Funding Agreement or the Securities Purchase Agreement have the respective meanings attributed to them in the Agreement, the Credit Agreement, the Bridge Funding Agreement or the Securities Purchase Agreement.

II. TRANSACTIONS PRIOR TO THE CLOSING

The following actions were taken prior to the Closing.

1. On October 1, 1999, the Agreement among Holdings, Target, TAC and Seller was executed and delivered.

2. On October 1, 1999, TAC, Seller and Agent Bank (the "Escrow Agent") entered into an Escrow Agreement pursuant to which TAC deposited with the Escrow Agent $1,000,000 pursuant to Section 3.3 of the Agreement.

3. On October 1, 1999, the Board of Directors of each of Holdings and TAC approved the terms of the Merger and the Agreement and the Board of Directors of TAC approved the Escrow Agreement.

4. On October 1, 1999, the Board of Directors of each of Target and Seller approved the terms of the Merger and the Agreement and the Board of Directors of Seller approved the Escrow Agreement.

5. On October 2, 1999, Seller issued a press release announcing the Holdings, Target, Seller and TAC agreement to the terms of the Merger and announcing the execution of the Agreement.

6. On November 16, 1999, Bank delivered to Holdings a commitment letter pursuant to which Bank agreed to provide a $40,000,000 term loan and a $10,000,000 revolving line of credit to facilitate the Acquisition and to provide working capital thereafter.

7. On November 24, 1999, Lead Investment Banker delivered to Holdings a commitment letter pursuant to which Lead Investment Banker undertook to provide a bridge loan for an aggregate amount of $60,000,000.

8. On November 24, 1999, Holdings delivered to Lead Investment Banker a retention letter pursuant to which Holdings retained Lead Investment Banker to sell the Note and Note Purchaser Warrants.

9. On December 24, 1999, a date at least three (3) business days before the Closing, Seller delivered to TAC pursuant to Section 4.3 of the Agreement a notice setting forth the amount of the Intercompany Loan to be paid immediately after Closing.

10. On December 28, 1999, the Board of Directors and shareholders of Holdings adopted an amendment of the certificate of incorporation of Holdings to authorize the Series A Preferred Stock.

11. On December 28, 1999, Holdings caused to be filed an Amended and Restated Certificate of Incorporation providing for 1,500 shares of Series A Preferred Stock par value $1.00 per share.

12. As of December 30, 1999, the Certificate of Merger was executed by the President of TAC and attested by the Secretary of such corporation and was executed by the President of Target and sealed and attested by the Secretary of such corporation.

13. On December 30, 1999, the Board of Directors of Holding authorized the issuance of 1,000 shares of Series A Preferred Stock to Seller with the rights designated in the Amended and Restated Certificate of Incorporation of Holdings.

14. On December 30, 1999, Seller, as sole stockholder of Target, consented to the Agreement and Certificate of Merger.
15. On December 30, 1999, Holdings, as sole stockholder of TAC, consented to the Agreement and Certificate of Merger.

III. CLOSING DOCUMENTS AND TRANSACTIONS

The following documents were delivered at or prior to the Effective Date, but all such documents are deemed delivered at the Effective Date. All documents are dated as of the Effective Date and delivered in New York, New York, unless otherwise indicated. All transactions in connection with the Closing shall be considered as accomplished concurrently, so that none shall be effective until all are effective. Executed copies (or photocopies, or conformed copies where necessary) of each document will be delivered after the Closing as follows:

> one to IC
> one to Holdings
> one to Seller
> one to Target
> one to Bank
> one to Lead Investment Banker

with photocopies to be distributed as follows:

> one to Investment Banker Counsel (IBC)
> one to Seller Counsel (SC)
> one to Bank Counsel (BC)
> one to Investor Corporation Counsel (ICC)

IV. SCHEDULE OF CLOSING DOCUMENTS

1. Corporate Good Standing, Articles, Bylaws and Incumbency of Target, Its Subsidiaries and Seller

1.01. Certificate of Incorporation and all amendments to date of Target certified by the Secretary of State of Delaware on December 3, 1999.

1.02. Certificate of the Secretary of State of Delaware, dated December 3, 1999, certifying that Target is an existing corporation and in good standing under the laws of the State of Delaware.

1.03. Telex from the Secretary of State of Delaware, dated the Effective Date, updating the information described in item 1.02 above.

1.04. Certificates of the Secretaries of State of California and New York dated December 1 and 2, 1999, respectively, certifying that Target is qualified to conduct business and in good standing in such states.

1.05. Telexes or verbal consents from the Secretaries of State of California and New York, dated the Effective Date, updating the information described in item 1.04 above.

1.06. (a)-(b) Articles or Certificates of Incorporation or other organization documents and all amendments to date of the following Subsidiaries of Target ("Subsidiaries") certified by the appropriate authority of the governing jurisdiction:

(a) New York Target Subsidiary Ltd. (N.Y.)

(b) Delaware Target Subsidiary, Inc. (Del.)

1.07. (a)–(b) Certificates of the authorities described in item 1.06, certifying that each of the Subsidiaries is an existing corporation and in good standing.

1.08. (a)–(b) Telexes or verbal consents of the authorities described in item 1.06, dated the Effective Date, updating the information set forth in item 1.07 above.

1.09. Certificate of Incorporation and all amendments to date of Seller certified by the Secretary of State of Delaware, dated December 3, 1999.

1.10. Certificate of the Secretary of State of Delaware, dated December 3, 1999, certifying that Seller is an existing corporation and in good standing under the laws of Delaware.

1.11. Telex from the Secretary of State of Delaware, dated the Effective Date, updating the information described in item 1.10 above.

1.12. Certificate of Secretary of Target, dated the Effective Date, as to the Certificates of Incorporation and Bylaws of such corporation, the election, incumbency and signatures of officers of such corporation, and certifying as to the resolutions of the Board of Directors and stockholders of such corporation relating to the transaction pursuant to Section 8.4 of the Agreement.

1.13. Certificate of Secretary of Seller, dated the Effective Date, as to the Certificate of Incorporation and Bylaws of such corporation, the election, incumbency and signatures of officers of such corporation, and certifying as to the resolutions of the Board of Directors of such corporation relating to the transaction pursuant to Section 8.4 of the Agreement.

2. Good Standing, Articles, Bylaws and Incumbency of Holdings and TAC

2.01. Certificate of Incorporation and all amendments to date of Holdings certified by the Secretary of State of Delaware on December 21, 1999.

2.02. Certificate of the Secretary of State of Delaware, dated December 21, 1999, certifying that Holdings is an existing corporation and in good standing under the laws of the State of Delaware.

2.03. Telex of the Secretary of State of Delaware, dated the Effective Date, updating the information set forth in item 2.02 above.

2.04. Certificate of the Secretary of State of each of California and New York, dated December 22, 1999, certifying that Holdings is qualified to conduct business and in good standing in such states.

2.05. Certificate of Incorporation and all amendments to date of TAC certified by the Secretary of State of Delaware on December 10, 1999.

2.06. Certificate of the Secretary of State of Delaware, dated December 21, 1999, certifying that TAC is an existing corporation and in good standing under the laws of the State of Delaware.

2.07. Telex of the Secretary of State of Delaware, dated the Effective Date, updating the information set forth in item 2.06 above.

2.08. Certificate of the Secretary of Holdings, dated the Effective Date, as to the Certificate of Incorporation and Bylaws of such corporation, the election, incumbency and signatures of officers of such corporation and certifying as to the resolutions of the Board of Directors of such corporation relating to the transaction pursuant to Section 9.4 of the Agreement, Sections 5.01(e), (f) and (h) of the Credit Agreement and the Bridge Agreement.

2.09. Certificate of the Secretary of TAC, dated the Effective Date, as to the Certificate of Incorporation and Bylaws of such corporation, the election, incumbency and signatures of officers of such corporation, and certifying as to the resolutions of the Board of Directors and stockholders of such corporation relating to the transaction pursuant to Section 9.4 of the Agreement, Sections 5.01(e), (f) and (h) of the Credit Agreement and the Bridge Agreement.

2.10. Certificate of the Secretary of Target (the Surviving Corporation), dated the Effective Date, certifying as to the resolutions of the Board of Directors of such corporation relating to Sections 5.01(e), (f) and (h) of the Credit Agreement and the Bridge Agreement.

2.11. (a)-(b) Certificates of the Secretaries of the Subsidiaries listed in (a)-(b) of item 1.06 as to the Certificate of Incorporation and Bylaws, the election, incumbency and signatures of officers and certifying as to resolutions of the Board of Directors of such corporations relating to Sections 5.01(e), (f) and (h) of the Credit Agreement.

3. Principal Documents

3.01. Agreement of Merger, dated as of October 1, 1999.
3.02. Certificate of Merger.

3.03. Escrow Agreement, dated October 1, 1999.

3.04. Certificate No. PA-1-1 evidencing 1,000 shares of Series A Preferred Stock of Holdings.

3.05. Seller Registration Rights Agreement.

3.06. Seller Warrant.

3.07. Credit Agreement, together with Schedules and Exhibits thereto.

3.08. Target Security Agreement, between Bank as Agent and for the Ratable Benefit of Lenders and Target.

3.09. (a)–(b) Subsidiary Security Agreement between Bank as Agent and for the Ratable Benefit of Lenders and each of the Subsidiaries listed in (a)-(b) of item 1.06.

3.10. Holdings Pledge Agreement.

3.11. Certificate No. 8 evidencing 1,000 shares, constituting all of the issued and outstanding shares of Target together with a stock power duly endorsed.

3.12. Target Pledge Agreement.

3.13. (a)-(b) Certificates evidencing all of the issued and outstanding shares of each of the Subsidiaries listed in item 1.06, together with stock powers or other instruments of transfer duly endorsed.

3.14. Individual Stock Pledge Agreements, executed by each of the Investor Shareholders and Management Shareholders in favor of the Bank.

3.15. Certificates evidencing all of the issued and outstanding common shares of Holdings, together with stock powers from each shareholder duly endorsed.

3.16. Mortgage.

3.17. Joinder Agreement executed by Target.

3.18. Private Placement Memorandum of December 27, 1999.

3.19. Supplement to the Private Placement Memorandum dated December 30, 1999.

3.20. Bridge Agreement.

3.21. Bridge Notes Indenture.

3.22. Senior Subordinated Bridge Note.

3.23. Bridge Note Registration Rights Agreement.

3.24. Warrants issued by Holdings to Lead Investment Banker.

3.25. Subordinated Pledge Agreement between Holdings and Investment Bank Group.

3.26. Intercreditor Agreement between Bank and Investment Bank Group.

4. Documents Relating to the Escrow Agent

4.01. Joint Written Notice executed by Seller and TAC pursuant to Section 4(a) of the Escrow Agreement to the effect that the Merger has been effected and instructing the Escrow Agent to pay the Escrow Deposit and interest accrued thereon to Target.

4.02. Receipt of Target, dated the Effective Date, for funds received from the Escrow Agent in the amount of $1,025,000.

5. Documents Relating to Compliance with Agreement of Merger

5.01. Certificate of the President of Seller, dated the Effective Date, pursuant to Sections 8.1 and 8.2 of the Agreement, as to compliance with and performance of the Agreement and as to the representations and warranties set forth in the Agreement.

5.02. Certificate of the Vice President of TAC dated the Effective Date, pursuant to Sections 9.1, 9.2 and 9.7 of the Agreement as to compliance and performance of the Agreement; the representations and warranties set forth in the Agreement; and its business, financial conditions and operations.

5.03. Releases executed by each person holding an option to purchase common stock of Target under the Target Stock Option Plan pursuant to Section 8.9 of the Agreement.

5.04. Certificate No. 7 of Target evidencing 1,000 shares of common stock of Target issued to Seller together with such stock transfer tax stamps as may be required.

6. Documents Relating to Compliance with Credit Agreement

6.01. Certificate executed by CEO and CFO of Holdings as to representations and warranties and no event of default pursuant to Section 5.01(d) of the Credit Agreement.

6.02. (a)–(d) UCC-1 Financing Statements covering personal property and appropriate documents for perfecting security interest in U.S. intellectual property as follows:

   (a) Holdings—California Secretary of State; Clerk of Los Angeles County, California; New York Department of State; and City Register of New York City;

   (b) Target—California Secretary of State; Clerk of Los Angeles County, California; New York Department of State; and City Register of New York City;

   (c) New York Target Subsidiary Ltd.—New York Department of State; and City Register of New York City; and

(d) Delaware Target Subsidiary Inc.—Delaware Secretary of State; Clerk of New Castle County, Delaware.

6.03. Certificate of President of Target to the effect that all indebtedness of Target has been paid or refinanced pursuant to Section 5.01(o) of the Credit Agreement.

6.04. Appointments of CT Corporation System in State of California as agent for service of process executed by CT Corporation, Holdings, Target and the Subsidiaries pursuant to Section 5.01(s) of the Credit Agreement.

6.05. Pro Forma Closing Date Balance Sheet for Holdings and its consolidated Subsidiaries pursuant to Section 5.01(t) of the Credit Agreement.

6.06. Borrowing Base Report, dated not more than two (2) days prior to the Effective Date pursuant to Section 5.01(y) of the Credit Agreement.

6.07. Appraisal of Appraisal Co. as to fair market value and orderly liquidation value of the real and personal property of Target pursuant to Section 5.01(b) of the Credit Agreement.

6.08. Written undertakings, executed by each of Target and the Subsidiaries pursuant to Section 5.01(d) of the Credit Agreement.

6.09. Solvency letters from CFOs and accountants for Holdings and Target pursuant to Section 5.01(k) of the Credit Agreement.

6.10. Bank Credit Audit pursuant to Section 5.01(p) of the Credit Agreement.

6.11. Certificate of Borrower as to consents pursuant to Section 6.03 of the Credit Agreement.

6.12. Evidence of payment of or indemnification against tax liens: City of New York—$10,000,000, State of New York—$500.

7. Consents, Waivers and Estoppel Certificates of Landlords of Target and Real Estate Matters

7.01. Consent of Lessor Ltd., lessor to New York Target Subsidiary Ltd., with respect to the facility located at One Main Street, New York, New York.

7.02. Owners' title insurance policy with respect to the California property, dated the Effective Date, pursuant to Section 8.8 of the Agreement.

7.03. Lenders' title insurance policy with respect to the California property.

7.04. Title Insurance Questionnaire.

7.05. Estoppel Certificate.

7.06. Survey.

7.07. Indemnities of Seller to the Title Insurance Company.

7.08. Discharges of Trust Company Mortgages.

7.09. Seller Agreement regarding effluent discharge.

8. Insurance

8.01. Insurance endorsements naming Agent as additional insured or loss payee pursuant to Section 5.01(x) of the Credit Agreement.

9. Documents Relating to Compliance with Bridge Agreement

9.01. Certificate of Vice President of Holdings pursuant to Section 3.1.4 of the Bridge Agreement as to the satisfaction of certain conditions of the Bridge Agreement.

9.02. Warrant Repurchase Letter Agreement, dated the Effective Date, between Holdings and Investment Bank Group.

10. Opinions of Counsel

10.01. Opinion of SC, dated the Effective Date, addressed to Holdings, the Agent, Lead Investment Banker and the Indenture Trustee pursuant to Section 8.5 of the Agreement, Section 5.01(mm) of the Credit Agreement and Section 3.1.8 of the Bridge Agreement.

10.02. Opinion of ICC, dated the Effective Date, pursuant to Section 9.5 of the Agreement.

10.03. Opinion of ICC, dated the Effective Date, addressed to the Agent pursuant to Section 5.01(c) of the Credit Agreement.

10.04. Opinion of ICC, dated the Effective Date, addressed to Lead Investment Banker and the Indenture Trustee pursuant to Section 3.1.7 of the Bridge Agreement.

10.05. Opinion of California Counsel, dated the Effective Date, addressed to the Agent pursuant to Section 5.01(v) of the Credit Agreement.

10.06. Opinion of Copyright Counsel, dated the Effective Date, addressed to the Agent and Holdings as to the trademark and copyright registrations in the United States pursuant to Section 5.01(w) of the Credit Agreement.

10.07. Opinion of BC dated the Effective Date, addressed to the Lenders pursuant to Section 5.01(u) of the Credit Agreement.

11. Documents Relating to IC and Management Shareholders

11.01. Employment Agreement between Target and John Smith, President of Target.

11.02. Powers of Attorney from each Management Shareholder appointing John Smith Attorney-in-fact.

11.03. Recourse Notes in the aggregate of $1,000,000 executed by each of the Management Shareholders (originals delivered to IC).

11.04. Pledge Agreement executed by Management Shareholders in favor of IC.

11.05. Cross Receipt of IC acknowledging receipt of the notes described in 11.03 and by John Smith as Attorney-in-fact for each of the Management Shareholders acknowledging receipt of an aggregate amount of $1,000,000.

11.06. Stockholders Agreement among Holdings, Investor Shareholders and Management Shareholders.

11.07. Agreement for Management Consulting Services between IC and Target.

11.08. IC Intercreditor Agreement by and between IC and Bank.

11.09. Letter as to Recourse Promissory Notes in favor of IC, dated the Effective Date, from IC to counsel for the Management Shareholders.

12. Funding of Holdings and TAC and Merger Payment

12.01. Cross Receipt executed by Holdings acknowledging receipt of $4,000,000, and by the Investor Shareholders acknowledging receipt of Certificate Nos. 1–4 evidencing 800,000 shares of the common stock of Holdings.

12.02. Cross Receipt executed by Holdings acknowledging receipt of $1,000,000, and by the Management Shareholders acknowledging receipt of Certificate Nos. 5–8 evidencing 200,000 shares of the common stock of Holdings.

12.03. Cross Receipt executed by Seller, dated the Effective Date, acknowledging receipt of (a) the Cash Portion of the Merger Payment in the amount of $100,000,000 determined pursuant to Section 3.2(b) of the Merger Agreement; (b) the Warrant; and (c) Certificate No. PA-1 evidencing 1,000 shares of Series A Preferred Stock, and by Holdings acknowledging receipt of (i) $10,000,000 as consideration for the issuance of the Series A Preferred Stock and (ii) a certificate evidencing 1,000 shares of Common Stock of Target.

12.04. Receipt executed by IC acknowledging receipt of $3,000,000 as a structuring fee.

13. Funding of Loan and Sale of Warrants

13.01. Term Note in the amount of $40,000,000 (original delivered to Lender).

13.02. Revolving Note in the amount of $10,000,000 (original delivered to Lender) (only $1,000,000 borrowed at Closing).

13.03. Cross Receipt of Lender acknowledging receipt of the Term Note and the Revolving Note and of Holdings acknowledging receipt of $41,000,000.

13.04. Cross Receipt of Investment Bank Group and Lead Investment Banker acknowledging receipt of the Investment Banker Warrants and Bridge Note and of Holdings acknowledging receipt of $60,000,000.

V. FILING OF CERTIFICATE OF MERGER

When all parties and their counsel were satisfied that the documents described in Section IV above were complete and in order, the Certificate of Merger was filed in the office of the Secretary of State of Delaware, in accordance with the General Corporation Law of the State of Delaware.

E N D N O T E S

1. See Maury Nunes, "But They Signed a Letter of Intent," *Director's Monthly*, April 2000, pp. 11–13.
2. This applies only when the seller will realize taxable gain from the sale—that is, when the tax basis of the assets in the acquired company is lower than the selling price, necessitating a "step up" to the selling price.
3. The bulk sales law, subject to variations among states, applies to acquirers of businesses dealing in bulk sales—the sale of merchandise from inventory. If a purchaser buys a major part of the material, supplies, merchandise, or other inventory of any such company, the purchaser is to give at least 10 days' advance notice of the sale to each creditor of the seller. The notice must identify the company and its buyer, and state whether the debts of the company will be paid as they fall due. If orderly payment will not be made, further information must be disclosed. In addition, many states require the buyer to ensure that the seller of the company uses proceeds from the sale to satisfy existing debts, and to hold in escrow an amount sufficient to pay any disputed debts.
4. This response is quoted verbatim from Stanley Foster Reed and Alexandra Reed Lajoux, *The Art of M&A: A Merger/Acquisition/Buyout Guide* (New York: McGraw-Hill, 1999), p. 465. As mentioned in the Preface and Acknowledgments to the present book, we drew from Chapter 8 (pp. 445–610) and Chapter 9 (pp. 611–642) of Reed and Lajoux. The original version of the Chapter 8 material was written by Richard Perkal, Esq., formerly with Lane and Edson in Washington, D.C., and now a partner with Kirkland & Ellis, Washington, D.C.
5. Mendez and Sawyers, op. cit. (Chapter 1, note 8), p. 315.

CHAPTER 6

Detecting Exposure Under Securities Law

The stock market is but a mirror which . . . provides an
image of an underlying economic situation.

John Kenneth Galbraith
The Great Crash (1955)

INTRODUCTION

Knowledge of securities law is imperative in any transaction involving one or
more public companies—whether as a buyer, a seller, or both. This knowledge
may even be helpful in transactions involving only private companies, if those
companies have issued or bought securities in a manner that brings them under the control of the securities law.

A security, after all, is a common element of corporate life. All companies
have some form of security on their balance sheets—including equity and,
generally, debt. And many companies use securities to make their acquisitions.

Equity securities, also called shares, are, by definition, owned by shareholders. As mentioned in Chapter 4, more than one-third of all lawsuits
against directors and officers come from shareholders, and the average
amount received in such cases is $8,672,576—the largest average received by
any nongovernment group filing such lawsuits.[1]

Shareholders, like other constituencies, sue over a variety of issues.

- *Inadequate disclosure* leads the list: One-third of all claim awards paid
  to shareholders in D&O lawsuits (6 percent of all claim awards) result from this accusation.

The rest of D&O claims from shareholders come from a great variety of
issues, including:

- *Business decisions:* divestitures or spin-offs, recapitalizations, and investment or loan decisions.
- *Other business issues:* contract disputes (with shareholders), dishonesty/fraud, executive compensation (such as golden parachutes), and fraudulent conveyance.
- *Fiduciary issues:* general breach of fiduciary duty and breach of duty to minority holders.
- *Financial or financing issues:* dividend declaration, change in financial performance or bankruptcy, financial transactions (such as derivatives), share repurchase, and stock or other public offering.
- *Merger or change of control issues:* challenging a company's takeover bid or its response to a bid from another company, trading on the basis of inside information, and proxy contests.

Clearly, the sweep of securities law is broad. To maintain some depth, this chapter will focus on securities law as it pertains to the last topic, merger and change of control issues. By mastering the basics of securities law pertaining to changes of control, acquirers will be better prepared to perform a litigation analysis of a candidate company and to reduce the chances of securities law violations before, during, and after their merger transaction.

OVERVIEW OF SECURITIES LAW

What precisely are corporate securities?

Corporate securities are a type of financial instrument—one "secured" by the value of an operating company. These securities are issued as *equity securities* (such as shares of company stock) or as *debt securities* (such as company bonds, certificates, notes, or paper).[2]

Equity represents ownership, whereas debt represents a promise to repay a certain sum, with interest, at a definite time. The distinction between equity and debt securities is important, because the two instruments require different tax and accounting treatment.

What is the purpose of the federal securities laws?

The federal securities laws require that issuers of the securities make certain disclosures at certain times. These disclosure rules ensure that anyone who buys or sells securities has the basic information necessary to determine their value.

All these laws are enforced by the Securities and Exchange Commission (SEC), which was established under the Securities Exchange Act of 1934 as an independent, nonpartisan, quasi-judicial regulatory agency charged with administering federal securities laws. The purpose of these laws is to protect investors in securities markets that operate fairly and to ensure that investors have access of all material information concerning publicly traded securities. The SEC also regulates firms engaged in the purchase or sale of securities, people who provide investment advice, and investment companies.

What are the primary federal securities laws?

The primary securities laws (to recap and expand the description in Chapter 1) are as follows:

- *Securities Act of 1933.* This law requires that investors receive financial and other information concerning securities being offered for public sale. It has led to the promulgation of hundreds of rules and regulations related to the registration of securities and the publication of information related to registration.

- *Securities Exchange Act of 1934.* This law requires that investors have access to current financial and other information regarding the securities of publicly held corporations particularly those that trade on the national exchanges or over the counter. The 1934 Act has led to the promulgation of hundreds of rules and regulations concerning the operation of the markets and participants, including proxy solicitations by companies and shareholders, tender offers, and buying securities on credit (so-called margin purchases).

- *Investment Company Act of 1940.* This law governs activities of companies, including mutual funds, that are engaged primarily in investing, reinvesting, and trading in securities, and that offer their own securities to the investing public. Under this law, investment companies are subject to certain statutory prohibitions and to regulation by the Securities and Exchange Commission (SEC). Public offerings of investment company securities must be registered under the Securities Act of 1933.

- *Investment Adviser Act of 1940.* This law contains provisions similar to those in the Securities Exchange Act of 1934 governing the conduct of securities brokers and dealers. It requires that persons or firms compensated for advising others about securities investment must register with the SEC and conform to statutory standards designed to protect investors.

- *Public Utility Holding Company Act of 1935.* This law covers interstate holding companies engaged, through subsidiaries, in the electric utility business or in retail distribution of natural or manufactured gas.
- *Trust Indenture Act of 1939.* This law applies to debt securities, including debentures and notes, offered for public sale. Even though such securities may be registered under the Securities Act of 1933, they may not be offered for sale to the public unless a formal agreement between the issuer of the bonds and the bondholder, known as a trust indenture, conforms to the statutory standards of this law.

This may seem like a broad array of laws to enforce. The SEC, however, is a relatively small agency in comparison to other agencies and Cabinet-level departments, such as the Department of Labor. It relies on what it calls a "public-private partnership." That is, the Commission sets standards for the issuance and trading of securities, but much of the direct, day-to-day regulation of the securities market participants is done under SEC oversight by the so-called self-regulatory organizations—stock exchanges. In addition, the investing public itself has the enforcement mechanism of the private right of action.

What is the role of state securities laws?

State securities laws, commonly known as blue sky laws, set forth registration requirements for brokers and dealers, registration requirements for securities to be sold within the state, and prohibition against fraud in the sale of securities. A majority of states, with the notable exception of New York and California, have adopted the Uniform Securities Act (USA) of 1956, amended in 1985 and 1988.[3] The revised Uniform Securities Act encouraged greater coordination between federal and state securities law regulation and greater cooperation among states.[4]

In addition, there are state corporate statutes governing corporate existence, charters, and bylaws. These make reference to the rights of holders of securities. Corporate statutes vary from state to state, but there is some uniformity, thanks to the influence of Delaware corporate law (often used as a prototype for state corporate statutes) and the Model Business Corporation Act first created in 1946, and continually updated under the auspices of a committee of the Business Law Section of the American Bar Association (ABA).

FEDERAL SECURITIES LAW PERTAINING TO PUBLIC COMPANIES

What are the most important federal laws to consider when conducting due diligence on an acquisition involving a public company?

At the federal level, securities laws are encompassed in two laws mentioned above: the Securities Act of 1933 (commonly referred to as the 1933 Act or the Securities Act), which sets forth registration requirements for companies seeking to sell securities to the public, and the more extensive Securities Exchange Act of 1934 (commonly called the 1934 Act or the Exchange Act), which sets the disclosure and filing requirements. The basic text of these laws has been amended and expanded over time—and now include hundreds of related rules.[5] Rules of the Securities Act and the Securities Exchange Act have undergone many amendments and additions over time.

You mentioned that the securities laws had been amended or expanded. What is the most recent amendment relevant to mergers and acquisitions?

Most recently (as of mid-2000), Regulation M-A added Items 1000 to 1016 under the Securities Act and the Securities Exchange Act. Effective January 24, 2000, this regulation (created entirely by the SEC, not Congress) is applicable to take-over transactions, including tender offers, mergers, acquisitions, and similar extraordinary transactions.[6] The revised rules will permit increased communications with security holders and the markets. The amendments also will:

- Balance the treatment of cash versus stock tender offers.
- Eliminate inconsistencies in treatment of tender offers versus mergers.
- Simplify and centralize disclosure requirements.[7]

What exactly is a tender offer?

More than 20 years ago, on November 29, 1979, the SEC proposed the following definition of tender offer (never adopted but never withdrawn):

> The term "tender offer" includes a "request or invitation for tenders" and means one or more offers to purchase or solicitations of offers to sell securities of a single class, whether or not all or any portion of the securities sought are purchased,

which (i) during any 45-day period are directed to more than 10 persons and seek the acquisition of more than 5 percent of the class of securities, except that offers by a broker (and its customer) or by a dealer made on a national securities exchange at the then current market or made in the over-the-counter market at the then current market shall be excluded if in connection with such offers neither the person making the offers nor such broker or dealer solicits or arranges for the solicitation of any order to sell such securities and such broker or dealer performs only the customary functions of a broker or dealer and receives no more than the broker's usual and customary commission or the dealer's usual and customary mark-up; or (ii) are not otherwise a tender offer under [clause (i)] of this section, but which (A) are disseminated in a widespread manner, (B) provide for a price which represents a premium[8] in excess of the greater of 5 percent of or \$2 above the current market price and (C) do not provide for a meaningful opportunity to negotiate the price and terms.

A short, somewhat tautological definition of a tender offer appears in Exchange Act Rule 13e-4(a)(2). In that rule, the term "issuer tender offer" refers to "a tender offer for, or a request or invitation for tenders of, any class of equity security, made by the issuer of such class of equity security or by an affiliate of such an issuer."[9]

In a tender offer, the acquirer sends an "offer to purchase" that sets forth the material terms of the offer, and a "letter of transmittal" that the shareholder sends back to accept the offer. By accepting the offer, the shareholder sells or "tenders" its shares to the acquirer.

A tender offer typically occurs within a 20-day period.[10] Most tender offers involve a general, publicized bid by an individual or group to buy shares of a publicly owned company at a price above or premium to the current market price. During a tender offer, the offeror may not directly or indirectly purchase or arrange to purchase, other than pursuant to the tender offer, securities that are the subject of that offer until the end of the offer (Rule 10b-13). This prohibition also includes privately negotiated purchases. Some purchases made before a public announcement may be permissible, even if a decision has been made by the purchaser to make the tender offer, but purchase agreements scheduled to close during the offering period are illegal no matter when they were or are made.

The disclosure rules for tender offers used to be different from the rules for mergers, but Regulation M-A has made the rules more consistent.

What does Regulation M-A require of companies engaged in tender offers and mergers?

Under Regulation M-A, acquiring companies (referred to as "filing persons") must provide security holders with a summary term sheet, written in plain

English, that describes in bullet points the most material terms of the proposed transaction. The summary term sheet must provide security holders with sufficient information to understand the essential features and significance of the proposed transaction. The bullet points must cross-reference more detailed disclosures found in the disclosure document disseminated to security holders.

Items include:

- *Subject company information.* Includes name and address, securities now trading, trading market and place, dividends, prior public offerings, and prior stock purchases. This is basic information about the company whose securities may be acquired.
- *Identity and background of the filing person.* Includes name and address, business background of entities, business background of natural persons, tender offer and class of securities to which the offer relates, and Internet contact, if any.
- *Terms of the transaction.* Includes material terms, purchases from insiders, differing terms for shareholders, appraisal rights, provisions for unaffiliated security holders, and eligibility for listing or trading.
- *Past contacts transactions, negotiations, and agreements.* Includes details on past transactions between subject company and filing person; significant corporate events involving the two, such as a merger, consolidation, acquisition, tender offer, election of a director to the board of the subject company, or sale or transfer of a material amount of assets of the subject company; name of person who initiated contacts or negotiations; conflicts of interest; and agreements involving the subject company's securities.
- *Purpose of the transaction and plans or proposals.* Includes purposes, use of securities, and subject company negotiations.
- *Source and amount of funds or other considerations.* Includes source of funds, conditions, and expenses. The filer may request confidentiality regarding the source of borrowed funds.
- *Interest in the securities of the subject company.* Includes securities ownership and securities transactions.
- *Persons and/or assets retained, employed, compensated, or used.* Includes solicitations or recommendations, employees and/or corporate assets.
- *Financial statements.* Includes financial information, pro forma information, and summary information.
- *Reports, opinions, appraisals, or negotiations.* Includes a description of the report and its preparer.

Regulation M-A also has a section on *going-private transactions*.

This may seem like an overwhelming amount of information, but it is even more overwhelming to consider that prior to Regulation M-A, individuals interested in understanding a transaction had to go to many different reports to get information.

Clearly, Regulation M-A provides a way for anyone to see "at a glance" the material aspects of a merger or acquisition transaction.

Are all securities lawsuits brought under the Securities Act and Exchange Act or related regulations?

No. Other laws may be applied in securities cases. For example, in the late 1980s, RICO was often applied.

What is RICO and how does it pertain to M&A?

The Racketeer Influenced and Corrupt Organizations Act was passed as part of broad anticrime legislation in 1970. RICO sets steep penalties, which include asset freezes, treble damages, and up to 20 years in jail, for those who engage in a "pattern" of crime. It was first applied in securities fraud cases in 1987. Under then-U.S. Attorney Rudolph Giuliani in the late 1980s, RICO indictments in the Southern District of New York averaged about 90 per year; some 20 percent of these were so-called "white collar" cases that did not involve organized crime. Since then the pace of RICO convictions has slowed, and judicial application of the statute has been moderate in recent cases. For example, in March 1992 the U.S. Supreme Court ruled in *Holmes v. Securities Corp.* that plaintiffs must prove that the alleged wrongdoing did *direct* harm to the plaintiffs.

RICO has been used in M&A cases. For example, in December 1991 Carl Lindner, an 8.4 percent holder in Pennsylvania Enterprises, accused that utility's directors of violating RICO by making only "sham" attempts to sell the concern. His suit called for the court to force the company to seek a buyer and to appoint an "independent oversight committee." Certainly evidence of due diligence by candidate acquirers could be used to show good faith in this regard.

How do securities laws influence transactional due diligence for buying a publicly held company versus a privately held company?

The negotiation of a public transaction involves fiduciary and disclosure considerations that are normally inapplicable to a private setting. The board of directors of a public company being acquired via a tender offer—often called a *target*, reflecting the involuntary nature of its involvement—must be mindful of its fiduciary responsibilities under state corporate law. Traditionally under state law, as represented by Delaware law and the Model Business Corporation Act, the directors' primary fiduciary duty is to shareholders. In the landmark case of *Revlon Inc. v. MacAndrews & Forbes Holdings* (1986), the court described the role of the board of directors as that of a price-oriented "neutral auctioneer" once a decision has been made to sell the company. Obviously, this interpretation constrains decisions in a way that would not apply to most sales of private companies. (But note that boards have some decision-making discretion under state "constituency" statutes as well as under the business judgment rule, discussed later in this chapter.)

Furthermore, the structure, timing, financing, and negotiation of a public company sale is greatly affected by federal and state securities laws. Because of these laws, the transaction is conducted in a fishbowl, and most material aspects of the transaction quickly become public knowledge. For example, even before public companies reach an agreement on price and structure, they may find themselves subject to certain disclosure obligations. They may be placed in a position in which they must disclose their activities. If questioned, they may be permitted to say nothing, but must also refrain from untruthful denial, as shown in *Basic, Incorporated v. Levinson* (1986), discussed below. Moreover, in a public company deal, statutory and practical delays provide ample opportunity for a new bidder to arrive on the scene.

As a result of the publicity surrounding its offer, the buyer may become a "stalking horse" for the seller in order to attract other bidders. Unfortunately for such a buyer, it will have incurred substantial transaction expenses such as legal and accounting fees and it may have laid out significant sums as commitment fees to lenders to arrange for financing. The buyer may have also passed up other investment opportunities while pursuing the acquisition of the target. These considerations may cause the buyer to focus on tactical issues at the expense of due diligence.

What form does a public company acquisition usually take?

A public company acquisition can be accomplished through either a one-step or a two-step transaction.

In the *one-step* acquisition, the buyer organizes an acquisition subsidiary that will merge into the target. Upon consummation of the merger, the stockholders of the target receive cash and, perhaps, other property such as notes, and the stockholders of the acquisition subsidiary receive all the stock of the target. The merger will require the approval of the stockholders of the target; the exact percentage of stockholder approval required will depend upon the articles of incorporation of the target and could be as low as a majority of the voting power of the common stock. To effect the approval, the target will be required to solicit proxies from the stockholders and to vote the proxies at a stockholder meeting called for the purpose of voting on the transaction. The proxy solicitation must comply with federal securities law.

A *two-step* acquisition involves a tender offer followed by a merger:

1. The buyer organizes an acquisition subsidiary that makes a tender offer for the shares of the target. Usually, the offer is conditioned upon enough shares being tendered to give the buyer sufficient voting power to ensure that the second-step merger will be approved. For example, if approval by a majority of the voting stock of the target is required, the offer is conditioned on the buyer obtaining at least a majority of the target stock in the tender offer.

2. The buyer obtains stockholder approval, the acquisition subsidiary is merged into the target, the stockholders of the acquisition subsidiary become stockholders of the target, and the original stockholders of the target who did not tender their shares receive cash. If the buyer obtains sufficient stock of the target (90 percent in Delaware), the merger will not require approval of the target's remaining stockholders (a so-called short-form merger).[11]

In any event, the acquiring company must make certain proxy disclosures, under Regulation 14A of the Exchange Act. A proxy statement is a document that informs shareholders of material facts, so that they may vote by "proxy" rather than attend a meeting of shareholders. If the shareholder meeting to which the proxy statement relates is being held in connection with any merger, consolidation, acquisition, or similar matter, the issuer must disclose certain information in the proxy statement as set forth in Regulation 14A.

In a public transaction, must the stock be acquired only through a tender offer or a merger?

No. The buyer may precede its tender offer or the merger with ordinary market purchases through the relevant stock exchange or may acquire, or enter into arrangements to acquire, stock from the target or from some of its major stockholders (lockup arrangements).[12] The timing and method of such purchases, however, must conform to federal securities laws, which preclude certain transactions after a tender offer begins and also may characterize certain open market purchases as tender offers.

How does the M&A process in a hostile transaction differ from due diligence in a friendly transaction?

The due diligence process in a hostile deal is very different from due diligence in a friendly deal. A friendly acquirer will typically conduct most of its due diligence after approaching its candidate company, and with the cooperation of the candidate company. By contrast, a hostile acquirer—that is, a company targeting another company for takeover via tender offer, proxy fight, or otherwise—must conduct its due diligence in advance of approaching the target.

What kind of due diligence, if any, can be conducted in a tender offer?

The acquirer in a tender offer will typically form a team that includes a dealer-manager[13] and some kind of financial advisor. Part of their work involves due diligence, since they review the target company's financials and business and advise the purchaser as to the desirability and feasibility of the proposed transaction. A deal may be more or less desirable and completable depending on the technicalities of federal and state securities laws as they apply to the transaction. Also, any tender offer requires the advice and counsel of experienced lawyers who will prepare the many legal documents required in conjunction with the tender offer. As essential members of the team, the lawyers should be familiar with federal and state securities laws, antitrust laws, and numerous other areas of the law that may apply to a specific transaction.[14] Because litigation is often a by-product of tender offers, the lawyers on a tender offer team should be prepared to consult with or retain a strong, experienced group of litigation attorneys.

What disclosure form must the bidder in a tender offer file?

Any person who is the "beneficial owner" of 5 percent or more of the shares of a class of voting equity securities registered under Section 12 of the Exchange Act must file a Schedule 13D with the SEC and with each securities exchange on which the securities are traded. Schedule13D must be filed with all parties, with a copy sent to the issuer, within 10 days after a bidder acquires 5 percent or more of an outstanding voting equity security.[15]

Also, on the day that the tender offer commences, the buyer must file a tender offer statement on Schedule 14D-1 with the SEC, and hand-deliver copies of the statement to the target and other bidders. Schedule 14D-1 is a fairly comprehensive disclosure document that includes much of the information listed above as required bullet points in Regulation M-A. The acquirer must also mail a copy of the statement to stock exchanges on which the target's stock is traded (or the NASD if the securities are traded over the counter) after giving them notice of the information required by Rule 14d-2(i) and (ii).

What is a beneficial owner and why does it matter?

A beneficial owner of equity is a person or group of persons possessing "voting power" or "investment power" over a security as defined in Rule 13d-3 of the Exchange Act. Thus, shares beneficially owned include not only shares directly owned, but also all shares with respect to which a person has or shares direct or indirect power to vote or sell. For instance, all shares subject to a shareholders' voting agreement become beneficially owned by each person who is a party to the agreement.

The concept of beneficial ownership is especially important in view of the 5 percent threshold to the filing requirements. Thus, if each member of a "group" of five persons owns 1 percent of the shares of a class of a company, that group must file a Schedule 13D or 13G if the group has agreed to vote or dispose of those securities as a block. These schedules require the filing person or group to disclose certain information about the transaction:

- Information about itself (name, address).
- The number of shares of the company to be acquired that it beneficially owns.
- Its purpose in acquiring those shares; any plans or proposals to acquire or dispose of shares of the target company.
- Any plans for an extraordinary corporate transaction (such as a merger, reorganization, or liquidation) affecting the target company or any of its subsidiaries.
- Any proposed change in the target's directors or management, in the target's capitalization or dividend policy, or in its business or corporate structure.
- Any past involvement of the individual or group members in violation of state or federal securities laws; the source and amount of funds; or other considerations for the acquisition.
- Any contracts, arrangements, understandings, or relationships that the filer has with any other person concerning the shares of the company to be acquired.

A person is deemed to own beneficially any security that he or she, directly or indirectly, has the right to acquire within 60 days, whether such acquisition is pursuant to a purchase contract, exercise of a warrant or option, or conversion of a convertible security (Rule 13d-3).

Also, once a tender offeror becomes a beneficial owner of 10 percent of the target's securities, it is an insider for purposes of Section 16 of the Exchange Act and must file a Form 3 with the SEC within 10 days of becoming an insider. The amount and type of ownership interest of the offeror must be disclosed on Form 3. An offeror must file a Form 4 upon any subsequent change in its beneficial ownership of the target's securities. The Form 4 must be filed within 10 days after the end of any month in which a change in beneficial ownership occurred. Forms 3 and 4 must be filed with the SEC and each exchange on which the target securities are traded.

Under Rule 16b-7 an insider is exempt from liability under Section 16(b) if it acquires or disposes of shares pursuant to a merger or consolidation of companies and one of the companies owns 85 percent or more of the combined assets of the other. Rule 16b-7 usually applies to second-step mergers after completion of a partial tender offer. Also, a transaction that does not follow a typical sale-purchase or purchase-sale sequence may be exempt from the liability provisions of Section 16(b).[16]

What exactly is a "group" under federal securities law?

Acquirers of less than 5 percent of a target company's stock may be part of a group and not realize it. Here are salient points about a group for the purposes of Schedules 13D and 13G rules:

- The existence of a written agreement is not required; circumstantial evidence of an agreement in itself may be enough (Section 13(d)1(E)3).

- A group can be formed as soon as the members of the group reach an agreement, even if the agreement is merely preliminary. Managers of an acquired company may be considered a group if they act as such to acquire shares and if collectively they own more than 5 percent of the company.

- A written agreement to acquire additional shares may not be necessary to define a group. If shareowners who collectively hold a total of 5 percent or more of a class of voting stock agree to act together in the future to further the group's purpose, this agreement may be enough to form a group regardless of whether acts to carry out the agreement (such as voting and acquiring stock) occur after the date of the agreement.

You mentioned earlier that the acquirer must disclose "any proposed change in the acquired company's . . . business or corporate structure." Suppose one of the changes involves a confidential strategic plan or a trade secret. Must it be disclosed?

It is possible to avoid the public disclosure of certain material if it can be demonstrated that such disclosure would be detrimental to the operations of the company, and that disclosure of the material is unnecessary for the protection of investors. Disclosure of a specific plan to convert a manual product to an Internet or "e-business" application may fit these two criteria. A company seeking to avoid the public disclosure of such information must seek an Order of Confidential Treatment from the SEC. Generally, if appropriate grounds for relief are asserted, the SEC will grant confidential treatment of such information for a limited period of time.

What rules constrain the behavior of sellers in a tender offer?

There are rules against "short tendering." This occurs when a shareholder in a partial tender offer tenders more shares than he or she actually owns in the hope of increasing the number of shares that the bidder actually will accept pro rata. A person is prohibited from tendering a security unless that person, or the person on whose behalf he or she is tendering, owns the security (or an equivalent security) at the time of the tender and at the end of the probation period. A person is deemed to own a security only to the extent that he or she has a net long position in such security.

MERGER DISCLOSURE ISSUES

Under what circumstances may a public company deny that it is engaged in merger negotiations?

Only if it is not so engaged. That was the gist of the Supreme Court's 1988 decision in *Basic Inc. v. Levinson*. In this landmark case, the Court said that outright denial of negotiations is improper even if the negotiations in question are discussions that have not yet resulted in an agreement on the price and structure of a transaction. The appropriate response to inquiries about such a matter is either "no comment" or a disclosure that negotiations are, in fact, taking place.

Prior to the *Basic* decision, the U.S. Court of appeals for the Third Circuit had implied that merger proposals and negotiations were not "material" and thus actionable until the parties had reached a firm agreement in principle on the price and structure of a transaction. In *Basic*, the Supreme Court rejected this test of materiality, often called a "bright line" test because it set forth a fairly clear dividing line between material and nonmaterial discussions. The high court held that the materiality and hence actionability of untrue statements about merger negotiations must be evaluated on a case-by-case basis after considering all relevant facts and circumstances.

When does a company have a duty to disclose merger negotiations?

Generally, the timing of disclosure of material information is at the discretion of the company and will be protected by the business judgment rule, described in the next section. Nevertheless, a company that is the subject of takeover speculation or whose stock is trading erratically typically finds itself pressured by brokers, news services, stock exchange officials, securities analysts, and others to disclose merger proposals and negotiations. The *Basic* decision has accelerated the trend toward voluntary disclosures in these circumstances, although it is still acceptable under certain circumstances for a company to adopt a policy of silence or state that "no comment" will be made with respect to merger proposals or rumors.

However, a company may not remain silent when (1) there is an affirmative disclosure rule (such as the tender offer regulations), (2) the company is about to purchase its own shares in the public market, (3) a prior public disclosure made by the company is no longer accurate (such as when a company has publicly denied that merger negotiations with a party were occurring), or (4) rumors that have been circulating concerning the proposed transactions are attributable to a leak from the company.

Disclosure may also be appropriate when it is apparent that a leak has occurred, even if the leak is not from the company. In such a situation, consideration should be given to a variety of factors, including the requirements of any agreement with a stock exchange, the effect of wide price fluctuations on shareholders generally, and the benefits to the market provided by broad dissemination of accurate information. If the company does elect to disclose either the existence or the substance of negotiations, it must take care that its disclosures are neither false nor materially misleading.

It should be noted that if the company refuses to respond to a stock exchange's request for disclosure or issues a "no comment," it may be subject to

disciplinary action by the exchange. This disciplinary action may include public notice of a violation, temporary suspension of trading in the corporation's
stock, or delisting. However, some have suggested that stock exchanges may
be "paper tigers" in this area because of a reluctance to enforce the rules. This
reluctance is attributed to the competition of "third market" securities firms
that trade listed securities off the exchanges. Moreover, courts have not found
a private right of action for violation of exchange rules.

"DUE DILIGENCE" UNDER STATE CORPORATE LAW: DIRECTOR DUTIES

What are the primary responsibilities of a corporate board of directors upon receipt of a takeover bid?

The board of directors' primary responsibility is to evaluate and recommend
what action a company should take in the event of an offer to acquire the
company. The directors' conduct in this and other contexts is typically
evaluated under the business judgment rule.

What is the business judgment rule?

The *business judgment rule* is a judicial doctrine applied by courts in cases
where shareholders have sued directors for violating their fiduciary duty of
care in making a particular business decision. The rule is that the board of directors' business decision will be protected from liability unless the shareholders can prove that in making that decision a director did not act with good
faith, informed judgment, and the rational belief that the decision was in the
corporation's best interest. The business judgment rule protects directors
from liability if they act in a manner consistent with its requirements in making a particular decision.

   A thorough due diligence process can satisfy the second prong of the
business judgment rule—that is, informed judgment.

What is a director's duty of due care?

For a director, exercising due care means acting on behalf of the company's
stockholders in good faith and with that amount of care similarly situated reasonable directors would exercise. In practice, this means, in conjunction with
the business judgment rule, making informed decisions after obtaining all reasonably available information required to make an intelligent decision and after
evaluating all relevant circumstances. Under this standard, the director's duty

is not merely to make the best possible decision in the director's judgment for the corporation but to make that decision only after careful, informed deliberation. It is the process of decision making that is taken into consideration by courts in evaluating whether a director acted with due care. If such a process is not shown, then the results of that decision may be reviewed by the court.

As mentioned in Chapter 4, a famous example of alleged lack of due care—and, more specifically, lack of seller due diligence—is *Smith v. Van Gorkom* (1985). Since *Van Gorkom*, the application of the business judgment rule has been discussed in a series of landmark cases—notably *Hanson Trust* (1986), *Time Inc.* (1990), and *Paramount* (1994). (See the Landmark Due Diligence Cases in the back of the book.) There are literally dozens of landmark cases in this area, which is extremely complex.[17]

What is a director's duty of loyalty?

A director of a corporation owes a duty of loyalty to the corporation and its shareholders. As such, the director is prohibited from acting with fraud, bad faith, or in the director's self-interest to the detriment of the corporation and its shareholders. Transactions with the corporation in which the director has a personal interest, or ones involving a director that conflict with the corporation's interest, are implicated by this duty. In reviewing such transactions, a court will shift the burden of proof to the director to show that the transaction is fair and that it serves the best interests of the corporation and its shareholders.

Why are the board's duties of loyalty and due care so important?

First, these rules affect timing—the need for the board to act with due care will restrict the board's ability to act quickly on a friendly offer. At the very least, a fairness opinion must be obtained, and the investment banker will need several days, at a minimum, to complete the task. The loyalty rules are particularly implicated in the case of a management buyout.

The rules also restrict the ability of the board to take action that eliminates the possibility of a competing bid—so-called lockups or other arrangements (bustup and topping fees[18] and "no shop" clauses[19]) that are designed (in part) to frustrate the efforts of other bidders. These arrangements are among the most negotiated provisions of the public deal.

For reasons outlined above, the buyer will seek to minimize the risk of a successful competing bid and will seek to ensure that it is compensated if it loses to another bidder. The next several questions deal with these issues in the context of the board's fiduciary responsibilities to the shareholders.

USE OF A SPECIAL COMMITTEE

When is it appropriate for a selling company to appoint a special committee of its board of directors to review a proposed transaction?

When a majority of board members have a personal interest in the proposed merger (i.e., when the management directors predominate and will obtain benefits from the merger), an independent special committee of the board should be appointed to handle the negotiation and recommendation of any proposed transaction. A special committee is also appropriate when a proposed transaction is complex enough to require careful study for the board to act responsibly. Having a special committee with adequate authority over the transaction may shift to a plaintiff the burden of showing that the transaction is unfair. Such a shift could preclude the issuance of injunctive relief against a proposed merger.

What steps should a special committee take to ensure that it is acting responsibly?

The special committee should examine all information about the proposed transaction. This examination must be thorough, and members of the special committee should question carefully the persons supplying such information to be sure the information is complete and accurate. The committee should also take care not to act hastily and should make sure that it documents its deliberations. Recent judicial decisions have indicated that directors who make decisions without adequate deliberation may have difficulty in establishing that they acted with the care necessary to provide the protection of the business judgment rule. In the context of mergers and acquisitions, the special committee of a board of directors should retain independent legal counsel and financial advisers.

Should a special committee obtain a fairness opinion?

Yes, but the opinion must be from a qualified, independent source such as an investment banking firm, a commercial bank, or a professional services firm. In rendering such an opinion, the advisor limits its evaluation to the adequacy of the consideration, or fairness of the exchange, not the strategic merits of the transaction. However, an opinion regarding financial fairness can only be developed upon considering the entire context of the transaction.

What purpose does a fairness opinion serve?

Although the fairness opinion can be a useful tool in determining whether to complete a transaction and in obtaining the protection of the business judgment rule, it is not an assurance that the best possible price was achieved. Additionally, a fairness opinion alone does not suffice as proof of the exercise of due care. Instead, a fairness opinion is one component (albeit a very important component) of the fiduciary's decision-making process and must be supplemented by management presentations, advice of legal counsel, and the deliberations of a board of directors or an independent special committee appointed by the board.

When are fairness opinions necessary?

Fairness opinions are necessary when there is a clear conflict of interest, when minority shareholders are being bought out, when a transaction will result in a significant structural change, or for any material transaction where the fiduciary wants an independent advisor to support its actions.

What criteria should be employed to assess fairness opinion providers?

In considering potential advisors, a fiduciary should consider the following factors:

- Can the advisor be perceived as having a conflict of interest? For example, does the advisor have significant transaction fees contingent on the closing of the transaction in question?
- Can the advisor be regarded as having the best interest of the client in mind?
- Does the advisor demonstrate the requisite technical, industry, and transaction experience?
- Does the advisor have the appropriate policies and procedures in place to ensure thorough transaction review and a completely impartial conclusion?

What should the fairness opinions say?

The fairness opinion should first clearly define the terms of the transaction on which it is opining. The fairness opinion should also describe the process used by the advisor in making its determination that a proposed transaction is fair and should indicate what matters have been investigated and independently verified, and what matters the advisor has not verified. Finally, the opinion should also describe the fees being paid and all possible conflicts of interest. To ensure impartiality, compensation for a fairness opinion should not be contingent upon the closing of a transaction.

Does the fairness opinion ensure the fairness of the transaction?

No. Because the opinion is an expert judgment and not a statement of fact, the opinion letter does not guarantee the fairness of the transaction. In addition to providing the opinion, the advisor should provide a presentation to the fiduciary detailing information regarding procedures performed during the engagement, data considered, judgments made, analytical methodologies employed, and all other relevant considerations connected to its conclusion that the transaction is fair. The fiduciary has a duty to question the advisor to determine that it has a reasonable basis for its opinion and is free from conflicts of interest. Ultimately, the burden is on the fiduciary, not the advisor, to accept or reject a transaction.

SELLER DUE DILIGENCE IN THE SALE OF A CONTROL BLOCK

What concerns will a seller have in the sale of a control block?

State corporation laws would suggest an expanded duty for the seller of a controlling block of stock. When a controlling block of stock is sold but other shareholders remain the *selling stockholder has a duty to conduct reasonable investigation of the potential purchaser*. The courts have imposed liability on a controlling stockholder in circumstances in which such stockholder could reasonably foresee that the person acquiring the shares would engage in activities that were clearly damaging to the corporation, such as looting, fraud, or gross mismanagement of the corporation. In planning a sale, a potential seller should fully investigate the potential purchaser's motive, resources, reputation, track record, conflicts of interest, and any other material items relevant to the transaction and the corporation. Note also that under certain circumstances, selling shareholders may be deemed underwriters for the purpose of Rule 145 of the Securities Act.[20]

A second consideration *is the duty of loyalty that a controlling stockholder owes to the minority stockholders.* This duty generally arises when a controlling stockholder is selling shares at a premium. For example, if a corporation owns a large quantity of a product that is in short supply and could be sold at above-market rates, a controlling stockholder may have a fiduciary obligation to refrain from selling shares at a premium on the theory that the shareholder's receipt of the premium would constitute a misappropriation of a corporate opportunity (i.e., the stockholder would be appropriating a certain amount of the corporate goodwill). In addition, some have suggested the imposition of a requirement of "equal opportunity" on a controlling stockholder. Under this requirement, a controlling stockholder must offer all the other stockholders an opportunity to sell the same proportion of their shares as the controlling stockholder. Generally, the courts have refused to apply this unwieldy principle. Accordingly, if a block purchase is challenged, the courts will review the particular facts surrounding the purchase to determine its fairness.

In addition to all the areas already covered, are there any other aspects of federal and state securities laws that may be relevant to mergers?

Insider trading laws are a source of potential liability for insiders of buying and selling companies alike. Since many individuals obtain knowledge of a target company during the time it is being considered for purchase—for example, during the due diligence phase—it is important to ensure that all parties involved have a good sense of *insider trading* law.

INSIDER TRADING

What exactly is insider trading?

Traditionally, insider trading was trading in a company's securities by an insider of the company on the basis of undisclosed material information. Such trading today is prohibited and illegal.

An insider has been defined as an officer, a director, or a principal shareholder (generally, any beneficial owner of more than 10 percent of the company's equity securities).

Also subject to the prohibition on insider trading is any employee who, in the course of his or her employment, acquires material nonpublic information about a publicly traded corporation. Such an individual owes a fiduciary duty to the employer not to appropriate this information for his or her own use and then trade on this information prior to its release and absorption by the market.

In addition, certain "outsiders" may become "temporary insiders" if they are given information by the subject corporation in confidence solely for a corporate purpose. Attorneys, accountants, consultants, and investment bankers are examples of "temporary insiders" who are involved in a merger or acquisition.

Trading on inside information concerning mergers and acquisitions may be closely scrutinized by the SEC and may result in criminal prosecutions and very substantial civil penalties.

What laws prohibit insider trading?

Most insider trading cases are covered by one well-known rule promulgated by the SEC under authority of the Exchange Act: Rule 10b-5 prohibits fraudulent or manipulative conduct in connection with the purchase or sale of securities. (For the full text of Rule 10b-5, see Chapter 1.)

Also, Rule 14e-3 prohibits trading on the basis of inside information in the context of a tender offer, whether as an insider, as the "tippee" of an insider, or anyone merely in possession of the inside information. The Insider Trading Sanctions Act of 1984 and the International Securities Enforcement Cooperation Act of 1989 set penalties for these violations. (See below for a discussion of Rule 14e-3.)

Finally, Section 16(b) of the Exchange Act prohibits any officer or director, or any shareholder owning more than 10 percent of the issuer's stock, from profiting from a purchase and sale or a sale and purchase (a short sale) of securities of the issuer within a six-month period. This is known as the *short-swing profit* rule. Any profits from such a purchase-sale or sale-purchase must be paid to the issuer. The short-swing profit rule applies whether or not that person was in possession of material inside information.

What is the "disclose or abstain" rule and how is it applied?

The "disclose or abstain" rule applies when an insider (or other types of individuals described above) possesses material nonpublic information about a corporation and he or she desires to trade that company's securities based on that information. The individual must either disclose the information to the market or abstain from trading in securities of the affected company. In the famed 1968 *Texas Gulf Sulfur* case, the first federal insider trading prosecution, the U.S. Court of Appeals for the Second Circuit Court in New York ruled that anyone who possesses material inside information must either disclose that information (and trade if desired) or keep the information confidential and refrain from trading.

In practical terms, the "disclose or abstain" rule means *abstain*. To be effective, disclosure of a material development affecting a security must result in dissemination broad enough to inform the entire public trading in that security. Most individuals cannot adequately disseminate such information themselves, and disclosure itself may constitute a breach of fiduciary duty. If the inside information is incomplete or inaccurate, disclosure could be misleading to other investors and result in separate liability under other SEC disclosure rules.

What is the misappropriation theory, and how is it applied?

The misappropriation theory of liability holds that an individual violates the securities laws when he or she secretly converts information received for legitimate business or commercial purposes by trading on the information for personal benefit. The U.S. Supreme Court upheld the misappropriation theory in *United States v. O'Hagan* (1997), when it found an attorney guilty for buying call options in a company (Pillsbury Co.) when he knew that another firm (Grand Metropolitan PLC) was planning to make a hostile bid for it. The court said:

> Although informational disparity is inevitable in the securities markets, investors likely would hesitate to venture their capital in a market where trading based on misappropriated nonpublic information is unchecked by law. An investor's informational disadvantage vis à vis a misappropriator with material, nonpublic information stems from contrivance, not luck; it is a disadvantage that cannot be overcome with research or skill.[21]

What if the recipient of a tip has no fiduciary relationship to the source of confidential information? Can this individual still be charged with insider trading?

First, let us define some basic terms.

- *Tipping* is the selective disclosure of material nonpublic information for trading or other personal purposes.

- A *tipper* is a person who, in return for some direct or indirect benefit, provides material nonpublic information about a security to another person who then trades in that security.

- A *tippee* is a person who receives material nonpublic information
  about a security and then trades in that security. Note that a tippee
  may also become a tipper if he or she divulges the information to
  another person (who becomes a second- or third-level tippee). If the
  tippee knows or should have known of the tipper's breach of duty
  and participates in the violation through silence or inaction, the tippee becomes liable as an aider and abettor if he or she then trades or
  divulges the information to one who trades.

Under Rule 10b-5, a tippee is liable for fraud only if he or she *knew* that
the information received was material nonpublic information. That is, Section
10(b) has a *scienter* requirement. This means that to be found liable for violating Rule 10b-5, an insider must have either "actual knowledge" of the fraud or
omission or have acted with "recklessness and disregard of the truth." Furthermore, judicial interpretation of Rule 10b-5 has often centered on the issue
of fiduciary duty of the tipper to the issuer of the securities or some other
party. Courts have interpreted Rule 10b-5 to prohibit tipping if (1) the tipper
has made a disclosure that breached a fiduciary or fiduciary-like duty that he
or she owed to another, including the issuer or other party. That duty is
breached where the tipper, traditionally an insider, but also potentially a
misappropriator, receives a personal benefit, directly or indirectly, from the
disclosure.

But another key insider trading rule, Rule 14e-3, does *not* contain such a
requirement. Rule 14e-3(a) simply prohibits an individual from trading while
he or she possesses material nonpublic information concerning a tender offer
if the individual knows or has reason to know that such information is
nonpublic and has been obtained, directly or indirectly, from any of the
following: the entity making the tender offer, the corporation that is the
subject of the tender offer, any persons affiliated with these entities, or any
person acting on behalf of either entity. The transfer of such information from
a tipper to a tippee violates this rule.

Rule 14e-3 makes it unlawful for certain persons to "communicate material, non-public information relating to a tender offer . . . under circumstances
in which it is reasonably foreseeable that such communication is likely to result in [improper trading or tipping]." This portion of the rule expressly excludes communications "made in good faith to certain individuals."

Rule 14e-3 is triggered when any person has taken a "substantial step" to
commence a tender offer, even if the offer never actually begins. A "substan-

tial step" includes the offeror's formulating a plan to make an offer; having its directors vote on a resolution with respect to the tender offer; arranging financing for a tender offer; authorizing negotiations for a tender offer; and directing that tender offer materials be prepared.

CONCLUDING COMMENTS

As acquirers study the financial, operational, legal, and transactional aspects of a candidate company, they must be mindful of securities law—particularly federal securities laws pertaining to mergers, acquisitions, and tender offers. In this chapter, we have attempted to provide an overview of such laws. Having mastered these, an acquirer will be in a stronger position to continue checking for legal compliance in a full range of other areas—as explained in the next six chapters.

E N D N O T E S

1. The figures in this section are based on Tillinghast-Towers Perrin, *1999 Directors and Officers Liability Survey: U.S. and Canadian Results* (New York: Tillinghast-Towers Perrin, 2000). Trends cited are for the United States only, unless otherwise noted.

2. For an overview of securities, including noncorporate (government) securities, see Alexandra R. Lajoux and J. Fred Weston, *The Art of M&A Financing: A Guide to Sources and Instruments of Corporate Growth* (New York: McGraw-Hill, 1999), pp. 91–166. Note: This entire chapter draws heavily from a much longer chapter that appears in Stanley Foster Reed and Alexandra Reed Lajoux, *The Art of M&A: A Merger/Acquisition/Buyout Guide* (New York: McGraw-Hill, 1999), pp. 723–798.

3. The original text of the USA has been accepted in 37 jurisdictions—most of which have also adopted the updated text, drafted by the National Conference of Commissioners on Uniform State Laws. For more about USA and the conference, see law.upenn.edu/bll/ulc/fnact99/usa88.htm.

4. The National Conference of Commissioners on Uniform State Laws stated the following in 1988: "While a state which previously has adopted the 1956 Act obviously could choose to update only certain of its law by adopting provisions from one or more Parts above, the Drafting Committee strongly encourages that a state not do so. The revisions encompassed in this Act reflect a conscious effort to carefully balance the various interests involved in state securities regulation."

5. Securities Act rules are numbered from 100 on up (to 236—or 1001 now, if you count shell-type rules "reserved" under Regulation ST for electronic filers). Ex-

change Act rules are numbered from 01 on up (to 36 now), with many subcategories. Exchange Act rules are named after sections. Thus, for example, under Section 10(b) there are rules from 10b-1 on up (to 10b-21 now). Regulations and forms are also named in accordance with sections. Items 1000 to 1016 of new Regulation M-A, as a regulation under both laws, are not part of this number system.

6. *Regulation M-A: Items 1000–1016 Under the Securities Act of 1933 and the Securities Exchange Act of 1934* (New York: Bowne Publishing, November 15, 1999).

7. For a brief description of these new rules, see Release No. 33-7760; 34-42055; IC-24107, dated October 22, 1999, effective January 24, 2000. The full text is available from the SEC or from Bowne Publishing, 800-370-8402. Ask for *Cross-Border Tender and Exchange Officers, Business Combinations and Rights Offerings, and Regulation M-A* (165 pages).

8. A tender offer premium is the "plus factor" in an offer—it is the incremental amount paid for securities in excess of an established market price as of a stated date. Traditionally in academic practice, premiums were measured five days before announcement. This was to prevent distortions in the stock price resulting from trading on the basis of rumors, guesses, or nonpublished inside information (i.e., illegal insider trading). Such trading tends to boost the target's stock price prior to a merger, so premiums—unless measured well in advance—can appear to be smaller than they really are.

9. *Exchange Act Rules, Vol. II: Rules 13a-1 through 15b9-2: General Rules and Regulations Under the Securities Exchange Act of 1934* (New York: Bowne Publishing, November 15, 1999).

10. A tender offer must remain open continuously for at least 20 business days. In addition, a tender offer must remain open for at least 10 business days following an announced increase or decrease in the tender offer price or in the percentage of securities to be bought (Rule 14e-1(b)). If any other change in the tender offer terms is made, the offeror should keep the offer open for five business days to allow dissemination of the new information in a manner reasonably designed to inform shareholders of such changes. The offering period may be extended, but the buyer must announce the extension not later than 9:00 A.M. on the business day following the day on which the tender offer expires (Rule 14e-1(d)).

    Shareholders who tender shares may withdraw them at any time during the tender-offer period unless the shares are actually purchased (Rule 14d-7(a)).Tendered shares may also be withdrawn at any time after 60 days from the date of the original tender offer if those shares have not yet been purchased by the bidder (Section 14d-5).

11. A two-step approach is not the same thing as a two-tier offer, in which the bidder, generally a hostile one, sets a deadline for an initial, high price. Those who sell their stock to the bidder after the deadline get a second, lower price. This technique was popular in the 1980s, but it has met with legal challenges (e.g.,

the 1991 decision in *USX v. Marathon,* a case that originated in 1982) and has become relatively rare.

12. In the stock lockup, the bidder receives an option to purchase authorized but unissued shares. This option favors the bidder in two ways: If the option is exercised, either the bidder may vote the shares in favor of the transaction or, if another bidder wins the contract for the company, the favored bidder may realize a profit by tendering the stock to the higher bidder. If the purpose of the lockup agreement is to stifle competitive bidding by definitively preferring one bidder over another, however, the board will likely be found to have breached its duty of loyalty to the shareholders. See *Revlon, Inc. v. MacAndrews & Forbes Holdings* (1986).

13. The dealer-manager is mostly involved in deal making, not due diligence. Its activities include soliciting large stockholders, communicating with the financial community, and assisting the buyer in accumulating a significant stock position before beginning the actual tender offer.

14. Other members of the team are not generally involved in due diligence. These deal participants include a shareholder solicitation firm that will arrange for delivery of tender offer materials and will contact shareholders to solicit their shares, a depository bank that will receive and pay for tendered securities, a forwarding agent that will receive shares as an agent for tendering stockholders, and a financial printer with the ability to prepare tender offer documents quickly and confidentially.

15. This requirement is somewhat relaxed for certain institutional investors whose purchases are made in the ordinary course of their business without the purpose or effect of changing or influencing the control of the issuer, and for investors that owned their shares prior to the time that the company became subject to the Exchange Act. Such investors need only file a Schedule 13G, which is a substantially shorter form than Schedule 13D, 45 days after the end of the calendar year in which the threshold ownership interest was acquired. If, however, such an institutional security holder changes its intention and decides to influence control of the company, it must file a Schedule 13D within 10 days of making that decision. During the 10-day period, the shares already owned may not be voted, and the owner may not buy any additional shares of the target company. A Schedule 13D must be amended "promptly" upon the occurrence of any "material change" in the information contained in the original Schedule 13D.

16. "Unorthodox" transactions—such as option transactions, stock conversions and reclassifications, and mergers of a target into a white knight and other corporate reorganizations—are frequently judged by a pragmatic or subjective test that may enable an insider to avoid liability when the automatic rules of Section 16(b) might otherwise apply. Under this alternative test, liability may be avoided if the insider did not have access to inside information or if the insider did not have a control relationship with the issuer of the securities.

17. See Dennis J. Block, Nancy L. Barton, and Stephen A. Radin, *The Business Judgment Rule: Fiduciary Duties of Corporate Directors* (New York: Aspen Law and Business, 1998), pp. 631–1202.

18. Topping fees, which were very common in the mid-to-late 1980s, are agreements with the target to compensate the buyer for potential losses if a new bidder usurps the deal. Because these fees are liabilities of the target, the winning bidder will have to bear their economic burden. This burden has the effect of increasing the cost of, and thus discouraging, other bids. Another arrangement is for the payment of bustup or breakup fees if the transaction is terminated by the target (other than for cause).

19. A no-shop agreement is a provision either in the acquisition contract or in a letter of intent that prohibits the board of directors from soliciting or encouraging other bids. It is always found in private company acquisition agreements and, far more often than not, in the acquisition agreement for public company transactions.

20. If a merger or acquisition involves the issuance of securities to the target's shareholders, such securities may not be resold freely, but may be restricted. Rule 145 of the Securities Act states that any party to a merger or acquisition transaction receiving securities is deemed to be engaged in a distribution and therefore to be an underwriter. Because of this "underwriter" status, it is necessary to use a Form S-4 registration statement to register securities issued to the target's shareholders. This form is basically a wraparound of the proxy statement and permits noncontrolling shareholders of the target to sell without restriction. Control persons or "affiliates" must sell, however, either under the registration statement or in accordance with restrictions in Rule 144 under the Securities Act.

21. *United States v. O'Hagan*, 117 S. Ct. 2199, 138 L Ed. 2d 724 (1997).

Detecting Exposure Under Tax Law and Accounting Regulations

Render therefore unto Caesar the things which are Caesar's . . .

Matthew 22:21

INTRODUCTION

After a century and a half of existence, the power of Congress to tax individuals and enterprises is still alive and well—and affecting M&A due diligence. Buyers, sellers, and their advisers inevitably consult the Internal Revenue Code (Title 26 of the U.S. Code)[1] when structuring their transactions. They know that it is important to ensure compliance with the tax code sooner rather than later. During the due diligence stage, buyers and sellers can benefit from understanding the tax and accounting aspects of transaction structure.[2]

Chapter 6 offered guidance on securities laws pertaining to mergers in order to minimize chances of postmerger litigation from shareholders. In this chapter, we will continue the transaction-oriented discussion by advising readers of major tax law and accounting regulations relevant to M&A, and therefore to due diligence. After all, the aim of due diligence is to reduce postmerger exposure to insolvency or liability—and knowing tax and accounting regulations can help in this regard.

In this chapter, we define basic tax terms, and go on to explain the tax consequences of transaction structure, choice of entity, and financing. In closing, we explain some postmerger tax issues, as well as other issues of general interest.

Frankly, we have intentionally taken a superficial approach here— touching only the most general tax topics. We have refrained from providing details on particular sections of the tax code or on the many pronouncements of the Financial Accounting Standards Board (FASB). Our aim is to provide a high-level overview. Adding too many details only distracts from that purpose.

This is an extremely complex area. Here are some estimates based on more precise figures from the Heritage Foundation in Washington, D.C. (heritage.org). From 1954 to the present, the number of tax code sections has increased more than fivefold,[3] and the tax code was amended nearly 1,000 times. Between 1986 and the present, there have been 5,400 *cumulative* changes to the tax law (where one change prompted others).

Given this high rate of change, even the specialists cannot hope to have complete knowledge in this area. We have made every attempt to be accurate here, but *always* consult with qualified M&A tax and accounting professionals. If dealing with a major accounting firm or law firm, remember that nearly every local office has M&A specialists. Use them! Your due diligence efforts will improve as a result.

TAX BASICS

What is the principal regulator in the taxation of companies involved in mergers and acquisitions?

The chief regulator here is the Internal Revenue Service (IRS), which is part of the U.S. Treasury Department. The IRS charter reads, in part, as follows:

> Responsibility: administer and enforce the internal revenue laws and related statutes, except those relating to alcohol, tobacco, firearms, and explosives.[4] Its mission is to collect the proper amount of tax revenue at the least cost to the public, and in a manner that warrants the highest degree of public confidence in the Service's integrity, efficiency, and fairness.

The IRS does not get involved in transactions. Unlike federal agencies such as the Federal Communications Commission and the Federal Trade Commission, the IRS does not need to give advance approval of a transaction. In fact, ordinarily, the IRS will not have occasion to review a transaction, unless and until an agent audits the tax return of one of the participants.

One exception to this rule is that the parties to a transaction can often obtain a private letter ruling issued by the National Office of the IRS. Such a ruling states the agency's position with respect to the issues raised and is generally binding upon the IRS. Requesting such a ruling is a serious business and should never be undertaken without expert legal help.

What are the principal goals of tax planning for a merger, acquisition, or divestiture?

From the acquirer's point of view, the principal goal of tax planning is to minimize, on a present value basis, the total tax costs of not only acquiring but also operating and even selling another corporation or its assets. In addition, effective tax planning provides various safeguards to protect the parties from the risks of potential changes in circumstance or the tax laws. Moreover, the acquirer should attempt to minimize the tax costs of the transaction to the seller in order to gain advantage as a bidder.

From the seller's point of view, the principal goal of tax planning is to maximize, on a present value basis, the after-tax proceeds from the sale of the corporation or its assets. This tax planning includes, among other things, determining the structure of the transaction and the entities involved in it, developing techniques to provide tax benefits to a potential buyer at little or no tax cost to the seller, and structuring the seller's receipt of tax-deferred consideration from the buyer.

More often than not, the most advantageous tax plan for the buyer is the least advantageous plan for the seller. For example, the tax benefit of a high basis in the assets of the acquired corporation may be available to the acquirer only at a significant tax cost to the seller. But buyers rarely if ever pursue tax benefits at the seller's expense, because the immediate and prospective tax costs of a transaction are likely to affect the price. Generally, the parties will structure the transaction to minimize the aggregate tax costs of the seller and buyer, and allocate the tax burden between them through an adjustment in price.

What tax issues typically arise in an acquisition or divestiture?

There is no definitive checklist of tax issues that may arise in every acquisition or divestiture. The specific tax considerations for a transaction depend upon the facts and circumstances of that particular deal. However, certain tax terms and issues, many of which are interrelated, are far more common than others.

To engage in any useful discussion of tax matters, participants in any transaction must grasp the *definitions of basic tax terms* used in M&A. A primary issue is the *basic structure of the transaction:* whether the transfer is effected as a stock acquisition, an asset acquisition, or a merger. The optimal structure is generally that which maximizes the aggregate tax benefits and minimizes the aggregate tax costs of the transaction to the acquired corporation, the seller, and the buyer. Key issues include net operating loss, credit carrybacks and carryforwards, amortization of goodwill, and the alternative minimum tax.

Another initial question to be resolved in many acquisitions is the *choice of entity* issue: whether the operating entity will be a C corporation, an S corporation, or a general or limited partnership. The tax implications of the *financing arrangement* must also be analyzed. Two key issues are the debt/equity distinction and the effect of the original issue discount rules.

Managers and advisers should also give attention to *other tax matters*, including the effects of state tax laws, the tax consequences of future distributions of the acquired company's earnings, and the ultimate *disposition* of the acquired corporation or its assets. Finally, deal makers should be aware of *accounting issues* related to taxation.

This chapter will cover each of these issues in order.

DEFINITIONS OF TAX TERMS

What are earnings and profits?

Earnings and profits is a term of art in the Internal Revenue Code. The amount of a corporation's earnings and profits is roughly equivalent to a corporation's net income and retained earnings for financial reporting purposes, as distinguished from current or accumulated taxable income. The primary purpose of the earnings and profits concept is to measure the capacity of a corporation to distribute a taxable dividend. If the IRS believes that a corporation, by virtue of its current and accumulated earnings and profits, *can* pay a taxable dividend, it may view certain "nonliquidating distributions" as dividends and tax them as such.

What is a distribution?

A corporate distribution means an actual or constructive transfer of cash or other property (with certain exceptions) by a corporation to a shareholder acting in the capacity of a shareholder. For tax purposes, a transfer of property to a shareholder acting in the capacity of an employee or lender, for example, is not a corporate distribution. This has special implications in employee stock ownership plans (ESOPs) or management buyouts (MBOs).[5]

What is a liquidation?

Corporate liquidation occurs when a corporation ceases to be a going concern. At this point, its actions are limited to winding up its affairs, paying its debts, and distributing its remaining assets to its shareholders. A liquidation for tax purposes may be completed prior to the actual dissolution of the corporation under state law.

What is a liquidating distribution?

A liquidating distribution is generally a distribution (or one of a series of distributions) made by a liquidating corporation in accordance with a plan of complete liquidation.

What is a nonliquidating distribution?

A nonliquidating distribution is any corporate distribution to shareholders that is not a liquidating distribution. A nonliquidating distribution is generally either a dividend or a distribution in redemption of some (but not all) of the corporation's outstanding stock.

What are the tax consequences to corporations of distributions of property to their shareholders?

The taxation of corporate distributions involves myriad complex rules, many with exceptions and qualifications. In general, however, the tax consequences to corporations of distributions of property depend upon three factors: (1) whether the property distributed is cash or property other than cash, (2) whether the recipient shareholder is an affiliated corporation (see below), and (3) whether the distribution is a liquidating or nonliquidating distribution.

Distributions of cash, both liquidating and nonliquidating, generally have no tax consequences to the distributing corporation, except that the amount distributed reduces the corporation's earnings and profits.

Distributions of appreciated property, both liquidating and nonliquidating, generally trigger the recognition of gain to the distributing corporation to the extent of the appreciation in the asset.

What is an affiliated corporation?

An affiliated corporation is one of a group of corporations consisting of two or more "member" corporations where the "parent" corporation controls, directly or indirectly, the stock of each of the "subsidiary" corporations. More precisely, the parent corporation must generally own a certain percentage (usually 80 percent) of the voting power and equity value of at least one of the subsidiary corporations. Other members of the group have similar ownership levels in the other subsidiaries. Certain corporations, such as foreign corporations, are not permitted to be members of an affiliated group.

What is a consolidated federal income tax return?

A consolidated return is a single federal income tax return made by an affiliated group of corporations in lieu of a separate return for each member of the group.

What are the advantages of filing consolidated federal income tax returns?

The principal advantages of a consolidated return are as follows:

- Losses incurred by one member of the group may be used to offset the taxable income of another member.
- The tax consequences of many intragroup transactions are either deferred or wholly eliminated.
- Earnings of a subsidiary corporation are reflected in the parent's basis in the stock of the subsidiary, so that such earnings are not taxed again on the sale of such stock by the parent.

Is there such a thing as a consolidated state income tax return?

Yes, but not all states allow an affiliated group of corporations to file a combined (consolidated) tax return. Some states do not allow combined returns at all; others allow them only in limited circumstances.

What is a tax year?

Every individual and entity that is required to file a tax return must do so on the basis of an annual accounting period. For individuals the annual accounting period is almost always the calendar year. For other entities, however, the tax accounting period may be either a calendar year or a fiscal year ending on the last day of a month other than December. An entity's tax year need not coincide with its fiscal year for purposes of financial accounting. Extensive rules govern the selection of tax years other than calendar years by

C corporations, S corporations, partnerships, and trusts. (These entities are discussed below in the section on choice of entity).

What is the current U.S. federal income tax rate structure?

The Taxpayer Relief Act of 1997 preserved corporate tax rates. These are still 34 percent for businesses with taxable income of up to $10 million, and 35 percent for larger companies (plus a surtax on taxable income above $15 million). Capital gains are still taxable at 28 percent, with exceptions in both directions.[6]

Is the distinction between capital gains and ordinary income still relevant in tax planning?

Yes. In its most recent tax bills, Congress retained the myriad rules and complexities in the Internal Revenue Code pertaining to capital gains and losses. More important for tax planning is that the tax code retains various limitations on the use of capital losses to offset ordinary income. So M&A planners must still pay attention to the characterization of income or loss as capital or ordinary.

What is the significance of the relationship between the corporate and individual tax rates?

Corporations can be used to accumulate profits when the tax rate on the income of corporations is less than the tax rate on the income of individuals. (Offsetting this benefit is the "double tax" on corporate earnings—paid once by the company and then by the stockholders receiving the company's dividends.) Conversely, noncorporate "pass-through" entities can be used to store profits when the tax rate on the income of corporations is greater than the tax rate on the income of individuals.

How does the capital gains tax fit in?

A shareholder's tax on the sale or liquidation of his or her interest in the corporation is determined at preferential capital gains rates.

How does the double tax on corporate earnings work?

The Internal Revenue Code sets forth a dual system of taxation with respect to the earnings of corporations. Under this system, a corporation is taxed as a separate entity, unaffected by the tax characteristics of its shareholders. The corporation's shareholders are subject to tax on their income from the corporation, if and when corporate earnings are distributed to them in any form.

What are the practical consequences of the dual system of corporate taxation?

The primary consequence of the dual system of taxation is that corporate earnings are generally taxed twice—first at the corporate level and again at the shareholder level. The shareholder-level tax may be deferred but not eliminated when the corporation retains its earnings rather than paying them out in dividends. The shareholders will pay a second level of tax when they sell their interests in the corporation.

How can leverage reduce the effects of double taxation?

A leveraged company's capital structure is tilted toward debt instead of equity. Leverage reduces or eliminates the negative effect of double taxation of corporations in two ways. First, unlike dividend payments to shareholders, which are generally taxable,[7] debt repayments to lenders are not generally taxable to the recipient. Second, in most cases, interest payments are tax-deductible to the corporation making them.[8] It is very important to remember, however, that the Internal Revenue Service may take the position that a purported debt is actually equity, thus eliminating the benefit of leverage.

What is the alternative minimum tax, or AMT?

The alternative minimum tax was enacted in 1969 to curb exploitation of deductions and preferences by certain high-income individuals and corporations. In later tax legislation, Congress amended the minimum tax provisions and created a rather severe regime of alternative minimum tax, particularly for corporations. The alternative minimum tax for both individuals and corporations is determined by computing taxable income under the regular method (with certain adjustments), and adding back certain deductions or "preferences" to obtain alternative minimum taxable income. To this amount is applied the alternative minimum tax rate for individuals or for corporations. The taxpayer is required to pay the greater of the regular tax or the alternative minimum tax. The 1997 tax law repealed the alternative minimum tax for small businesses for taxable years beginning after December 31, 1997.[9] For the purpose of the new law, a small business is a corporation that had average annual income of less than $5 million in its first taxable year after December 31, 1996, and less than $7.5 million for taxable years thereafter.

BASIC STRUCTURE OF THE TRANSACTION

What are the various forms that a transaction can take?

There are three general forms used for the acquisition of a business: (1) a purchase of the *assets* of the business, (2) a purchase of the *stock* of the company owning the assets, and (3) a *statutory merger* of the buyer (or an affiliate) with the asset-owning company.

It is possible to combine several forms so that, for example, some assets of the business are purchased separately from the stock of the company that owns the rest of the assets, and a merger occurs immediately thereafter between the buyer and the acquired company. Or a transaction may involve the purchase of assets of one corporation and the stock of another, where both corporations are owned by the same seller.

What happens in an asset transaction, and what are the reasons for this type of deal?

In an asset transaction, the seller transfers all the assets used in the business that is the subject of the sale. These include real estate, equipment, and inventory, as well as "intangible" assets such as contract rights, leases, patents, and trademarks. These may be all or only part of the assets owned by the selling company. The seller executes the specific kinds of documents (e.g., deeds, bills of sale, and assignment) needed to transfer the assets in question.

Many times, the choice of an asset transaction is dictated by the fact that the sale involves only part of the business owned by the selling corporation. Asset sales are the only way to go in the sale of a product line that has not been run as a subsidiary corporation with its own set of books and records.

In other cases, an asset deal is not necessary but is chosen because of its special advantages.

- An asset sale is preferable when the seller will realize taxable gain from the sale—that is, when the tax basis of the assets in the acquired company is lower than the selling price. In such a case, the buyer generally will obtain significant tax savings from structuring the transaction as an asset deal, thus "stepping up" the asset basis to the purchase price. Conversely, if the seller will realize a tax loss, the buyer is generally better off inheriting the tax history of the business by doing a stock transaction, and thus keeping the old high basis.

- In an asset sale, with some exceptions (explained in Chapter 5), the buyer generally assumes only the financial liabilities that it specifically agrees to assume.

What happens in a stock transaction, and what are the reasons for this type of arrangement?

In a stock transaction, the seller transfers its shares in a corporation to the buyer in exchange for an agreed-upon payment. Usually all shares are transferred, with some exceptions.[10]

A stock transaction is appropriate whenever the tax costs or other problems in an asset transaction make the transaction undesirable. As mentioned in Chapter 5, asset transfers may have a high tax cost, and can impose the administrative hassle of obtaining third-party consents for the asset transfer (often unnecessary in a stock deal).[11]

There are two major disadvantages of a simple stock deal, however.

First, it may be more difficult to consummate the transaction if there are a number of stockholders. Assuming that the buyer wants to acquire 100 percent of the company, it must enter into a contract with each of the selling stockholders, and any one of them might refuse to enter into the transaction or might refuse to close. The entire deal may hinge on one stockholder. As will be shown below, the parties can achieve the same result as a stock transfer through a merger transaction and avoid the need for 100 percent agreement among the stockholders.

Second, the stock transaction may result in tax disadvantages after the acquisition—disadvantages that can be avoided by choosing an asset transaction. Under Section 338 of the Internal Revenue Code, however, it is possible to have most stock transactions treated as asset acquisitions for federal income tax purposes. Under a so-called Section 338 election, the tax benefits can be achieved while avoiding the nontax pitfalls of an asset transaction.

What happens in a merger transaction, and what are the reasons for this kind of deal?

A merger is a transaction in which one corporation is legally absorbed into another, and the surviving corporation succeeds to all the assets or liabilities of the absorbed corporation. There are no separate transfers for the assets or liabilities; the entire transfer occurs by operation of law when the certificate of merger is filed with the appropriate authorities of the state.

In a *reverse merger* the buyer is absorbed by the company it is buying. The shareholders of the buyer get stock in the company, and the shareholders of the acquired company receive the consideration agreed to. For example, in an all-cash deal, the shareholders of the acquired company will exchange their shares in the company for cash. At the end of the day, the old shareholders of the acquired company are no longer shareholders, and the shareholders of the buyer own the company. For federal tax purposes, a reverse merger is often treated essentially like a stock deal.

In a *forward merger* the acquired firm merges into the acquirer's company, and the acquired company's shareholders exchange their stock for the agreed-upon purchase price. When the dust settles, the buyer has succeeded to all the assets and liabilities of the acquired firm. For federal income tax purposes, such a transaction is treated as if the acquired firm sold its assets for the purchase price, and then liquidated and distributed the sales proceeds to its shareholders as a liquidation distribution.[12]

In a *subsidiary merger* the buyer corporation simply incorporates an acquisition subsidiary that merges with the acquired company. Such a transaction must be approved by a majority of shareholders of the firm owning the subsidiary, and by the board of directors (not the shareholders) of the successor firm. In a *forward* subsidiary merger, the acquired company is merged into the acquisition subsidiary, which may function as a holding company.[13] In a *reverse* subsidiary merger, the acquisition subsidiary merges into the acquired company. This allows the owner of the successor firm to avoid asset transfer problems while still treating the transaction as an asset deal for taxation purposes, thanks to Section 338.

The agreement between buyer and seller in the case of any merger is essentially the same as in a stock or asset deal, except that the means of transferring the business will be the statutory merger as opposed to an asset or stock transfer. Thus, a merger helps buyers avoid the inconveniences of asset or stock transfers—and the permissions each entails.

To effect a statutory merger, the board of directors of each corporation that is a party to the merger must adopt a resolution approving an agreement of merger. Shareholders owning a majority of the stock must also approve the transaction.[14] In some cases the corporate charter may require a higher percentage ("supermajority," such as 75 percent) of shareholder approval. The merger becomes effective upon the filing of a certificate of merger.

How can a stock acquisition be combined with a merger?

This is the two-step transaction described in Chapter 6. To recap, the first step is an acquisition of part of the stock (usually at least a statutorily sufficient majority) of the acquired company; the second step is a merger. As explained in Chapter 6, two-step transactions are very common in public company acquisitions where the first step is the acquisition of a control block through a tender offer and the second step is a merger in which the minority is bought out.

How does an asset acquisition differ from a stock acquisition with respect to taxes?

The primary tax distinction between an asset acquisition and a stock acquisition concerns the acquirer's *basis* in the assets acquired.

A taxpayer's basis in an asset is the value at which the taxpayer carries the asset on its tax balance sheet. An asset's basis is initially its historical cost to the taxpayer. This *initial basis* is subsequently increased by capital expenditures and decreased by depreciation, amortization, and other charges, becoming the taxpayer's *adjusted basis* in the asset. Upon the sale or exchange of the asset, gain or loss for tax purposes is measured by the difference between the amount realized for the asset and its adjusted basis.

The basis of the asset represents, in effect, the amount at which the cost of the asset may be recovered free of tax through depreciation, deductions, and adjustments to gain or loss upon disposition.

When an acquirer directly acquires the assets of a corporation, and the corporation is subject to tax on the sale or exchange of the assets, the basis of the assets to the acquirer is their cost. This is called *cost basis*. When an acquirer indirectly acquires a corporation's assets through the acquisition of stock, the basis of the assets in the possession of the acquired corporation is generally not affected. This is called *carryover basis* because the basis of an asset in the acquired corporation "carries over" on the change of stock ownership.

A cost basis transaction is often referred to as an "asset acquisition," and a carryover basis transaction is often referred to as a "stock acquisition." Neither of these terms necessarily reflects the actual structure of the transaction.

Are there any other significant tax differences between a cost basis, or "asset," transaction and a carryover basis, or "stock," transaction?

Yes. In a carryover basis transaction, the acquirer acquires, by operation of law, the corporation's tax attributes—net operating loss carryovers, business credit carryovers, earnings and profits, accounting methods, and others—each of which may be either beneficial or detrimental to the acquirer. The most beneficial tax attributes, however, are generally subject to various limitations that are triggered upon a significant change of stock ownership of the acquired corporation. In all cost basis transactions, the acquirer acquires the assets of a corporation without the corporation's tax attributes.

What types of transactions are carryover basis, or "stock," transactions?

As a rule, a carryover basis, or stock, acquisition includes any transaction in which the stock or assets of a corporation are acquired by the acquirer and the bases of the assets of the corporation are not increased or decreased on the change of ownership. There are several types of carryover basis transactions. The direct purchase of the corporation stock in exchange for cash and debt is the most straightforward stock acquisition. Another transaction that is treated as a sale of stock for tax purposes is the merger of the acquiring corporation into the acquired corporation—a reverse merger—in which the shareholders of the corporation relinquish their shares in exchange for cash or debt in a fully taxable transaction. Another common stock transaction is the acquisition of the stock or assets of a corporation in a transaction free of tax to its exchanging shareholders.

What types of transactions are cost basis, or "asset," transactions?

As a rule, a cost basis, or asset, acquisition includes any transaction in which the preacquisition gains and losses inherent in the assets acquired are triggered and recognized by the acquired corporation. There are several types of cost basis transactions. The direct purchase of the assets from the acquired corporation in exchange for cash or indebtedness is the quintessential asset acquisition. Another common asset transaction is the statutory merger of the acquired corporation into an acquiring corporation—a forward cash merger—in which the shareholders of the acquired corporation exchange their shares for cash or other property in a fully taxable transaction. In certain circumstances, a corporation may acquire the stock of another corporation and elect under Section 338 of the tax code to treat the stock acquisition, for tax purposes, as an asset acquisition.

What is the significance to the acquirer of the basis of the assets in an acquired corporation?

The basis of the assets in an acquired corporation may have a significant and continuing effect on the tax liabilities and, therefore, the cash flow of either the acquirer or the acquired corporation. The basis of an asset represents the extent to which the asset may be depreciated or amortized (if at all), thereby generating noncash reductions of taxable income. Basis also represents the extent to which the consideration received in a taxable sale or exchange of an asset may be received by the seller free of tax.

What is the prospective cost basis of an asset to the acquirer?

The prospective cost basis of an asset to the acquirer is the price that it will pay for the asset, directly or indirectly, which is presumed to be its fair market value.

What is the prospective carryover basis of an asset to the acquirer?

The prospective carryover basis of an asset to the acquirer is simply the "adjusted basis" of the asset in the possession of the acquired corporation prior to its acquisition. As explained above, the adjusted basis of an asset is generally its historical or initial cost, reduced or "adjusted" by subsequent depreciation or amortization deductions.

You mentioned earlier that a "step-up" might be necessary in an asset purchase. What is this about?

When the basis of an asset is increased from the acquired corporation's lower initial basis (or adjusted basis, if different) to a basis determined by an acquirer's cost or fair market value, the basis of the asset is said to have been "stepped up." The term may refer, however, to any transaction in which the basis of an asset is increased. In most asset, or cost basis, transactions, the basis of the assets of the acquired corporation is stepped up to the acquirer's cost. An acquisition in which the basis of the assets of the acquired corporation is increased is referred to as a *step-up transaction*.

Who benefits from a step-up?

Generally, the buyer. High tax basis in an asset is always more beneficial to its owner than low basis. The higher the basis, the greater the depreciation or amortization deductions (if allowable), and the less the gain (or the greater the loss) on the subsequent disposition of the asset. An increase in these deductions and losses will reduce the tax liabilities of the acquirer or the acquired corporation during the holding period of the assets, thereby increasing after-tax cash flow.

Will an acquirer's cost basis in an asset generally be greater than its carryover basis?

Yes. When an asset has appreciated in value, or when the economic depreciation of an asset is less than the depreciation or amortization deductions allowed for tax purposes, an acquirer's prospective cost basis in the asset will exceed its prospective carryover basis. The depreciation and amortization deductions allowed for tax purposes for most types of property are designed to exceed the actual economic depreciation of the property. As a result, the fair market value of most assets, which represents the prospective cost basis of the asset to an acquirer, generally exceeds the adjusted tax basis. The aggregate difference between the acquirer's prospective cost and carryover bases of the acquired corporation's assets is often substantial.

Will an acquirer generally receive greater tax benefits by acquiring a corporation through a cost basis transaction than through a carryover basis transaction?

Yes. An acquirer in a cost basis acquisition of a corporation will generally acquire a basis in the corporation's assets that is higher than the basis in a carryover basis transaction. This is because the cost or fair market value of the corporation's assets is generally greater than the adjusted basis of the assets prior to the acquisition. In that circumstance, a cost basis transaction will "step up" the basis of the assets of the acquired corporation. The amount of the increase in basis—the excess of cost basis over carryover basis—is referred to as the *step-up amount.*

Do all asset, or cost basis, transactions step up the bases of the acquired firm's assets?

No. When the purchase price of the assets of the acquired corporation, which is presumed to equal their fair market value, is less than the carryover basis of the assets, a cost basis, or asset, transaction will result in a net reduction of basis. In such cases, the transaction should generally be structured as a carryover basis, or stock, acquisition.

In what circumstances are carryover basis transactions more beneficial to an acquirer, from a tax standpoint, than cost basis transactions?

There are two situations in which a carryover basis, or stock, transaction may be more beneficial to the acquirer than a cost basis, or asset, acquisition. In the first situation the carryover basis of the acquired corporation's assets to the acquirer exceeds their cost basis. This excess represents potential tax benefits to the acquirer—noncash depreciation deductions or taxable losses—without a corresponding economic loss. That is, the tax deductions or losses from owning the assets may exceed the price paid for such assets. In the second situation the acquired corporation possesses valuable tax attributes—net operating loss carryovers, business tax credit carryovers, or accounting methods, for example—that would inure to the benefit of the acquirer. Situations in which carryover basis transactions are preferable to the acquirer over cost basis transactions, however, are more the exception than the rule.

What are loss carryovers and carrybacks?

If a taxpayer has an excess of tax deductions over its taxable income in a given year, this excess becomes a net operating loss of the taxpayer. Section 172 of the tax code allows that taxpayer to use its net operating loss (NOL) to offset taxable income in subsequent years (a carryover or carryforward) or to offset taxable income in earlier years (a carryback). For most taxpayers an NOL may be carried back for up to two taxable years and may be carried forward for up to 20 years.[15] Generally speaking, each state has its own NOL carryback and carryforward rules, which may not necessarily match the federal rules.

What role do loss carryovers play in mergers and acquisitions?

As stated earlier, a potential advantage in carryover basis acquisitions—both taxable stock purchases and tax-free reorganizations—is the carryover of basis and of favorable tax attributes in the hands of the buyer. To the extent that a buyer can acquire an acquired corporation and retain favorable NOL carryovers, it can increase the after-tax cash flow generated by the activities of the acquired company and, to some extent, use those losses to offset tax liability generated by the buyer's own operations.

What is the accounting treatment of net operating losses?

Statement No. 109, issued by the Financial Accounting Standards Board (FASB) in 1992, mandates recognition of the tax consequences of a transaction or an event in the same period that the transaction or event is recognized in the enterprise's financial statements. Under FAS No. 109, for example, deferred tax liabilities are recognized for future taxable amounts and deferred tax assets are recognized for future deductions and operating loss and tax credit carryforwards, and the liabilities and assets are then measured using the applicable tax rate.

What are the tax consequences of a cost basis, or asset, acquisition to the acquired corporation?

The general rule is that the basis of an asset in the possession of an acquired corporation may not be stepped up to cost or fair market value without the recognition of taxable gain to the corporation. In a cost basis transaction, the acquired company will generally be subject to an immediate tax on an amount equal to the aggregate step-up in the bases of the assets. In addition, the sale or exchange of an asset may trigger the recapture of investment or business tax credits previously taken by the acquired corporation on the acquisition of the asset.

What are the tax consequences of a cost basis, or asset, acquisition to the shareholders of the acquired corporation?

The shareholders of the acquired corporation will be subject to tax upon the receipt of the asset sales proceeds (net of the corporate level tax) from the acquired corporation. This is so whether the proceeds are distributed in the form of a dividend, in redemption of the shareholders' stock in the acquired company, or in complete liquidation of the acquired corporation. If the asset sales proceeds are retained by the acquired corporation, then the value of those proceeds is indirectly taxed to the shareholders upon the sale or exchange of the stock of the acquired corporation.

In what circumstances will an acquired corporation and its shareholders be subject to double tax on a cost basis, or asset, acquisition?

The corporation and its shareholders will typically be subject to double tax when (1) the acquired corporation sells its assets to the acquirer in a taxable transaction, (2) the shareholders of the acquired corporation will ultimately receive the proceeds of the sale, and (3) the receipt of the proceeds by the shareholders of the acquired corporation will be taxable to them. The cost basis transaction in these circumstances generally causes the proceeds of the sale to be taxed twice, first to the corporation and again to its shareholders.[16]

On balance, which type of structure is preferable: a stock acquisition or an asset acquisition?

Generally, a stock, or carryover basis, acquisition is preferable to an asset, or cost basis, acquisition. The immediate tax cost to the acquired corporation and its shareholders on the basis step-up amount of asset acquisition is generally greater than the present value of the tax benefits to the acquirer.

Under what circumstances does a cost basis, or asset, acquisition transaction make better sense for tax purposes?

An asset, or cost basis, transaction is generally advisable for tax purposes in situations where the double tax burden to the seller can be partially or wholly avoided, and in situations where double tax is inevitable regardless of the structure. When double tax is unavoidable, the seller can postpone the recognition of gain via an installment sale or via a tax-free or partially tax-free acquisition.

What is an installment sale?

An installment sale is a disposition of property (by a person who is not a "dealer" in such property) where at least one payment is to be received after the close of the taxable year in which the sale occurs. Basically, an installment sale is a sale or exchange for a promissory note or other debt instrument of the buyer. In the case of an installment sale, the gain on the sale is recognized, pro rata, whenever principal payments on the note are received or, if earlier, upon a disposition of the installment obligation.

For example, if A sells property to B for a note with a principal amount of $100 and A's basis in the property was $60, A realizes a gain of $40. Since the ratio of the gain recognized ($40) to the total amount realized ($100) is 40, this percentage of each principal payment received by A will be treated as taxable gain. The other $60 will be treated as a nontaxable return of capital.

What kinds of transactions are eligible for installment sale treatment?

The installment method is generally available for sales of any property other than installment obligations held by a seller, and other than inventory and property sold by dealers in the subject property. Subject to certain exceptions, installment treatment is generally available to a shareholder who sells his or her stock or to a corporation or other entity that sells its assets. Installment treatment is not available for sales of stock or securities that are traded on an established securities market.

What are the tax consequences of a typical tax-free reorganization?

In the classic tax-free acquisition, the Parks own all the stock of Mom and Pop Grocery, Inc. (Grocery), which is acquired by Supermarkets, Inc. (Supermarkets). In the transaction, the Parks surrender to Supermarkets all their stock in Grocery solely in exchange for voting stock of Supermarkets. This is a fully tax-free B reorganization, in which the Parks recognize no immediate gain or loss.

The corollaries to tax-free treatment here as elsewhere are carryover and substituted basis and holding period. In other words, the Parks obtain a basis in their Supermarkets stock equal to their basis in the Grocery stock surrendered (substituted basis) and continue their old holding period in the stock. Similarly, Supermarkets takes a basis in the Grocery stock acquired equal to the Parks' basis (carryover basis) and also picks up the Parks' holding period.

What are the advantages of tax-free transactions to sellers and buyers?

By participating in a tax-free transaction, the seller is provided the opportunity to exchange its own company's stock for stock of the buyer without the immediate recognition of gain. Because the seller will have a basis in the buyer's stock that is the same as the seller's old basis in the acquired corporation stock (a "substituted basis"), tax is deferred only until the acquired corporation stock is ultimately sold. When the acquired corporation is closely held and the buyer is publicly held, the seller may obtain greatly enhanced liquidity without a current tax.

For the buyer, there are two principal advantages to a tax-free acquisition. First, when the buyer is able to use its stock in the transaction, the corporation can be acquired without the incurrence of significant debt. When equity financing in general is attractive from a buyer's point of view, it will often make sense to do so in a business acquisition. Second, although subject to certain limitations, the acquired corporation's tax attributes (including net operating loss carryovers) will remain usable after the acquisition.

What kinds of transactions may qualify for tax-free treatment?

Every transaction involving an exchange of property is taxable unless otherwise specified in the Internal Revenue Code. Thus, corporate acquisitions are generally taxable to the seller of stock or assets. However, several types of acquisition transactions may be tax-free to the seller, but only to the extent that the seller receives stock in the acquiring corporation (or in certain corporations closely affiliated with the acquiring corporation).

In general, tax-free acquisitions fall into three categories: statutory mergers, exchanges of stock for stock, and exchanges of assets for stock. Most available tax-free acquisition transactions are provided under Section 368 of the tax code.[17] In all, considering the various permutations of its provisions, Section 368 ultimately sets forth more than a dozen different varieties of acquisition reorganizations. The most commonly used forms are the A, B, C, and D reorganizations. (Others are F and G reorganizations, and various hybrids.)

- An *A reorganization* (named, of course, after its alphabetic place in Section 368) is very simply a "a statutory merger or consolidation."[18] This type of reorganization has other, more complex names—such as a *reorganization not solely for voting stock*, as distinct from a B reorganization, which *is* solely for voting stock (see below). It is also referred to as a *tax-free forward merger*, as opposed to the taxable forward merger and taxable reverse merger forms discussed earlier (there is no tax-free reverse merger).
- A *B reorganization* is a stock-for-stock exchange in which one company buys the stock of another company using only ("solely") its own stock.
- A *C reorganization* is a transaction in which one company buys the assets of another company using only its own stock.
- A *D reorganization* is a transaction in which a company transfers its assets down into a subsidiary. This kind of transaction would usually disqualify a company from meeting the requirements of Section 355 of the tax code, which provides for a tax-free "spin-off" (distribution) of a subsidiary's stock to shareholders.

To qualify as tax-free reorganizations under Section 368, all acquisition reorganizations must meet three nonstatutory requirements. First, the reorganization must have a business purpose. Second, the acquiring corporation must satisfy the continuity of business enterprise requirement, involving the continuation of a significant business of the acquired corporation or the use of a significant portion of the acquired corporation's business assets. Third, and probably most burdensome, the reorganization must satisfy the continuity of interest requirement.

What is the continuity of interest requirement?

As noted above, tax-free treatment is generally available to an acquired corporation's stockholders only to the extent that they either retain their stock or exchange it for stock in the acquiring entity or group. Continuity of interest requires that this qualifying stock consideration constitute a substantial portion of the total consideration received by the acquired corporation's shareholders in the overall transaction. For this purpose, a substantial portion is at least 40 percent; if a private ruling from the Internal Revenue Service is desired, the stock consideration must be at least 50 percent of the total.

TAX AND ACCOUNTING ISSUES IN CHOICE OF ENTITY

What types of entities may operate the business of an acquired company?

Four types of entities may be used to acquire and operate the business of the acquired corporation: (1) C corporations, (2) S corporations, (3) partnerships, either general or limited, and (4) limited liability companies (LLCs). The LLC is a hybrid entity authorized in 1988 by the Internal Revenue Service. It offers the legal insulation of a corporation and the preferred tax treatment of a limited partnership.

What are the primary differences among the four types of business entities?

A regular, or C, corporation is a separate taxpaying entity. Therefore, its earnings are taxed to the corporation when earned and again to its shareholders upon distribution. Partnerships and S corporations (and presumably LLCs), in contrast, are generally not separate taxpaying entities.

The earnings of partnerships and S corporations are taxed directly to the partners or shareholders, whether or not earnings are distributed or otherwise made available to such persons. Moreover, partnerships and S corporations may generally distribute their earnings to the equity owners free of tax. Because S corporations and partnerships are generally exempt from tax, but pass the tax liability with respect to such earnings directly through to their owners, these entities are commonly referred to as *pass-through entities*.

What are pass-through entities?

Pass-through entities are structures that permit a single—rather than double—tax. Under the dual system of taxation, corporate earnings from the sale of appreciated property are taxed twice, first to the corporation when the sale occurs, and then to the shareholders upon the distribution of the net proceeds.[19] This places importance on the use of entities to pass through earnings to a point where they are recognized and taxed only once.

There are three types of pass-through entities: (1) a partnership, both general and limited, (2) an S corporation, and (3) a C corporation that files a consolidated income tax return with its corporate "parent." The earnings of all C corporations are subject to double tax, but the consolidated return provisions generally permit the earnings of subsidiary members of the consolidated return group to be taxed to the ultimate parent only. The earnings of an S corporation, with certain exceptions, are subject to taxation only at the shareholder level. The earnings of a partnership are also subject to a single tax, but only to the extent that such earnings are allocated to noncorporate partners (unless the partner is an S corporation). Partnership earnings that are allocated to corporate partners are subject to double taxation, just as though the income were earned directly by the corporations.

What is a C corporation?

A C corporation is defined in the Internal Revenue Code as any corporation that is not an S corporation. The term *C corporation* as used in this chapter, however, excludes corporations granted special tax status under the tax code, such as life insurance corporations, regulated investment companies (mutual funds), or corporations qualifying as real estate investment trusts (REITs).

What is an S corporation?

An S corporation is simply a regular corporation that meets certain requirements and elects to be taxed under Subchapter S of the Internal Revenue Code. Originally called a "small business corporation," the S corporation was designed to permit small, closely held businesses to be conducted in corporate form, while continuing to be taxed generally as if operated as a partnership or an aggregation of individuals. As it happens, the eligibility requirements under Subchapter S, keyed to the criterion of simplicity, impose no limitation on the actual size of the business enterprise.[20]

Briefly, an S corporation may not (1) have more than 75 shareholders, (2) have as a shareholder any person (other than an estate and a very limited class of trust) who is not an individual, (3) have a nonresident alien as a shareholder, (4) have more than one class of stock, (5) be a member of an affiliated group with other corporations, or (6) be a bank, thrift, insurance company, or certain other types of business entities.

What is a partnership for tax purposes?

Except under rare circumstances, a partnership for tax purposes must be a bona fide general or limited partnership under applicable state law.

How are LLC mergers treated?

Under most state laws, a limited liability company may merge with or into a stock corporation, limited partnership, business trust, or another LLC. All members of the LLC must approve the merger unless they agree otherwise. Filing of articles and the effective date operate the same as for corporate mergers.

What is the most tax-efficient structure to acquire or operate an acquired corporation's business?

If practicable, not even a single level of corporate tax should be paid on income generated by the acquired corporation's business. For this reason, a pass-through entity owned by individuals (as discussed below) should be the structure whenever possible. With respect to an acquisition of assets by individuals, this means that the acquisition vehicle should be either a partnership (presumably limited) or an S corporation. In the case of a stock acquisition by individuals, the acquired corporation generally should be operated as an S corporation.

When the buyer is a C corporation, the acquired corporation's business, whether acquired through an asset or a stock purchase, should be operated as a division of the buyer or through a separate company included in the buyer's consolidated return. In either case, the income of the acquired corporation will be subject to only one level of corporate tax prior to dividend distributions from the buyer to its shareholders.

Under what circumstances may a consolidated return be filed?

In order for two or more corporations to file a consolidated return, they must constitute an "affiliated group" for tax purposes. Although subject to numerous qualifications and complications, an affiliated group is essentially a chain of corporations in which a common parent owns at least 80 percent of the voting power and at least 80 percent of the value of the stock of the other members of the group.

When should an S corporation be considered?

Typically, an S corporation should be considered when the acquired corporation is, or can become, a freestanding domestic operating corporation owned by 75 or fewer U.S. individual shareholders. Because the S corporation requirements are designed to ensure that such entities will have relatively simple structures, they are not inherently user-friendly vehicles for larger, complex operations. Nevertheless, because there is no limit on the size of the business that may be conducted in an S corporation, it is often possible to plan around obstacles to qualification under Subchapter S and to use this favorable tax entity.

When should a partnership be considered?

The partnership is an alternative to the S corporation, with several notable advantages. First, it is always available without restriction as to the structure or composition of the acquired corporation's ownership; therefore, it can be used when the S corporation is unavailable for technical reasons. In addition, the partnership is unique in enabling the partners to receive distributions of loan proceeds free of tax. Finally, if the acquired corporation is expected to generate tax losses, a partnership is better suited than an S corporation to pass these losses through to the owners. The last two advantages result from the fact that partners, unlike S corporation shareholders, may generally include liabilities of the partnership in their basis in the partnership.

In addition to the choice of entity, what major structural issues should be considered?

From a tax standpoint, probably the most important issue is whether the buyer should seek to obtain a cost basis or a carryover basis in the assets of the acquired corporation. Because of the potential for obtaining either of these results regardless of whether assets or stock is actually acquired, the determinations of the tax goal and the actual structure may initially be made on a separate basis.

What are the mechanics of achieving a cost or carryover basis?

In a taxable acquisition, carryover basis can be achieved only through a stock acquisition. For federal tax purposes, however, stock may be acquired in two ways: first, through a direct purchase of seller's stock, and second, through a reverse cash merger.

As indicated earlier, a cost basis can be achieved by purchasing either assets or stock from the seller. As in the case of a stock purchase, the tax law permits an asset purchase to be effected in two ways: first, through a direct purchase of the seller's assets, and second, through a forward cash merger. In the context of a stock acquisition, a cost basis can be achieved by making an election under Section 338 of the tax code.

How are purchase price allocations made for tax purposes?

Although businesses are usually bought and sold on a lump sum basis, for tax purposes each such transaction is broken down into a purchase and sale of the individual assets, both tangible and intangible. There is no specific requirement under the tax laws that a buyer and seller allocate the lump sum purchase price in the same manner. Because each party tends to take a position most favorable to it, allocation issues have been litigated by the IRS fairly often over the years. At the same time, courts and, to a lesser extent, the IRS have tended to defer to allocations of purchase price that are agreed upon in writing between a buyer and seller in an arm's-length transaction.

Are there any rules governing the allocation of purchase price?

Yes. If the seller transfers assets constituting a business and determines its basis as the consideration (e.g., purchase price) paid for the assets, then this transfer is considered a Section 1060(c) "applicable asset" acquisition. Both buyer and seller in such a transaction must use the "residual method" to allocate the purchase price received in determining the buyer's basis or the seller's gain or loss. This method, which is the same as the one used for a stock purchase, requires that the price of the assets acquired be reduced by cash and cashlike items; the balance must be allocated to tangible assets, followed by intangibles, and finally by goodwill and going-concern value. IRS regulations state that both buyer and seller are bound by the allocations set forth in the acquisition agreement.

What about amortization of intangibles following an acquisition?

Until the passage of the Omnibus Reconciliation Act of 1993, acquirers found it impossible to amortize intangibles at anything close to their economic obsolescence because of arbitrary standards set forth in Accounting Principles Board Opinion No.17 (APB 17), which set a 40-year maximum for amortization of goodwill. Although some write-offs were mandated at shorter periods, the burden was on the company to justify shorter periods not explicitly covered by the mandates. The 1993 law proposed a new tax code section (Section 197) that sets a uniform standard of 15 years for amortization of intangibles at a rate of 100 percent, with certain exceptions treated with either longer periods (e.g., land) or shorter periods (e.g., computer software). All other forms of goodwill and other intangibles are amortizable at 15 years, a great improvement over the old 40-year standard. The FASB is currently revising these rules again, as part of its effort to reform purchase accounting and to abolish pooling accounting. (See below at "Related Accounting Considerations.")

What is the main difference between a partnership and an S corporation as far as their pass-through status goes?

The partnership is a more complete pass-through entity. With respect to issuance of stock or debt, the S corporation is treated in exactly the same way as a C corporation: such events are not taxable transactions to it. Likewise, no taxable event is recognized to an S corporation when its warrants are issued or exercised. In contrast, most transactions undertaken by a partnership are viewed for tax purposes as if they were undertaken by the partners themselves. If the partnership is treated solely as an entity apart from its partners, the business arrangement will be undermined. Thus, the issuance and exercise of a warrant to buy a stated percentage of the outstanding stock of a corporation becomes a far more complex transaction to structure when it involves an interest in a partnership.

TAX IMPLICATIONS OF FINANCING ARRANGEMENTS

What tax issues should be analyzed in structuring straight debt financing?

Generally, straight debt is an unconditional obligation to repay principal and interest, has a fixed maturity date not too far removed, is not convertible, and has no attached warrants, options, or stock. A straight debt instrument ordinarily does not include interest that is contingent on profits or other factors, but it may provide for a reasonable variable interest rate. It will not have a principal that is subject to contingencies.

In short, straight debt is an instrument without significant equity features. Straight debt instruments are generally classified as debt for tax purposes. Accrued interest on a straight debt instrument is deductible by the borrower and taxable to the lender. As a practical matter, the only tax issue in straight debt financing is the computation of the accrued interest.

The Internal Revenue Code and proposed regulations contain an extremely complex set of comprehensive rules regarding interest accruals. These rules generally require that interest must accrue whether or not a payment of interest is made. Thus, interest may be taxed, or deducted, before or after interest is paid.

How is debt distinguished from equity for tax purposes?

U.S. federal tax law offers no specific, objective criteria to determine whether a given instrument should be treated as debt or equity, despite attempts to legislate such standards.[21] State tax law offers more exemptions than rules. The debt-equity characterization issue has produced an abundance of tax litigation, with a resulting body of case law in which there are very few common principles. The judicial response in defining debt and equity has much in common with its response in defining an obscenity under the First Amendment; that is, judges have been unable to enunciate a complete definition, but they know it when they see it.

A few useful generalizations can be made. Virtually all the litigation and activity by the IRS has been in the recharacterization of purported debt as equity, and not the other way around. Therefore, it is quite safe to say that recharacterization is not a problem in dealing with a purported equity instrument.

In examining a purported debt instrument, the courts look for objective evidence that the parties intended a true debtor-creditor relationship. In particular, they have placed great weight on whether the instrument represents an unconditional promise to pay a certain sum at a definite time. Other significant factors that are considered include whether the loan was made by shareholders of the borrower, the borrower's debt-to-equity ratio, whether the loan is subordinated to third-party creditors, and whether it has a market rate of interest. Debt may be recharacterized as equity, but the tax consequences may be severe.

Can an acquirer deduct interest paid on loans made for acquisitions?

Only within limits. Section 279 of the tax code disallows interest deductions in excess of $5 million a year on debt that is used to finance an acquisition, to the extent that the company's interest deductions are attributable to "corporate acquisition indebtedness." Because its effects are direct and harsh, Section 279 must be considered in evaluating any debt instrument used in connection with a corporate acquisition, or a refunding of such a debt instrument.

OTHER TAX ISSUES

What role do state and local taxes play in structuring mergers and acquisitions?

State and local taxes generally play a secondary role in planning acquisitions and divestitures. First, most state income tax systems are based largely on the federal system, particularly in terms of what is taxable, to whom, when, and in what amount. Second, when an acquired corporation operates in a number of states, it can be inordinately difficult to assess the interaction of the various state tax systems. On the other hand, serious and embarrassing mistakes have been made by tax planners who ignored a transaction's state tax consequences. Although a detailed discussion of state income tax consequences deserves a book of its own, several extremely important state tax issues merit attention here.

First and foremost, there are income taxes. These vary from state to state and may affect companies located outside the state.[22]

Beyond income taxes, numerous other taxes imposed by states and localities may affect an acquisition. Although these rarely amount to structural prohibitions or incentives, they often increase cost. For example, when real estate is being transferred, there will often be unavoidable real property gain, transfer, or deed recordation taxes. Perhaps the most notorious of the real property gain and transfer taxes are those imposed by New York State and New York City, respectively, upon certain sales of real estate and of controlling interests in entities holding real estate.

Purchases of assets may not be exempt from a state's sales tax. Many states offer exemptions, but this should not be taken for granted. Check it out.

Certain types of state and local taxes that are not associated directly with an acquisition can be significantly affected by an acquisition or by the particular structure of the acquisition. For example, a state's real property and personal property taxes are based on an assessment of the value of the property owned by a taxpayer. Often, a transfer of ownership of the property will trigger a reassessment of the value of the property.

RELATED ACCOUNTING CONSIDERATIONS

What are the principal authoritative accounting pronouncements covering the accounting for mergers and acquisitions?

Traditionally, the principal authoritative accounting pronouncements covering the subject of accounting for mergers and acquisitions (business combinations) have been Accounting Principles Board Opinions No. 16 and No. 17.

APB 16 had given two acceptable methods of accounting for business combinations: the purchase method and the pooling of interests method. In general, the purchase method accounts for a business combination as the acquisition of one company by another. The purchase price and costs of the acquisition are allocated to all the identified assets acquired and liabilities assumed, based on their fair market values. If the purchase price exceeds the fair value of the purchased company's net assets, the excess is recorded as goodwill. Earnings or losses of the purchased company are included in the acquiring company's financial statements from the closing date of the acquisition.

The pooling of interests method accounts for a business combination as a uniting of ownership interests of two companies by the exchange of voting equity securities. No acquisition is recognized because the combination is accomplished without disbursing resources of the constituents. In pooling accounting, the assets, liabilities, and retained earnings of each company are carried forward at their previous carrying amounts. Operating results of both companies are combined for all periods prior to the closing date, and previously issued financial statements are restated as though the companies had always been combined.

In April 1999, the Financial Accounting Standards Board declared its intention to abolish pooling by January 1, 2001, and to reform purchase accounting. As of April 2000, some members of Congress, including Virginia Republicans Sen. Tom Bliley and Hon. Tom Davis, were urging Congress to postpone pooling abolition in favor of purchase reform.

How is the purchase price of the acquired corporation determined under the purchase method?

The purchase method follows principles normally applicable under historical cost accounting to recording acquisitions of assets and issuances of stock. The general principles to apply the historical cost basis of accounting to an acquisition depend on the nature of the transaction:

- If a corporation is acquired by exchanging cash or other assets, the purchase price is the amount of cash disbursed or fair value of other assets distributed.
- If a corporation is acquired by incurring liabilities, the purchase price is the present value of the amounts to be paid.
- If a corporation is acquired by issuing shares of stock, the value assigned to the stock is the fair value of the consideration received. As a practical matter, in most business combinations it is easier to value the stock exchanged, and this is normally done for convenience.

Cash paid, liabilities incurred, and securities issued constitute the major portion of the purchase price of most acquisitions. Numerous other items, however, must be considered for inclusion in the purchase price. Here are some of them:

- Direct expenses, such as finder's and directly related professional fees (legal, investment banking, accounting, appraisal, and environmental consulting).
- A premium or discount on a debt security issued or assumed, with the imputed liability adjusted to present value on the basis of current interest rates, if stated rates differ significantly from current market rates.
- A negotiated adjustment to the purchase price related to assumption of a contingent liability, such as a lawsuit or tax examination.

Under the purchase method, how should the buyer's cost be allocated to the assets acquired and liabilities assumed?

The buyer's cost is allocated to individual assets and liabilities at their fair market values at the time of acquisition. Independent appraisals may be used in determining the fair value of some assets and liabilities. Subsequent sales of assets may also provide evidence of values.

Previously recorded goodwill of the acquired company is not recognized in the purchase price allocation. If the acquired company sponsors a single-employer defined benefit pension plan, the assignment of the purchase price to the individual assets acquired and liabilities assumed shall include a liability for the projected benefit obligation in excess of plan assets, or an asset for plan assets in excess of the projected benefit obligation.

How are the differences between the market or appraised values of specific assets and liabilities and the income tax bases of those assets accounted for?

The FASB's FAS No. 96, "Accounting for Income Taxes," requires, as a rule, that a deferred tax liability or asset be recognized for the tax consequences of differences between the assigned fair values and the tax bases of assets and liabilities recognized in a business combination. A deferred tax liability or asset is not recognized for a difference between the assigned amount and the tax basis of goodwill, unallocated "negative" goodwill, and leveraged leases. Statement No. 96 contains complexities that could affect the accounting for business combinations. The facts and circumstances of each transaction need to be evaluated.

How much time does a buyer have to complete the accounting under the purchase method?

The *allocation period,* during which the buyer identifies and values the assets acquired and the liabilities assumed, ends when the acquiring enterprise is no longer waiting for information that it has arranged to obtain and that is known to be available or obtainable. Although the time required varies with circumstances, the allocation period should usually not exceed one year from the consummation of a business combination. The existence of a preacquisition contingency for which an asset, a liability, or an impairment of an asset cannot be estimated does not, of itself, extend the allocation period.

What are preacquisition contingencies and how should they be considered in the allocation of purchase price?

A contingency is an existing condition, situation, or set of circumstances involving uncertainty as to possible gain or loss to an enterprise that will ultimately be resolved when one or more future events occur or fail to occur. A preacquisition contingency is a contingency of the acquired enterprise that is in existence before consummation of a business combination; it can be a contingent asset, a contingent liability, or a contingent impairment of an asset.

Examples of preacquisition contingencies are pending or threatened litigation, obligations relating to product warranties and product defects, and actual or possible claims or assessments. These include income tax examinations, assessments by environmental agencies, guarantees of indebtedness of others, and impairment of the carrying amount of productive assets used in the business.

Contingencies that arise from the acquisition and that did not exist prior to the acquisition are the buyer's contingencies rather than preacquisition contingencies of the acquired company.

At what date should a buyer that has applied the purchase method report combined results?

The acquisition date of a company ordinarily is the date that assets are received and other assets are given or securities are issued. The reported income of the buyer includes operations of the acquired corporation beginning with the date of acquisition. In a purchase business combination, there is no restatement of prior period financial statements. In certain situations, however, the acquisition date may be "as of" a date earlier than the closing date. These include, for example, situations in which the parties intend to fix a determinable price as of a specified date other than the closing date or to develop a formula whereby changes in earnings or market price between the specified date and the closing date will be considered in the final purchase price. If a date earlier than the closing date is considered appropriate, the parties should reach a firm purchase agreement that includes specifying the date of acquisition other than the closing date, and the time period between the specified date and the closing date should be relatively short.

What are typical forms of contingent consideration in an acquisition, and how should such consideration be included in determining the cost of an acquired company?

A business combination may provide for the issuance of stock or the transfer of cash or other consideration contingent on specified transactions or events in the future. Agreements often provide that a portion of the consideration be placed in escrow and distributed or returned when the specified event has occurred. In general, to the extent that the contingent consideration can be determined at the time of the acquisition, such amount shall be included in determining the cost of the acquired company.

What accounting is required for expenses related to a purchase?

Direct acquisition costs incurred by an acquiring company effecting a business combination accounted for under the purchase method are included as part of the purchase price of the acquired company. Direct acquisition costs incurred by an acquired company, or its major or controlling shareholders, should generally not be included as part of the cost of the acquired company. Acquisition costs incurred by the acquired company are presumed to be taken into account indirectly by the acquiring company in setting the purchase price. If, however, the acquiring company agrees to reimburse the acquired company's major or controlling shareholders for acquisition costs incurred by them, these costs should be included as part of the purchase price of the acquired company. Direct acquisition costs include fees paid to investment bankers, legal fees, accounting fees, appraisal fees, and other consulting fees.

Fees paid to an investment banker in connection with a business combination accounted for as a purchase when the investment banker is also providing interim financing or debt underwriting services must be allocated between direct costs of the acquisition and debt issue costs.

What are the disclosure requirements for business combinations?

For a *purchase* business combination, the following disclosures are required in the notes to the financial statements of both public and nonpublic enterprises:

- Name and brief description of the acquired enterprise.
- Period for which results of operations of the acquired enterprise are included in the income statement of the acquiring enterprise.
- Cost of the acquired enterprise and, if applicable, number of shares of stock issued or issuable and amount assigned to the issued and issuable shares. Pushdown accounting must be used.[23]
- Description of the plan for amortization of acquired goodwill, the amortization method, and the amortization period.
- Any contingent payments, options, or commitments specified in the acquisition agreement and their proposed accounting treatment.

In addition, notes to the financial statements of the acquiring enterprise (if publicly held) should include pro forma information (i.e., information showing the financial results of combining the companies).

CONCLUDING COMMENTS

The tax and accounting aspects of merger transactions may seem like a maze of restrictions on deal makers' freedom to buy and sell. Some believe they are excessive, and in drastic need of simplification. For now, however, they are a fact of life, deal making, and due diligence—hence this chapter.

E N D N O T E S

1. Title 26 of the U.S. Code was established following ratification of the Sixteenth Amendment of the U.S. Constitution in 1913, empowering Congress to tax "incomes, from whatever source derived, without apportionment among the several States, and without regard to any census or enumeration." This broadened the authority of the Internal Revenue Service, which was established in 1862 by an act of Congress. Source: Legal Information Institute, Cornell University.

2. This chapter is an update and summary of Reed and Lajoux, op. cit., Chapter 5, note 4. Special thanks to the Lane and Edson LLP attorneys who provided the original framework for this discussion during the first edition of *The Art of M&A: A Merger/Acquisition/Buyout Guide.*

3. Source: The Heritage Foundation, Washington, D.C., at heritage.org.

4. Taxation of these areas is administered by the Bureau of Alcohol, Tobacco, and Firearms, within the Department of the Treasury, and supervised under the Office of the Undersecretary for Enforcement, Department of the Treasury.

5. For a discussion of the tax aspects of stock ownership in employee stock ownership plans, see Reed and Lajoux, op. cit. (note 2), p. 304 and pp. 421–431. For a discussion of the special tax issues in management buyouts, see Reed and Lajoux, pp. 305–314.

6. Taxpayer Relief Act of 1997, Section 311. Gains from the sales of assets can be taxed at 8, 10, 14, 18, 20, 25, 28, 31, 36, or 39.5 percent, depending on the holding period, date sold, type of asset, and amount of other income. In the year 2000, Congress is still considering several tax bills that would simplify or eliminate these distinctions. One candidate for president in the November 2000 elections favors a flat tax rate, which, if enacted into law, would make much of this chapter moot.

7. Shareholders may not have to pay taxes on their dividends if they hold their stock for a certain period of time. This "dividends received deduction" is available to shareholders who have held the stock (and been at economic risk from it) for more than 45 days—or more than 90 in some cases (such as preferred stock). The Taxpayer Relief Act of 1997, in Section 1015, preserved this deduction but made it more stringent.

8. Under current law, an issuer of debt can deduct the interest that it pays, but an issuer of equity may not deduct dividend payments it makes. The interest/dividend distinction became somewhat complicated after the Taxpayer Relief Act of 1997, which stated that no deduction will be allowed for interest on an instrument that is payable in stock of the issuer or a related party. This raises the issue of treatment of convertible debt, notes Kenneth R. Goldberg of Jones, Day, Reavis & Pogue, New York. Source: *1997 Tax Reform: Summaries of Selected Provisions Affecting Corporations, Other Entities, and Business Executives* (August 1997), (Jones Day white paper) p. 31.

9. See Section 401 of the Taxpayer Relief Act of 1997, effective for years beginning after December 31, 1997, and for property placed in service after December 31, 1998.

10. Exceptions include a tender offer for a public company (since not all shareholders will necessarily tender) and a management buyout type of deal, in which managers will retain some stock.

11. Do review third-party documents for "change of control" provisions. Contracts, leases, or permits involving real estate, for example, may require consent if there is a change in the control of the tenant.

12. Although both forms of merger convey the assets in the same simple manner, in the forward merger, assets end up in another corporate shell. In certain jurisdictions, this may violate lease and other contract restrictions the same way a direct asset transfer does. Similarly, in some jurisdictions, recordation taxes may be due after a forward merger when the buyer seeks to record the deeds in its name to reflect the merger.

13. If the buyer wants a holding company structure—that is, wants the acquired entity to be a subsidiary of a holding company—it forms a holding company with an acquisition corporation subsidiary. After the merger, the holding company will own all the stock of the acquired corporation, and the buyer will own all the stock of the holding company.

14. Under Delaware law the approval of the surviving corporation's stockholders is necessary only if its certificate of incorporation will be amended by the merger and if the shares of the survivor issued to the sellers comprise less than 20 percent of the outstanding shares of the survivor.

15. See Section 1082 of the Taxpayer Relief Act of 1997.

16. There are several significant exceptions to this general rule. The most common exception is those situations in which a selling shareholder of the acquired corporation stock is a C corporation: The proceeds from the sale of the acquired corporation stock by a corporate shareholder will likely be taxed again upon their ultimate distribution to noncorporate shareholders.

17. The one exception is a Section 351 transaction. Section 351 of the tax code provides nonrecognition treatment on the transfer of property to a corporation by one or more parties in exchange for stock or stock and securities of the transferee corporation, provided the transferors possess 80 percent control of the transferee corporation immediately after the transaction.

18. Code Section 368 (a) 1 (A) and Reg. Section 1.368-2(b) 1 cited in Martin D. Ginsberg and Jack S. Levin, *Mergers, Acquisitions, and Buyouts: A Transactional Analysis of the Governing Tax, Legal, and Accounting Considerations* (New York: Aspen Law and Business, 1999), Section 801. 1. Ginsberg and Martin are the main source for our definitions of A, B, C, and D reorganizations.

19. A longstanding exception to this system was the so-called General Utilities rule. Named after a 1935 Supreme Court decision about the General Utilities com-

pany, this tax code rule permitted nonrecognition of gain to corporations upon certain distributions to shareholders of appreciated property. It was repealed in 1986.

20. Not all states recognize the S corporation. For those that do not, the corporation pays state income taxes as if it were a C corporation. For those states that do recognize S corporations, both resident and nonresident shareholders of the state where the corporation does business must file returns and pay taxes to that state. In such cases, a shareholder's state of residence will usually (but not always) provide a credit against its own tax.

21. In 1969 Congress enacted Section 385 of the tax code authorizing the IRS to issue regulations regarding the debt-versus-equity issue. Eleven years later, the IRS promulgated the first version of the Section 385 regulations. These regulations were rewritten twice and were finally withdrawn in 1983.

22. One of the laws limiting the reach of state income taxes was broadened in early 1992 when the U.S. Supreme Court declared a "de minimis" exception to a 1959 law establishing a federal limitation on state income taxes in *Wisconsin Department of Revenue v. William Wrigley, Jr., Co.* (1992).

23. Pushdown accounting refers to the establishment of a new accounting and reporting basis in an acquired corporation's separate financial statements, resulting from the purchase and substantial change of ownership of its outstanding voting equity securities. The buyer's purchase price is "pushed down" to the acquired company and used to restate the carrying value of its assets and liabilities. For example, if all the voting equity securities of an acquired corporation are purchased, the assets and liabilities of the acquired corporation are restated using fair market values so that the excess of the restated amounts of the assets over the restated amounts of the liabilities equals the buyer's purchase price.

PART THREE

A Closer Look at Legal Compliance

One of the most difficult areas of due diligence is ensuring legal compliance—the focus of this final section of our book.

In Part One (Chapters 1 through 4), we provided an overview of financial, operational, and legal due diligence. In Part Two (Chapters 5 through 7), we addressed the highly technical but necessary area of transactional due diligence. In this section, we return to the subject of legal due diligence, explaining the law of antitrust and trade, intellectual property, consumer protection, the environment, and employment (Chapters 8 through 12).

As mentioned in earlier chapters, the number of statutes and regulatory agencies has grown exponentially over time. As a result, the law has significantly influenced basic principles and practices of financial and operational management. For this reason, managers would be wise to pay attention to the law in all their activities, including due diligence.

We recognize that a legalistic focus is not natural to most corporate leaders and managers. If you, our readers, are operating managers, you probably concentrate on operations. When it comes to legal risk, you probably let your advisers do the research, while reserving decisions to yourselves. The combination can sometimes lead to legal entanglements despite the best advice.

As believers in self-regulation through knowledge, we believe that to avoid liability in general, and postmerger liability in particular, managers need to understand the basic legal principles personally, not just via advisers. Managers can benefit greatly by knowing the principles underlying the major laws of the land. Such knowledge can be the cornerstone of thorough due diligence in any transaction.

CHAPTER 8

Detecting Exposure Under Antitrust Law and International Economic Law

Monopoly is business at the end of its journey.

Henry Demarest Lloyd
Wealth Against Commonwealth (1894)

INTRODUCTION

Antitrust ranks high among the legal areas that acquirers must investigate when conducting M&A due diligence. The reasons are compelling.

1. Every acquisition—simply by increasing the market strength of the acquirer—raises the potential, however distant, for an antitrust law violation. Only sure knowledge of antitrust law can set that concern to rest.
2. The acquisition candidates themselves, prior to the acquisition, may have taken actions that violate antitrust law. Antitrust law, after all, is not limited to M&A issues. It deals with restraint of competition in a number of areas.

In many transactions it may be impossible to proceed without obtaining the necessary approval from antitrust authorities. Therefore, potential buyers and sellers should be sure at the initial planning stages to provide adequate time and resources to do this.

The following overview of antitrust law can make acquirers and sellers alike more sensitive to this important legal area.

ANTITRUST FUNDAMENTALS

What are the basic concepts behind antitrust law?

Antitrust law in the United States derives from a late-nineteenth-century effort to break up "trusts"—the large, market-dominating companies that had evolved in that era.

Classic antitrust policy looks at both the means and the potential results of large size. It reflects two fundamental beliefs (which we put in quotes to distinguish belief from known fact.)

- "Any large company, in order to grow, may have restrained the trade of others in its industry."
- "Once a company is large, by sheer size it may harm the competitiveness of its smaller peers."

Since one way for companies to grow is through acquisition, antitrust regulators often focus on acquisitions, which they classify into three basic categories: *horizontal, vertical,* and *complementary.*[1]

- A horizontal transaction (merger, acquisition, joint venture, partnership, or alliance) involves an acquisition or alliance with a competitor. Such a transaction may create a monopoly or oligopoly in a market by eliminating or reducing competition.
- A vertical transaction involves similar connections with a supplier or customer. Such a transaction may put competitors of the acquired firm at a severe disadvantage.
- A complementary transaction involves growth through diversification. Such a transaction may remove potential competition or discourage competition by others because of the financial or marketing strength of the resulting firm.

Equally important to antitrust policy are two other concepts: *structure* and *practice.* A transaction may change the competitive balance in an industry or market, or a company may engage in a predatory trade practice (see diagram).

There are two main predatory practices, which should raise red flags in any due diligence investigation.

- *Collusion and cooperation.* This occurs when a group of companies agree to take a course of action that harms the consumer, such as fixing prices at a high level, rather than competing among themselves to offer low prices. A classic case in this regard is *Matsushita v. Zenith* (1986).

The Antitrust Grid

	Structure	Practice
Vertical		
Complementary		
Horizontal		

- *Predation and exclusion.* This occurs when a company takes action in order to prevent a competitor from entering or growing in a market. Examples include tying arrangements (linking one product or service to another, instead of allowing the consumer to buy each separately), exclusive dealing (between producer and buyer), and selling at or below cost. A classic tying and exclusive dealing case is *Jefferson Parish Hospital v. Hyde* (1984).[2] A classic pricing case is *Monsanto v. Spray-Rite* (1984). (There has been some concern that franchise-franchisee relations are a form of tying, but sound legal arguments can be made against this notion.[3])

Before 1980, regulators believed that mergers encouraged such anticompetitive behavior.

More recent antitrust theory (particularly in the 1990s) has looked at mergers on their economic merits.

Could you give some background on how antitrust law has evolved in the twentieth century?

Antitrust policy went through several phases in the twentieth century. In the early part of the century, policymakers broke up firms that dominated markets—whether individually as monopolies or in groups as oligopolies (more about these forms later). That policy said big was bad, whether or not it involved mergers. Then, in midcentury, policymakers began to focus on merger transactions as a cause of market domination, challenging acquisitions related to vertical and horizontal integration through mergers.

In recent decades, say scholars, there has been an "antitrust revolution." Indeed, this is the title of a book edited by John E. Kwoka, Jr. and Lawrence J. White, now in its third edition.[4] In the early 1980s, policymakers began to use economics in their analysis of transactions, creating a revolutionary impact on antitrust policy.

Now, large size in a company or a transaction no longer triggers antitrust actions. Rather, as Kwoka and White observe, *economics*, not mere size, "frames the central issues for investigation." Using both data analysis and theory, economics "structures the examination of the likely competitive effects of various practices or structural changes in companies and the industries in which they operate."

In this new economically inclined view, transactions that make sense for consumers will be approved, even if they create horizontal or vertical integration.

MONOPOLIES AND OLIGOPOLIES

What is a monopoly, and how does relate to M&A activity?

Economists define a monopoly as a single firm selling a product for which there are no good substitutes in a market where entry by other sellers is difficult or impossible.[5] Such a company is capable, says classic economic theory, of charging more for less (and thus earning higher profits) than other sellers would, if those sellers could enter the market. (A single buyer in a market, called a *monopsony*, can do the converse, and extract a lower price for sellers than multiple competitive buyers could.)

The concept of monopoly is important in M&A due diligence. In the words of the antitrust guidelines of the Department of Justice and Federal Trade Commission: "[Economic] efficiencies are most likely to make a difference in merger analysis when the likely adverse competitive effects, absent the efficiencies, are not great. Efficiencies almost never justify a merger to monopoly or near-monopoly."

Pure monopolies are rare, but they do exist for specific products and/or locations. Examples include, in some local markets, local residential telephone, electricity, natural gas, water, and cable television distribution; and postal service for first-class and bulk mail.[6] Another example is a single store lacking nearby competitors. All these forms just listed are permitted under current law because of special circumstances.

Some dominant firms are quasi-monopolies—singularly large sellers with a fringe of smaller competitors. Recent examples include Microsoft in personal computer operating systems, Intel in microprocessors, and United Parcel Service for small package deliveries.[7]

Technological advances and competitive forces eventually overcome particular monopolies, but new ones always rise up. New monopolies arise in three ways, say experts:

- Through internal growth that achieves market-dominating economies of scale.
- Through government action that takes over an industry, such as mail.
- Through consolidation into massive organizations via mergers.

In the past, the U.S. government has had very strict policies against this last type of monopoly, but today the government will examine cases on their economic effects, taking a more liberal attitude toward size.

What is an oligopoly?

In an oligopoly, the number of sellers is small enough to enable collusion. Since mergers can reduce the number of sellers in the market, regulators have seen them as a cause of oligopoly conditions, and have challenged them on that basis.

What are the main federal regulators for antitrust?

The two main agencies are the Department of Justice (DOJ), through its Antitrust Division, and the Federal Trade Commission (FTC).

THE CLAYTON ACT AND HART-SCOTT-RODINO

What are the main U.S. antitrust laws affecting M&A?

The two main laws are the Sherman Antitrust Act of 1890 and the Clayton Act of 1914, which outlaw monopolies. The Sherman Act contains general language outlawing monopoly, while the Clayton Act more specifically outlaws mergers that have monopolistic effects. In addition, there is the Hart-Scott-Rodino Antitrust Improvements Act of 1976, which requires certain merger disclosures.

What exactly does the Clayton Act say?

Section 7 of the Clayton Act prohibits a corporation from acquiring stock or assets of another corporation if the acquisition might "substantially lessen competition or tend to create a monopoly" in any line of commerce in any section of the country. A violation of Section 7 may give rise to a court-ordered injunction against the acquisition, an order compelling divestiture of the property or other interests, or other remedies.

Section 7 is enforced by the Antitrust Division of the DOJ and by the FTC. In November 1990 Congress passed the Interlocking Directorate Act of 1990, amending Section 8 of the Clayton Act to state that "no person shall, at any time, serve as a director or officer in any two corporations (other than banks, banking associations and trust companies) that are: A) engaged in whole or in part in commerce; and B) by virtue of their business and location of operation competitors."

The provision does not apply if both companies are small (with capital and surplus and undivided profits under $10 million) or if the competitive sales involved are low (less than 4 percent for each or less than 2 percent for either). Individual and corporate fines were increased under the act to $350,000 and $1 million, respectively.

In conjunction with the federal laws, there are state laws that can restrict mergers. Under federal law (the McCarran-Ferguson Act, enacted as Title 15 of the U.S. Code, Section 1011 ff.), states are given broad authority to regulate mergers involving insurance companies. States have similar authority in certain other areas where they have special regulatory jurisdiction, such as the alcoholic beverages industry.

Mergers of companies with foreign operations or subsidiaries sometimes require review and approval by foreign governments. In addition, some foreign countries (most notably Canada) have their own premerger notification programs that may have to be complied with.

What does the Hart-Scott-Rodino Act say?

The Hart–Scott–Rodino Antitrust Improvements Act of 1976 (the HSR Act), as mentioned, requires the parties to a proposed acquisition transaction to furnish certain information about themselves and the deal to the FTC and the Antitrust Division of the Department of Justice before the merger is allowed to go forward. The information supplied is used by these government agencies to determine whether the proposed transaction would have any anticompetitive effects after completion. If so, in general, they must be cured prior to closing. A mandatory waiting period follows the agencies' receipt of the HSR filings.

What mergers or acquisitions require premerger notification under the HSR Act?

Generally, all mergers and acquisitions that meet the following three criteria must be reported under the HSR Act and the related premerger notification rules:

- The transaction is between two persons with minimum sizes of $100 million and $10 million, respectively, in gross assets or, for manufacturing companies, in annual sales.
- As a result of the transaction, the acquiring person will own either (1) more than $15 million of the acquired person's voting securities or assets or (2) 50 percent or more of the voting securities of a company that has consolidated annual sales or gross assets of $25 million or more.
- One of the persons involved is engaged in U.S. commerce or in an activity affecting U.S. commerce.

The "persons" include not only the corporations involved, but also any other corporation that is under common control. "Control," for purposes of the HSR Act, is defined as owning 50 percent or more of a company's voting securities or having the contractual power to designate a majority of a company's board of directors. Special control rules apply to partnerships and other unincorporated entities.

What information is required to be included in the HSR premerger notification form?

The form requires a description of the parties and the proposed merger or acquisition, certain current financial information about the parties, and a breakdown of revenues of the parties according to industry codes (currently changing from the old Standard Industrial Classification codes). This breakdown of revenues is used by the DOJ and the FTC to determine whether the proposed combination of the businesses would have anticompetitive effects. The information filed is exempt from disclosure under the Freedom of Information Act, and no such information may be made public except pursuant to administrative or judicial proceedings.

After the premerger notification form has been filed, how long must the parties wait before the merger or acquisition can be consummated?

Where the acquisition is being made by a cash tender offer, the parties must wait 15 days before the purchaser may accept shares for payment. In all other cases, the parties must wait 30 days before the transaction can be completed. If the acquisition raises antitrust concerns, the government may extend the waiting period by requesting additional information from the parties. In that case, the waiting period is extended for 20 days (10 days in the case of a cash tender offer) past the time when the additional information is provided.

The parties may request early termination of the waiting period. When the acquisition raises no antitrust concerns, the government may grant the request at its discretion.

Are certain mergers and acquisitions exempt from the HSR Act?

Yes. Acquisitions made through newly formed corporate acquisition vehicles are frequently exempt from the reporting requirements of the HSR Act because the vehicle does not meet the "size-of-person" test; that is, it does not have $10 million in gross assets or sales. This is true, however, only when no other person having $10 million in gross assets or annual sales owns 50 percent or more of the voting stock of the vehicle or has the contractual power to designate a majority of the vehicle's directors. If the vehicle is not controlled by another person, it will be the only company matched against the $10 million size-of-person test. If another company or person does control the vehicle, through either a 50 percent stock ownership or a contractual power to appoint a majority of its directors, that controlling person will be matched against this test. Special rules apply in determining control of partnerships and other unincorporated acquisition vehicles.

Special rules are also used to determine the "size" of a newly formed corporation, and care must be taken to avoid making contractual commitments for additional capital contributions or for guarantees of the new corporation's obligations until after the formation has been completed. In general, the "assets" of a newly formed acquisition vehicle do not include funds contributed to the vehicle or borrowed by the vehicle at the closing to complete the acquisition. The HSR Act and FTC rules also provide numerous exemptions for special situations.

Just because a transaction is exempt from HSR does not mean that it will be approved by regulators, however. Regulators are perpetually concerned about market concentration caused by horizontal mergers, and have issued additional guidelines concerning such mergers.

APPLICATION OF ANTITRUST LAW TO M&A

How can we tell whether a particular horizontal merger is likely to be challenged by the federal government?

Current administration policy is set forth in the Horizontal Merger Guidelines, revised as recently as April 1997. The essential text of these guidelines was issued in April 1992 by the DOJ and the FTC. The 1992 guidelines, the first comprehensive joint statement ever issued by the two agencies, update those issued by the DOJ in 1984 and the FTC in 1982.

As in previous guidelines, horizontal mergers are assessed according to a sliding scale of permissiveness. Thus, the less concentrated the industry, the larger the permissible merger. The index used to measure concentration, the Herfindahl-Hirschmann Index (referred to as the HHI), sums the squares of the individual companies' market shares to measure both postmerger share and the growth in market share resulting from the transaction. The 1992 guidelines retain the HHI scoring system introduced in the 1984 guidelines: "unconcentrated" (under 1,000), "moderately concentrated" (between 1,000 and 1,800), and "highly concentrated" (over 1,800). As in the 1984 guidelines, a score is only one factor to be considered. It is not enough by itself to make or break a charge of market concentration.

Can you give an example of a merger that would create a "highly concentrated" industry?

An industry of five firms having market shares of 30 percent, 25 percent, 20 percent, 15 percent, and 10 percent, respectively, has an HHI score of $30^2 + 25^2 + 20^2 + 15^2 + 10^2$, or 2,250. If the third and fifth firms merge, the resulting score is $30^2 + 25^2 + 30^2 + 15^2$, or 2,650, with an increase in score of 400.

A good example of a highly concentrated industry today is the defense industry, discussed below.

Is the HHI analysis conducted on the acquirer's industry only?

No. An HHI analysis must be performed for each distinct "relevant market" in which *both* of the merging companies operate.

How likely is it that any given merger will be challenged as being in a highly concentrated industry?

Given basic business demographics, chances are relatively low. In unconcentrated industries (with an HHI below 1,000) the largest four firms have 50 percent or less of the market. Historically, this description fits about 60 percent of U.S. industries. In such unconcentrated industries, the DOJ is unlikely to challenge any merger. In moderately concentrated industries (where the HHI falls in the range of 1,000 to 1,800), the four largest firms normally account for between 50 percent and 70 percent of the market. This is the case with approximately 25 percent of U.S. companies.

Within this range the DOJ will review other factors bearing upon the likelihood of predatory practices. Generally, within this range only mergers that increase the HHI by more than 100 points are likely to be challenged. Thus, for example, the over-100 prohibited zone would be reached in such an industry by a merger of two firms each with a 7.1 percent market share, a 10 percent firm with a 5 percent firm, a 25 percent firm with a 2 percent firm, and a 50 percent firm with a 1 percent firm.[8]

What do the DOJ and FTC guidelines say about market concentration by a single firm?

The 1992 guidelines express an intent to scrutinize mergers that can in some circumstances confer market power on a single firm, even if that firm does not have a sizable market share. If, for example, the two merging firms had previously sold products that were perceived by a substantial number of customers to be close substitutes for one another, the merged firm could raise prices on one product line and risk only some diversion of sales to its other product line.

Whatever the level of concentration, regulators will challenge any merger that is likely to create or enhance one-firm domination of a market. Thus, a leading firm that accounts for 35 percent of the market and that is twice the size of its next-largest competitor will normally not be allowed to acquire any firm accounting for even 1 percent of that market.

Are the DOJ/FTC guidelines exclusively concerned with concentration?

No. Analysis of horizontal mergers is no longer governed by the single-minded focus on market concentration. The guidelines do consider economic factors, including the following:

- Ease of entry into the market (the 1992 guidelines make it clear that the easier it is for new firms to enter the market, the less the likelihood of challenge).
- The availability of out-of-market substitutes (the more readily available, the less prospect there is of collusion).
- The degree to which the merging firms confront one another within the relevant market (if they occupy separate sectors of the market, the merger is less a cause of concern than if they are head to head in the same corner).
- The level of product homogeneity (the more homogeneous the product, the easier it is to collude).
- The pace of technological change (the slower the rate of change, the more likely collusion becomes).
- The importance of nonprice terms (the more important they are, the harder it is to collude).
- The degree to which firms have access to information concerning their competitors' transactions (the more information available, the greater the likelihood of collusion).
- The size and frequency of orders (the smaller and more frequent, the greater the likelihood of collusion).
- Whether the industry is characterized either by a history of collusion or by patterns of pricing conduct that make collusion more likely (if it is, the likelihood of a challenge increases).
- Historical evidence of noncompetitive performance (challenge is more likely).

This is quite a departure from classic antitrust, as expressed in the Supreme Court's 1963 ruling in the *Philadelphia National Bank* case. In that ruling, the Court said that if a merger violates antitrust law, it should be barred, even if the merger delivers social benefits.

What about vertical or conglomerate mergers?

The 1984 DOJ guidelines addressed acquisitions involving vertical mergers, but these are not covered in the new guidelines. Vertical and conglomerate mergers have been relatively free from challenge for the past 20 years.

What about foreign competition?

The 1992 guidelines state that "market shares will be assigned for foreign competitors in the same way in which they are assigned to domestic competitors."

These shares may have to be calculated over a longer period of time to account for exchange rate fluctuations. They may also have to be adjusted to account for import quotas. Finally, market shares may have to be combined if foreign firms appear to be acting in a coordinated or collusive way.

You mentioned 1997 revisions to the 1992 guidelines. What did the revisions say?

The revisions, which are reprinted as Appendix 8-A, addressed the subject of efficiency as a reason regulators might approve a merger that might otherwise be considered anticompetitive. The FTC and DOJ note that a merger can increase efficiency:

> Mergers have the potential to generate significant efficiencies by permitting a better utilization of existing assets, enabling the combined firm to achieve lower costs in producing a given quantity and quality than either firm could have achieved without the proposed transaction. Indeed, the primary benefit of mergers to the economy is their potential to generate such efficiencies.[9]

INDUSTRY FOCUS: DEVELOPMENTS AND CASES

How much do antitrust concerns vary by industry?

Potential antitrust issues vary enormously by industry. Acquirers should remain informed of major regulatory and deregulatory developments in their industry and in industries of interest to them for potential acquisitions. Regulatory and deregulatory developments can change the business climate dramatically.

Such events include new industrial policies arising from executive branch initiatives, new federal and state laws relating to industries, and new court decisions interpreting those laws. These all work together to create an antitrust climate for various industries. Sellers, too, should be aware of these issues. Since antitrust is an area of great caution for many acquirers, sellers need to be ready to answer acquirers' general antitrust questions.

Could you give an example of regulatory and deregulatory events in a key industry—for example, defense?

Good question. Antitrust concerns are very relevant in the defense industry. There was dramatic consolidation in that industry throughout the 1990s. A key deregulatory event was the April 1994 agreement from a panel of officials from the DOJ, the FTC, and the Department of Defense to develop and apply special standards to defense acquisitions. The group declared:

> A broad range of efficiencies may be taken into account by the enforcement agencies in the exercise of prosecutorial discretion, and are sometimes taken into account by courts. Efficiencies will not carry much weight if they can be achieved through less anticompetitive means than mergers (for example, a temporary teaming arrangement), and must be demonstrated by clear evidence. In a situation where a merger between the only two firms in a market is proposed, a "winner take all" competition between the firms will almost always be preferable to a merger. A merger to monopoly could be preferable only in special circumstances and when the net benefit of efficiencies is greater than the anticompetitive effect.[10]

After development of the new standards, approval for defense mergers came more swiftly. From 1994 to 1997, for example, there were 35 mergers. The most well known of these transactions were horizontal mergers between competitors, including Northrop-Grumman (1994), Lockheed Martin Marietta (1995), Boeing-Rockwell (1996), Hughes-Raytheon (1997), and Boeing-McDonnell Douglas (1997). Such mergers caused a higher degree of concentration in the marketplace. There are now only five large defense contractors, plus numerous small ones.

In 1997, the Defense Science Board became concerned about vertical acquisitions, noting that some defense contractors were buying their own suppliers. The DSB expressed fears that some transactions could cause contractors to prefer their internal sources, weakening independent suppliers.[11] It may not be a coincidence that in 1998, there were only $1.5 billion in mergers in the aerospace and aircraft sector, compared to $18.8 billion in 1997. Although the number of transactions in both years was comparable (21 in 1998 versus 24 in 1997), the sudden drop in typical size suggests a cautionary approach.

What has been happening in telecommunications with respect to antitrust?

In the telecommunications arena, for example, a key *regulatory* event was the 1982 consent decree (called Modification of Final Judgment) after the breakup of AT&T and the creation of the system of Bell operating companies offering local telephone service. A key *deregulatory* event was the Telecommunications Act of 1996. Since the law was enacted, there have been several large telecommunications mergers, notably Worldcom/MFS Communications (1996), Bell Atlantic/NYNEX (1997), and Worldcom/MCI (1998), and SBC/Ameritech (1999).

Both the consent decree and the Telecommunications Act have cast a long shadow on telecommunications mergers. This industry still appears to be in a deregulatory mode in the new millennium, following intense activity in the late 1990s. Telecommunications acquirers spent $125 billion in 1998 and $88 billion in the first half of 1999—making this the most acquisitive industry, in dollar-terms, next to commercial banking.

Telecommunications transactions have tended to pass regulatory tests, but only after close scrutiny. A recent example is the late-1997 approval of the Bell Atlantic–NYNEX merger, 16 months after the April 1996 announcement of that deal.

Regulators reviewing the merger saw it as a horizontal acquisition, and were concerned about the effect of the merger on potential competition. The two companies had not yet competed directly, since they were in different regions: Bell Atlantic was in six states from Virginia to New Jersey, and NYNEX was in seven states from New York to Maine. But the Telecommunications Act was supposed to pave the way for them to compete with each other; the merger would prevent that potentially positive event from occurring.

Regulators were also concerned about the vertical integration likely to occur following the merger. If the two firms had not merged, they would have had to pay each other to originate or terminate calls in each other's territory. The competitive concern here was that the vertical combination might "create or increase incentives for the merged firm to disadvantage rival long-distance carriers that had little option but to purchase access from the merged firm."[12] Regulators and courts did finally approve the acquisition, but only after a long-term scrutiny of these issues.

What about the retail industry?

Retail is a very visible industry that impacts customers and communities directly, and perhaps for this reason it has received particularly strict antitrust treatment. In late 1999, for example, three companies called off major mergers, citing FTC opposition or overly stringent conditions. The canceled transactions were Viacom Blockbuster's proposed franchise agreement with Hollywood Entertainment Corp., Royal Ahold NV's planned $1.75 billion purchase of Pathmark Stores outlets in New Jersey (following the successful acquisition of Giant Food in 1998), and Abbot Laboratories' proposed purchase of Alza Corp. for $7.3 billion.

Could you give an example of a recent transaction that triggered antitrust scrutiny, and describe the results?

One of the largest and most well-known examples is the $82 billion Exxon-Mobil merger, which was conditionally approved by the Federal Trade Commission on November 30, 1999. The new firm, called Exxon Mobil Corp.

(XOM), came into being after predecessor firms complied with a government request to sell a combined total of $2 billion in assets. This was an all-time record—twice the size of the largest previous FTC-ordered divestiture.

To satisfy FTC antitrust concerns, the new company was required to divest itself of 2,431 gasoline stations, pipeline interests in Alaska and the Southeast, an oil refinery in California, and other assets.

The FTC also required that:

- Exxon sell its Benicia[13] refinery, which yielded 128,000 barrels per day.
- Exxon divest 85 gasoline stations in the San Francisco Bay area and 275 supply agreements for other California locations.
- Exxon be prohibited from using the Exxon name to sell diesel fuel and gasoline in California for up to 12 years.
- Exxon and Mobil sell control of some of the production of paraffinic base oil, the foundation for most of the world's finished lubricants.
- Exxon and Mobil sell their interests in one of two pipelines that ship gasoline to the midAtlantic.
- Mobil sell its unused space in the trans-Alaska pipeline.

FTC Chairman Robert Pitofsky said in an interview with Associated Press reporters that this large, FTC-ordered asset sale would prevent unfair competition among gasoline retailers, as well as unfair pricing to consumers.

The agreement gave the firm nine months to complete its divestitures, except for the sale of Exxon's Benicia refinery and gasoline stations in California, which Exxon was allowed to sell to a single buyer within 12 months.

The FTC also ordered 1,740 gasoline stations sold on the East Coast, where Exxon and Mobil sell more gasoline than other suppliers. Exxon was required to sell stations it owned, operated, or leased in New York, Connecticut, Rhode Island, Massachusetts, Vermont, New Hampshire, and Maine. Mobil was similarly ordered to make divestitures in New Jersey, Pennsylvania, Delaware, Maryland, Virginia, and the District of Columbia.

The FTC also considered how Exxon and Mobil would be treating their service station owners and their employees, who stood to suffer in the wake of the merger and related antitrust action. Exxon and Mobil station dealers in the Northeast, represented by the National Coalition of Petroleum Retailers, had threatened to sue if their rights were not protected in the merger and resulting sell-offs. To resolve this issue, the FTC said that one or at most two other oil firms could take over operations of Exxon and Mobil on the East Coast. The new owners could use the names "Exxon" and "Mobil," and accept their credit cards for up to 10 years.

The FTC took public comment for 30 days (during December 1999) before giving final approval to bidders for the assets at the end of that month.

INTERNATIONAL ECONOMIC LAW

How does international economic law come into the picture?

International law, including international antitrust law, is an intricate network of regulations and guidelines composed of international agreements, multinational treaties, and policies imposed by international bodies. Here is a list of such areas, adapted from Joel P. Trachtman, Professor of International Law and Academic Dean at the Fletcher School of Law and Diplomacy, Tufts University.

- Domestic laws involving international transactions.
- International trade law, including both the international law created by members of the World Trade Organization and the United Nations, and domestic trade laws.
- International economic integration law, including the law of the European Union, the North American Free Trade Association, and the Latin American regional agreement MERCOSUR.
- Private international law, including international choice of law, choice of forum, enforcement of judgments, and the law of international commerce.
- International regulation involving business. (Examples, among the topics covered in this book, are antitrust actions, intellectual property, product safety, labor, environment, securities, and taxes.)
- International financial law, including private transactional law, regulatory law, the law of foreign direct investment, and international monetary law, such as the law of the International Monetary Fund and the World Bank.

Clearly, few acquirers can or should master all these areas. But acquirers would be wise to run this checklist by the management of or advisers to a candidate company to see if any red flags arise. Then acquirers can focus on those issues.

What are the primary U.S. laws and international agreements affecting U.S. companies?

In the United States, there are laws pertaining to customs, tariffs, and quotas. These are administered by the Department of Commerce.

In addition, there are several international agreements of general relevance. The two broadest agreements are the United Nations Convention on Contracts for the International Sale of Goods, and the General Agreement on Tariffs and Trade (GATT).

The UN Convention on Contracts for the International Sale of Goods covers a broad variety of issues pertaining to the sale of goods, including:

- Formation of contracts.
- Sale of goods.
- Obligations of the seller (delivery of the goods and handing over of documents, conformity of the goods and third-party claims, and remedies for breach of contract by the seller).
- Obligations of the buyer (payment of the price, taking delivery, remedies for breach of contract by the buyer, and passing of risk).
- Obligations of both seller and buyer (provisions common to the obligations of the seller and of the buyer).
- Installment contracts.
- Damages.
- Interest.
- Exemptions.[14]
- Effects of avoidance.
- Preservation of goods.

Any acquirer of a company that sells goods abroad should check for compliance with these standards.

GATT, a more well-known treaty, is the trade agreement that founded the aforementioned World Trade Organization (WTO), representing 117 nations. This group, which monitors 10,000 goods and services, met most recently in the fall of 1999 in Seattle, Washington, where it faced organized protests from labor and environmental groups. Despite its unpopularity with some, compliance with GATT is important, and checking for adherence to it can be an important part of the due diligence work for a candidate company involved in international trade.

CONCLUDING COMMENTS

Antitrust issues are paramount in many mergers, particularly those involving candidate companies of significant size ($10 million or more in gross assets or sales). Interested parties should determine early on how likely it is that they will be required to obtain the necessary antitrust-related consents, how long the process will take, and how difficult and expensive it will be. Furthermore, thorough diligence in the area of business conduct requires some general knowledge of international economic law.

As in any other legal area, consulting with qualified legal counsel is imperative. When the procedures and the criteria for obtaining consents are well defined, this regulatory "audit" can be performed relatively quickly and reliably—enabling the acquirer to focus on other issues of importance, as outlined in the following chapters.

APPENDIX 8A

Revision to the Horizontal Merger Guidelines Issued by the U.S. Department of Justice and the Federal Trade Commission*

April 8, 1997

4. Efficiencies

Competition usually spurs firms to achieve efficiencies internally. Nevertheless, mergers have the potential to generate significant efficiencies by permitting a better utilization of existing assets, enabling the combined firm to achieve lower costs in producing a given quantity and quality than either firm could have achieved without the proposed transaction. Indeed, the primary benefit of mergers to the economy is their potential to generate such efficiencies.[1]

---

1 The Agency will not deem efficiencies to be merger-specific if they could be preserved by practical alternatives that mitigate competitive concerns, such as divestiture or licensing. If a merger affects not whether but only when an efficiency would be achieved, only the timing advantage is a merger-specific efficiency.

*Reprinted verbatim from www.FindLaw.com.

Efficiencies generated through merger can enhance the merged firm's ability and incentive to compete, which may result in lower prices, improved quality, enhanced service, or new products. For example, merger-generated efficiencies may enhance competition by permitting two ineffective (e.g., high cost) competitors to become one effective (e.g., lower cost) competitor. In a coordinated interaction context (see Section 2.1), marginal cost reductions may make coordination less likely or effective by enhancing the incentive of a maverick to lower price or by creating a new maverick firm. In a unilateral effects context (see Section 2.2), marginal cost reductions may reduce the merged firm's incentive to elevate price.

Efficiencies also may result in benefits in the form of new or improved products, and efficiencies may result in benefits even when price is not immediately and directly affected. Even when efficiencies generated through merger enhance a firm's ability to compete, however, a merger may have other effects that may lessen competition and ultimately may make the merger anticompetitive.

The Agency will consider only those efficiencies likely to be accomplished with the proposed merger and unlikely to be accomplished in the absence of either the proposed merger or another means having comparable anticompetitive effects. These are termed merger-specific efficiencies. Only alternatives that are practical in the business situation faced by the merging firms will be considered in making this determination; the Agency will not insist upon a less restrictive alternative that is merely theoretical.

Efficiencies are difficult to verify and quantify, in part because much of the information relating to efficiencies is uniquely in the possession of the merging firms. Moreover, efficiencies projected reasonably and in good faith by the merging firms may not be realized.

Therefore, the merging firms must substantiate efficiency claims so that the Agency can verify by reasonable means the likelihood and magnitude of each asserted efficiency, how and when each would be achieved (and any costs of doing so), how each would enhance the merged firm's ability and incentive to compete, and why each would be merger-specific. Efficiency claims will not be considered if they are vague or speculative or otherwise cannot be verified by reasonable means.

Cognizable efficiencies are merger-specific efficiencies that have been verified and do not arise from anticompetitive reductions in output or service. Cognizable efficiencies are assessed net of costs produced by the merger or incurred in achieving those efficiencies.

The Agency will not challenge a merger if cognizable efficiencies are of a character and magnitude such that the merger is not likely to be anticompetitive in any relevant market.[2] To make the requisite determination, the Agency considers whether cognizable efficiencies likely would be sufficient to reverse the merger's potential to harm consumers in the relevant market, e.g., by preventing price increases in that market.

In conducting this analysis,[3] the Agency will not simply compare the magnitude of the cognizable efficiencies with the magnitude of the likely harm to competition absent the efficiencies. The greater the potential adverse competitive effect of a merger—as indicated by the increase in the HHI* and post-merger HHI from Section 1, the analysis of potential adverse competitive effects from Section 2, and the timeliness, likelihood, and sufficiency of entry from Section 3—the greater must be cognizable efficiencies in order for the Agency to conclude that the merger will not have an anticompetitive effect in the relevant market. When the potential adverse competitive effect of a merger is likely to be particularly large, extraordinarily great cognizable efficiencies would be necessary to prevent the merger from being anticompetitive.

In the Agency's experience, efficiencies are most likely to make a difference in merger analysis when the likely adverse competitive effects, absent the efficiencies, are not great. Efficiencies almost never justify a merger to monopoly or near-monopoly.

---

2   Section 7 of the Clayton Act prohibits mergers that may substantially lessen competition "in any line of commerce . . . in any section of the country." Accordingly, the Agency normally assesses competition in each relevant market affected by a merger independently and normally will challenge the merger if it is likely to be anticompetitive in any relevant market. In some cases, however, the Agency in its prosecutorial discretion will consider efficiencies not strictly in the relevant market, but so inextricably linked with it that a partial divestiture or other remedy could not feasibly eliminate the anticompetitive effect in the relevant market without sacrificing the efficiencies in the other market(s). Inextricably linked efficiencies rarely are a significant factor in the Agency's determination not to challenge a merger. They are most likely to make a difference when they are great and the likely anticompetitive effect in the relevant market(s) is small.

3   The result of this analysis over the short term will determine the Agency's enforcement decision in most cases. The Agency also will consider the effects of cognizable efficiencies with no short-term, direct effect on prices in the relevant market. Delayed benefits from efficiencies (due to delay in the achievement of, or the realization of consumer benefits from, the efficiencies) will be given less weight because they are less proximate and more difficult to predict.

*   Editor's Note: For an explanation of the Herfindahl-Hirschmann Index, see Chapter 8 of this book.

The Agency has found that certain types of efficiencies are more likely to be cognizable and substantial than others. For example, efficiencies resulting from shifting production among facilities formerly owned separately, which enable the merging firms to reduce the marginal cost of production, are more likely to be susceptible to verification, merger-specific, and substantial, and are less likely to result from anticompetitive reductions in output.

Other efficiencies, such as those relating to research and development, are potentially substantial but are generally less susceptible to verification and may be the result of anticompetitive output reductions. Yet others, such as those relating to procurement, management, or capital cost, are less likely to be merger-specific or substantial, or may not be cognizable for other reasons.

ENDNOTES

1. The first two terms—*vertical* and *horizontal*—are well established in the literature. The third term is subject to variation. In their book *The Art of M&A: A Merger/Acquisition/Buyout Guide* (cited in earlier chapters), authors Reed and Lajoux use *diagonal* as the third term, in keeping with the geometry of the antitrust model.

2. These cases are discussed extensively in John E. Kwoka and Lawrence J. White, *The Antitrust Revolution: Economics, Competition, and Policy* (New York: Oxford University Press, 1999).

3. Tony Lin, in "Distinguishing Kodak Lock-In and Franchise Contractual Lock-In," *Southern Illinois Law Journal,* Fall 1998 (Vol. 23, No. 1), notes the following (in abstract): "In *Eastman Kodak Co. v. Image Technical Services, Inc.,* the United States Supreme Court held that Kodak's replacement parts for its own photocopier equipment could be a relevant market for antitrust purposes. This article discusses tying arrangements and compares the Kodak tying arrangement with that of a franchisor and franchisee. The author argues that conducting a preliminary economic analysis does not violate the . . . rule against tying arrangements, and that an economic analysis reveals that franchise tying arrangements are not likely to lead to antitrust concerns. The author then concludes that franchise lock-in and Kodak lock-in are distinguishable under both a legal and economic analysis." Source: University Law Review Project (lawreview.org). The University Law Review Project is a free service provided by the Coalition of Online Law Journals and FindLaw (http://www.FindLaw.com/) with the support of Stanford University and the Legal Information Institute at Cornell Law School. There are archives of these abstracts at FindLaw LegalMinds (http://www.LegalMinds.org/). The participants encourage redistribution of this material.

4. Kwoka and White, op. cit. (note 2).

5. This definition is based on one offered by Kwoka and White (ibid., p. 9), who explain: "Most economists would agree that the social loss from this pricing behavior is related to the output reduction: the deadweight loss 'triangle' created by the foregone net value received by the consumers because of the reduced output. Some economists, and most politicians, would also count the monopolist's excess profits (above competitive levels) as social loss, whereas efficiency theory considers these excess profits as neutral transfers from consumers to the owners of the monopoly enterprise. Some would claim that at least part of the monopolist's potential excess profits are likely to be dissipated either through socially wasteful efforts to defend the monopoly or through inefficiency that arises because of the absence of competitive behaviors."

6. These examples come from Kwoka and White, op. cit. (note 2), p. 9.

7. For a detailed analysis of the Microsoft monopoly case, see Richard J. Gilbert, "Networks, Standards, and the Use of Market Dominance: Microsoft," in Kwoka and White, op. cit., pp. 386–408.

8. This discussion of the HHI index is based on a Hogan & Hartson (Washington, D.C.) client memo dated April 2, 1992—still a valuable presentation after nearly a decade. For a financial point of view on HHI, see J. Fred Weston, "The Payoff in Mergers and Acquisitions," in M. L. Rock, R. H. Rock, and M. Sikora, eds., *The Mergers and Acquisitions Handbook* (New York: McGraw-Hill, 1994), pp. 51–76, esp. p. 69.

9. From the 1982 antitrust guidelines. See Appendix 8A.

10. *Report of the Defense Science Board Task Force on Antitrust Aspects of Defense Industry Consolidations* (Washington, D.C.: Defense Science Board Task Force, 1994).

11. *Report of the Defense Science Board Task Force on Vertical Integration and Supplier Decisions* (Washington, D.C.: Defense Science Board Task Force, 1997).

12. Stephen R. Brenner, "Potential Competition in Local Telephone Service: Bell Atlantic-NYNEX," in Kwoka and White, op. cit. (note 2), p. 116. Mr. Brenner consulted for MCI Telecommunications Corporation and filed testimony for MCI with the New York Public Services Commission analyzing this merger.

13. The facts in this answer are based on a report by Reuters Limited, as reported on the America OnLine news service in December 1999, and confirmed in a number of business periodicals.

14. The UN Convention on Contracts also covers such legal matters as anticipatory breach, exemptions, and effects of avoidance—items that acquirers can delegate to counsel for mastery.

CHAPTER 9

Detecting Exposure Under Intellectual Property Law

Nam et ipsa scientia potestas est.
(Knowledge is power.)

Francis Bacon
Meditationes Sacrae (1597)

INTRODUCTION

When conducting legal due diligence on any company, acquirers should carefully review the status of its intellectual property (IP). Such property is becoming increasingly important in the so-called new economy, which will be predominantly based on proprietary technology employed in a global marketplace. IP infringement was the cause of 1 percent of claims paid in D&O insurance in 1999.[1]

This chapter summarizes the major laws governing the users of intellectual property. Such knowledge can help acquirers secure rights to assets, protect themselves from litigation, and—beyond due diligence—build company value.

- An acquirer can make sure that the candidate company actually owns the property it claims to own. That is, the acquirer can check to determine if all copyrights, patents, and trademarks are registered with the proper authorities, as appropriate. If it does this, the acquirer can defend against future charges of copyright, patent, or trademark infringement.

- An acquirer should check to ensure that all maintenance fees have been paid, so that all the patents owned by the candidate company are truly active. Sometimes companies believe they own a patent and have it listed on a property schedule, but fail to make the maintenance fee payment, thereby allowing the patent to lapse. In some cases, they are unable to reclaim the patent.

- An acquirer can make sure that the candidate company did not infringe the rights of the copyrights, patents, and trademarks held by others, and that it did not commit any other unfair trade practices. For example, when DEC sued Intel for patent infringement on several of its chip patents, Intel responded by searching through its own portfolio to find patents that it could use to sue DEC. Eventually, the dispute was settled when Intel bought a portion of DEC's manufacturing facilities and worked out a cross-licensing agreement.[2]

Potential lawsuits are only the most primitive reason to conduct a search for patents. One authority in this area, Julie Davis, a Chicago-based partner with Arthur Andersen LLP, sees a "pyramid" of value in patent management, beginning with the defensive level and moving up to the visionary level. (See Appendix 9A.)

SCOPE OF INTELLECTUAL PROPERTY LAW

What precisely is intellectual property?

Intellectual property is a term that describes the intangible assets owned by an individual or an organization that are protectable as proprietary. There are three main types of intellectual property: copyrights, patents, and trademarks. Licenses to use such property are a derivative form of intellectual property.

All intellectual property is legally protectable. In fact, federal law specifically protects such property. The constitutional basis for this protection is found in Article I, Section 8, of the U.S. Constitution. This article states that, among other powers, "Congress shall have power to . . . promote the progress of science and useful arts, by securing for limited times to authors and inventors the exclusive right to their respective writings and discoveries." The article also states that Congress has the right to regulate interstate and foreign commerce.

Copyright law grew out of the protection granted to "writings," patent law developed out of the protection granted to "discoveries," and trademark law grew out of Congress's power to regulate commerce. As mentioned in Chapter 4, copyright, patent, and trademark infringement is a source of litigation against corporate officers and directors—particularly from suppliers to a corporation.

COPYRIGHTS

What is a copyright?

A copyright is the right of ownership extended to an individual who has written or otherwise created a tangible or intangible work, or to an organization (e.g., an employer or publisher) that has paid the individual for the work while retaining right of ownership.

Copyrights are protectable under the U.S. Copyright Act of 1976, which was enacted as part of Title 17 of the U.S. Code. State law in this area is inconsistent, and the federal law covering this area includes a provision that effectively gives federal law preeminence over state law when the latter is unclear.

In early copyright law, the term *writings* focused on the written word. The U.S. Copyright Act extended this term to include works in a variety of fields, including:

- Architectural design
- Computer software[3]
- Graphic arts
- Movies (motion pictures)
- Sound recordings (e.g., on CDs and tapes)
- Videos

Any type of work may be copyrighted, as long as it is "original" and in a "concrete medium of expression." (Computer software, although intangible, is apparently considered a concrete medium.)

A copyright gives the owner exclusive rights to the work, including the right of:

- Display
- Distribution
- Licensing
- Performance (including digital audio transmission)
- Reproduction

A copyright may also grant to the owner the exclusive right to produce (or license the production of) *derivatives* of the work. "Fair use" of the work is exempt from copyright law. There is no "bright line" test for fair use, despite rules of thumb such as "150 words." Rather, the fairness of use is judged in relation to a number of factors, including:

- Nature of the copyrighted work.
- Purpose of the use.
- Size and substantiality of the portion of copyrighted work used in relation to that work as a whole.
- Potential market for or value of the copyrighted work.

A number of organizations promote the protection of copyrights, including the Berne Convention for the Protection of Literary and Artistic Works, of which the United States is a member, and the World Intellectual Property Organization, which covers patents and trademarks as well as copyrights.

How long do copyrights last?

For works created on or after January 1, 1978:

- In general, the term is life of the author and 70 years after the author's death.
- For joint works, the term is life of the last surviving author and 70 years after the surviving author's death.
- For anonymous works, pseudonymous works, and works made for hire, the term is 95 years from the year of first publication, or 120 years from date of creation, whichever expires first, unless the identity of one or more authors for an anonymous or pseudonymous work is revealed in the record of the registration, then the term is based on the life of the identified author(s).[4]

How does an organization or individual get a copyright?

It is customary to attach a copyright notice to a work. For example, in the beginning of this book, there is a notice: Copyright © 2000 The McGraw-Hill Companies. It is also traditional to register the copyright by filling out a copyright form and sending multiple copies of a work to the Copyright Office of the Library of Congress. Note, however, that even without taking such measures, an owner of an original work may assert a copyright claim.

How does an organization defend itself against the downloading of a copyrighted work that appears on the Internet?

Companies often use encryption to control access to a copyrighted work, and a new law—the Digital Millennium Copyright Act of 1998, effective January 1,

2000—makes it illegal to sell, manufacture, or offer for sale any technology designed to circumvent encryption.[5]

What documents pertaining to the candidate company's copyrights should the due diligence investigator review?[6]

Key areas include:

- All registered copyright and applications for copyright registration, including titles of works, authors, owners, publication dates, filing dates, issue dates, and countries of registration or application.
- All material unregistered copyrights, including those for software.
- Documentation concerning chain of title, including assignments to the company of works created by contract programmers and chain of title opinion letters.
- Copyright clearance opinion letters evaluating possible infringement.
- Documentation concerning recordation of copyright registrations with the U.S. Customs Service.
- Files concerning review of software usage for unlicensed copies of copyrighted software.
- Files concerning copyright assignments, licenses, and security interests. In some jurisdictions, security interests in copyrights must be perfected in the copyright office and must pertain to a registered copyright.
- Files concerning any threatened or pending copyright infringement litigation.

PATENTS

What exactly is a patent?

A patent is the right of ownership extended to an individual who has invented or otherwise discovered something, or to an organization that has paid that individual to do the work involved in the invention or discovery. A patent is typically defined as a grant extended to the owner of an invention (the individual inventor, or an entity that owns the invention) that excludes others from making, using, or selling the invention, and includes the right to license others to make, use, or sell the invention.

As with copyrights, the constitutional basis for patent protection comes from Article I, Section 8, of the U.S. Constitution, described above. Patents are protectable under the Patent Cooperation Treaty of 1970, which was incorporated into Title 35 of the U.S. Code. Federal courts have exclusive jurisdiction over disputes involving patents.

Patent protection can be extended to inventions that are novel (new and original), useful, and not obvious. Patents may be issued for four general types of inventions/discoveries:

- Compositions of matter
- Machines
- Man-made products
- Processing methods

These last two items merit some commentary. The definition of "man-made products" is expanding to include inventions in the area of design and for bioengineering ("plant patents"). Also, "processing methods" are being interpreted more broadly. This is a hot topic in skirmishes over the patenting of procedures used in Web-based products.

For example, priceline.com claims a patent on reverse auctions. If upheld, that patent may act to force other dot-coms out of business. The holder of the patent could sue others conducting reverse auctions, claiming patent violations.

How long do patents last?

Under current international trade law—as enacted in the 1994 Agreement on Trade-Related Aspects of Intellectual Property (TRIPS) that accompanied the Uruguay Round of the General Agreement on Tariffs and Trade (GATT)—patents are issued for a nonrenewable period of 20 years measured from the date of application. Inventors being granted patents in the United States must pay maintenance fees due at 3.5, 7.5, and 11.5 years from grant of the patent.[7] Fees vary widely by country, however, and if an acquirer buys a company with patents in 70 countries, it will need to master their varying patent fee schedules.

How can an individual or a company get a patent?

The inventor must send a model or a detailed description of the invention to the U.S. Patent and Trademark Office (USPTO), the federal agency charged with administering the patent laws. The USPTO employs examiners who review applications requesting patent protection for an alleged new invention. The average time between patent application and issuance is about 2.5 years, although the process may be much shorter or longer, depending on the situation. Acquirers of intellectual property with a patent pending will want to keep this time frame in mind.

The USPTO looks to see if the applicant for the patent has shown proper "diligence" in filing the application. (For excerpts from the *Manual of Patent Examination Procedures* on the subject of diligence, see Appendix 9B.) If a dispute with a rival arises during the process, proper diligence needs to be taken into consideration, as in any dispute. If an application is rejected, the inventor may appeal the decision.[8]

What aspects of the candidate company's patents should the due diligence investigator review?[9]

Key areas include:

- All patents and pending patent applications, including filing date, issue date, status, country of issuance or application, and claims coverage.
- File wrappers (basic cover sheet information) for patent applications and patents with references, including assignments from inventors to the company.
- Files for any USPTO actions, interferences, continuations, terminal disclaimers, or other USPTO proceedings.
- Patent searches and opinion letters concerning noninfringement and patentability.
- Maintenance fee records for any issued patents.
- Engineers' and scientists' notebooks and invention disclosures schedules kept by the company.
- Files concerning any patent assignments, which should include the right to sue for past infringements.
- Files concerning any patent licenses (cross licenses), which should not exceed the term of the patent. (As mentioned, a patent lasts only 20 years from the date of application.)
- Files concerning any threatened or pending patent infringement litigation, whether brought by the company against another firm or brought by another firm against the company.

TRADEMARKS AND SERVICE MARKS

What exactly is a trademark?

A trademark is the right to use a name associated with a company, product, or concept, as well as the right to use a symbol, picture, sound, or even smell associated with these factors. The mark can already be in use or be one that will be used in the future. (A trademark may be assigned to a trade name, which is the name that a company uses to operate its business.)

Trademarks may be protected by both federal statute under the Lanham Act of 1946, which is now part of Section 15 of the U.S. Code, and a state's statutory and/or common law.

Trademark status may be granted to unique names, symbols, and pictures, and also to unique building designs, color combinations, packaging, presentation and product styles, and even Internet domain names. It is also possible to receive trademark status for identification that does not appear to be distinct or unique, but that over time has developed a secondary meaning identifying it with the product or seller.

The owner of a trademark has exclusive right to use it on the product it was intended to identify and often on related products. Service marks receive the same legal protection as trademarks but are meant to distinguish services rather than products.

How long do trademarks last?

A trademark is indefinite in duration, so long as the mark continues to be used on or in connection with the goods or services for which it is registered, subject to certain defenses. Federally registered trademarks must be renewed every 10 years. A statement of continuing use must be filed between the fifth and sixth year after registration, or the registration is canceled. Rights in trademarks arise through use. Federal registration is recommended.

How does a company receive a trademark?

As in the case of a patent, a company registers its trademark with the USPTO. If the trademark is initially approved by an examiner, it is published in the official gazette of the USPTO to notify other parties of the pending approval so that the application may be opposed. As with patents, rejected applicants may appeal.

State trademark laws differ, but most states have adopted a version of the Model State Trademark Bill and/or the Uniform Deceptive Trade Practices Act of 1964, which cover trademarks. Under state law, trademarks are protected (even without federal registration) as part of the common law concept referred to as *unfair competition*.

What is the common law of unfair competition?

The law of unfair competition involves wrongs (torts) committed by a party that causes an economic injury to a business through a deceptive or wrongful business practice. (In this usage, unfair competition does not refer to the economic harms imposed by monopolies and oligopolies, covered in the previous chapter.)

Can you give an example of a deceptive or wrongful business practice?

There are many kinds of unfair trade practices, including:

- Bait and switch—unauthorized substitution of one brand of goods for another.
- Breach of confidentiality—for example, use of confidential information by a company's former employee to solicit customers away from the company.
- Breach of a restrictive covenant.
- False advertising—using a false offer to lure customers.
- False representation—making false claims about products or services.
- Misappropriation—unauthorized use of an intangible asset not protected by trademark or copyright laws.
- Theft of trade secrets—stealing proprietary information from a business (see below).
- Trade libel—negative untrue statements about a business.
- Trademark infringement—using another company's trademark.

The law regarding unfair competition is part of the common law of each state. In the areas of copyrights, trademarks, and false advertising, federal law may apply (and may preempt state law). In fact, one reason that Congress established the Federal Trade Commission (FTC), described in Chapter 4, was to protect consumers and other businesses from deceptive trade practices. A few states have enacted legislation modeled after the previously mentioned Uniform Deceptive Trade Practices Act of 1964 to ban certain kinds of unfair competition.

What are some review areas for trademarks?

The investigator should review:[10]

- All trademark and service mark registrations and applications, including dates of first use, filing dates, issue dates, classes of goods and services, status, countries of issuance or application, and assignments.
- All trade names, company names, brand names, and unregistered trademarks and service marks.
- File wrappers for trademark applications and registrations.
- Files for any office actions, oppositions, cancellations, or other USPTO proceedings.
- Searches and opinion letters concerning clearance and registrability.
- Files relating to any Internet domain names registered by the company, including any threatened or pending disputes under domain name dispute policies.
- Documentation concerning recordation of trademarks with the U.S. Customs Service.
- Files concerning any trademark assignments, which should include an assignment of goodwill and, if the mark is the subject of an intent-to-use application, an assignment of the business to which the mark pertains.
- Files concerning any trademark licenses, which should include quality control language.
- Files concerning any threatened or pending opposition or cancellation proceeding in the USPTO, or any federal or state trademark infringement, dilution, false advertising, or unfair competition proceedings involving either the company's trademarks or the marks of another.

TRADE SECRETS

What exactly is a trade secret?

A trade secret is "information, including a formula, pattern, compilation, program, device, method, technique, or process" that is kept a secret and that derives value from being kept secret.[11] Many states have adopted the Uniform Trade Secrets Act to govern this area. Acquirers need to pay special attention to trade secrets given the recent case of *Electro Optical Industries v. White* (1999). As described in the Landmark Cases section at the end of this book, the court found that certain types of trade secret disclosures are "inevitable" and therefore not legally actionable.

What documents pertaining to trade secrets should be reviewed in a due diligence investigation?

Key areas of review include:

- All inventions that are not the subject of issued patents, but may be the subject of patent applications.
- All software developed by or for the company for which confidentiality has been maintained.
- All other material business that has been kept secret and from which the company derives economic benefit by keeping it secret.
- Documents reflecting procedures to protect the company's trade secrets, such as the company's written confidentiality policies and nondisclosure agreements.
- Documents reflecting the company's implementation of such policies, such as by marking materials as "confidential," restricting access to materials (such as barring entry into sensitive parts of its manufacturing plants), and similar actions.
- Documents relating to hiring and exit interviews of technology and other sensitive personnel.
- Nondisclosure agreements (often called NDAs).
- Documents reflecting any company policies addressing protection of the trade secrets of others that may be received by the company through authorized disclosure, inadvertent receipt, or competitive intelligence.
- Documents relating to policies and procedures for receiving unsolicited submissions.
- Files concerning any trade secret misappropriation litigation, which may involve departed employees, relations with suppliers and customers, or competitive intelligence.

LICENCES AND LICENSE AGREEMENTS

What exactly are licenses and license agreements?

The word *license* means permission. A *license* is the direct granting of permission by a governing entity to a governed entity—as when a local government permits a business to operate within its jurisdiction. A *license agreement* is an agreement between two peers to use, adapt, sell, or otherwise benefit from an invention or other item of value.

An acquirer should try to become a successor to all the candidate company's licenses and license agreements. As stated in the sample Due Diligence Checklist in the back of this book, licenses may be absolutely essential to the ability of a corporation to continue legally to conduct its business. The buyer should ensure that all such necessary licenses are current and in good order and that these licenses will be readily transferable, or remain valid, in the context of the acquisition transaction. It is generally useful to obtain the advice of special counsel or experts in the particular field (e.g., Federal Communications Commission counsel in the case of broadcasting licenses).

What documents pertaining to licenses should be reviewed in a due diligence investigation?

Key documents include:

- All intellectual property licenses in which the company is a licensee, including names of parties, dates of expiration, rights granted, and any pertinent restrictions such as territory or transferability.
- All intellectual property licenses in which the company is licensor, including names of parties, dates of expiration, rights granted, and any pertinent restrictions.
- Evidence of any registered user filings in countries where such filings are required.

OTHER INTELLECTUAL PROPERTY

In addition to copyrights, patents, trademarks, trade secrets, and licenses, what other intellectual property should an acquirer examine?

The above list covers most intellectual property, but acquires should also look to the following:

- *Goodwill* is one important asset. We are not referring to the concept of goodwill used in purchase accounting. (In that concept, goodwill is the difference between purchase price and book value.) As intellectual property, goodwill is defined as the "expectancy of continued patronage."

- *Know-how* is another distinct asset. It is knowledge within a company of how to perform actions that build company value.

ASSIGNMENTS AND TRANSFERS OF INTELLECTUAL PROPERTY

In addition to documents pertaining to copyrights, patents, trademarks, and licenses, what other documents might help establish a company's claim of intellectual property ownership?

The due diligence investigator should take a close look at any agreements with individual employees or subcontractors, or with other companies, to identify any assignments or transfers of intellectual property of any kind. These documents include:

- Documents showing assignments of intellectual property to or from the company, including grants of security interests.
- Documents showing recordation (written record) of assignments of applications for intellectual property rights, including grants of security interests.
- Documents showing releases of security interests in intellectual property, and showing recordation of such releases.
- Agreements with persons or entities that may create, work with, or have access to the company's intellectual property (including employees and independent contractors), showing assignment to the company of rights in intellectual property and confidentiality of trade secrets.
- Agreements relating to databases, processing services, and/or software.
- Agreements pertaining to know-how, research and development, and technology.
- Joint venture, partnership, and strategic alliance agreements.
- Government grants and related agreements.
- Agreements pertaining to domain names, source codes, and the like.
- Noncompete and nonsolicitation agreements.

What other types of documents might be usefully examined in a due diligence investigation?

The acquirer should check any files pertaining to actual or potential litigation against the company for infringement of the intellectual property rights of others. As mentioned in Chapter 4, infringement is a common source of litigation from suppliers and competitors. The due diligence investigator should also look at relevant insurance policies covering such litigation matters.

Once the due diligence investigators have gathered all these files, what should they do?

First, they should maintain copies of the files, for use in the event that the candidate company's claims to intellectual property ownership ever come under challenge.

Investigators should also examine all these files to see if the company can document ownership of the property it claims to have. If the company lacks such ownership, the acquirer can ask the company to obtain it, or to accept a reduced purchase price reflecting the lack of documentation.

Having determined all the property owned by the candidate company, the acquirer is then in a good position to value it. Valuation can be based on current or potential future royalty revenues or other income generated by the property. Most professional service companies have teams specializing in intellectual property valuation, and there are a number of valuation services that specialize in it.

How can a candidate company make sure that the acquirer will not use some of the confidential knowledge it gains during the intellectual property review?

This should be covered under the confidentiality agreement signed at the outset of the transaction. For a sample confidentiality agreement, see Appendix 1A.

CONCLUDING COMMENTS

Intellectual property—including copyrights, patents, trademarks, licenses, and trade secrets—composes an increasingly important part of the value of many companies today. It can add substantially to a company's value if its ownership is well documented. At the same time, it can detract from value if ownership documentation is faulty, or if the company has violated intellectual property rights of others.

Therefore, the due diligence investigator needs to examine the ownership claims to such assets, to ensure that they will be effectively transferred to the acquirer. At the same time, the investigator needs to make sure that the company is not vulnerable to major claims for intellectual property infringement.

The investigator who does this work thoroughly will provide a major service to any corporate acquirer—especially in today's information-based economy.

A P P E N D I X 9A

The Intellectual Property "Pyramid"[*]

Visionary Level

Integration Level

Profit Center Level

Cost Control Level

Defensive Level

At the *defensive* level, the company uses patents as a shield to protect itself from litigation. These companies hope that by creating a "pile of patents" and other intellectual property (IP) bigger than their competitors' piles, they can shield themselves from litigation because they will be able to negotiate cross licenses rather than go to court.

At the *cost control* level, the company focuses on how to reduce the costs of filing and maintaining its intellectual property rights. Well-executed strategies in this area can save large companies millions of dollars annually.

---

[*]   Julie L. Davis of Arthur Andersen LLP, Chicago, Illinois.

At the *profit center* level, companies devise ways to continue reducing costs while at the same time generating more revenue from their existing IP through sales, licencing, and patent rights enforcement.

At the *integration* level, the IP function stops focusing exclusively on self-centered activities and reaches out beyond its own department to serve a greater purpose within the organization as a whole. In essence, its activities have been integrated with the activities of other functions and imbedded in the day-to-day operations, procedures, and strategies of the company.

At the *visionary* level, the IP function takes on the challenge of identifying future trends in the industry. It identifies future industry and consumer trends, and anticipates technological revolutions. As such, it seeks to develop or acquire the IP that will be necessary to ensure the company's long-term survival and success.

Clearly, understanding such levels can help acquirers gain the most value from the intellectual property they acquire.

APPENDIX 9B

Diligence in Filing a Patent Application: Excerpts from the Manual of Patent Examination Procedures

The U.S. Patent and Trademarks Office (USPTO) has defined diligence in applications for patents and trademarks. The following text is composed of verbatim excerpts from the Manual of Patent Examination Procedures *(Washington, D.C.: Government Printing Office, 1999). For ease of reading, we have omitted references to cases, and we have not used ellipses (≈ ≈ ≈) to show breaks between paragraphs. Key terms include* conception *(meaning the initial idea for the invention) and* reduction to practice *(meaning application of the idea into a working invention).*

DILIGENCE

Diligence comes into question only after prior conception is established.

In patent law, an inventor is either diligent at a given time or he is not diligent [in filing for a patent]; there are no degrees of diligence. An applicant may be diligent within the meaning of the patent law when he or she is doing nothing, if his or her lack of activity is excused. Note, however, that the record must set forth an explanation or excuse for the inactivity; the USPTO or courts will not speculate on possible explanations for delay or inactivity. Diligence must be judged on the basis of the particular facts in each case. See *Manual of Patent Examination Procedures* (MPEP) Section 2138.06 for a detailed discussion of the diligence requirement for proving prior invention.

Under Title 37 Code of Federal Regulations (CFR) 1.131, the critical period in which diligence must be shown begins just prior to the effective date of the reference and ends with the date of a reduction to practice, either actual or constructive (i.e., filing a United States patent application). Note, therefore, that only diligence before reduction to practice is a material consideration. The "lapse of time between the completion or reduction to practice of an invention and the filing of an application thereon" is not relevant to an affidavit or declaration under 37 CFR 1.131.

DILIGENCE IN FILING

When a reissue application is filed within two years from the date of the original patent, a rejection on the grounds of lack of diligence or delay in filing the reissue should not normally be made, in the absence of evidence to the contrary.

However, as stated in the fourth paragraph of 35 U.S.C. 251, "No reissued patent shall be granted enlarging the scope of the claims of the original patent unless applied for within two years from the grant of the original patent."

A reissue filed on the two-year anniversary date is considered filed within two years.

A reissue application can be granted a filing date without an oath or declaration, or the filing fee being present in accordance with 37 CFR 1.53(d)(1). Applicant will be given a period of time to provide the missing parts and to pay the surcharge under 37 CFR 1.16(e).

"REASONABLE DILIGENCE"

The diligence of 35 U.S.C. 102(g) relates to reasonable "attorney-diligence" and "engineering-diligence," which does not require that "an inventor or his attorney . . . drop all other work and concentrate on the particular invention involved . . . ."

Critical Period for Establishing Diligence Between One Who Was First to Conceive But Later to Reduce to Practice the Invention

The critical period for diligence for a first conceiver but second reducer begins not at the time of conception of the first conceiver but just prior to the entry in the field of the party who was first to reduce to practice and continues until the first conceiver reduces to practice.

What serves as the entry date into the field of a first reducer is dependent upon what is being relied on by the first reducer, e.g., conception plus reasonable diligence to reduction to an actual reduction to practice or a constructive reduction to practice by the filing of [an application].

The Entire Period During Which Diligence Is Required Must Be Accounted for By Either Affirmative Acts or Acceptable Excuses

An applicant must account for the entire period during which diligence is required. A two-day period lacking activity has been held to be fatal. Efforts to exploit an invention commercially do not constitute diligence in reducing it to practice. An actual reduction to practice in the case of a design for a three-dimensional article requires that it should be embodied in some structure other than a mere drawing.

The period during which diligence is required must be accounted for by either affirmative acts or acceptable excuses.

Work Relied Upon to Show Reasonable Diligence Must Be Directly Related to the Reduction to Practice

The work relied upon to show reasonable diligence must be directly related to the reduction to practice of the invention in issue.

DILIGENCE REQUIRED IN PREPARING AND FILING PATENT APPLICATION

The diligence of attorney in preparing and filing patent application inures to the benefit of the inventor. Conception was established at least as early as the date a draft of a patent application was finished by a patent attorney on behalf of the inventor. Conception is less a matter of signature than it is one of disclosure. Attorney does not prepare a patent application on behalf of particular named persons, but on behalf of the true inventive entity. Six days to execute and file application is acceptable.

E N D N O T E S

1. The 1 percent figure is from Tillinghast-Towers Perrin, op. cit. (Chapter 4, note 8). The authors extend thanks to the Legal Information Institute at Cornell University for providing the full text of the laws and cases cited here, and for providing an insightful explanation of these laws. Readers are encouraged to use this excellent Web site, which can be found at law.cornell.edu.

2. Source: Julie L. Davis, Managing Partner, Worldwide Intellectual Property Practice, Arthur Andersen LLC. Ms. Davis is based in Chicago, Illinois.

3. For software-based works, there is the Coalition for Networked Information. The CNI Web site is cni.org.

4. Source: Carl Davis, Kennedy, Davis & Hodge, Atlanta, Georgia. This firm provides intellectual property legal services, including copyright registration, evaluation of inventions as to patentability and prosecution of patents for inventions, and clearance and registration of trademarks, as well as related litigation.

5. Carol Anne Been, "High Technology and Intellectual Property Due Diligence Checklist," *Conducting Due Diligence 1999*, pp. 905ff.

6. The items in this checklist and others in this chapter rely heavily on the expertise of Carol Anne Been, ibid.

7. Source: Carl Davis, op. cit. (note 4).

8. Appeals can be made to the Patents and Trademark Office's board of appeals, with further or alternative review available from the U.S. Court of Appeals for the Federal Circuit, or the U.S. District Court for the District of Columbia. Source: Legal Information Institute, op. cit. (note 1). Since its formation in 1982, the Court of Appeals for the Federal Circuit (known as the Federal Circuit) has had primary jurisdiction over patents.

9. The remainder of this chapter relies heavily on the expertise of Carol Anne Been, op. cit. (note 5). We highly recommend this article in its entirety.

10. Ibid, pp. 909–911.

11. Uniform Trade Secrets Act, Section 1ff., 14 U.S.A. 541.

Detecting Exposure Under Consumer Protection Law

Rather a tough customer in argyment.

Charles Dickens
Barnaby Ridge (1841)

INTRODUCTION

Consumers—paying customers—are a company's wellspring of revenues, a vital factor in the life of any business. Therefore, an important part of due diligence investigation is the analysis of the candidate company to ensure compliance with consumer protection laws and the proper relationships with its customers. In this chapter, we give an overview of consumer protection law and regulation.

Such an overview may come in handy to many acquirers, who would be wise to exercise care in this area. As noted in Chapter 4, customers, suppliers, competitors, and other contractors together make up 18.6 percent of lawsuits against companies, based on trends from 1990 to 1999.[1] The average settlement in 1999 received by customers was $3,106,376.[2]

By understanding the consumer protection laws, the acquirer can do a more thorough job of litigation analysis—the examination of existing claims against a company to determine their validity and potential dollar impact. Acquirers cannot be too careful here. For example, all the major product liability cases—such as those involving asbestos, thalidomide, birth control shields, and tobacco—began with a first case that changed life for one company, in some cases an acquirer. In the early 2000s, emerging areas for litigation include not only obviously risky products such as handguns, but also bioengineered food (genetically modified crops), managed health care, and vitamins.

The following review should interest most acquirers. Remember, when you buy a company, in most cases, you buy its potential for future lawsuits. Courts are increasingly finding successor (that is, acquirer) liability, particularly with respect to product liability claims.

CONSUMER PROTECTION LAW: AN OVERVIEW

What are the main types of consumer protection laws?

Consumer protection laws can be found in a variety of sources—notably the following:

- Product liability law (including tort law)
- Food and drug law
- Consumer credit law

PRODUCT LIABILITY LAWS

What is product liability?

Product liability refers to the liability of any or all parties involved in the making of a product for harm caused by that product.[3] The parties that might be named in a product liability suit include:

- The manufacturer of the parts that make up the product (component parts).
- The assembler of the product.
- The wholesaler of the product.
- The retailer of the product.
- The "wholetailer" of the product (company, often Internet based, acting as both wholesaler and retailer).

The harm may be done to someone who bought, borrowed, or otherwise came into contact with the product, even if the harm occurs after an alteration of the product by a reseller. (See, for example, *Saratoga Fishing Co. v. J. M. Martin & Co.*, 1997.) Court decisions have established certain ground rules for proving causation—the link between the alleged defect and the alleged harm—and for determining harm.

Product liability claims can be based on negligence, strict liability (under tort law, discussed below), or breach of warranty, depending on the jurisdiction where the claim is based. The common point in all suits is the argument that the product is defective.

For the purpose of product liability lawsuits, what are the technical definitions of "product" and "defective"?

The term *product* generally includes some form of manufactured product, such as a lawn mower, but exceptional court cases—according to the Legal Information Institute at Cornell University—have expanded the definition to include nonmanufactured products such as gas, personal residences, pets from pet stores, and even navigational charts.

A *defect* is a flaw in the design, manufacture, or marketing of a product. Design defects are inherent; they exist before the product is manufactured. While the item might serve its purpose well, it may be unreasonably dangerous to use because of a design flaw. On the other hand, manufacturing defects may occur during the construction or production of the item. Only a few out of many products of the same type are flawed in this case. Defects in marketing deal with improper instructions and failures to warn consumers of latent dangers in the product.

Product liability is generally considered a "strict liability" offense. Strict liability wrongs do not depend on the degree of care exercised by the defendant. Translated to product liability terms, a defendant is liable when it is shown that the product is defective. It is irrelevant whether the manufacturer or supplier exercised great care. If there is a defect in the product that causes harm, the maker will be liable for it. We will discuss the due diligence implications of this distinction at the end of the chapter.

What are the main sources of product liability law?

There is no single federal products liability law. Instead there is a patchwork of federal and state law.

Federal laws address specific aspects of product safety. These laws include:

- The Consumer Product Safety Act
- The Flammable Fabrics Act
- The Poison Prevention Packaging Act
- The Federal Hazardous Substances Act (see also Chapter 9)

If there is a conflict between state and federal law, federal law takes precedence.

What regulators have jurisdiction over consumer product safety?

The relevant federal agency is called the Consumer Product Safety Commission (CPSC). This agency has jurisdiction to enforce the product safety laws listed above. Its charter states that the purpose of the agency is to:

- Protect the public against unreasonable risks of injury from consumer products.
- Develop uniform safety standards for consumer products and minimize conflicting state and local regulations.
- Promote research and investigation into the causes and prevention of product-related deaths, illnesses, and injuries.

The charter further states that to help protect the public from unreasonable risks of injury associated with consumer products, the CPSC:

- Requires manufacturers to report defects in products that could create substantial hazards.
- Requires, where appropriate, corrective action with respect to specific substantially hazardous consumer products already in commerce.
- Collects information on consumer product-related injuries and conducts research on consumer product hazards.
- Encourages and assists in the development of voluntary standards related to the safety of consumer products.
- Establishes, where appropriate, mandatory consumer product standards.
- Bans, where appropriate, hazardous consumer products.

The CPSC Web site publishes details of the agency's actions against companies, among other information.

What about state law regulating consumer product safety and related liability?

Since state laws can vary greatly, the U.S. Department of Commerce has promulgated a Model Uniform Product Liability Act (MUPLA) for voluntary use by the states.[4] Many states have enacted comprehensive product liability statutes.

The general law of product liability derives from two sources: tort law and the Uniform Commercial Code.

Could you review the basics of tort law as they apply to product liability?

Torts, as mentioned in Chapter 4, are wrongs recognized by law as grounds for a lawsuit. Tort law is state law created generally through judicial decisions (common law) and by legislatures through statutory enactment (statutory law). Tort law includes consideration of injury or harm caused by products.

While some torts may also be crimes punishable by imprisonment, the aim of tort law is to provide monetary relief to victims for the damages incurred by another person's actions, and to deter others from committing the same harms. The injured person may sue for monetary damages and/or an injunction to prevent the continuation of the wrongful conduct. Monetary damages collectible by the injured party may cover: loss of earning capacity, pain and suffering, and/or reasonable medical expenses. Damages may include both present and future expected losses and even a punitive component. There has been movement to cap the award of punitive damages, but so far without universal application. (See *Honda Motor Company Co., Ltd., et al. v. Oberg,* 1994).

Torts fall into three categories: *intentional torts, negligent torts,* and *strict liability torts.* Intentional torts are purposeful wrongs that the defendant intended through his or her action. Negligent torts occur when the defendant's actions were unreasonably unsafe. Strict liability wrongs, as mentioned above, do not depend on the fault of the defendant; they are established when a particular action or product causes damage.

What does the Uniform Commercial Code say about product liability?

The Uniform Commercial Code sets some standards on the sale of goods that have an impact on the manufacture and sale of products. Of special importance is Article 2, dealing primarily with the sale of goods. A major part of Article 2, which has been adopted by a majority of states, describes the implied and express *warranties of merchantability* in the sale of goods as follows:

(1) Unless excluded or modified, a warranty that the goods shall be merchantable is implied in a contract for their sale if the seller is a merchant with respect to goods of that kind . . .

(2) Goods to be merchantable must [at least]:
   a. pass without objection in the trade under the contract description; and
   b. in the case of fungible goods, [be] of fair average quality within the description; and
   c. [be] fit for the ordinary purposes for which such goods are used; and

    d. run, within the variations permitted by the agreement, of even kind, quality and quantity within each unit and among all units involved; and

    e. [be] adequately contained, packaged, and labeled as the agreement may require; and

    f. conform to the promise or affirmations of fact made on the container or label if any.

(3) Unless excluded or modified . . . other implied warranties may arise from course of dealing or usage of trade.[5]

What is the authoritative text on product liability under tort law and what basic points does it cover?

In 1998, the American Law Institute published a comprehensive statement on tort law in the product liability area, entitled *Restatement of the Law 3d, Torts: Product Liability* (New York: American Law Institute, 1998). The individuals ("reporters") responsible for the drafting of this text were Professor James A. Henderson, Jr. of Cornell Law School (affiliated with the Legal Information Institute cited in note 1) and Professor Aaron D. Twerski of Brooklyn Law School.

Restatement 3d deals with the liability of commercial product sellers and distributors for harm caused by their products, updating a previous document of the same title (but called *Restatement of the Law 2d*, published in the mid-1960s). *Restatement 3d* identifies three types of defects:

- *Design Defects.* Here the foreseeable risks of harm posed by the product could have been reduced or avoided by the adoption of a reasonable alternative design, and failure to use the alternative design renders the product not reasonably safe.

- *Manufacturing Defects.* The product departs from its intended design, even if all possible care was exercised.

- *Inadequate Instructions or Warnings Defects.* The foreseeable risks of harm posed by the product could have been reduced or avoided by reasonable instructions or warnings, and their omission renders the product not reasonably safe. The harm may be caused by misrepresentations, postsale failure to warn, and postsale failure to recall products.

Importantly, the *Restatement* covers (in Chapter 3) the liability of a successor to the business of a product seller. In particular, it covers liability for harm caused by defective products that a predecessor sold commercially by a successor's own postsale failure to warn, and by the sale or distribution as one's own of a product manufactured by another.

It also covers the related topic of affirmative defenses, dealing with apportionment of responsibility between or among plaintiff, sellers and distributors of defective products, and others, as well as with disclaimers, limitations, waivers, and other contractual outs as defenses to product liability claims for harm to persons.

Finally, the *Restatement* covers product liability in consumer-sensitive industries such as food and drugs—the focus of our next section.

FOOD AND DRUG LAWS

What is the basis for consumer protection via food and drug laws?

Food production has been regulated in the United States since the dawn of the Industrial Revolution in the mid-1800s. The federal government, however, did not pass major legislation until 1906, when the U.S. Congress enacted the Food and Drug Act and the Meat Inspection Act as Section 21 of the U.S. Code. The Food and Drug Act was repealed later, but replaced with a wide range of consumer protection statutes, including:

- The Food, Drug, and Cosmetic Act of 1938, regulating cosmetics and therapeutic devices.
- The Food Additives Amendment of 1957, requiring the evaluation of food additives to establish safety.
- The Delaney Clause of the Food Additives Act of 1958, forbidding the use of substances found in foods causing cancer in laboratory animals.
- The Kefauver-Harris Drug Amendments of 1962, requiring drug manufacturers to show that their drugs were safe.
- The Nutrition Labeling and Education Act of 1990, requiring all packaged foods to carry labels with nutrition information.

What federal agency regulates consumer protection in the area of food and drugs?

Food and drugs in the United States are regulated by the Food and Drug Administration (FDA). It began as an independent agency, but since 1979 has been part of the Department of Health and Human Services. The products regulated by the FDA account for more than one-fourth of all consumer spending.

The FDA's charter is short. It states that the agency exists to "protect the health of the Nation against impure and unsafe foods, drugs, and cosmetics, and other potential hazards." The agency's jurisdiction over food includes labeling of all packaged foods. Similarly, its jurisdiction over drugs spans a broad range, from cosmetics to medical devices. The FDA also protects the rights and safety of patients in clinical trials of new medical products, monitors the promotional activities of drug and device manufacturers, and oversees the safety of the nation's blood supply.

Does the FDA have jurisdiction over alcohol and tobacco?

No. That is the business of the Bureau of Alcohol, Tobacco, and Firearms. There is some talk currently about giving the FDA jurisdiction over tobacco, but if it gains jurisdiction, some have suggested that it may have to ban tobacco entirely—on the theory that tobacco has no beneficial use, only harmful side effects.

CONSUMER CREDIT LAWS

What is consumer credit law?

Consumer credit law is an area of law that ensures equal access to credit by creditworthy individuals and protects consumers from false advertising, exorbitant interest, and other ills associated with credit. Credit enables consumers to purchase goods or services without paying full cost at the time of the purchase. Consumer credit may be in the form of a credit card, a line of credit, or a loan.

What are the main sources of consumer credit law?

The law of consumer credit is embodied primarily in federal and state statutory law that provides consumers with protection in their transactions. These laws protect consumers and establish guidelines for the credit industry.

States have passed various statutes regulating consumer credit. The Uniform Consumer Credit Code has been adopted in seven states and Guam. It's purpose is to protect consumers who are obtaining credit financing for transactions, to ensure that adequate credit is provided, and to govern the credit industry in general.

Congress passed the Consumer Protection Act (as Part of U.S. Code Section 15, Chapter 41) in part to regulate the consumer credit industry. The act requires creditors to disclose credit terms to consumers obtaining credit. The Consumer Protection Act also protects consumers from loan sharks, restricts the garnishing of wages, and empowers the National Commission on Consumer Finance to investigate the consumer finance industry. The act also prohibits discrimination based on sex or marital status in the extending of credit, and regulates credit card companies, credit reporting agencies, and certain debt collectors.

CONCLUDING COMMENTS

Consumer issues are too often overlooked in acquisitions, yet they form an important part of any company's life. Consumers drive the top line of business, bringing in revenues. They also create an important aspect of the company's general reputation in the financial marketplace. Finally, consumers can become a formidable adversary in court, with the help of the plaintiffs bar and regulators. Knowledge of consumer protection laws and related global standards can help any acquirer conduct a comprehensive, consumer-friendly due diligence investigation of any transaction.

Looking beyond the letter of the law, an acquirer can achieve excellence in consumer relations by following the principles laid out in the Caux Roundtable Principles for Business (from Caux, Switzerland), a multinational group of business leaders.[6] The principles, in part, read as follows:

- We believe in treating all customers with dignity, irrespective of whether they purchase our products and services directly from us or otherwise acquire them in the market. We therefore have a responsibility to:
- Provide our customers with the highest quality products and services, consistent with their requirements.
- Make every effort to ensure that the health and safety of our customers, as well as the quality of their environment, will be sustained or enhanced by our products and services.
- Assure respect for human dignity in products offered, in marketing, and in advertising.
- Respect the integrity of the culture of our customers.

Companies that abide by these five simple principles are well on their way to avoiding litigation from or on behalf of consumers.

E N D N O T E S

1. The figures in this section are based on Tillinghast-Towers Perrin, *1999 Directors and Officers Liability Survey: U.S. and Canadian Results* (New York: Tillinghast-Towers Perrin, 2000).

2. Customers sue over a number of issues, including general issues such as contract disputes, deception and dishonesty, and restraint of trade. In this chapter, we focus only on lawsuits based on laws specifically enacted to protect consumers.

3. The authors acknowledge the Legal Information Institute at Cornell University (law.cornell.edu) as an important source of basic information for this section.

4. For the past two decades, members of Congress have tried to pass a major product liability reform bill, but so far reformers have not been successful—partly because of opposition from the American Trial Lawyers Association, also known as the plaintiffs bar.

5. Quoted verbatim from UCC Article 2, Section 314, General Obligation and Construction of Contract; Implied Warranty: Merchantability; Usage of Trade.

6. The Caux Roundtable consists of senior business leaders from Europe, Japan, and the United States. The roundtable was founded in 1986 by Frederick Philips, former president of Philips Electronics, and Olivier Giscard d'Estaing, vice chairman of INSEAD. It has been chaired by U.S. business executives as well, including Winston Wallin, former chairman and CEO of Medtronic, Inc. The roundtable has offices in the Hague, Netherlands; Tokyo, Japan; and Washington, D.C.

Detecting Exposure Under Environmental Law

The Good Man pouring from his pitcher clear,
But brims the poisoned well.

Herman Melville
Timoleo (1891)

INTRODUCTION

One major source of potential acquirer liability involves noncompliance with applicable environmental laws. Unfortunately, as in many areas of due diligence, good intentions may be of no avail. An innocent acquirer may well be tainted by the environmental crimes committed by those employed by an acquired corporation—sometimes at a level beyond the easy scrutiny of officers and directors. Therefore, we begin the chapter with an overview of this complex legal area—followed by some tips on environmental due diligence.

A word of advice: Environmental law is not just for "smokestacks." Most industries—in the manufacturing and service sectors alike—engage in activities that have at least some impact on the environment. The environment, after all, encompasses land, water, and air, which all affect one another. A study of the law brings this point home—and shows the way toward due diligence in this area.

ENVIRONMENTAL LAW: AN OVERVIEW

What are the origins of federal environmental law in the United States?

The National Environmental Policy Act (NEPA) was passed in 1969, followed by the Environmental Quality Improvement Act, the Environmental

Education Act, and the establishment of the Environmental Protection Agency (EPA).

With these actions, the federal government sought to protect the nation's natural resources. According to the Code of Federal Regulations, Title 40, these include "land, fish, wildlife, biota (plants), air, water, ground water, drinking water supplies, and other such resources belonging to, managed by, held in trust by, appertaining to, or otherwise controlled by the United States, any State or local government, or any foreign government."

State statutory law reflects the same concerns. In addition, the common law (particularly in decisions pertaining to nuisance) may provide some remedies.

What current federal laws govern environmental matters?

The U.S. Code has many relevant sections including Title 15, dealing with commercial law; Title 16, dealing with conservation; Title 40, dealing with public property; Title 42, dealing with public health; and Title 43, dealing with public lands. The laws that concern most acquirers are found in Title 42. Here are the major laws:

- *Comprehensive Environmental Response, Compensation, and Liability Act (CERCLA).* Also known as "Superfund," CERCLA outlaws certain types of pollution, generally defined as the contamination of air, water, or earth by harmful substances. It is found in Title 42 of the U.S. Code, Sections 9601 ff.
- *Nuclear Waste Policy Act.* Enacted as Title 42 of the U.S. Code, Sections 10101 ff., this statute aims to achieve safe disposal of nuclear wastes.
- *Resource Conservation and Recovery Act (RCRA).* Enacted as part of Title 42 of the U.S. Code, Sections 6901 ff., RCRA is a comprehensive regulatory statute aimed at controlling solid waste disposal.
- *Federal Clean Water Act (FCWA).* Found in Title 33 of the U.S. Code, Sections 1251 ff., this law aims to curb the pollution of water, both directly through dumping and indirectly through ground pollution that seeps into reservoirs.
- *Clean Air Act (CAA).* Enacted to control air pollution, CAA is located in Title 42 of the U.S. Code, Sections 7401 ff.
- *Toxic Substances Control Act (TSCA).* TSCA requires chemicals manufacturers to test new chemicals and submit results to the EPA. It is located in Title 15 of the U.S. Code, Sections 2601 ff.

State law varies, although some states have adopted model statutes.[1] In addition, some states have enacted environmental protection statutes that create a "superlien" on property of individuals or companies liable for pollution.

What agencies are involved in environmental protection?

The primary federal governmental agency involved in environmental protection is the Environmental Protection Agency (EPA), founded in 1970.

The purpose of the agency, according to its charter, is to:

- Enable coordinated and effective government action on behalf of the environment.
- Endeavor to achieve systematic control and abatement of pollution, by properly administering and integrating a variety of research, monitoring, standard-setting, and enforcement activities.
- Provide coordination and support for research and antipollution activities conducted by state and local governments, private and public groups, individuals, and educational institutions.
- Reinforce efforts on the part of other federal agencies to assess the impact of their operations on the environment.
- Furnish written comments on environmental impact statements and publish its findings.

In addition, the Occupational Safety and Health Administration (OSHA) within the Department of Labor (DOL) has promulgated regulations affecting the storage and security of hazardous substances. (For more on OSHA, see Chapter 12). Furthermore, the Department of Energy and Department of the Interior have adopted regulations that affect some businesses. It is beyond the scope of this chapter to delineate all these regulations, but we urge acquirers to request due consideration of such regulations from their advisers.

What kinds of reporting obligations do companies have with respect to any environmental problems they discover?

Problems may have to be reported (either by the seller or, after closing, by the buyer) to one or more of the following parties:

- EPA
- Insurers
- Lenders
- Outside directors
- Securities and Exchange Commission and the stock exchanges[2]
- Shareholders

- Tenants
- Unions

CHECKING FOR ENVIRONMENTAL COMPLIANCE

How long does environmental due diligence take?

The amount of time required by environmental due diligence can vary greatly depending on the level needed. Here are some time lines according to one expert (Sean Monoghan of Shanley & Fisher, Morristown, New Jersey):

- American Society for Testing and Materials (ASTM) testing for a real estate purchase: one or two days.[3]
- Internet search for record of violations: one to two weeks.
- Preliminary assessment under state law: three to five weeks.
- Full site investigation, including soil or groundwater sampling: one to two months.
- Remedial investigation/feasibility study, including review of internal and external compliance records and interviews with employees and regulators: six months or more.[4]

Who should be involved in conducting the due diligence investigation?

Ideally, the investigation is conducted by an expert professional specializing in environmental issues. The investigator should talk first and foremost to the manager with line responsibility for environmental compliance in the company being sold.

In ASSESSING a company's potential exposure to environmental liability, where should an acquirer start?

Before getting into details, an acquirer should conduct a broad environmental exposure analysis. Generally speaking, there are two kinds of environmental problems to be feared in a proposed acquisition:

- A *balance sheet problem* that adversely affects the balance sheet.
- A *projection problem* that adversely affects financial projections.

Either kind can destroy the economic benefits that the buyer hopes to achieve.

How do environmental liabilities affect a balance sheet?

Balance sheet problems can result from liabilities, either disclosed or undisclosed, that the buyer inherits from the seller. Such liabilities typically include the cost of cleaning up environmental damage caused by the seller or one of the seller's predecessors. The costs can include charges for removing contaminated soil or purifying tainted groundwater, and can cover not only the site purchased by the buyer but also adjoining properties or remote locations on which hazardous substances generated by the business were used and/or dumped, potentially contaminating the air, ground, or water.

Moreover, under the Superfund, officers, directors, and even stockholders can be personally liable for cleanup costs, and companies that contributed to the pollution of a common dump site are jointly and severally liable for such cleanup costs.

Finally, even secured lenders that wind up operating or controlling the contaminated property can be liable for such cleanup costs. As a result, the buyer must approach these problems not just from his or her own point of view; but from the vantage point of the lender.

In addition to cleanup costs, a company can be liable to third parties who have become ill or died as a result of drinking contaminated groundwater, or whose property has been contaminated by pollution emanating from the company's facilities.

Therefore, any acquirer of an entity with assets that include real estate should automatically check for environmental compliance at each site.

How can environmental liabilities affect financial projections?

These liabilities can prevent the company from achieving its projected cash flow and earnings goals over time. Such liabilities typically arise in situations where the acquired company has a history of noncompliance with applicable air or water emissions standards.

When the due diligence process discloses such a history of operating problems, the prospective purchaser needs to calculate the cost of bringing the company into compliance and keeping it in compliance. For example, the purchaser may encounter significant unbudgeted capital costs (to procure needed emissions control equipment), operating costs higher than anticipated (to ensure that the offending equipment is operated in conformity with applicable environmental standards), or both.

In extreme cases, the buyer's diligence may disclose that the company (or a particular plant) cannot be economically operated in compliance with environmental law.

What are the first questions the acquirer should ask?

Any diligent buyer should work from a comprehensive environmental checklist, or retain a qualified environmental professional to do so.

An initial list of questions might be as follows:

- Were any toxic or hazardous substances used or generated by the candidate company?
- Were any hazardous wastes shipped off site for disposal? If wastes were shipped to a dump that has been or may be declared a federal Superfund site, the buyer might inherit a substantial liability. This liability may flow through to the purchaser irrespective of transaction structure (assets versus stock). Moreover, the purchaser may be liable even though it expressly does not assume the liability, if in fact the purchaser does not intend to continue the same business as the predecessor.
- Are there lagoons or settling ponds that may contain toxic wastes?
- Are there underground tanks that may have leaked and discharged their contents into the groundwater? What about unregistered, abandoned tanks?

Such locations are considered "brownfields"—that is, industrial and commercial properties that are abandoned, idle, or underused because of real or perceived environmental contamination.

What kinds of industries are most likely to have environmental exposure?

The historic "smokestack" manufacturing business is the one most likely to present environmental concerns. Here are two common environmental hazards in such a business:

- Landfills used for disposing of waste.
- Heavy metals (such as lead, arsenic, and cadmium) from various industrial processes and paints.

Another environmentally sensitive industry is health care. There are regulatory requirements affecting storage and disposal of medical wastes, and licensing and inspection requirements for X-ray machines.

Aside from such obvious examples, what other types of acquisitions can pose environmental risks?

Environmental problems are by no means limited to the manufacturing sector. Warehouses, retail businesses, and service companies may own structures that contain the following problems:

- Asbestos in wall insulation or pipe wrapping.
- Electrical transformers filled with polychlorinated biphenyls (PCBs). These elements are used in electrical transformers and commercial solvents such as those found in paint thinner and degreasing agents, which are potent carcinogens and which migrate readily into groundwater if spilled.
- Lead-based paint.
- Radon gas.
- Underground fuel storage tanks. Such tanks may contain gasoline, in the case of a business that operates or has operated a fleet of trucks or cars. Or they may contain heating oil, in the case of any business or even a residence. Eventually all such structures may leak.
- Insulation made from urea-formaldehyde foam.
- Septic systems and wells that have been abandoned.

What special problems are posed by Superfund liability?

First, liability for Superfund violations may reach beyond the corporate entity. Officers, directors, and even shareholders can be held personally liable. Second, cleanup costs can be enormous—well beyond the value of the assets purchased. Third, liabilities of companies that generated wastes dumped in a common site are joint as well as several; every contributor of hazardous waste to that site is theoretically liable for the whole cleanup. Finally, it can take years before liability is determined and apportioned.

What can the buyer do to protect itself?

The buyer can hire an environmental consulting firm to do an environmental liability audit of the candidate company. More and more lenders are requiring delivery of such an audit report, showing an essentially clean bill of health, as a lending precondition. Although the EPA has relaxed lender liability under Superfund, lenders still remain cautious.[5]

The buyer can also make sure that the seller's warranties are broad enough to cover (1) environmental liabilities arising as a result of on-site or off-site pollution, and (2) all actions causing pollution, whether or not such actions, when taken, were in violation of any law or commonly accepted standard. One such standard is the CERES Principles listed in Appendix 11A. The second point is critical because Superfund liability can reach back to actions taken before the adoption of modern environmental protection laws, when the shipment of such wastes by unlicensed carriers to unlicensed sites was not considered to be illegal.

Finally, the buyer can make sure that environmental warranties and any escrows or offset rights survive as long as possible. It may take years before the pollution is discovered and traced back to the company.

Suppose a seller has already obtained environmental clearances. Are these automatically transferable?

Not necessarily. Federal, state, and local permits and consent decrees relating to water quality, air emissions, and hazardous wastes should be checked carefully to make sure they remain effective after closing. In addition, in at least one state (New Jersey) the seller of an industrial or commercial facility, with certain exceptions, cannot pass an effective title to the buyer without state approval or waiver of a cleanup plan.

VOLUNTARY DISCOVERY AND DISCLOSURE OF ENVIRONMENTAL VIOLATIONS

Do states or the federal government provide incentives for companies that voluntarily discover and disclose environmental violations?

Some states do offer such incentives, but these protections are limited to state law concerns. When state and federal laws overlap (which is to say, in most cases), acquirers should turn to federal law.[6]

The EPA's "Audit Policy" extends lesser penalties to acquirers that discover and report violations on their own. The policy is reprinted as Appendix 11B.

According to the EPA policy, at what point does an entity have to disclose that a violation may have occurred?[7]

The regulated entity must disclose violations when there is an objectively reasonable factual basis for concluding that violations may have occurred. When the facts underlying the violation are clear, but the existence of a violation is in doubt because of differing interpretations of the law, the regulated entity should disclose the potential violations.

If an owner or operator discovers a violation that began when the facility was owned and/or operated by a previous entity, can the subsequent owner/operator receive penalty mitigation under the EPA Audit Policy? Can the previous owner also obtain such mitigation?

In both cases, the regulated entity must meet all conditions in the final Audit Policy, including the requirement for prompt disclosure. Separate entities are considered independently. Suppose that one company buys a unit from another company, and the buyer and seller of the unit remain separate entities. There may be situations where a subsequent owner/operator can receive penalty mitigation while the previous owner/operator cannot. For example, the new owner may disclose violations promptly to the EPA, whereas the previous owner failed to disclose such violations.

Clearly, to avoid such a situation down the road, it is in the interests of sellers to help buyers conduct environmental due diligence.

CONCLUDING COMMENTS

Environmental liability exposure deserves its reputation as an area of extreme caution for all M&A participants. The vast reach of federal and state law touches buyers and sellers, lenders, and advisers. All can benefit from a general knowledge of environmental law, and from a commitment to respecting it.

In the words of the Caux Roundtable's *Principles for Business* (introduced in the previous chapter), one of the goals of any corporation is to "promote and stimulate sustainable economic development and play a leading role in preserving and enhancing the physical environment and conserving the earth's resources."

For every acquirer, this goal can be furthered during the due diligence process by noting the candidate company's environmental record and practices and by protecting itself against inheritance of any future negative developments in this regard.

In brief, then, environmental due diligence is an important part of the M&A process. Although the number and complexity of the laws may seem daunting, a competent professional adviser can do much to identify and mitigate the risk of legal exposure in this area.

A P P E N D I X   11A

The CERES Principles

Endorsing Company Statement

By adopting these Principles, we publicly affirm our belief that corporations have a responsibility for the environment, and must conduct all aspects of their business as responsible stewards of the environment by operating in a manner that protects the earth. We believe that corporations must not compromise the ability of future generations to sustain themselves.

We will update our practices constantly in light of advances in technology and new understandings in health and environmental science. In collaboration with CERES, we will promote a dynamic process to ensure that the Principles are interpreted in a way that accommodates changing technologies and environmental realities. We intend to make consistent, measurable progress in implementing these Principles and to apply them to all aspects of our operations throughout the world.

THE CERES PRINCIPLES

Protection of the Biosphere

We will reduce and make continual progress toward eliminating the release of any substance that may cause environmental damage to the air, water, or the earth or its inhabitants. We will safeguard all habitats affected by our operations and will protect open spaces and wilderness, while preserving biodiversity.

Sustainable Use of Natural Resources

We will make sustainable use of renewable natural resources, such as water, soils, and forests. We will conserve nonrenewable natural resources through efficient use and careful planning.

Reduction and Disposal of Wastes

We will reduce and where possible eliminate waste through source reduction and recycling. All waste will be handled and disposed of through safe and responsible methods.

Energy Conservation

We will conserve energy and improve the energy efficiency of our internal operations and of the goods and services we sell. We will make every effort to use environmentally safe and sustainable energy sources.

Risk Reduction

We will strive to minimize the environmental, health, and safety risks to our employees and the communities in which we operate through safe technologies, facilities, and operating procedures, and by being prepared for emergencies.

Safe Products and Services

We will reduce and where possible eliminate the use, manufacture, or sale of products and services that cause environmental damage or health or safety hazards. We will inform our customers of the environmental impacts of our products or services and try to correct unsafe use.

Environmental Restoration

We will promptly and responsibly correct conditions we have caused that endanger health, safety, or the environment. To the extent feasible, we will redress injuries we have caused to persons or damage we have caused to the environment and will restore the environment.

Informing the Public

We will inform in a timely manner everyone who may be affected by conditions caused by our company that might endanger health, safety, or the environment. We will regularly seek advice and counsel through dialogue with persons in communities near our facilities. We will not take any action against employees for reporting dangerous incidents or conditions to management or to appropriate authorities.

Management Commitment

We will implement these Principles and sustain a process that ensures that the Board of Directors and Chief Executive Officer are fully informed about pertinent environmental issues and are fully responsible for environmental policy. In selecting our Board of Directors, we will consider demonstrated environmental commitment as a factor.

Audits and Reports

We will conduct an annual self-evaluation of our progress in implementing these Principles. We will support the timely creation of generally accepted environmental audit procedures. We will annually complete the CERES Report, which will be made available to the public.

Disclaimer

These Principles establish an environmental ethic with criteria by which investors and others can assess the environmental performance of companies. Companies that endorse these Principles pledge to go voluntarily beyond the requirements of the law. The terms "may" and "might" are not meant to encompass every imaginable consequence, no matter how remote. Rather, these Principles obligate endorsers to behave as prudent persons who are not governed by conflicting interests and who possess a strong commitment to environmental excellence and to human health and safety. These Principles are not intended to create new legal liabilities, expand existing rights or obligations, waive legal defenses, or otherwise affect the legal position of any endorsing company, and are not intended to be used against an endorser in any legal proceeding for any purpose.

A P P E N D I X   11B

Audit Policy of the EPA—Incentives for Self-Policing: Discovery, Disclosure, Correction, and Prevention

The following text is excerpted from the revised final Audit Policy of the Environmental Protection Agency (EPA, or Agency), effective May 11, 2000. The revised policy replaces the Audit Policy issued December 22, 1995. For the full text of the revised policy, see epa.gov.

I. EXPLANATION OF POLICY

A. Introduction

On December 22, 1995, EPA issued its final policy on "Incentives for Self-Policing: Discovery, Disclosure, Correction, and Prevention of Violations," commonly referred to as the Audit Policy. The purpose of this Policy is to enhance protection of human health and the environment by encouraging regulated entities to voluntarily discover, disclose and prevent violations of Federal environmental law. Benefits to entities that make disclosures under the terms of the Policy include reductions in the amount of civil penalties and a determination not to recommend criminal prosecution of disclosing entities . . .

B. Background and History

The Audit Policy provides incentives for regulated entities to detect, promptly disclose, and expeditiously correct violations of Federal environmental requirements. The Policy contains nine conditions, and entities that meet all of them are eligible for 100 percent mitigation of any gravity-based penalties that otherwise would be assessed. ("Gravity-based" refers to that portion of the penalty over and above the portion that represents the entity's economic gain from noncompliance, known as the "economic benefit.") Regulated entities that do not meet the first condition—a systematic discovery of violations—but meet the other eight conditions are eligible for 75 percent mitigation of any gravity-based civil penalties . . .

C. Purpose

The revised policy . . . is designed to encourage greater compliance with Federal laws and regulations that protect human health and the environment. It promotes a higher standard of self-policing by waiving gravity-based penalties for violations that are promptly disclosed and corrected, and which were discovered systematically—that is, through voluntary audits or compliance management systems. To provide an incentive for entities to disclose and correct violations regardless of how they were detected, the Policy reduces gravity-based penalties by 75 percent for violations that are voluntarily discovered and promptly disclosed and corrected, even if not discovered systematically . . .

D. Incentives for Self-Policing

Section C of the Audit Policy identifies the major incentives that EPA provides to encourage self-policing, self-disclosure, and prompt self-correction. For entities that meet conditions of the Policy, the available incentives include waiving or reducing gravity-based civil penalties, declining to recommend criminal prosecution for regulated entities that self-police, and refraining from routine requests for audits . . .

Remaining sections cover conditions, opposition to audit privilege and immunity, effect on states, scope of policy, and implementation of policy.

II. STATEMENT OF POLICY

A. Purpose

This policy is designed to enhance protection of human health and the environment by encouraging regulated entities to voluntarily discover, disclose, correct, and prevent violations of federal environmental requirements.

B. Definition

For purposes of this policy, the following definitions apply:

"Environmental audit" is a systematic, documented, periodic, and objective review by regulated entities of facility operations and practices related to meeting environmental requirements.

"Compliance management system" encompasses the regulated entity's documented systematic efforts, appropriate to the size and nature of its business, to prevent, detect, and correct violations through all of the following:

(a) Compliance policies, standards, and procedures that identify how employees and agents are to meet the requirements of laws, regulations, permits, enforceable agreements, and other sources of authority for environmental requirements.

(b) Assignment of overall responsibility for overseeing compliance with policies, standards, and procedures, and assignment of specific responsibility for assuring compliance at each facility of operation;

(c) Mechanisms for systematically assuring that compliance policies, standards, and procedures are being carried out, including monitoring and auditing systems reasonably designed to detect and correct violations, periodic evaluation of the overall performance of the compliance management system, and a means for employees or agents to report violations of environmental requirements without fear of retaliation;

(d) Efforts to communicate effectively the regulated entity's standards and procedures to all employees and other agents;

(e) Appropriate incentives to managers and employees to perform in accordance with the compliance policies, standards, and procedures, including consistent enforcement through appropriate disciplinary mechanisms; and

(f) Procedures for the prompt and appropriate correction of any violations, and any necessary modifications to the regulated entity's program to prevent future violations.

"Environmental audit report" means the analysis, conclusions, and recommendations resulting from an environmental audit, but does not include data obtained in, or testimonial evidence concerning, the environmental audit.

"Gravity-based penalties" are that portion of a penalty over and above the economic benefit; i.e., the punitive portion of the penalty, rather than that portion representing a defendant's economic gain from noncompliance.

"Regulated entity" means any entity . . . regulated under federal environmental laws.

C. Incentives for Self-Policing

1. No Gravity-Based Penalties

Where the regulated entity establishes that it satisfies all of the conditions of Section D of the policy [see below], EPA will not seek gravity-based penalties for violations of federal environmental requirements discovered and disclosed by the entity.

2. Reduction of Gravity-Based Penalties by 75 percent

If a regulated entity establishes that it satisfies all of the conditions of Section D of this policy except for D(1)—Systematic Discovery—EPA will reduce by 75 percent gravity-based penalties for violations of Federal environmental requirements discovered and disclosed by the entity.

3. No Recommendations for Criminal Prosecution

(a) If a regulated entity establishes that it satisfies at least conditions D(2) through D(9) of this Policy, EPA will not recommend to the Department of Justice or other prosecuting authority that criminal charges be brought against a regulated entity as long as the EPA determines that the violation is not part of a pattern or practice that demonstrates or involves:

(i) a prevalent management philosophy or practice that concealed or condoned environmental violations; or

(ii) high-level corporate officials' or managers' conscious involvement in, or willful blindness to, the violations.

(b) Whether or not the EPA recommends the regulated entity for criminal prosecution under this section, the Agency may recommend for prosecution for the criminal acts of individual managers or employees under existing policies guiding the exercise of enforcement discretion.

4. No Routine Requests for Audits

EPA will not request or use an environmental audit report to initiate a civil or criminal investigation of the entity . . .

D. Conditions

1. Systematic Discovery

The violation was discovered through:

(a) an environmental audit; or

(b) a compliance management system reflecting the regulated entity's due diligence in preventing, detecting, and correcting violations. The regulated entity must provide accurate and complete documentation to the Agency as to how its compliance management system meets the criteria for due diligence outlined in Section B and how the regulated entity discovered the violation through its compliance management system. EPA may require the regulated entity to make publicly available a description of its compliance management system.

2. Voluntary Discovery

The violation was identified voluntarily, and not through a legally mandated monitoring or sampling requirement prescribed by statute, regulation, permit, judicial or administrative order, or consent agreement . . .

3. Prompt Disclosure

The regulated entity fully discloses the specific violation in writing within 21 days (or such shorter time as may be required by law) after an entity has discovered that the violation has, or may have, occurred.

4. Discovery and Disclosure Independent of Government or Third-Party Plaintiff

The regulated entity discovers and discloses the potential violation to EPA prior to a legal action by the government or any other plaintiff . . .

5. Correction and Remediation

The regulated entity corrects the violation within 60 calendar days from the date of discovery, certifies in writing that violations have been corrected, and takes appropriate measures as determined by EPA to remedy any environmental or human harm due to the violation. [Extensions may be granted if requested within 60 days.]

6. Prevent Recurrence

The regulated entity agrees in writing to take steps to prevent a recurrence of the violation . . .

7. No Repeat Violations

The specific violation (or a closely related violation) has not occurred previously within the past three years at the same facility, and has not occurred within the past five years as part of a pattern at multiple facilities owned or operated by the same entity. For the purposes of this section, a violation is:

(a) any violation of Federal, State, or local environmental law identified in a judicial or administrative order, consent agreement or order, complaint, or notice of violation, conviction or plea agreement; or

(b) any act or omission for which the regulated entity has previously received penalty mitigation from EPA or a State or local agency.

8. Other Violations Excluded

The violation is not one which (a) resulted in serious actual harm, or may have presented an imminent and substantial endangerment, to human health or the environment, or (b) violates the specific terms of any judicial or administrative order, or consent agreement.

9. Cooperation

The regulated entity cooperates as requested by EPA and provides such information as is necessary and requested by EPA to determine applicability of this Policy.

Remaining sections cover economic benefit recovery; effect on state law, regulations, or policy; applicability (to the assessment of penalties); and public accountability.

ENDNOTES

1. Uniform laws include the Uniform Transboundary Pollution Reciprocal Access Act (adopted by Colorado, Connecticut, Michigan, Montana, New Jersey, Oregon, and Wisconsin) and the Uniform Conservation Easement Act (adopted by Alaska, Arizona, District of Columbia, Georgia, Idaho, Indiana, Kansas, Kentucky, Maine, Minnesota, Mississippi, Nevada, New Mexico, South Carolina, Texas, Virginia, and Wisconsin).
2. E.g., Staff Accounting Bulletin 92 of the Securities and Exchange Commission regarding disclosure of environmental liability exposure.

3. The ASTM Committee E-50 on Environmental Assessment has produced several useful checklists, including guides for environmental site assessment, sustainable restoration of brownfield properties, and evaluations of underground storage tanks. The ASTM may be contacted at 100 Barr Harbor Drive, West Conshohocken, PA 19428.

4. This list is based on one that appeared in Sean Monoghan, "Environmental Due Diligence," *Conducting Due Diligence 1999*, op. cit. (Chapter 1, note 8), p. 1018. The estimate on Internet search time is our own.

5. The Asset Conservation, Lender Liability, and Deposit Insurance Protection Act, enacted September 30, 1996, amends Superfund by reinstating the EPA Final Rule on Lender Liability Under CERCLA, 1992, which had been struck down by the U.S. Court of Appeals for the District of Columbia in *Kelley v. EPA*, 15 F.3d 1100 (CA DC 1994). For a recent directive, see EPA Policy on Interpreting CERCLA Provisions Addressing Lenders and Involuntary Acquisitions by Government Entities (62 Federal Register 36424, July 7, 1997).

6. Source: Monaghan, op. cit. (note 4), p. 1024.

7. The answers to this question and the rest of the questions in this section are taken verbatim from the EPA's "Audit Policy Interpretive Guidance," published in January 1997 and still current as we go to press.

CHAPTER 12

Detecting Exposure Under Employment Law

"A fair day's wages for a fair day's work": it is
as just a demand as governed men ever made
of governing. It is the everlasting right of man.

Thomas Carlyle
Past and Present (1843)

INTRODUCTION

In this chapter, we aim to summarize the major employment law issues confronted by an acquirer conducting due diligence. Our goal is ambitious: Entire books (not to mention multiple volumes of regulations) have been written about single, narrow aspects of this topic—for example, health and safety law. Nonetheless, we believe that a brief overview of a variety of employment law areas can be helpful to acquirers.

Employees are the most common source of litigation against corporate directors and officers today. As noted in Chapter 4, employees or unions, current or prospective, filed over half (55.2 percent) of all lawsuits targeting corporate directors and officers over the past decade, with an average settlement amount of $305,760.[1] Although this amount is comparatively low (compared to the average of $3.1 million gained by customers and nearly $9 million gained by stockholders), it is significant, considering the vital importance of employees. Human capital, after all, is arguably the single most valuable asset of any company.

Employees sue their employers for a variety of reasons. As stated in Chapter 4, employee lawsuits have alleged a variety of improper actions, including discrimination or harassment, unhealthy or unsafe work environments, denial of benefits, breach of employment contract, and wrongful termination. Such lawsuits typically refer to federal or state law setting standards for equal opportunity, health and safety, wages, and hours (including issues of benefits and leave), or workforce reduction. In this chapter, we summarize the relevant federal law in these four key areas, as well as two more specialized areas: collective bargaining and immigration.

EMPLOYMENT LAW: AN OVERVIEW

What areas are covered by employment law?

Employment law consists of literally thousands of federal and state laws, administrative regulations, and judicial decisions. These laws, regulations, and decisions set boundaries on corporate behavior with respect to a variety of issues. State law concerns include contractual rights created by agreements between employers and employees—a very important area in disputes involving departing employees. The focus of this chapter, however, is the vast scope of federal law. As mentioned above, these issues may be usefully classified into the areas of *equal opportunity*, *health and safety*, *wages and hours*, and *workforce reduction*. In addition, federal law has protected the rights of workers to influence these issues by affirming their right to *collective bargaining*. (This last category is not a cause of private lawsuits, because the federal government is typically the plaintiff in such cases.)

EQUAL OPPORTUNITY LAWS

What do you mean by equal opportunity laws?

Equal opportunity laws protect the rights of individuals to obtain and retain employment in jobs for which they are qualified and capable, irrespective of their age, disabilities, gender, national origin, race, religion, or sexual orientation. These laws forbid discrimination against individuals because of their status in these areas. Discrimination means prejudice that has an economic effect on an employee, such as bias in hiring, promotion, job assignment, termination, and compensation, or that results in harassment against an employee.

What is the primary equal opportunity law?

Title 7 of the Civil Rights Act of 1964[2] prohibits discrimination based on any of the following characteristics:

- National origin
- Race/skin color

- Religion
- Gender

The act makes it illegal for employers to discriminate in the following areas:

- Hiring
- Discharging (firing)
- Pay
- Terms of employment
- Conditions of employment
- Privileges of employment (perquisites)

The Civil Rights Act applies to most employers engaged in interstate commerce with more than 15 employees, as well as to labor organizations and employment agencies. It is enforced by the Equal Employment Opportunity Commission, which also enforces other discrimination laws described below.[3] Court cases have provided a number of significant interpretations on these points.

State statutes also provide extensive protection from employment discrimination. Some laws extend federal-type protections to employees not covered by federal law—for example, employees who may experience discrimination on the basis of sexual orientation. Other statutes expand federal requirements by covering more employers and by providing employees with greater rights.

What specific law protects employees against discrimination based on age?

The Age Discrimination in Employment Act of 1967 (ADEA) bans discrimination based on age. The prohibited practices are nearly identical to those outlined in Title 7. An employee is protected from discrimination based on age if he or she is over 40. The ADEA contains guidelines for benefit, pension, and retirement plans. The ADEA was amended by the Older Workers Benefit Protection Act of 1990, which protects the pensions of older workers. (See below for applications to reductions in force.)

What specific federal law protects employees against discrimination based on disabilities?

Discrimination based on disability is covered at the federal level by the Americans with Disabilities Act of 1990 (ADA), which became effective in 1992. This law prohibits discrimination against a qualified individual with a disability who can perform the essential functions of a position with or without accommodation. The purpose of the act, among other goals, is to prevent employers from discriminating against disabled individuals and requiring them to provide certain accommodations to qualified individuals.

The law extends beyond employment issues to issues involving other constituencies, such as customers. The law bans discrimination against certain disabled individuals with respect to the following:

- Education
- Employment
- Housing
- Access to public buildings
- Access to transportation

The ADA applies to all employers engaged in interstate commerce and having 15 employees or more. Some states have disability laws, which may expand on the rights of employees and the obligations of employers.

The ADA defines a disability as "a physical or mental impairment that substantially limits one or more of the major life activities of the individual." It asserts protection of such individuals, as well as individuals who have "a record of such impairment" or who are "regarded as having such an impairment." The law specifically withholds ADA protections to those who engage in illegal and/or socially undesirable behavior, such as active addiction to illegal drugs, kleptomania, pyromania, or sexual behavior disorders. On the other hand, if an individual is a rehabilitated drug user, is participating in a supervised drug rehabilitation program, or is erroneously regarded as a drug user, then the individual may receive ADA protections.

The law does not specifically exclude alcoholism, but in at least one case—*Burch v. Coca-Cola Co.* (1997)—the court said that the evidence presented did not show limitation in a major life activity, and hence failed to demonstrate disability.

There is also the Rehabilitation Act of 1973, enacted to "promote and expand employment opportunities in the public and private sectors for handicapped individuals" by banning discrimination. The law also sets up affirmative action programs, which are designed to actively encourage the hiring of individuals who in the past have been subject to discrimination. Companies covered by the act include employers receiving federal contracts over $2,500 or federal financial assistance.[4] Since many companies and organizations in the private sector receive federal contracts or assistance, the reach of this law is long.

What specific laws ban discrimination based on gender?

As mentioned, Title 7 of the Civil Rights Act of 1964 prohibits discrimination based on sex. This can be discrimination against either men or women on the basis of their gender. To ensure lack of discrimination against women, Congress passed the Pregnancy Discrimination Act in 1978, to include under sex discrimination in Title 7 any bias against employees because of pregnancy, childbirth, or related medical conditions.

The Equal Pay Act of 1963, amending an older law entitled the Fair Labor Standards Act, applied to companies involved in interstate commerce, regardless of size. The Equal Pay Act prohibits sex-based bias in the award of pay. The law states that equal pay must be paid for equal work if jobs require "equal skill, effort, and responsibility, and are performed under similar working conditions." The work need not involve the same title and job description. It can be applied to work that is superficially dissimilar in title and job description, while being similar in fact. For example, if a woman in an organization is paid a certain amount to be a "project coordinator," and a man is paid twice as much to be a "strategic director," and if their work requires the same skill, effort, and responsibility under similar working conditions, then the woman could have grounds for a suit—especially if there were a pattern of such discrimination. The same would be true for a male "coordinator" vis-à-vis a female "director."

Furthermore, over the past two decades, a series of court decisions have increased liability exposure in the area of sexual harassment (a form of discrimination). For example, in *Oncale v. Sundowner Offshore Services, Inc.* (1998), the court clarified that same-sex harassment is covered by Title 7.

What are the key issues and court decisions in the area of sexual harassment?

Two key issues are the *hostile work environment* and the *quid pro quo* arrangement.

Hostile work environment was the issue confronting the U.S. Supreme Court in *Meritor Savings Bank v. Vinson* (1986). In this case, the Court stated that harassment is illegal when it "is sufficiently severe or pervasive to alter the conditions of the victim's employment and create an abusive working environment." The highest court has been expansive in identifying such an environment. For example, in *Harris v. Forklift Systems, Inc.* (1993), the Supreme Court held that plaintiffs need not prove that the harassment seriously affected their "psychological well-being" in order to have an actionable cause.

Quid pro quo means "this for that," and in sexual harassment cases it refers to a situation in which the employee is expected to grant sexual favors in return for a benefit or lack of a disbenefit. (As in "Do this and you will get a promotion; refuse and you will be fired.") If a supervisor harasses an employee, but the employee experiences no tangible employment action as a consequence of the harassment (such as promotion or firing, depending on the situation), then the employer can raise an affirmative defense to liability or damages. This was the finding in both *Faragther v. City of Boca Raton* (1998) and in *Burlington Industries Inc. v. Ellert.*

During due diligence, it is important to determine whether the company to be acquired has policies and training programs that can aim to prevent sexual harassment from occurring in the workplace—by detecting and preventing a hostile work environment, quid pro quo arrangements, and other forms of sexual harassment. In the *Faragther* case the court held that the employer must establish that it exercised reasonable care to prevent and correct promptly any sexual harassing behavior, and that "the plaintiff employee unreasonably failed to take advantage of any preventive or corrective opportunities provided by the employer or to avoid harm otherwise."[5]

HEALTH AND SAFETY LAWS

What are the main health and safety laws?

The primary law protecting the health and safety of workers in the workplace is the Occupational Safety and Health Act of 1970, which fills five volumes of the Code of Federal Regulations. The law covers all nongovernment employers that engage in interstate commerce. In most provisions, there is no size limit: even small companies come under the regulations. There are, however, exemptions for small businesses with respect to record keeping. (In addition, some discrimination laws pertain to health since certain disabilities are related to health and are protectable. Also, the Black Lung Act prohibits discrimination by mine operators against miners who suffer from pneumoconiosis, known as "black lung,"[6] and, as mentioned, the Civil Rights Act of 1964 prohibits discrimination involving pregnancy, childbirth, and related conditions.)

The Occupational Safety and Health Act established the Occupational Safety and Health Administration (OSHA), a unit of the Department of Labor (DOL) empowered to set forth regulations to promote health and safety in the workplace. A state may enact its own health and safety laws, but they must be in areas not covered by OSHA, or must receive federal approval.[7] OSHA has even asserted that its authority extends to the homes of telecommuters, but then clarified that it has no plans to issue regulations or conduct inspections in this regard.[8]

The DOL, through OSHA, may authorize inspections of workplaces to determine what future regulation may be needed. Through its inspections, the DOL also aims to ensure compliance with current regulations, and to examine conditions that have inspired past complaints. If the DOL finds that an employer is violating a safety or health regulation, it then issues an injunction or a citation. DOL citations may be reviewed by the Occupational Safety and Health Review Commission (established at the same time as OSHA) or by federal judges. The DOL may also impose fines for noncompliance.

The DOL regulates a number of seemingly dispersed areas. Most recently, for example, it has been active in creating and enforcing laws in the area of "ergonomics."

Could you describe the new rules for ergonomics?

On November 23, 1999, the DOL released new ergonomics rules—310 pages of regulations in development since 1992.[9] About one-third of general industry work sites—or 1.9 million work sites employing 27 million workers—are affected. The Labor Department estimates that less than 30 percent of the nation's employers have ergonomics standards now.

The science of ergonomics seeks to reduce the chances of injury when workers do repetitious, strenuous, or awkward tasks. A well-known example is carpal tunnel syndrome, which occurs in work as diverse as word processing and poultry plucking.

Eliminating such injuries, says OSHA, can save U.S. companies some $9 billion annually in lost productivity, insurance premiums, and workers' compensation claims—an amount more than twice the estimated $4.2 billion that implementing the guidelines could cost.[10]

Each year, about 1.8 million U.S. workers experience work-related musculoskeletal disorders, such as injuries from overwork or repetitive motion affecting the back or arms. About one third of these ailments are serious enough to result in the worker missing time on the job. OSHA standards require that workers with repetitive stress receive 90 percent of their pay and 100 percent of their benefits if their ailments force them to take leave from work.

The new rules set forth guidelines for good ergonomics, and require employers that report injuries to train their employees in the new guidelines. The rules also set standards for computer keyboards, desks, manufacturing equipment, and other machines and furnishings in the work environment—thus affecting makers and buyers of such equipment.

What regulations apply to manufacturing operations overseas?

OSHA laws do not extend overseas, but this creates the opposite problem of poor working conditions that decline to the level of "sweatshops." Proper due diligence in the acquisition of any manufacturer—particularly one with non-U.S. sites—requires assurance that no sweatshop conditions exist.

Sweatshops are manufacturing operations that pose undue hardships on workers. The term is generally reserved for small manufacturing operations in developing countries where workers receive substandard wages while working in crowded and unsafe conditions.

Sweatshops do pose risks to acquirers. Aside from the obvious ethical issues they raise, accusations of "sweatshop" conditions can damage the reputation of a company and expose it to lawsuits and federal fines. Several companies took major steps in October 1999 to reform their manufacturing processes.[11] Nike released the location of some of its factories, and Reebok International and Liz Claiborne allowed human rights groups to audit some of their plants (in Indonesia and Guatemala, respectively). All three companies are founding members of the Fair Labor Association, an apparel industry group responsible for self-policing in this area. In the toy industry, Mattel has announced plans to publish a comprehensive review of eight plants in four countries, using hundreds of specific labor standards.

WAGE AND HOURS LAW

What are the main areas covered by wage and hours laws?

Areas covered include minimum wage and family/medical leave, as well as laws affecting pensions and insurance that employers must pay on behalf of their employees, such as workers' compensation insurance and unemployment insurance. Also, employers need to be aware of current regulations regarding health plans and health insurance.

Could you give an overview of minimum wage law?

The minimum wage is an hourly amount that certain employers must match or exceed when compensating employees. The federal minimum wage provisions are contained in the Fair Labor Standards Act of 1938 (FLSA). The law applies to employees of enterprises that do at least $500,000 in business a year.

The law also applies to employees of smaller firms if the employees are engaged in interstate commerce or in the production of goods for commerce, such as employees who work in transportation or communications or who regularly use the mails or telephones for interstate communications. When state law requires a higher minimum wage, that higher standard applies. As we go to press, the minimum wage (set in 1997) is $5.15, but it is likely to rise to $6.15 by April 2002.[12]

The FLSA contains a number of exemptions from the minimum wage that may apply to some workers. The law establishes a youth subminimum wage that employers may pay employees under 20 years of age during their first 90 consecutive calendar days of employment. The current youth subminimum wage is $4.25.

Minimum wage laws are enforced by the Wage and Hour Division of the U.S. Department of Labor.[13]

How does overtime pay fit in?

For the purposes of overtime pay, federal law defines two classes of employees: exempt versus nonexempt.

- Exempt employees receive wages that are exempt from federal overtime law because they are managerial or professional workers. Even if they work more than a certain number of hours per week (as defined by federal law), they do not have a right to receive overtime pay.
- Nonexempt employees receive wages that are covered by federal overtime law. If they work over a certain number of hours per week (currently set at 40), then they must receive overtime pay (currently set at 1.5 times normal pay).

To be classified as a nonexempt employee, a worker must have a job that entails a great deal of decision-making discretion, such as a managerial or professional job.

What laws affect leave?

The primary law here is the Family and Medical Leave Act of 1993. Under this law, an employee may take up to 12 weeks of unpaid leave per year for a serious medical condition in the family, or for the birth or adoption of a child. The DOL released its final interpretive regulations on this law in January 1995. These regulations put the burden on the employer to determine whether the employee is eligible under the law.

Under the FMLA, an employee must have worked over a period of 12 months for at least 1,250 hours, and must work at a site where 50 or more employees are employed within a 75-mile radius.

What laws govern pensions paid by companies?

Pensions paid by companies are regulated under the Employee Retirement and Income Security Act of 1974 (ERISA), as amended, described in Section 29 of the U.S. Code.

There are two types of pension plans: *qualified* (meaning that they meet certain federal standards and qualify for tax-favorable treatment) and *nonqualified*.

There are two types of qualified pension plans: a defined benefit plan, and a defined contribution plan.

- A *defined benefit plan* (DBP) is a pension plan that determines the total value of benefits by a formula and requires the employer to meet certain actuarial standards in making contributions to the plan. Contributions must be sufficient to pay obligations when they fall due.
- A *defined contribution plan* (DCP) is a pension plan that requires minimum contributions year by year for each year in which the plan is in existence. These plans can take the form of profit-sharing plans with or without salary deferral (the well-known 401(k) plan) and usually have variable contribution levels.

Both defined benefit and defined contribution plans are subject to a compensation cap under recent tax law.[14] More broadly, they are subject to rules set forth under the Internal Revenue Code and ERISA, administered by the Department of Labor.

Nonqualified plans—generally plans for senior executives—are often funded by contributions, either as additional compensation or as salary deferrals to a *rabbi trust*.[15]

What are some concerns acquirers might face with respect to pensions?

Concerns for acquirers include underfunded and overfunded pensions, plan termination, plan mergers, severance agreements, and the treatment of pension beneficiaries in the sale of a business. It is beyond the scope of this chapter to go into any of these complex and important subjects in depth, but we will say a few words about each.

Underfunded pensions and overfunded pensions occur only in DBPs, not DCPs. As mentioned, in a DBP, unlike a DCP, the acquirer guarantees a certain pension amount. Underfunded plans occur when the company winds up having less in a plan than it needs to pay promised benefits; overfunded plans occur when the company has more. Plan termination occurs when a plan is liquidated, and when it is merged with another plan (see below).

Prior to 1987, acquirers had a great deal of flexibility with respect to pension plan assets. This changed with the Omnibus Budget Reconciliation Act of 1987 (OBRA), which imposed a standard range of interest assumptions for funding purposes. OBRA also precluded termination and reversion except under exceptional conditions.[16] This was to prevent employers from gutting plans—a tactic employed in the mid-1980s prior to the passage of OBRA.

What should acquirers know about severance agreements?

Severance agreements also rank high among potential litigation sources. Landmark cases in the field have held that severance plans are "employee welfare benefit plans" and that such plans are subject to the disclosure, reporting, and fiduciary requirements imposed by ERISA. For instance, in *Adcock v. Firestone Tire & Rubber Co.* (1987), a Tennessee district court held that employees have a contractual right under federal common law to severance benefits established by their employer.

Treatment of pensioners in the sale of a business is another area for litigation. Section 510 of ERISA bans companies from discharging or otherwise taking action against an employee for the purpose of "interfering" with the employee's right to obtain benefits under a pension plan. Plant closings that entail mass layoffs have generated claims by plaintiffs that the closing was motivated by the employer's desire to save benefit costs. In *Millsap vs. McDonnell Douglas* (1998), the court refused to dismiss a class action against McDonnell Douglas Corp., finding that the plaintiffs established a prima facie case that the company closed its Tulsa, Oklahoma plant in order to deprive employees of retirement benefits in violation of Section 510.

On the other hand, Section 510 does not require every purchaser of a going concern to credit service with a predecessor employer; nor does it require that a successor's plan be identical in every respect to the predecessor's.

If a buyer and seller both have defined contribution plans—for example, two 401(k)s—how can these be merged?

This is a complex area best understood on a plan-by-plan basis.[17] Consider the example of the most common defined contribution plan, the 401(k). It depends on whether the acquirer bought the stock of the acquired company or its assets. In asset acquisitions, with certain exceptions,[18] plans must remain separate, and the acquired company plan must be managed by the seller. In stock acquisitions, three approaches are possible: maintaining separate plans, terminating the acquired plan, or merging the two plans.

To maintain separate plans, the acquirer simply has to make sure that each plan files its own Form 5500 and satisfies federal requirements for minimum coverage and nondiscrimination in the amount of contributions. The Internal Revenue Code provides a transition period to meet these requirements of the remainder of the plan year through the last day of the first plan year, beginning on the day of the acquisition.

The "successor plan rule" of the Internal Revenue Service says that an acquired company's plan will be disqualified if more than 2 percent of its employees participate in another defined contribution plan (except for an employee stock ownership plan) within one year of the termination. This rule can be avoided by terminating the plan prior to the acquisition.

Merging two plans can save administrative expense,[19] but it also has its complications. All "valuable benefits" in each plan must be preserved in the merged plan, complicating plan administration. Furthermore, if a company with a 401(k) plan is acquired by a nonprofit, procedures become extremely complex.[20]

Moving away from pensions and toward insurance, what laws cover the insurance aspects of employee compensation?

As mentioned, major employers may be required to pay insurance for unemployment and for disability. Although they are not required to provide group health insurance, if they do provide such insurance, they must follow certain regulations.

What laws require unemployment compensation insurance?

Unemployment insurance laws require employers to pay taxes so that in the event that they discharge workers, the workers will be able to receive payments for a specified period of time or until they find a new job. Tax payments, both state and federal, are deposited in an Unemployment Trust Fund, which is maintained in separate accounts for each state.

The main federal unemployment insurance law is the Social Security Act of 1935. States also have unemployment insurance programs. The federal and state programs are coordinated to avoid overlap, with federal law taking precedence.

What about workers' compensation laws—how do they differ from unemployment compensation?

Workers' compensation insurance is similar to unemployment insurance, but it is paid in order to provide pay to workers who still have their jobs, but who must miss work because of injury or disablement on the job. Workers' compensation laws also provide benefits for dependents when workers die from job-related accidents or illnesses. Some laws protect employers and fellow workers by limiting the amount that an injured employee can recover from an employer and by eliminating the liability of coworkers in most accidents. Several states—for example, California—have comprehensive workers' compensation statutes that require employers to provide workers' compensation insurance. Federal statutes cover both federal employees and workers employed in some significant aspect of interstate commerce.

What do acquirers need to know about health plans, or health insurance?

Medical plans fall into two basic types: funded and unfunded.

Funded plans are funded through a trust. An acquirer buying a company with a trust may have to terminate or transfer the trust. Because of strict deductibility rules under the Internal Revenue Code, Section 419A, the buyer should ask the seller to provide assurance (through representations in the acquisition agreement) that contributions to the plan are deductible.

Benefits under *unfunded plans* are provided through insurance, either as an insured plan with a third-party carrier or as a self-insured plan (also called an "administrative services only" or ASO plan). The term *insured* can be misleading, since most insured plans today contain features—such as retrospective rating programs, minimum premium adjustments, or reserves—that essentially adjust the premium cost of the policy to the claim experience under the policy. These features may create unexpected benefits or costs for a buyer.

With medical plans of any type, it is critical to determine exactly what benefits are covered, as of what time, and what will happen if the policy is terminated.

Many of the laws applying to health plans can be found in the Consolidated Omnibus Reconciliation Act of 1985 (COBRA). Although this act was passed almost two decades ago, final regulations were not issued until the turn of the millennium, and employers are still learning about them.[21] Final regulations were also recently issued on the Health Insurance Portability Act of 1996, more than three years after its passage. COBRA requirements apply only to employers that employed 20 or more workers on a typical business day during the preceding year.

WORKFORCE REDUCTION LAWS

What laws govern workforce reduction?

There are two primary laws—one regarding layoffs (also known as reduction in force, or RIF) and the other regarding notice of layoffs.

What laws govern layoffs?

Actually, companies are free to reduce their workforce, as long as in doing so they comply with other laws—notably equal opportunity law prohibiting discrimination.[22]

To avoid lawsuits over discrimination in layoffs, companies can offer an employee extra compensation in return for getting the employee to sign a waiver of any discrimination claims. The Age Discrimination in Employment Act (ADEA) includes guidelines for the use of such a procedure. In any event, it is advisable to provide a kind of "due process" to departing employees. An acquirer desiring to set up a policy for RIF might consider studying these government regulations (found in Title 5, Volume 1, of the Code of Federal Regulations), which can be customized to the needs of the company.[23] To the reader unfamiliar with human resources (or "human capital") issues, the Title 5 lists may seem like a bureaucratic exercise more concerned with form than function. But to the employee, Title 5 represents a form of due process that can make the loss or reduction of income more acceptable—and prevent postacquisition litigation.

Could you give the details on the law regarding discrimination waivers signed by older workers when they are being discharged?

In presenting a severance agreement to an employee who is to be discharged, an acquirer (or any company) should know that the ADEA requires the company to advise the employee in writing that the employee should consult with an attorney. Also, the company must provide the employee with at least 21 calendar days to consider the agreement before the agreement can be in force. After signing the agreement, the employee is entitled to revoke it at any time during the next seven days by giving the employer written notice of the revocation. The severance agreement and the release do not become effective until the day after the seven-day revocation period has expired. Also, for the release to be binding, the employee should receive some consideration (i.e., additional compensation in some form) in turn for signing the waiver.

Additional requirements apply if the discharge is part of a reduction in force[24] (an "exit incentive or other employment termination program offered to a group or class of employees"). In this case, the employer must provide, at the beginning of the 45-day election period, a written description of the eligibility requirements and time limits applicable to the program as well as the job titles and ages of all employees eligible or selected for the program.

An employee who has signed a waiver promising not to sue may still sue—and keep the money received for signing the waiver—if the release agreement is invalid.

What laws govern notice of layoffs?

The primary law here is a provision contained within the Omnibus Trade and Competitiveness Act of 1988, called the Worker Adjustment and Retraining Notification Act (WARN).[25] WARN applies to companies with 100 or more employees that close a single site of 50 or more employees, or that institute a mass layoff affecting one-third or more of the employees at a given site (provided that at least 50 are affected). Under WARN, such employers must give their employees and communities at least 60 days' notice of a plant closing or mass layoff.

The law defines all its key terms. *Employees* under WARN means all full-time employees. Part-time employees do not count, unless all employees together work 4,000 hours per week, including overtime. *Plant closing* means permanent or temporary shutdown of a single site that results in loss of employment during any 30-day period for 50 or more full-time employees. A *mass layoff* is one that affects one-third of employees in an action that affects 50 or more employees, or that affects 500 or more employees (even if the number of employees laid off is less than one-third of all employees). *Notice to employees and communities* means notice to the chosen representative of the employees (e.g., a labor union) or to the employees themselves, as well as to the state government of the affected employees and the chief elected official of the local government.

The law includes exemptions for faltering companies and for unforeseen circumstances. An employer need not warn of a plant shutdown if it is actively seeking capital in order to avoid the shutdown, and if by giving notice it believed it would harm its chances of obtaining the capital. An employer is also exempt if the business circumstances that forced the shutdown were not reasonably foreseeable at the time that the notice would have been required. An employer must still give as much notice as practical and, when giving notice, explain why it is shorter than the 60 days required.

COLLECTIVE BARGAINING LAWS

What is collective bargaining?

As this term suggests, *collective bargaining* means negotiating on behalf of a group. In the labor law context, it means negotiating with employers on behalf of employees who are members of labor unions. The bargaining is done in the interests of obtaining an agreement, called a *collective bargaining agreement*. Negotiations are used to determine various conditions of employment. Such conditions may include any aspect of work, but collective bargaining tends to focus on pay and other areas not already fully covered by federal law. For example, negotiators might seek to ensure payment for union members at a level well above minimum wage, and it is in their discretionary power to do so.

What laws cover collective bargaining?

Collective bargaining is governed by federal and state statutory law, administrative agency regulations, and judicial decisions. In areas where federal and state law overlap, federal law controls. State laws regulate collective bargaining for agricultural workers, who are not covered under federal law. Federal employment law often has precedence over bankruptcy law.[26]

Collective bargaining laws entered federal law through the National Labor Relations Act of 1935 (NLRA), which outlaws certain unfair labor practices and grants employees the right to join trade unions and to bargain collectively. The law covers most industries. Exceptions include agriculture, covered under state law, and certain types of transportation, covered under the Railway Labor Act of 1926 governing labor relations in the railway and airline industries.

The NLRA has grown in importance over the years, following amendments by the Labor Management Relations (Taft-Hartley) Act of 1947 and the

Labor Management Reporting and Disclosure (Landrum-Griffin) Act of 1959. The NLRA created a National Labor Relations Board (NLRB), which to this day works to clarify the law and to add to its reach through a myriad of regulations. The NLRB also schedules, conducts, and supervises representation elections (in which workers are voting for or against being represented by a union). The board is the primary adjudicatory body for processing and persecuting unfair labor practice charges. It has virtually unlimited powers when it comes to interpreting and applying the NLRA.

The NLRA requires the employer to bargain with the appointed representative of its employees (typically an organized labor union). The law also sets limits on the subject matter and tactics of collective bargaining[27] and gives procedural guidelines for good faith bargaining.

What is the role of arbitration in collective bargaining?

Arbitration is commonly designated in collective bargaining agreements as the way to resolve disputes over rights between employees and employers (as opposed to disputes over interests).

In disputes over rights, the parties select a neutral third party (an arbiter) to hold a formal or informal hearing on the disagreement. The third party then arbitrates the dispute by issuing a binding decision. Laws covering arbitration include the Federal Arbitration Act, which federal courts often apply in labor disputes (although the law does not expressly cover employment contracts), and the Uniform Arbitration Act, a model law adopted by 35 states.

You mentioned disputes over interests. How are these usually resolved?

Disputes over interests may be resolved through negotiation or by force. Forced solutions include strikes, when workers refuse to come to work, and lock-outs, when workers are prevented from entering the premises where they work.

Could you list some due diligence issues in an acquisition involving one or more unionized companies?

First of all, if the acquired company is unionized, the acquirer will want assurance that it is in compliance with the collective bargaining regulations described above. As in checking any aspect of acquired company legal compliance, the acquirer should first focus on an overall process for legal compliance and, if this is found wanting, then on the particulars.

In addition, the acquirer will have to deal with issues of accretion and/or successor liability under the following scenarios:

- *The acquirer and the acquired both have unions.* Does the bargaining unit of the company fold into the acquirer's bargaining unit, or does it remain freestanding? (This is called an *accretion* issue.)
- *The acquirer has a union, the acquired does not.* Should the acquired company employees automatically join the acquired company's unit? (This is also considered an accretion issue.)
- *The acquirer does not have a union, the acquired does.* The acquirer may be deemed a successor employer. That is, it may not have to recognize the union right away, but may be deemed a successor employer depending on whether the acquirer hires a majority of the unionized workers. (This is called a *successor liability* issue.)
- *Neither company has a union.* No collective bargaining issues arise.

IMMIGRATION LAWS

What are some basics of immigration law that an acquirer should know?

Under federal law, companies may not employ illegal aliens. U.S. federal law defines who is a citizen and who is an alien (noncitizen). It also sets forth the different types of aliens: resident versus nonresident, immigrant versus nonimmigrant, and documented versus undocumented (or illegal). The typical legal alien is a resident, immigrant, documented alien. That is, an alien who has an immigrant visa is permitted to work in the United States, and receives documents to that effect. Visas are issued for temporary periods and must be renewed periodically unless and until the holder becomes a citizen. Federal law, in U.S. Code Title 28, defines how an alien can become a citizen, or can obtain the right to live and work in the country legally. States have some limited legislative authority regarding immigration, as described in Title 28, Section 1251 of the U.S. Code.

The primary immigration law of the United States is the Immigration and Nationality Act of 1952 (INA), as amended. In addition, the Immigration Reform and Control Act of 1986 (IRCA) among other provisions, toughened criminal sanctions for employers that hire illegal aliens. The Immigration Act of 1990 increased the level of immigration (approaching 1 million annually now) and evened the allocation of visas among countries.

CONCLUDING COMMENTS

As in other legal areas, the acquirer should check for the candidate company's compliance with employment law—especially laws concerning equal opportunity, health and safety, wages and hours, workforce reduction, collective bargaining, and immigration, as discussed in this chapter.

If the candidate company has a strong compliance program in place, the due diligence process in this legal area can be brief. If, however, the candidate company has no such program, the acquirer will need to exercise extreme caution, given the high incidence of litigation in this area. To protect its future, the acquirer may need to negotiate stronger representations and warranties regarding employment. The usual warning applies: Reps and warranties are only as good as the money behind them. And so, once again: *Caveat emptor*.

E N D N O T E S

1. The figures in this section are based on Tillinghast-Towers Perrin, *1999 Directors and Officers Liability Survey: U.S. and Canadian Results* (New York: Tillinghast-Towers Perrin, 2000).

2. In addition, there is the Civil Rights Act of 1991, which amends previous law from the post–Civil War era (1866) to ensure to all persons equal rights under the law, and outlines the damages available to complainants in actions brought under the Civil Rights Act of 1964, the Americans with Disabilities Act of 1990, and the Rehabilitation Act of 1973.

3. The Equal Opportunity Employment Commission interprets and enforces the Civil Rights Act of 1964, the Equal Payment Act of 1963, the Age Discrimination in Employment Act of 1967 Title VII, the Americans with Disabilities Act, and sections of the Rehabilitation Act of 1973 (all described later in the chapter).

4. The Department of Labor enforces Section 793 of the law, which refers to employment under federal contracts. The Department of Justice enforces Section 794 of the law, which refers to organizations receiving federal assistance. Source: Legal Information Institute, Cornell University (law.cornell.edu).

5. See also the "EEOC Enforcement Guidance: Vicarious Employment Liability for Unlawful Harassment by Supervisors," June 18, 1999.

6. Source: Legal Information Institute, Cornell University (law.cornell.edu).

7. The Legal Information Institute at Cornell University cites California as an example of a state that has passed, with federal permission, its own set of health and safety laws. The California laws are generally considered even tougher than the federal laws.

8. In November 1999, the DOL's OSHA posted an advisory on its Internet Web site that asserted OSHA dominion over employees who work from home. The advisory entered the public "spotlight" via further Internet postings in early 2000, leading to the clarification.

9. Sources: John Carey, "OSHA's Ergo-Rules: Business, Hold Your Fire," published in the December 6, 1999 issue of *Business Week*, and obtained through the *Business Week* online service. Also, "OSHA Proposes New Ergonomic Standards Focus Is on Repetitive-Stress Injuries," *Bloomberg News*, November 22, 1999.

10. "So-called repetitive-motion injuries are occurring by the hundreds of thousands in the New Economy as workers spend longer and longer hours at the keyboard. On average, a carpal-tunnel injury keeps a worker off the job 25 days—longer than the 17-day average for a bone fracture." Carey (ibid.). The Bloomberg press account (ibid.) states that implementing the new ergonomics rules would cost only $150 per employer.

11. See Aaron Bernstein, "Sweatshops: No More Excuses," *Business Week*, November 8, 1999. Also, see "Corporate Codes of Conduct: A Hot Issue for Directors," *Director's Monthly*, July 1997, pp. 1–6. Mr. Palmer, currently of counsel with McCutchen, Doyle, Brown & Enersen, LLP, wrote this overview of worldwide manufacturing ethics when he was senior counsel at Sears, Roebuck and Co.

12. On November 10, 1999, the U.S. Senate approved an amendment to Section 625 of the Bankruptcy Reform Act of 1999 to hike the minimum wage rate to $5.50 on March 1, 2000, then to $5.85 on March 1, 2001, and $6.15 on March 1, 2002. The bill is pending further consideration by the House. For its part, the House Ways and Means Committee has approved H.R. 3081, the Wage and Employment Growth Act of 1999, sponsored by Representative Lazio (R-NY), which would increase the minimum wage to $5.48 on April 1, 2000, to $5.81 on April 1, 2001, and to $6.15 on April 1, 2002.

13. For more on the minimum wage, see the DOL's Web site. Click "Minimum Wage" at www.dol.gov. Note: The description of minimum wage on this Web site does not include arguments against a minimum wage, which can lessen employment opportunities for youth and the poor, some economists say. See, for example, the publications of the CATO Institute in Washington, D.C.

14. The Revenue Reconciliation Act of 1993 imposed a $150,000 cap on the amount of compensation that can be held in a qualified plan (amending the Internal Revenue Code, Section 401(a)17) as well as a $1 million cap on the deductibility of compensation (adding IRC Section 162(m)). The latter cap may be waived for plans that include performance incentives approved by an independent committee of the company's board of directors.

15. For an excellent article on regulatory aspects of nonqualified benefits in the merger context, see Pamela Baker, "Executive Compensation in Mergers & Ac-

quisitions," *The Practical Lawyer*, June 1993, pp. 75ff. Part 2 of this article, which appeared in the July 1993 issue of the same publication, is a more general discussion of equity-based pay and is also very helpful.

16. OBRA precludes termination and reversion unless 1) the plan is new and contains a provision that permits reversion of excess assets to the employer, or 2) the plan permits reversion for at least five years.

17. See Reed and Lajoux, *The Art of M&A: A Merger/Acquisition/Buyout Guide* (New York: McGraw-Hill, 1999), pp. 405ff.

18. Plans may be combined in an asset acquisition only if the buyer assumes the acquired company's plan or if the plan assets are spun off to the buyer's plan.

19. A notable example from the defined benefit world is the 1996 plan consolidation at RTC America Inc., a unit of the RTC Corporation, PLC, a London-based mining company. RTC America, which owns Kennecott Corp., Luzenac America Inc., and U.S. Borax, used to run its defined benefit plans separately. Prior to the consolidation, RTC was using 20 money managers to manage the plans' assets. After the consolidation, it terminated its relations with 13 of the firms and hired four in their place, thus cutting the number of money managers dedicated to these plans in half. Source: "RTZ Creates 1 Plan from 3 Subsidiaries," *Pensions & Investments*, April 1, 1996, p. 46. By contrast, when AT&T took over NCR in a $7.5 billion hostile deal in 1991, the two companies decided to maintain separate pension plans. Five years later, when AT&T spun off NCR, it was the unit, not the parent, that was responsible for funding the plans.

20. See Rebecca Hallowell, "Consolidations, Mergers, and Acquisitions: Maximizing Retirement Plan Design," *Horizons: Fidelity's News Magazine for Non-Profits*, Spring 1996 (Vol. 7), pp. 8ff.

21. For example, in advertising a February 10, 2000 program at the Wyndham Milwaukee Center, a seminar provider announced that "the Internal Revenue Service has issued Final Regulations under [COBRA]."

22. Employers can use certain procedures to ensure conformity to equal opportunity laws when they lay off employees. For a discussion of such procedures, see Joseph T. McLaughlin and Elizabeth W. Millard, "Employment Issues in M&A Transactions," *Current Developments in Employment Law* (New York: American Law Institute–American Bar Association Continuing Legal Education, 1998), available at westlaw.com. See also, Lynne C. Hermle, "Fighting the Personnel Fires: Dealing with Employment Issues Arising from Merger and Acquisitions in a High-Tech Environment," 28th Annual Institute on Employment Law, October–November 1999, available from Westlaw Publishing via westlaw.com.

23. The laws governing reduction in force (RIF) apply only to the federal government. The government, by its very economic nature—being financed by taxes rather than by competitive market forces—has traditionally been able to employ large numbers of people for long periods of time. This practice began to change in the 1980s, however, when the government made its first attempt at downsizing. At that time, the government passed rules that can be found in the

Code of Federal Regulations, Title 5, Vol. 1. The most recent version (as of January 2000) was issued in January 1998. See the Office of Personnel Management Web site at opm.gov/rif. Areas covered by the regulation (and adaptable to company policy) include transfer of function/employees; identification of positions with a transferring function; policies for retention, demotion, displacement, and furlough; length of service and quality of performance; notice to the employee, including content of notice and employee status during the notice period; and appeals and corrective action.

24. This applies, in ADEA language, to a waiver requested in connection with "an exit incentive or other employment termination program offered to a group or class of employees."

25. See Deborah H. Eisen, "Failure to 'Warn': Repercussions in Reorganization," *Director's Monthly*, August 1999, p.10ff. Ms. Eisen is an attorney with Weinstein, Eisen & Levine in Los Angeles, California.

26. For example, the National Labor Relations Act usually has precedence over bankruptcy law.

27. The law governs such activities as legal injunctions (court-ordered actions), lockouts, pickets, and strikes. The right to strike is supported by the NLRA. This is in part because of the Norris-LaGuardia Act of 1932, which limited the power of federal courts to issue injunctions prohibiting unions from engaging in strikes and other coercive activities. The President of the United States may prohibit a strike on behalf of public safety, as when President Ronald Reagan prohibited a strike by the National Air Traffic Controllers Union.

CONCLUSION

The revolutionary idea that defines the boundary between
modern times and the past is the mastery of risk

Peter L. Bernstein
Against the Gods, 1996

In this book we have tried to offer a great deal of basic information and advice about the practice of due diligence in mergers and acquisitions. In closing, we wish to repeat one important message implicit throughout these pages: Due diligence can limit risk, but it can never—and should never—extinguish it. Risk, after all, as J. Michael Cook observes in the first chapter of this book, is the other side of the coin of opportunity. As we conclude our book on M&A due diligence, this point bears further emphasis.

Peter Bernstein said it well. "Today, the tools we use are complex, and breakdowns can be catastrophic, with far-reaching consequences," he notes, making an observation that any seasoned acquirer already knows by experience. "We must be constantly aware of the likelihood of malfunctions and errors."

So true. But rather than letting the likelihood of negative events paralyze us as corporate acquirers and advisers, we must master the study of this likelihood through risk management. The mastery of risk, as Mr. Bernstein notes, has yielded great benefits to society.

> Without a command of probability theory and other instruments of risk management, engineers could never have designed the great bridges that span our wildest rivers, homes would still be heated by fireplaces or parlor stoves, electric power utilities would not exist, polio would still be maiming children, no airplanes would fly, and space travel would be just a dream.

These words offer hope to any participant in the due diligence process. The sound conduct of this process can lead to corporate success—and, we would add, success for us all in a free society. If decision makers of all organizations exercise appropriate diligence in all their affairs, then they will or should be free from second-guessing by the courts, and free, too, from overbearing governmental involvement in their activities.

The exercise of due diligence by its nature supports the very function of the free enterprise system, and lays an important foundation for a federalist approach to government. Such an approach, affirmed in the U.S. Constitution, supports the notion of limited government, based on the virtues that emanate from the prudent self-interest of the average informed citizen.

You, our valued reader, are surely such a citizen—whatever nation you call home. As such, we believe that you will put this book to sensible use. You will let common sense and decency be your guide as you study acquisition candidates with the informed diligence due that the situation requires—no more, and no less.

DUE DILIGENCE CHECKLIST

DOCUMENTS

Corporate Documents

Certificate of Incorporation (CI) Including All Amendments, Name Changes, and Mergers   The CI is particularly helpful in determining what name to search for title to real estate. Special care should be taken not to overlook name variations—for example, "Rocket Airlines Inc.," "Rocket Air Lines, Inc.," and "Rocket Airlines Corp." These are quite likely to be very separate legal entities. The date and state of incorporation are also critical. Different companies with identical names may be incorporated in different states.

Bylaws   Look for change-of-control provisions. Many bylaws contain "poison pill" provisions designed to place restrictions on changes in control, or to make such changes very expensive to the potential acquirer. Bylaws may be available via an online research service, if the company is public.

Minutes   Look for information on past acquisitions or mergers and other transactions affecting capital; the information will help trace ownership of assets and equity. Make certain that the election and appointment of current directors and officers is duly reflected, and that the issuance of all outstanding stock has been properly authorized.

Financial Statements

Develop breakdowns, by location, of assets (land, buildings, equipment, inventory, vehicles, and, if not billed out of a central office, receivables). Consider whether those provided are adequate for use in possible SEC filings and whether pro forma financials are needed. Examine footnotes as a source of information for more detailed inquiries into existing debt, leases, pensions, related party arrangements, and contingent liabilities. Especially in leveraged acquisitions, consider the company's debt.

Focus on areas of potential vulnerability, and check for compliance with Generally Accepted Accounting Principles as determined by the Financial Accounting Standards Board (FASB). Here are some key areas, typically expressed in a Financial Accounting Statement (FAS) or a Staff Accounting Bulletin (SAB) from the FASB:

- FAS 109 (disclosure of future cost of retiree benefits)
- FAS 121 (asset impairments)
- FAS 123 (employee stock-based compensation)
- FAS 125 (transfers and servicing of financial assets and extinguishment of liabilities)
- FAS 131 (segment reporting)
- FAS 133 (derivatives and hedging)
- FAS 88 (accounting for changes in defined benefit pension plans)
- SAB 92 (disclosure of environment costs)
- SAB 99 (definition of materiality)

Engineering Reports

Try to find "as built" drawings, especially if surveys are not available. Review them for environmental problems or other concerns that might require major capital expenditures.

Market Studies/Reports on Company's Product

Product reports may be written in house or by outside consultants. In the case of public companies, if findings are material, they may be mentioned in the "management discussion and analysis" section of the company's annual report. Check the 10Ks and proxies, too. Note that marketing is a minefield of potential liability concerns, as described in Chapter 8.

Key Intangibles

Patents, Trademarks, Trade Names, and Copyrights These items generally involve "registered" or "filed" rights that can be searched for at the U.S. Patent and Trademark Office and, for copyrights, at the Library of Congress in Washington, D.C. However, such rights may not have been filed for. Also, corporations frequently have other key intangibles, such as trade secrets, that are not filed for anywhere. This is especially true of companies that deal in high technology, software, and the like. Due diligence calls for inquiry as to the status and methods of protection for these items. Review all related trade secrets, know-how, and license agreements.

Licenses and Permits   Whether granted by the government or by a private third party, licenses and permits may be absolutely essential to the ability of a corporation to continue legally to conduct its business. The buyer should ensure that all such necessary licenses are current and in good order and that these licenses and permits will be readily transferable, or remain valid, in the context of the acquisition transaction. It is generally useful to obtain the advice of special counsel or experts in the particular field (e.g., FCC counsel in the case of broadcasting licenses).

Licenses and permits should be studied in connection with state and federal law and regulations. In the case of power plants, permits and licenses will be a key item for the due diligence checklist.

Key Tangibles

Mortgages   If mortgages are significant, request a closing binder. Look for notes or other evidence of indebtedness. In the case of International Development Bank (IDB) or other quasi-public financing, request the closing binder and be sure to review indenture and other issues.

Title Documents to Real Estate and Personal Property   Review title policies and documents creating any encumbrance upon title and deeds/bills of sale by which the company acquired assets. If assets were acquired by stock purchase or merger, find evidence of filing of appropriate corporate documents in jurisdiction(s) where assets are located as well as in state(s) of incorporation.

Real Property and Assets Identification   Ask the seller to give the complete address (including county) of every facility or piece of real estate owned or leased by the company and to describe each such facility using the following list of categories (indicate more than one category if appropriate):

- Corporate offices
- Production, manufacturing, or processing facilities
- Warehouses, depots, or storage facilities
- Distribution facilities
- Sales offices

- Repair/warranty work facilities
- Apartments or other residential real property
- Undeveloped real property
- Any other facilities

If the property is *owned,* the seller should key it with an "O" and provide the full legal name in which title is recorded. If the property is *leased,* the seller should indicate an "L" and provide the full name of lessor. The seller should indicate whether there is *inventory* at any such facility by "I."

The seller should indicate by "Supp C" whether any goods, products, or materials at any such facility are there on consignment from a supplier. Ask the seller to provide the complete address (including county) of every site not described above in which the company has any assets, including every facility of any customer/processor at which the company has raw materials, goods, products, or inventory on consignment, and the name of the party in possession of such assets, including any such customer/processor.

Compare actual documents with title insurance. Look for encumbrances, easements, rights of third parties, and personal property encumbrances appearing on UCC records that should be checked. When in doubt, send someone to the site.

Contracts

Supply and Sales Agreements   Do existing agreements meet the company's future business requirements? Review them for assignability, term, and expenditures required. (Some long-time distribution contracts will survive a merger but not an acquisition of assets.)

Employment and Consulting Agreements   Review any agreements with current key employees whom the acquirer wishes to retain to ensure that the terms are good enough to hold them, and check for claims of past employees or those whom the acquirer does not wish to retain. The agreements should also be reviewed to discover if they restrict the retaining of proprietary information such as customer lists.

Leases   Get legal descriptions. Have particular concern as to term and expiration dates and renewal rights, rent, and special provisions concerning assignment that may include change of corporate ownership.

License and Franchise Agreements   Look for correspondence concerning extension, expansion, disputes, and estoppels. Franchise relationships are likely to be stormy. Is there a franchise organization? Note assignment clauses and clauses creating a landlord's lien. Are any prior consents required? Are these sufficient to meet business requirements?

Loan Agreements Review terms, intention, and assignability provisions as to any need to refinance or to obtain consents to an acquisition from lenders. Schedules and exhibits should be reviewed to glean useful information regarding the company's assets and structure.

Shareholder Agreements Review provisions and their effect on the proposed transaction. If the agreement will survive, check its effect on future transactions—that is, registration rights and antidilution or dissenters' rights.

Sponsorship Agreements Are sponsorship agreements tax deductible to the giver and tax free to the receiver? In December 1991, the Internal Revenue Service said no to both questions, disappointing organizers and sponsors of the Mobil Cotton and John Hancock Bowls.

Agreements with Labor Obtain and study all agreements for unusual provisions that would unduly constrain management's options. Review benefits, severance, and plant closing provisions.

- Will the agreements terminate at sale or are they binding on the buyer?
- Do the agreements have provisions that restrict the buyer?
- Is the company presently in compliance with the agreements? Does any agreement expire soon? Will the buyer want it to be reopened? (Notice may be required.) Is a strike likely?
- Are there any grievances that raise general issues of contract interpretation?

Agreements with Management

- Are there golden parachutes?
- Is there excessive compensation? (Compare to current compensation studies by executive search firms such as Korn/Ferry International, and executive compensation firms such as Hay Group and William L. Mercer.)

Security Agreements or Other Agreements Giving Other Parties the Right to Acquire Assets of the Company Review financing statements or other evidence of perfected security interests. Lien searches conducted by professional services engaged in this business are usually the most efficient way of uncovering UCC financing statements of record, but it is also sometimes necessary to check for third-party interests recorded against particular assets of the seller, rather than against the name of the seller itself. For example, security interests in assets such as vessels or aircraft are recorded in special registries (outside the scope of the usual UCC lien search) against the particular vessel or aircraft itself, rather than against the owning company.

Sales and Product Warranty Agreements Review for provisions that vary from the description or understanding of such documents that are provided or held by management. Review for provisions that may be illegal and/or unenforceable and for indemnity obligations of the company.

Selected Correspondence Reviewing company correspondence is a useful means of uncovering past problems that may recur.

Acquisition Agreements Review prior acquisition agreements concerning surviving provisions—that is, noncompete clauses and indemnification obligations.

Pension and Profit-Sharing Plans Check out the fine print in all plans and trust documents, and review the personnel handbook and any policy manual.

- Form 5500
- Summary Plan Description (SPD)
- Actuarial valuation
- Auditor's report and accompanying management reports
- Investment manager agreements
- Fiduciary insurance and bonds
- Investment contracts
- Investment policy
- Accrued, unfunded liabilities
- Fringe benefits

Welfare Benefit Plans Be aware that potential liabilities in welfare benefit plans can be substantial, and that valuation of plans requires expert guidance. Check out fiduciary insurance and bonds.

Multiemployer Plans Multiemployer plans can be a major problem. See Chapter 12.

Deferred Compensation Plan and Stock Option Plan Pursuant to revisions to Regulation S-K issued October 15, 1992, SEC-registered companies are now disclosing more about deferred plans in their proxy statements.

Is the candidate company in compliance with FASB 123 on stock compensation?

Supplemental or Excess Pension Plan

- Is the plan exempt from ERISA?
- Will future law affect costs or benefits?
- Are large claims anticipated?
- Are reserves on company books adequate?
- Can the plan be terminated or amended?
- Are there any benefits in pay status?
- Are the benefits in effect funded with insurance?

Insurance Policies

Review all policies and ask at least these questions:

- Do policies cover the areas of risk exposure? (Consider a risk analysis consultant to review this very technical area.)
- What is the deductible?
- What are the liability limits per occurrence? In total?
- Are punitive or treble damages excluded by the policy or by state law?
- Are policies written for "claims incurred" or "claims made"?
- Must a "tail" be purchased to extend coverage?
- Is there a "reservation of rights" clause?
- Is there a regulatory exemption clause?
- What about coverage for director and officer liability?
- What about environmental liability?

KEY INFORMATION FROM THE COMPANY'S MANAGEMENT

Financial, Ownership, and Governance Information

Financial Information Perform an analysis of the company's past operating and financial performance. Document any planned substantive changes. In conducting such an analysis, keep in mind the latest tax and accounting changes. Under the "safe harbor" provisions of the Private Securities Litigation Reform Act of 1995, companies can make forward-looking statements about financial performance, as long as they include an appropriate disclaimer. Also, under a Financial Accounting Standards Board rule effective since December 25, 1992, companies may report their projections of how current losses may offset future gains, even if it is not certain that the losses will trigger an offsetting tax benefit. (Under a previous rule adopted in 1987, companies could not report such projections on the grounds that they were not certain to materialize.)

Relative Profitability of the Company's Various Classes of Products and Business Segments   Compare results against companies of similar size in the industry.

Ownership of Company's Securities   Trace the title of present owners of the corporation (if privately held). Review for existing pledges/liens that must be released to permit the transaction.

Governance Information   Does the company have a functioning board of directors? Does it have independent committees for audit, nomination, and compensation?

Litigation Matters

Potential Defaults Under Existing Contracts or Potential Litigation   Identify as many potential defaults as possible and obtain waivers, consents, and so on. Ask for a summary of all pending or threatened legal actions that are material:

- Names and addresses of all parties
- The nature of the proceedings
- The date of commencement
- Current status
- Relief sought
- Estimated actual cost
- Insurance coverage, if any
- Any legal opinions rendered concerning those actions

Summaries should also be provided for the following:

- All civil suits by private individuals or entities
- Suits or investigations by government bodies
- Criminal actions involving the company or its significant employees
- Tax claims (federal, state, and local)
- Administrative actions
- All investigations
- All threatened litigation

Product Backlogs, Purchasing, Inventory, and Pricing Policies Is the company accurately tracking the internal flow of goods? Falsification of records can abet fraudulent schemes of massive proportions.

Pending Negotiations for the Purchase or Disposition of Assets or Liens The buyer may want to drop real property that it is planning to dispose of into another entity (such as an affiliated partnership) to avoid gain recognition or provide for means of early investment return to acquiring persons.

Federal Tax Challenges A number of items may come up in the tax area. These fall into two basic categories: understatement of income and overstatement of deductible expenses.

State and Local Tax Challenges Does the company being acquired owe property taxes? If so, how will these be allocated between the acquirer and the seller? Is there room for negotiation with the municipality or township? If the acquirer is from outside the jurisdiction, it will not be in the best position to reach a settlement; tax challenges should be settled through the selling company. The incentive for settlement could be a sharing of gain if the settlement is in favor of the seller.

Recent or Pending Changes in Federal Laws or Regulations That Might Affect the Company's Business Ask for copies of all material correspondence during the past five years with government agencies, including the following:

- Department of Justice (including the Antitrust Division)
- Department of the Treasury (including the Internal Revenue Service)
- Department of Labor (DOL) (working conditions, including pensions)
- Occupational Safety and Health Administration of DOL (worker safety and health)
- Consumer Product Safety Commission (consumer safety)
- Environmental Protection Agency (environment)
- Equal Employment Opportunity Commission (employment fairness)
- Federal Trade Commission (commercial transactions)
- Securities and Exchange Commission (securities issues and exchanges)

In addition, acquirers in specific industries must be aware of their relevant regulators. These include:

- Federal Deposit Insurance Corporation
- Public utility commissions
- Federal Energy Regulatory Commission

Ask legal counsel to check the latest version of the Code of Federal Regulations for relevant new laws affecting the candidate company's business. These should be examined for compliance—and the potential for lawsuits alleging noncompliance. For a complete list of CFR titles, see Appendix 4A in this book.

KEY INFORMATION FROM OUTSIDE SOURCES

Market and Capital Information

Market and Product Studies Whether or not the company has conducted market and product studies, it is always a good idea to consult independent research. Try also to obtain product test data from regulatory agencies. Contact major customers to determine their level of satisfaction and copies of test programs they have run.

Capital Confirmation Confirm outstanding capitalization from the company's stock transfer agent.

Lien Search

Acquirers will want to confirm the absence of liens or judgments via searches of public records. Note that names of debtors to be searched are often difficult to determine.

- Prior names—four-month rule regarding after-acquired collateral—cannot rely on creditor.
- Fictitious names or other false information.
- Continuation statements.

Sometimes a search must be conducted at the state or local level. In such cases it may be necessary to do the following:

- Coordinate between the search firm and title company (sometimes not done).
- Consult *Uniform Commercial Code and Related Procedures*, published by Register, Inc., to determine if state(s) at issue have additional or unusual search requirements.
- Obtain the lender's/borrower's approval.

Ordering a Search Send a letter to the search firm/title company listing names, location, cost, and deadline, and request copies of all liens found. Send a copy to the client and lender's/borrower's counsel.

Reviewing a Search What is your client buying, selling, liening, or loaning against? Are certain equipment, goods, and intangibles, supposed to be free and clear? Are they vital to the business? To the closing? If so, watch for liens against those items.

- If certain secured debt is to remain in place, related UCC-1s should show up on the search report.
- If secured debt is to be paid off at closing, the seller must produce UCC-3s or other required forms of release from the relevant parties.
- What does the appraisal say? What does the commitment/finance package say?

Check the report for names and jurisdictions. Review the UCC-1s sent.

- Debtor
- Secured party
- Date (five-year rule)
- Description of collateral

Compare search data against schedules to be incorporated into loan documents, contracts, and bills of sale. Often, local counsel will need copies of lien searches in order to deliver a priority opinion.

Bringdown of Search A search bringdown is a telegram or telephone update of lien searches and of corporate good standing certificates. It is often difficult to obtain such an update closer than a few days before closing, but every effort should be made to close on the basis of the most recent bringdowns possible.

Creditor Check

Assumption of Debt If secured debt is not to be paid off, get security documents to see if, for example, incurring of acquisition debt, imposition of related liens, merger, change of control, or sale of assets is permitted. Are there burdensome covenants? Is prepayment permitted, with or without penalty? Confirm absence of defaults from the principal lenders and absence of defaults from lessors (landlords).

Recognize the unusual or potential problem. (The key here is detail and curiosity.)

- Is the affiliate of seller named as secured party?
- Are the names of the debtors not exactly right, but "must be" related?

Other Searches

Patent and Trademark Searches for Possible Infringement of Products or Product Names

Certificates of Good Standing for All Corporate Subsidiaries Whether Active or Inactive

Title Search/Acquisition of Title Insurance

Appraisals of Company-Owned Real Property and Improvements

Equipment Appraisals Made by or for Insurance Companies

SAMPLE ACQUISITION AGREEMENT AND COMMENTARY[*]

The following articles and sections exemplify the content of an acquisition agreement used in a merger. Phrasing related to the **due diligence process** (such as guarantee of access and investigation rights) is highlighted in bold.

RECITALS

---

*   Adapted with permission from a longer agreement that appears in Stanley Foster Reed and Alexandra Reed Lajoux, *The Art of M&A: A Merger/Acquisition/Buyout Guide* (New York: McGraw-Hill, 1999), pp. 506–610. Credit for this document goes to Richard L. Perkal, a partner with Kirkland & Ellis, Washington, D.C., as cited in the Preface and Acknowledgments section of this book.

ARTICLE I: THE BUSINESS COMBINATION

The following is a discussion of the material items that are usually included in Article I of a merger agreement (the "Agreement"). The section headings listed below provide the topics frequently covered in this article.

Article I of the Agreement typically (a) describes how the merger will be accomplished (the "Merger"), (b) identifies which corporation's legal existence will cease and which corporation will be the "Surviving Corporation" in the merger, and (c) identifies the state laws that will govern the surviving corporation's legal existence. This section also contains the agreement of the parties to meet the corporate legal requirements of the states of incorporation of the respective parties in order to obtain approval of the merger.

The disappearing corporation frequently commits itself to call a special meeting of stockholders and to use its best efforts to obtain stockholder approval of the merger. These undertakings tend to be more elaborate when the disappearing corporation is a publicly held corporation and therefore must provide a proxy statement or information statement to its stockholders.

Once the stockholders of the disappearing corporation have approved the merger and the parties satisfy additional corporate actions and the conditions contained in Articles IX and X, the Agreement provides that the articles of merger will be filed in the respective offices of the secretary of state (or comparable authority) of the states in which each corporation is incorporated. The merger will become effective upon such filing. The effect of the merger is described by reference to a section of the business corporation laws governing the corporate existence of each corporation involved in the transaction. Some states require the surviving corporation to appoint an agent for service of process if the surviving corporation will no longer be present or resident within the state following consummation of the merger. This requirement is intended to enable creditors in the state to continue to have recourse against the disappearing corporation. The merger will have no effect on the rights of creditors or on any liens on the property of either company; liens and debts of the disappearing corporation will become the obligations of the surviving corporation.

The parties stipulate in this article which corporation's articles and bylaws will apply to the surviving corporation and whether any changes or amendments to these documents will be made upon the consummation of the merger. The officers and directors of the surviving corporation may also be identified.

In order to preserve structural flexibility, the buyer can suggest the inclusion of language that gives the buyer the right to restructure the transaction for tax, financial, or other reasons. Because a change in the structure of the transaction could have a significant adverse impact on the seller if, for example, the direction of the merger were to be changed from downstream to upstream, the buyer and seller must reach a resolution that satisfies each of their concerns.

ARTICLE II: CONVERSION AND EXCHANGE OF SHARES

The following discussion pertains to the mechanics of the conversion of shares of the merging corporations and the transfer of the purchase price. The section headings listed below provide the topics generally covered in this article.

Section 2.1   Conversion of Shares
Section 2.2   Dissenting Stockholders
Section 2.3   Stock Transfer Books
Section 2.4   Surrender and Exchange of Stock Certificates
Section 2.5   Determination and Payment of Merger Payment

This article describes the manner in which shares in each of the merging corporations will be converted or, in the case of the surviving corporation, the number of shares that remain outstanding upon consummation of the merger. It also describes the nature of the cash or securities consideration to be received by each holder of stock of the nonsurviving corporation.

Where the disappearing corporation has a diverse group of stockholders, the buyer may wish to consider the potential effects of stockholders' exercise of their dissenters' or appraisal rights under the laws of a particular jurisdiction. In transactions where stockholders may exercise their rights to dissent, the buyer should include a provision that describes the effect of the merger on such rights and imposes an obligation upon the seller and company to give the buyer notice of any communications by stockholders with respect to their dissenters' or appraisal rights. The notice obligation is frequently included in the covenant section. The buyer should also attempt to procure for itself the opportunity to direct all negotiations and proceedings concerning these rights.

Also included in this article is the method of surrender and exchange of stock certificates that enables the stockholders of the disappearing corporation to receive the merger payment. For a closely held company this may simply involve the seller's surrender of the certificates to the buyer and the buyer's payment to the seller of the agreed-upon merger consideration. However, in the case of a public company or a company with a significant number of stockholders, the method for surrender of certificates is somewhat more complicated. The buyer and company will agree that the stock transfer books of the company will be closed as of a particular time, usually the time of the filing of the certificate of merger with the secretary of state. They will also agree that stockholders must surrender their certificates to a paying agent that will be responsible for the disbursement of the merger payment. Typically, the buyer will agree that simultaneously with the consummation of the merger it will transfer the entire amount of the merger consideration to an account that will be administered by a paying agent. Funds in the account are then disbursed to the company's stockholders upon the surrender of their stock certificates.

In the event that the company has outstanding preferred stock, options, warrants, or securities convertible into common stock, the buyer should make provision in this article for the effect that the merger will have on such securities. The buyer will want to try to extinguish, through the merger, any right that a third party may have to receive common stock of the surviving corporation, and will want to avoid being subject to any dilution as a result of the exercise or conversion of any such securities. This assures the buyer that it will hold 100 percent of the common stock of the surviving corporation immediately after the merger. In certain cases the terms of such securities require the surviving corporation to honor the holder's right to receive common stock; other securities merely fail to provide for their termination in the event of a merger. The buyer should always attempt to include, as a condition to the buyer's obligation to close the transaction, the agreement of all holders of such securities to surrender their securities for cancellation at the closing.

ARTICLE III: CLOSING

This article provides the date, time, and place for the closing of the transaction (the "Closing"). Typically, the parties agree to close the transaction at the offices of the legal counsel for the buyer. Closings generally commence early in the morning so that wire transfers of funds can be accomplished prior to the afternoon close of the federal wire. The parties further agree that at the closing the parties will deliver all the documents and instruments required to be delivered by the acquisition agreement. (The date that the certificate of merger is filed with the appropriate officials governing the merger is referred to as the "Closing Date.")

ARTICLE IV: REPRESENTATIONS AND WARRANTIES OF SELLER AND COMPANY

The representations and warranties included in this article are extremely comprehensive and may, in some instances, be inappropriate in light of the size of the transaction or the nature of the company's business.

In an acquisition of a publicly traded company, it would not be customary to include all these representations and warranties. As we previously mentioned, the reason for fewer representations and warranties in a public context is that there is usually no one to sue after closing for a misrepresentation or breach of warranty. It is unrealistic for the buyer to expect to recover from thousands of public stockholders. Accordingly, some agreements omit representations and warranties that are of less importance to the buyer or not directly related to the buyer's ability to terminate the acquisition agreement because of certain adverse changes in the company. For example, most agreements in the acquisition of a publicly traded company *omit* the following seller/company representations and warranties:

Section 4.4 Title to Securities of Company and Subsidiaries
Section 4.9 Solvency
Section 4.10 Debt
Section 4.12 Product and Service Warranties and Reserves
Section 4.13 Reserves for Public Liability and Property Damage Claims
Section 4.18 Intellectual Property
Section 4.19 Assets Necessary to the Business
Section 4.21 Customers and Suppliers

Section 4.22   Competing Lines of Business
Section 4.23   Restrictive Covenants
Section 4.24   Books and Records
Section 4.25   Bank Accounts
Section 4.35   Investment Purpose
Section 4.36   Dealership and Franchises

The following language is typical of the seller/company representations and warranties sections in a merger agreement.

The Seller and the Company represent and warrant to Buyer as follows:

Section 4.1. Organization; Subsidiaries and Other Ownership Interests.   The Company and the Seller are each corporations duly organized, validly existing and in good standing under the laws of the jurisdiction of their incorporation. Section 4.1 of the disclosure statement of even date herewith delivered to Buyer by Seller (the "Disclosure Statement") sets forth the name of each Person (as defined in Article XII) in which the Company or any other Subsidiary (on a combined basis) owns or has the right to acquire, directly or indirectly, an equity interest or investment of ten percent (10) or more of the equity capital thereof or having a book value of more than _____ Dollars ($_____) (a "Subsidiary"). Each Subsidiary is duly organized, validly existing and in good standing under the laws of its jurisdiction of incorporation or organization. Each of the Company and the Subsidiaries has the corporate or other necessary power and authority to own and lease its properties and assets and to carry on its business as now being conducted and is duly qualified or licensed to do business as a foreign corporation or other entity and is in good standing in each jurisdiction in which the properties owned or leased by it or the nature of the business conducted by it makes such qualification or licensure necessary except where the failure to be so qualified or licensed and in good standing would not have a Material Adverse Effect. For purposes of this Agreement, the term Material Adverse Effect shall refer to any event which would have a material adverse effect on the financial condition, business, earnings, assets, prospects or condition of the Company and its Subsidiaries taken as a whole. Section 4.1 of the Disclosure Statement sets forth the name of each jurisdiction in which the Company and each Subsidiary are incorporated and are qualified to do business. The Company has delivered to the Buyer true and correct copies of its Certificate of Incorporation and Bylaws and true and correct copies of the certificate of incorporation or comparable charter documents and bylaws of each of the Subsidiaries. Except as set forth in Section 4.1 of the Disclosure Statement, neither the Company nor any Subsidiary owns any equity investment or other interest in any Person other than the equity capital of the Subsidiaries which are owned by the Company or a Subsidiary.

It is customary in acquisition agreements to have the seller and candidate company warrant that the seller, the company, and its subsidiaries are duly organized, and that each is qualified to do business in every jurisdiction in which each is required to qualify. If the seller or the company is not duly organized, the acquisition agreement may not be binding against it since it will not have the authority to execute the document in a corporate capacity. The utility of this representation is often debated in a theoretical context but is rarely heavily negotiated. Underlying the debate is the following question: If the agreement is not binding on the seller or the company, whom do you sue and for what? The answer is not carved in stone; the buyer could probably sue the person who signed the document in an individual capacity for misrepresentation, although a sizable recovery is unlikely. More important, the buyer would certainly have the right to walk from the deal, and that right is the primary reason the buyer should require this representation.

> *Section 4.2. Authorization.* The execution, delivery and performance of this Agreement and any instruments or agreements contemplated herein to be executed, delivered and performed by Company or Seller (including without limitation [list important agreements to be executed on or before the Closing]) (the Related Instruments), and the consummation of the transactions contemplated hereby and thereby, have been duly adopted and approved by the Board of Directors and the Stockholders of the Company and the Board of Directors of the Seller, as the case may be. The Company and the Seller have all requisite power and authority to execute, deliver and perform this Agreement and the Related Instruments, as applicable, and to consummate the transactions contemplated hereby and in the Related Instruments. This Agreement has been and as of the Closing Date, and each of the Related Instruments will be, duly and validly authorized, executed and delivered on behalf of the Seller and the Company. This Agreement is, and the Related Instruments will be as of the Closing Date, the valid and binding obligation of the Company and Seller, as applicable, enforceable against the Company or Seller, as the case may be, in accordance with their respective terms.

Ordinarily, the seller and company will represent to the buyer that the agreement is properly authorized and enforceable. Certainly, the buyer is entitled to know that the seller and company have taken all the steps that are necessary to authorize the agreement and any documents that are material to the consummation of the transaction (referred to above as the "Related Instruments") in order to ensure that such documents are binding. The related instruments might include a noncompete agreement, a separate purchase agreement relating to certain other assets, and other documents containing agreements between the parties that are special to the transaction and therefore are not specifically covered by a stock purchase, asset purchase, or merger agreement.

The most important aspect of this representation relates to enforceability of the agreement and related instruments, as this will directly affect the buyer's rights under these documents.

A similar issue arises here as was discussed in connection with Section 4.1. What damages would be recoverable by the buyer if the seller breached this representation? Sometimes the breach arises because the signatory to the document on behalf of the seller or the company did not have authority to bind that party. In such a case, the buyer may have a cause of action against the signatory or against the party on whose behalf the signatory executed the document. In addition, the buyer may be faced with a seller or company who refuses to close the deal because the agreement was not signed by an authorized agent. Such a buyer may be able to force the seller or company to close the transaction if its acts created an appearance of authority, or if it ratified the agreement after it was signed. Partial performance of the terms of the deal—application for regulatory approval, permitting continued **due diligence investigation**, or complying with representations requiring the consent of the buyer to certain actions by the company, for example—may provide convincing evidence of such ratification. In any event, the buyer would definitely have the right to refuse to close the transaction.

Section 4.3. Capitalization of Company and Subsidiaries.

(i) The authorized, issued and outstanding shares of the Company's capital stock consist of _____ shares of common stock, $ _____ par value per share, of which _____ shares are issued and outstanding [and any other shares, such as preferred stock] (the "Company Capital Stock"). The issued and outstanding shares of the Company Capital Stock are duly authorized, validly issued and fully paid and nonassessable and were not issued in violation of the preemptive rights of any person or of any agreement, law or regulation by which the issuer of such shares at the time of issuance was bound. The authorized, issued and outstanding equity capital of each Subsidiary is listed in Section 4.3(i) of the Disclosure Statement. The outstanding shares of, and the outstanding units of equity capital of, the Subsidiaries have been duly authorized, validly issued and are fully paid and non-assessable. Neither the Company nor any Subsidiary has issued any securities, or taken any action or omitted to take any action, giving rise to claims for violation of federal or state securities laws or the securities laws of any other jurisdiction.

(ii) Except as set forth in Section 4.3(ii) of the Disclosure Statement, at the date hereof there is no option, warrant, call, convertible security, arrangement, agreement or commitment of any character, whether oral or written, relating to any security of, or phantom security interest in, the Company or any Subsidiary, and there are no voting trusts or other agreements or understandings with respect to the voting of the capital stock of the Company or the equity capital of any Subsidiary.

A representation that requires that a seller set forth the capitalization of the company and its subsidiaries is rarely negotiated. Rather, discussions between the buyer and seller generally involve the factual circumstances surrounding the matter being represented. In order for a buyer to understand the effect of its purchase of the capital stock of the company (including the capital stock of the subsidiaries), it must be aware of the capital structure of the company and its subsidiaries.

Section 4.4. Title to Securities of Company and Subsidiaries.

(i) Except as set forth in Section 4.4(i) of the Disclosure Statement, the Seller has good and valid title to all of the issued and outstanding shares of the Company Capital Stock free and clear of all claims, liens, mortgages, charges, security interests, encumbrances and other restrictions or limitations of any kind whatsoever (other than pursuant to this Agreement). The Seller is not party to, or bound by, any other agreement, instrument or understanding restricting the transfer of such shares.

(ii) Except as set forth in Section 4.4(ii) of the Disclosure Statement and other than pursuant to this Agreement, the issued and outstanding units of equity capital of each of the Subsidiaries are owned by the Persons listed as owner on Section 4.4(ii) of the Disclosure Statement, in each case free of preemptive rights and free and clear of all claims, liens, mortgages, charges, security interests, encumbrances and other restrictions or limitations of any kind whatsoever.

Generally, a buyer entering into an acquisition agreement is acquiring the entire company. Therefore, it is essential that the buyer know that it is purchasing all the outstanding capital securities of the company, and that no one can challenge its ownership thereof after closing.

Section 4.5. Financial Statements and Projections.

(i) Seller has furnished to Buyer true and complete copies of the audited consolidated financial statements (including balance sheets, statements of income, statements of changes in stockholder's equity and statements of changes in financial position) of the Company and its Subsidiaries as of and for the years ended [fill in fiscal year-end for last five years] accompanied by the related opinions of the Company's official independent auditors as of such dates and for such periods (collectively, the "Financial Statements"). The Financial Statements, together with the notes thereto, fairly present the consolidated financial position of the Company and its Subsidiaries at the dates of, and the combined results of the operations and the changes in stockholders' equity and financial position for each of the Company and its Subsidiaries for the periods covered by, such Financial Statements in accordance with generally accepted accounting principles ("GAAP") consistently applied with prior periods except as indicated in the accompanying opinion of the official independent auditors. Seller has furnished to Buyer true and complete copies of the unaudited consolidated and consolidating balance sheets of the Company and its Subsidiaries as at [fill in the date of the most recent quarterly or fiscal period then ended] (the "Most Recent Balance Sheet") and the related consolidated and consolidating statements of income, statements of changes in stockholders' equity and statements of changes in financial position of the Company and its Subsidiaries as of and for the period then ended (collectively, the "Unaudited Financial Statements"). The Unaudited Financial Statements fairly present the financial position of the Company and its Subsidiaries at the date of, and the consolidated results of the operations and the changes in stockholders' equity and financial position for the Company and of its Subsidiaries for the period then ended. Such Unaudited Financial Statements have been prepared in accordance with GAAP consistently applied with prior periods, except that the Unaudited Financial Statements do not contain any or all of the footnotes required by GAAP, are condensed and are subject to year-end adjustments consistent with prior practice.

(ii) Seller has delivered to Buyer true and correct copies of the projected balance sheets of the Company for the fiscal years ending [fill in appropriate information], and the related statements of projected earnings and projected cash flow for the periods then ended (the "Projected Financial Statements"). The Projected Financial Statements are reasonable and mathematically accurate, and the assumptions underlying such projections provide a reasonable basis for such projections. The factual data used to prepare the Projected Financial Statements are true and correct in all material respects.

Generally, the most important representation that a buyer must require of the seller is that the consolidated financial statements of the company fairly present the financial condition of the company in accordance with GAAP. Almost every other representation in an acquisition agreement is in some way related to the financial statements of the company. For example, representations relating to receivables, inventory, real property, and tangible and intangible assets and liabilities concern items that are included on the balance sheet of the company to the extent required by GAAP. Accordingly, although the financial statement representations are somewhat standard in their format, they are vital to the buyer because the buyer has based its entire investment decision on either the overall financial condition of the company or certain financial characteristics of the company such as operating performance or net assets. As a result, the financial statements are usually the basis for fixing the purchase price of the company. Although situations exist where financial statements are less vital to the buyer's investment decision (e.g., in the purchase of a start-up company), such statements are usually of critical importance.

Section 4.6. Absence of Undisclosed Liabilities.   As of the date hereof and as of the Closing Date, except as and to the extent reflected, reserved against or otherwise disclosed on the Most Recent Balance Sheet or the notes thereto, or set forth in Section 4.6 of the Disclosure Statement, or otherwise properly disclosed in any other Section of the Disclosure Statement and except for those incurred in the ordinary course of business, the Company and its Subsidiaries did not have and do not have, any indebtedness or liability of any nature, whether accrued, absolute, contingent or otherwise, whether due or to become due, which is in excess of _____ Dollars ($_____).

The "absence of undisclosed liabilities" is by and large a catchall. It includes any and all liabilities of the company and its subsidiaries that were not reflected on the most recent balance sheet of the company or the notes to this balance sheet, as well as liabilities not otherwise disclosed pursuant to any of the other representations in the acquisition agreement. A smart seller should never agree to this representation without some resistance. To begin with, why should the seller (after having made numerous representations about the company) now be asked to warrant something the buyer may have failed to ask the seller to disclose? The answer is one that relates to a shifting of risk. Who should bear the risk of the buyer's omission? There is no clear answer, except that if the seller has agreed to the concept that it will generally warrant that the most recent balance sheet includes all liabilities of any kind or nature, then this representation does little more than provide additional comfort for the buyer.

Section 4.7. Accounts Receivable.   Seller has delivered, or shall deliver at Closing, to Buyer a list of all accounts receivable of the Company and its Subsidiaries as at [fill in appropriate date] (the "Accounts Receivable") which list is true, correct and complete in all material respects and sets forth the aging of such Accounts Receivable. All Accounts Receivable of the Company and its Subsidiaries represent sales actually made or services actually performed in the ordinary and usual course of their business consistent with past practice. Since the date of the Most Recent Balance Sheet, (A) no event has occurred that would, under the practices of the Company or the Subsidiary in effect when the Most Recent Balance Sheet was prepared, require a material increase in the ratio of (I) the reserve for uncollectible accounts receivable to (II) the accounts receivable of the Company or the Subsidiary, and (B) there has been no material adverse change in the composition of such Accounts Receivable in terms of aging. There is no contest, claim or right of set-off contained in any written agreement with any account debtor relating to the amount or validity of any Account Receivable, or any other account receivable created after the date of the Most Recent Balance Sheet, other than accounts receivable which do not exceed, in the aggregate, the reserve for uncollected accounts. At the date of the Most Recent Balance Sheet, as of the date hereof and as of the Effective Time of the Merger, all accounts receivable of the Company and the Subsidiary, if any, were, are and will be, respectively, unless previously collected, valid and collectible and there is no contest, claim or right of set-off contained in any written agreement with any maker of an account receivable relating to the amount or validity of such account or any note evidencing the same.

In instances where the most recent balance sheet reflects a significant amount of receivables, the buyer should require this representation in order to get specific protection that the receivables of the company and its subsidiaries are collectible. A representation with respect to the receivables of the company is sometimes unnecessary depending upon the type of company that is being acquired. For example, if the company that is being acquired entered into a factoring arrangement with respect to all its receivables, then this representation may be altogether unnecessary or to a great degree simplified. Conversely, the buyer purchasing assets may, in circumstances where the collectibility of the accounts is in doubt, require the seller to guarantee the buyer's ability to collect the receivables.

> **Section 4.8. Most Recent Inventory.** The inventories of the Company and the Subsidiaries on a consolidated basis as reflected on the Most Recent Balance Sheet consist only of items in good condition and salable or usable in the ordinary course of business, except to the extent of the inventory reserve included on the Most Recent Balance Sheet, which reserve is adequate for such purpose. Such inventories are valued on the Most Recent Balance Sheet at the lower of cost or market in accordance with GAAP.

In the event that the company to be acquired is engaged in manufacturing or is otherwise involved in the distribution of goods whether retail or wholesale, it is extremely important for the buyer to have the seller make a specific representation with respect to the inventory of the company and its subsidiaries. A buyer needs to understand the relationship between the value of the inventory reflected on the most recent balance sheet and the condition of the inventory. Items that are or may become obsolete should be reserved against on the most recent balance sheet. In addition, it is important for the buyer to know whether the valuation of inventory on the financial statements reflects its actual value. Accordingly, the seller's representation that inventories are valued at the lower of cost or market in accordance with GAAP will assure the buyer that the inventories are valued in the most conservative fashion. In some cases, the buyer may include a representation that a particular dollar amount is the minimum value of the company's inventories. That type of representation is more common in an asset purchase.

> **Section 4.9. Solvency.** The Seller and each of the Company and its Subsidiaries is on the date hereof, and immediately prior to the Closing Date will be, Solvent. "Solvent" shall mean, in respect of an entity, that (i) the fair value of its property is in excess of the total amount of its debts and (ii) it is able to pay its debts as they mature.

Aside from the obvious pricing implications of acquiring an insolvent corporation, one of the primary purposes of obtaining a solvency representation from a seller regarding the company and its subsidiaries is that lenders providing acquisition debt often require such a representation from the buyer. Especially in leveraged buyouts, one of the principal concerns of lenders is the solvency of the leveraged company because transfers (e.g., security interests granted to lenders) from insolvent companies are voidable as fraudulent conveyances. Although the leveraged surviving corporation may certainly be in a more precarious position than the company, this representation provides the initial base from which the buyer will attempt to satisfy its lenders on the solvency issue.

The solvency representation regarding the seller is intended to protect the buyer against the risk of acquiring the company and its subsidiaries in a transaction that could be characterized as a fraudulent conveyance by the seller. A buyer's decision to include the seller in the solvency representation must be based upon the financial condition of the seller, the extent to which the company and its subsidiaries constitute a substantial portion of the seller's assets, and the seller's ability to pay its debts as they mature after the sale of the company and its subsidiaries.

> **Section 4.10. Debt.** Set forth in Section 4.10 of the Disclosure Statement is a list of all agreements for incurring of indebtedness for borrowed money and all agreements relating

to industrial development bonds to which the Company is a party or grantor, which list is true and correct in all material respects. Except as set forth in Section 4.10 of the Disclosure Statement, none of the obligations pursuant to such agreements are subject to acceleration by reason of the consummation of the transactions contemplated hereby, nor would the execution of this Agreement or the consummation of the transactions contemplated hereby result in any default under such agreements.

This representation serves to break down the debt components of the most recent balance sheet that relate to debt for money borrowed. It also requires the seller to identify debt items that may be accelerated by reason of the consummation of the transactions contemplated by the Agreement. Because this representation has an information-gathering purpose, it is not usually negotiable.

Section 4.11. Fairness Opinion. The Company has received an opinion of [name of independent and nationally recognized investment banker], dated the date hereof, addressed to the Company and has delivered a copy of such opinion to Buyer to the effect that, as of the date of the Agreement, the consideration per share to be received by the holders of the Company's Common Stock in the Merger is fair to the holders of the Company's Common Stock from a financial point of view. The Company believes that it is justified in relying upon such opinion.

The buyer should attempt to include this representation when the company has a significant number of stockholders or is a publicly traded company. The buyer should require the company to obtain a fairness opinion because, after consummation of the merger, the buyer will succeed to the company's liabilities, including liabilities that may result from stockholder suits against the company or its officers and directors alleging that the merger price was inadequate. Liabilities could result when stockholders have exercised dissenter's or appraisal rights and sued the company directly or have instituted a derivative suit against officers or directors who are indemnified by the company.

The last sentence of the representation regarding reliance is intended to elicit from the company any facts that might undermine the validity of the opinion, such as facts not disclosed to the investment bankers or knowledge of conflicts of interest that might tend to bias the opinion. Several factors make this reliance representation important. First, investment bankers typically require indemnification in connection with rendering fairness opinions, and the buyer will succeed to any liability of the company to its investment bankers after the merger. Second, although a company might argue that the buyer is in a position to evaluate the reasonableness of the opinion based on the representations of the company in the agreement and on its own **financial investigation** of the company, the buyer is not privy to all the circumstances involving the preparation and delivery of the fairness opinion. Consequently, the buyer should not be reticent about making inquiries into the fairness opinion process and the manner in which the company has attempted to satisfy itself that the opinion rendered is reasonable.

Section 4.12. Product and Service Warranties and Reserves. Except as disclosed in Section 4.12 of the Disclosure Statement, the amount of any and all product warranty claims relating to sales occurring on or prior to the Most Recent Balance Sheet Date shall not exceed the amount of the product warranty reserve included on the Most Recent Balance Sheet which reserve was prepared in accordance with GAAP consistently applied and which the Company believes is adequate in light of any and all circumstances relating to its warranties of which it was aware and the amounts actually paid by it for product warranty claims. The only express warranties, written or oral, including without limitation, [insert warranty], with respect to the products or services sold by the Company and its Subsidiaries are as set forth in Section 4.12 of the Disclosure Statement.

One area that may expose a buyer to tremendous liability is product and service warranties made by the company or any subsidiary. A seller is required under GAAP to have "adequate" reserves on its balance sheet to cover such liabilities, but this standard is a very subjective one. Accordingly, a prudent buyer should have the seller specifically warrant the accuracy of this element of the most recent balance sheet. In addition, the buyer should be apprised of any and all of the warranties made and reserves held by the company so that the buyer can make its own determination of the adequacy of the company's reserves. In certain situations, a buyer may require specific representations setting forth the annual amount paid in satisfaction of claims under a particular product warranty. Gambling on the law of averages, the buyer may derive some degree of comfort.

Section 4.13. Reserve for Public Liability and Property Damage Claims. The amount of the public liability, property damage and personal injury reserve included on the Most Recent Balance Sheet was prepared in accordance with GAAP consistently applied and the Company reasonably believes such reserve is adequate.

A buyer may be concerned about this type of liability if it is foreseeable that the company or a subsidiary could have exposure above and beyond the limits of its insurance policies. Similar to the product warranty reserve discussed in Section 4.12 above, the adequacy of this reserve is a subjective judgment.

Section 4.14. Insurance. Set forth in Section 4.14 of the Disclosure Statement is a complete and correct schedule of all currently effective insurance policies or binders of insurance or programs of self-insurance which relate to the Company and its Subsidiaries, which insurance is with financially sound and reputable insurance companies, against such casualties, risks and contingencies, and in such types and amounts, as are consistent with customary practices and standards of companies engaged in businesses similar to the Company and its Subsidiaries. The coverage under each such policy and binder is in full force and effect, and no notice of cancellation or nonrenewal with respect to, or disallowance of any claim under, or material increase of premium for, any such policy or binder has been received by the Company or its Subsidiaries, nor to the Seller. Neither the Company, the Seller nor the Subsidiaries has knowledge of any facts or the occurrence of any event which (i) reasonably might form the basis of any claim against the Company or the Subsidiaries relating to the conduct or operations of the business of the Company or the Subsidiaries or any of the assets or properties covered by any of the policies or binders set forth in Section 4.14 of the Disclosure Statement and which will materially increase the insurance premiums payable under any such policy or binder, or (ii) otherwise will materially increase the insurance premiums payable under such policy or binder.

A representation with respect to the insurance policies of the company is important to the buyer in order to safeguard the assets it is buying against a variety of damage claims. Since the buyer may be unaware of what type of insurance should be carried by the company, the seller should warrant that the company has all of the insurance that is customary for the business of the company and its subsidiaries. The seller will not usually quarrel about this part of the representation; what troubles the seller most is the buyer's desire for assurances that the premiums for such insurance will not increase dramatically because of an event or claim that the seller may be aware of. How can the seller be certain what events will increase the premiums? In a clear case—when the seller has recently become aware that its product is carcinogenic, for example—the seller should be aware that its insurance premiums will obviously increase dramatically when this fact comes to the attention of its insurance companies. The buyer should also **investigate** whether such policies will survive after the acquisition, since many policies lapse on a change of control of the company. Alternatively, in some cases, a buyer may be prudent to include a representation by the seller stating that such policies will survive after the acquisition.

A second important consideration is whether the insurance policies are "claims made" or "claims incurred" policies. A "claims made" policy covers only those claims that are made to the insurance company while the policy was in full force and effect. A "claims incurred" policy, by contrast, covers all claims made at any time, provided that the events giving rise to a liability occurred during the time the policy was in full force and effect.

Lastly, if insurance is an important aspect of the business and a certain portion of the insurance consists of self-insurance, the buyer should factor this in when analyzing the cost of running the business. In the event the buyer wishes to continue to self-insure, the buyer should require the seller's cooperation in obtaining any regulatory approvals necessary to continue to self-insure the operations of the company.

> *Section 4.15. Real Property Owned or Leased.*   Section 4.15 of the Disclosure Statement sets forth a complete and accurate list or description of all real property (including a general description of fixtures located at such property and specific identification of any such fixtures not owned by the Company or any Subsidiary) which the Company or any Subsidiary owns or leases, has agreed (or has an option) to purchase, sell or lease, or may be obligated to purchase, sell or lease and any title insurance or guarantee policies with respect thereto, specifying in the case of leases, the name of the lessor, licensor or other grantor, the approximate square footage covered thereunder, the basic annual rental and other amounts paid or payable with respect thereto and a summary of the other terms thereof. True copies of all such leases for real property with aggregate annual rental payments (excluding payments to third parties on account of real estate taxes (or increases therein), insurance, operating costs, or common area expenses), individually in excess of _____ Dollars ($_____) (including all amendments thereof and modifications thereto) have been delivered to Buyer prior to the date hereof. Except as set forth in Section 4.15 of the Disclosure Statement, no consent to the consummation of the transactions contemplated by this Agreement is required from the lessor of any such real property.

The scheduling of real property serves to support the buyer's **due diligence** efforts by identifying each property owned or leased by the company or any subsidiary. In the request for disclosure of leases, consideration should be given to the dollar threshold in annual rental payments that identifies a lease that the company must disclose. For smaller companies, it may be appropriate to include no threshold at all, requiring the disclosure of all leases of real property.

This representation is also designed to elicit disclosure of both (1) obligations for periodic payments or capital commitments that have been incurred by the company or any subsidiary, and (2) those leases where landlord consents may be required to avoid lease terminations by virtue of the acquisition. Rental commitments and agreements to purchase will have an impact on the cash flow requirements of the company but may not have been apparent to the buyer from a review of the company's financial statements.

The buyer should require the annual lease payment information in order to prepare a cash flow analysis. In addition, this disclosure will aid a buyer who is trying to determine the financeability of the company's and subsidiaries' real estate and the necessity of obtaining appraisals of the real estate to assist its financing efforts.

Section 4.16 Fixed Assets; Leased Assets.

(i) Section 4.16(i) of the Disclosure Statement sets forth a complete and accurate list or description of all equipment, machinery and other items of tangible personal property which the Company or any Subsidiary owns or leases, has agreed (or has an option) to purchase, sell or lease, or may be obligated to purchase, sell or lease having a book value of _____ Dollars ($_____) or more or requiring annual rental payments in excess of _____ Dollars ($_____), specifying in the case of leases, the name of the lessor, licensor or other grantor, the description of the property covered thereby, the basic annual rental and other amounts paid or payable with respect thereto and a summary of the other terms thereof. True copies of all leases for such assets with aggregate rental payments individually in excess of _____ Dollars ($_____) (including all amendments thereto and modifications thereof) have been delivered to Buyer prior to the date hereof. The book value of all such assets owned or leased by the Company and its Subsidiaries not included on such list does not, in the aggregate, exceed _____ Dollars ($_____) at the date hereof.

(ii) Except as set forth in Section 4.16(ii) of the Disclosure Statement, no consent to the consummation of the transactions contemplated by this Agreement is required from the lessor, licensor or other grantor of any such tangible personal property.

As with the representation relating to real estate in Section 4.15, this representation asks for disclosure of each item of tangible personal property owned or leased by the candidate company or any subsidiary that has a value or annual cost in excess of a given dollar threshold. Unlike the real property representation, in which the buyer may reasonably request and be interested in information on each piece of real property owned by the company or any subsidiary, requesting disclosure of every item of tangible personal property absent a dollar threshold would impose an unreasonable burden on the seller and would subject the seller to the risk of misrepresentation in the event that an asset were inadvertently omitted.

This risk will motivate the seller to negotiate for a higher dollar threshold. A buyer may determine that it can live with a dollar threshold on the book value of owned assets but must require a lower amount in respect of lease obligations, since the latter will have a direct impact on cash flow projections. The buyer, in any event, should base its threshold on the individual value of assets that it deems relevant to any financing that may be necessary for it to finance the purchase price.

Section 4.17. Title and Related Matters.

(i) Subject to the exceptions contained in the second sentence of this Section 4.17, the Company or a Subsidiary has, and immediately after giving effect to the transactions contemplated hereby will have, good and marketable title (or, in jurisdictions where title insurance policies insuring good and marketable title are not available, good and indefeasible title, or good and merchantable title or some quality of title substantially equivalent thereto) to or a valid leasehold interest in (a) all of the properties and assets reflected in the Most Recent Balance Sheet or acquired after the date of the appropriate Most Recent Balance Sheet by the Company or a Subsidiary, (b) all properties or assets which are subject to operating leases as defined in Financial Accounting Standards Board Statement No. 13 and are not reflected in the Most Recent Balance Sheet, and (c) all other properties and assets owned or utilized by the Company or any Subsidiary in the conduct of their respective businesses. All properties and assets referred to in the preceding sentence are presently owned or held by the Company or a Subsidiary, and at and immediately after the Closing Date, will be held by the Company or a Subsidiary, free and clear of all title defects or objections, mortgages, liens, pledges, charges, security interests, options to purchase or other encumbrances of any kind or character, except: (v) liens for current taxes not yet due and payable; (w) liens, imperfections of title and easements which do not, either individually or in the aggregate, materially detract from the value of, or interfere with the present use of, the properties subject thereto or affected thereby, or otherwise materially impair the operations of the entity which owns, leases or utilizes such property or materially impair the use of such property by such entity; (x) mortgages and liens securing debt which is reflected as a liability on the Most Recent Balance Sheet; (y) mechanics', carriers', workmen's, repairmen's and other similar liens arising or incurred in the ordinary course of business; and (z) as set forth in Section 4.17(i) of the Disclosure Statement.

Title to the property owned by the company and its subsidiaries is important for the purpose of verifying the value and financeability of the assets acquired. The scope of the title representations should include assets leased under operating leases, as these assets will generally not be disclosed on a balance sheet and may represent significant value if the company's rental payments are below market rates, especially if the company's leasehold interest is mortgageable. Typically, this section has several subsections listing various types of assets, such as plants and other tangible assets, leases, real property, right-of-way or other authorizations, and various types of approval for the ownership or use of real estate.

An acquisition lender advancing funds on a secured basis will require the buyer to make extensive representations regarding the quality of its title to the assets securing the loan. The buyer should therefore attempt to obtain as much comfort on the existence of liens and encumbrances from the seller as possible. It is important to elicit in the disclosure statement all liens that might have an impact on the buyer's ability to obtain sufficient financing. Furthermore, the buyer should carefully review the liens disclosed and assess the degree to which the liens impair financeability of the assets of the company and its subsidiaries. Close scrutiny may reveal the existence of liens that limit marketability and prevent the buyer from providing its lender with a first priority security interest. Once these liens have been identified, the buyer may wish to require as its condition to closing that certain liens be discharged.

There are alternatives to having the seller schedule existing liens. The buyer (as in the second sentence of paragraph (i) could permit an exception for certain "liens, imperfections of title and easements." In addition, the materiality standard might be made more definite by referring to a lien or imposition in excess of a specified dollar amount. However, although a materiality exception may provide sufficient protection to the buyer vis-à-vis the seller, a lender may find it unacceptable. The buyer employing the exception must be willing to take on the risk that a lender may, through certain loan representations and covenants, require the discharge of liens that are not material to either the seller or the buyer.

The representations in paragraphs (ii) and (iii) are intended to assure the buyer that the assets to be acquired are in good operating condition and that the company's and subsidiaries' leases are enforceable and not in default.

Paragraphs (iv) and (v) attempt to verify that no violations or proceedings exist that might prevent the buyer from using the real estate acquired as it had been used in the past by the company and the subsidiaries. The seller may seek to limit the statement about existing violations by imposing a materiality standard. A buyer might well concede this point; a useful compromise position might be to require the representation that any violation would not result in an award of damages, or require expenditures to remedy the violation, in excess of a specified dollar amount.

Section 4.18. Intellectual Property.

(i) Section 4.18(i) of the Disclosure Statement sets forth a complete and accurate list, including, where applicable, the date of registration or expiration, serial or registration number or patent number, of all United States (including the individual states and territories of the United States) and foreign registered trademarks, service marks and trade names; unregistered trademarks, service marks and trade names; trademark, service mark and trade name applications; product designations; designs; unexpired patents; pending and filed patent applications; current and active invention disclosures; inventions on which disclosures are to be prepared; trade secrets; registered copyrights; and unregistered copyrights (collectively, the "Intellectual Property"), which the Company or any Subsidiary owns or licenses, has agreed (or has an option) to purchase, sell or license, or may be obligated to purchase, sell or license. With respect to each of the foregoing items, there is listed on Section 4.18(i) of the Disclosure Statement (a) the extent of the interest of the Company and its Subsidiaries therein; (b) the jurisdictions in or by which each such patent, trademark, service mark, trade name, copyright and license has been registered, filed or issued; (c) each agreement and all other documents evidencing the interest of the Company and its Subsidiaries therein, including, but not limited to, license agreements; (d) the extent of the interest of any third party therein, including, but not limited to, any security interest or licenses; and (e) each agreement and all other documents evidencing the interest of any third party therein.

The intellectual property representation requires the disclosure of all intellectual property that the company or any subsidiary uses in its business and is designed to assure the buyer that the intellectual property, or the company's or its subsidiaries' use thereof, does not infringe upon the rights of third parties. The representation has been drafted to cover any intellectual property rights that may exist or are pending that would adversely affect the company or its subsidiaries. This representation may be extremely important if, for example, the value of the company's business is largely dependent upon its possession of a particular patent or its ability to market its product under a particular trademark.

This section may be very long, with multiple clauses setting forth rights in intellectual property, and information as to filing or transfer fees that might be incurred in connection with the transaction. When the company and its subsidiaries have extensive foreign intellectual property holdings, these fees can be of sufficient magnitude that the buyer may desire to attempt to obligate the seller to pay a portion of these costs.

Section 4.19. Assets Necessary to the Business.   Except as set forth in Section 4.19 of the Disclosure Statement, the Company and the Subsidiaries collectively own or lease, directly or indirectly, all of the assets and properties, and are parties to all licenses and other agreements, in each case which are presently being used or are reasonably necessary to carry on the businesses and operations of the Company and the Subsidiaries as presently conducted, and none of the stockholders of the Company, the Seller nor any of their affiliates (other than any of the Company and the Subsidiary) owns any assets or properties which are being used to carry on the business or operations of the Company and the Subsidiaries as presently conducted.

Notwithstanding the many representations made by the seller, a buyer has no way of knowing that it is getting everything that it needs to operate the business of the company and its subsidiaries as presently conducted without this broad representation. This type of representation is critical if the buyer is purchasing a company by means of an asset acquisition or a business that has been operated as a division of another company.

Section 4.20. Additional Contracts.   In addition to the other items set forth in the Disclosure Statement attached hereto pursuant to the other provisions of this Agreement, Section 4.20 of the Disclosure Statement identifies as of the date hereof the following:

(i) each agreement to which the Company or any Subsidiary is a party which involves or may involve aggregate annual future payments (whether in payment of a debt, as a result of a guarantee or indemnification, for goods or services, or otherwise) by the Company or any Subsidiary of _____ Dollars ($ _____) or more;

(ii) each outstanding commitment of the Company or any Subsidiary to make capital expenditures, capital additions or capital improvements in excess of _____ Dollars ($ _____);

(iii) any contract for the employment of any officer or employee or former officer or employee of the Company or any Subsidiary (other than, with respect to any employee, contracts which are terminable without liability upon notice of 30 days or less and do not provide for any further payments following such termination) pursuant to which payments in excess of _____ Dollars ($ _____) may be required to be made at any time following the date hereof;

(iv) any stock option or stock appreciation rights plan or arrangement of the Company or any Subsidiary;

(v) any mortgage or other form of secured indebtedness of the Company or any Subsidiary;

(vi) any unsecured debentures, notes or installment obligations of the Company or any Subsidiary, the unpaid balance of which exceeds _____ Dollars ($ _____) in the aggregate except trade payables incurred in the ordinary course of business;

(vii) any guaranty of any obligation of the Company or any Subsidiary for borrowings or otherwise, excluding endorsements made for collection, guaranties made or letters of credit given in the ordinary course of business, and other guaranties which in the aggregate do not exceed _____ Dollars ($ _____);

(viii) any agreement of the Company or any Subsidiary, including options, for the purchase, sale, disposition or lease of any of its assets (other than inventory) having a book value of more than _____ Dollars ($ _____) for any single asset or _____ Dollars ($ _____) in the aggregate or for the sale of inventory other than in the ordinary course of business;

(ix) any contract to which the Company or any Subsidiary is a party pursuant to which the Company or any Subsidiary is or may be obligated to make payments, contingent or otherwise, exceeding _____ Dollars ($_____) in the aggregate, on account of or arising out of the prior acquisition of businesses, or all or substantially all of the assets or stock, of other companies or any division thereof;

(x) any contract with any labor union of which the Company or any Subsidiary is a party;

(xi) any contract or proposed contract, including but not limited to assignments, licenses, transfers of exclusive rights, "work for hire" agreements, special commissions, employment contracts, purchase orders, sales orders, mortgages and security agreements, to which the Company or any Subsidiary is a party and which (A) contains a grant or other transfer, whether present, retroactive, prospective or contingent, by the Company or any Subsidiary, of any rights in any invention, trade secret, proprietary information, trademark, service mark, trade name, copyright or other intellectual property by whatever name designated, without regard to whether such invention, trade secret, proprietary information, trademark, service mark, trade name, copyright, material object or other intellectual property was in existence at the time such contract was made, or (B) contains a promise made by the Company or by any Subsidiary to pay any lump sum or royalty or other payment or consideration in respect to the acquisition, practice or use of any rights in any invention, trade secret, proprietary information, trademark, service mark, trade name, copyright, material object in which an original work of authorship was first fixed or other intellectual property by whatever name designated and without regard to whether such lump sum, royalty payment or other consideration was ever made or received;

(xii) any contract with the Seller or any officer, director or employee of the Company or any Subsidiary of the Seller (A) involving at least _____ Dollars ($_____) in aggregate payments over the entire term thereof or more than $_____ Dollars in any 12-month period or (B) the terms of which are not arms-length; or

(xiii) any other contract, agreement or other instrument which the Company or any Subsidiary is a party not entered into in the ordinary course of business which is material to the financial, business, earnings, prospects or condition of the Company or the Subsidiaries and not excluded by reason of the provisions of clauses (i) through (xii), inclusive, of this subsection.

Except as otherwise agreed to by the parties as set forth in Section 4.20 of the Disclosure Statement, true and complete copies of all contracts, agreements and other instruments referred to in Section 4.20 of the Disclosure Statement have heretofore been delivered, or will be delivered at least ten business days prior to Closing, to Buyer by the Seller. All such contracts, agreements and other instruments are enforceable by the Company or the Subsidiaries which is (are) a party thereto in accordance with their terms except as to enforceability thereof may be affected by applicable bankruptcy, reorganization, insolvency, moratorium or other similar laws now or hereafter in effect, or by general equity principles.

This is an information-gathering representation that is designed to identify all the important contractual relationships of the company and its subsidiaries. Depending upon the type of deal being negotiated, a seller may be reluctant to make this representation because of the inordinate amount of work required to satisfy the disclosure obligation. The seller may instead tell the buyer that it is welcome to review all the contracts and other agreements at the offices of the seller. However, as with any other representation that is founded on access as opposed to identification, the buyer takes responsibility at its own peril. Therefore, a prudent buyer will demand that the seller identify all such documents and, if need be, offer to assist in the seller's preparation of the disclosure statement.

The dollar thresholds in this representation are deal-specific and the same considerations previously discussed are appropriate here.

Section 4.21. Customers and Suppliers. Section 4.21 of the Disclosure Statement sets forth (i) a true and correct list of (A) the ten largest customers of the Company and each of the Subsidiaries in terms of sales during the fiscal year ended [fill in date of most recent fiscal year end] and (B) the ten largest customers of the Company and each of the Subsidiaries in terms of sales during the three (3) months ended [fill in the most recent quarter end], showing the approximate total sales to each such customer during the fiscal year ended [fill in date of most recent fiscal year end] and the three (3) months ended [fill in most recent quarter end]; (ii) a true and correct list of (A) the ten largest suppliers of the Company and each of the Subsidiaries in terms of purchases during the fiscal year ended [fill in date of most recent fiscal year end], and (B) the ten largest suppliers of the Company and each of the Subsidiaries on a consolidated basis in terms of purchases during the three (3) months ended [fill in most recent quarter end], showing the approximate total purchases from each such supplier during the fiscal year ended [fill in date of most recent fiscal year end], and the three (3) months ended [fill in most recent quarter end], respectively. Except to the extent set forth in Section 4.21 of the Disclosure Statement, there has not been any material adverse change in the business relationship of the Company or any Subsidiary with any customer or supplier named in the Disclosure Statement. Except for the customers and suppliers named in Section 4.21 of the Disclosure Statement, neither the Company nor any Subsidiary had any customer who accounted for more than 5 of its sales during the period from [insert appropriate period of 12 to 18 months prior to date of Agreement], or any supplier from whom it purchased more than 5 of the goods or services purchased by it during such period.

Depending upon the nature of the business conducted by the candidate company and its units or divisions, the buyer may agree to require disclosure of the largest customers and suppliers on "a consolidated basis." The principal reason for this representation is to identify the dependence of the business on a single or small group of customers or suppliers.

Section 4.22. Competing Lines of Business. Except as set forth on Section 4.22 of the Disclosure Statement, no affiliate of the Seller owns, directly or indirectly, any interest in (excepting not more than 5 stockholdings for investment purposes in securities of publicly held and traded companies), or is an officer, director, employee or consultant of, or otherwise receives remuneration from, any person which is, or is engaged in business as, a competitor, lessor, lessee, customer or supplier of the Company or any Subsidiary.

In certain situations, it may appear unnecessary to require a seller to enter into some sort of noncompete agreement because of the nature of the seller's business. However, it still may be useful for the buyer to assure itself that there are no hidden companies operated or controlled by the seller that compete with the company or a subsidiary. The protection afforded by this representation is limited; the seller may be able to adversely affect the business of the company or a subsidiary in light of the seller's inside knowledge or simply because it has greater resources. The buyer should be forewarned that, despite its receipt of this representation, a seller may remain a competitor given the practicalities of a particular situation.

Section 4.23. Restrictive Covenants.   Except as set forth in Section 4.23 of the Disclosure Statement, neither Company nor any Subsidiary is a party to any agreement, contract or covenant limiting the freedom of the Company or any Subsidiary from competing in any line of business or with any person or other entity in any geographic area.

A buyer must be aware of agreements that constrain the operation of the company and its subsidiaries. Many buyers purchase companies with the expectation that the business of the company can be expanded geographically. In some cases, the buyer may be relying on this expectation to the point of including such expansion in its projections. Therefore, the buyer should carefully review any agreements that are disclosed as a result of this representation.

Section 4.24. Books and Records.
(i) The books of account and other financial records of the Company and its Subsidiaries are in all material respects complete and correct, and have been maintained in accordance with good business practices.

(ii) The minute books of the Company and its Subsidiaries, as previously made available to the Buyer and its counsel, contain accurate records of all meetings and accurately reflect all other material corporate action of the stockholders and directors and any committees of the Board of Directors of the Company and its Subsidiaries.

(iii) The Buyer has been or will be prior to the Closing Date, afforded **access to all such records** referred to in subparagraphs (i) and (ii) above.

Section 4.25. Bank Accounts.   Section 4.25 of the Disclosure Statement contains a true and correct list of the names of each bank, savings and loan or other financial institution, in which the Company or its Subsidiaries has an account, including cash contribution accounts, or safe deposit boxes, and the names of all persons authorized to draw thereon or to have access thereto.

Sections 4.24 and 4.25 above are representations that confirm the accuracy of information usually furnished to the buyer in connection with its **due diligence** efforts.

Section 4.26. Employee Benefit Plans; Labor Relations
(i) The term "Employee Plan" shall mean any pension, retirement, profit-sharing, deferred compensation, bonus or other incentive plan, any medical, vision, dental or other health plan, any life insurance plan, or any other employee benefit plan, including, without limitation, any "employee benefit plan" as defined in Section 3(3) of the Employee Retirement Income Security Act of 1974, as amended ("ERISA") and any employee benefit plan covering any employees of the Company or any Controlled Entity in any foreign country or territory (a "Foreign Plan"), to which the Company or any Controlled Entity contributes or is a party or is bound and under which employees of the Company or any Controlled Entity are eligible to participate or derive a benefit, except any government-sponsored program or government-required benefit. Section 4.26(i) of the Disclosure Statement lists each Employee Plan and identifies each Employee Plan (other than a Foreign Plan) which, as of the date hereof, is a defined benefit plan as defined in Section 3(35) of ERISA (a "Defined Benefit Plan") or is a multi-employer plan within the meaning of Section 3(37) of ERISA (a "Multi-Employer Plan").

This particular representation is extremely important in situations in which the company or any subsidiary has a substantial number of employees. Over the past few years, potential liability with respect to employee benefits and related plans has increased dramatically. Therefore, it is important for the buyer to know that the employee plans maintained by the company or any subsidiary are in compliance with existing regulations and are adequately funded. This section can be very long, attesting compliance with various sections of Employee Retirement Income Security Act of 1974 (ERISA) and the tax code. (For a further discussion of employee benefits law, see Chapter 12 of this book.)

> *Section 4.27. Litigation.*   Except as set forth in Section 4.27 of the Disclosure Statement, there is no action, suit, proceeding or investigation pending or, to the best knowledge after **due inquiry** of Seller and the Company, threatened, which would be likely to have a Material Adverse Effect; there is no reasonable basis known to the Seller or the Company for any such action that may result in any such effect and that is probable of assertion; and the Company, or any Subsidiary is not in default in respect of any judgment, order, writ, injunction or decree of any court or any federal, state, local or other governmental department, commission, board, bureau, agency or instrumentality which would be likely to have a Material Adverse Effect.

Generally, a seller will have no problem disclosing to the buyer the existence of any pending or threatened action against the company or a subsidiary that would have a material adverse effect. The part of this representation that is more difficult for the seller to make relates to whether the seller has a reasonable basis to know of any action that may result in a material adverse effect. Although there may be no claim pending or action threatened, the buyer wants to know whether the seller, company, or subsidiary has taken any action that would result in a material adverse effect. For example, if immediately prior to the signing of the acquisition agreement the company were to willfully breach a contract essential to its business, the other party to the contract, unaware of the breach, would not yet have filed a claim. Without this particular representation, the seller would not have to disclose this event. Not surprisingly, the seller is often unwilling to evaluate which of its actions may result in a claim that would have a material adverse effect, or make warranties based on its evaluation. The seller may argue that routine corporate actions could result in a material adverse effect, or the seller may express unwillingness to take on liability for the knowledge of each of its directors, officers, and employees. As with other representations, the issue is risk allocation. A smart buyer will soften this representation to appease the seller but will nonetheless seek disclosure, since the seller should be aware of an action taken that would or may constitute a material adverse effect and can always choose to disclose it rather than guess as to its outcome.

> *Section 4.28. Compliance with Laws.*
>   (i) The Company and the Subsidiaries comply with, and have made all filings required pursuant to, all federal, state, municipal or local constitutional provisions, laws, ordinances, rules, regulations and orders in connection with the conduct of their businesses as now conducted.
>   (ii) The Company and the Subsidiaries have all governmental licenses, permits and authorizations necessary for the conduct of their respective businesses as currently conducted (the "Permits"), and all such Permits are in full force and effect, and no violations exist in respect of any such Permits, and no proceeding is pending or, to the knowledge of the Seller, threatened, to revoke or limit any thereof. Except as otherwise disclosed in Section 4.28(ii) of the Disclosure Statement, all such Permits are set forth on the Disclosure Statement.

(iii) Except as set forth in Section 4.28(iii) of the Disclosure Statement, neither the Company nor any Subsidiary has received notice of violation or of any alleged or potential violation of any such constitutional provisions, laws, ordinances, rules, regulations or orders, cured or not, within the last five years or any injunction or governmental order or decree.

(iv) Except as set forth in Section 4.28(iv) of the Disclosure Statement, there are no present or past Environmental Conditions in any way relating to the business of the Company or any Subsidiary. For purposes of this Agreement, "Environmental Condition" means (a) the introduction into the environment of any pollution, including without limitation any contaminant, irritant, or pollutant or other toxic or hazardous substance (whether or not such pollution constituted at the time thereof a violation of any federal, state or local law, ordinance or governmental rule or regulation) as a result of any spill, discharge, leak, emission, escape, injection, dumping or release of any kind whatsoever of any substance or exposure of any type in any work places or to any medium, including without limitation air, land, surface waters or ground waters, or from any generation, transportation, treatment, discharge, storage or disposal of waste materials, raw materials, hazardous materials, toxic materials or products of any kind or from the storage, use or handling of any hazardous or toxic materials or other substances, as a result of which the Company or any Subsidiary has or may become liable to any person or by reason of which any of the assets of the Company or any Subsidiary may suffer or be subjected to any Lien, or (b) any noncompliance with any federal, state or local environmental law, rule, regulation or order as a result of or in connection with any of the foregoing.

The buyer might limit the representation contained in paragraph (ii) by excepting "any such licenses, permits and authorizations the failure to obtain which will not have a Material Adverse Effect."

Similarly the buyer might agree to limit the scope of subparagraph (iii) by adding to the five-year limitation the phrase "which would be reasonably likely to result in any liability for penalties or damages exceeding _____Dollars ($ _____) in the aggregate."

The environmental representation in paragraph (iv) is extremely important in light of the tremendous cost that can be incurred in correcting environmental problems. As a result of significant legislative and judicial developments over the past two decades, unwary buyers may find themselves saddled with obligations to clean up environmental problems caused by their predecessors. Such problems can range from removing asbestos in buildings to expensive groundwater purification programs made necessary by leaks from underground storage tanks.

Section 4.29. Noncontravention; Consents.   Except as set forth in Section 4.29 of the Disclosure Statement, the execution, delivery and performance of this Agreement and the Related Instruments and the consummation of any of the transactions contemplated hereby and thereby by the Seller and the Company do not and will not:

(i) violate any provisions of Seller's or Company's certificate of incorporation or bylaws;

(ii) violate, or result with the passage of time in the violation of, any provision of, or result in the acceleration of or entitle any party to accelerate (whether after the giving of notice or lapse of time or both) any obligation under, or result in the creation or imposition of any lien, charge, pledge, security interest or other encumbrance upon any of the properties of Company or any Subsidiary pursuant to any provision of any mortgage, lien, lease, agreement, permit, indenture, license, instrument, law, order, arbitration award, judgment or decree to which the Seller, Company or any Subsidiary is a party or by which it or any of its properties are bound, the effect of all of which violations, accelerations, creations and impositions would result, in the aggregate, in subjecting the Company or the Subsidiaries to liabilities in excess of _____Dollars ($_____);

(iii) violate any law, order, judgment or decree to which the Company or any Subsidiary is subject;

(iv) violate or conflict with any other restriction of any kind or character to which Company or any Subsidiary is subject, or by which any of their assets may be bound, the effect of all of which violations or conflicts would result, in the aggregate, in subjecting Company or the Subsidiaries to aggregate liabilities in excess of _____Dollars ($_____);

(v) constitute an event permitting termination of an agreement to which Company or any Subsidiary is subject, if in any such circumstance, individually or in the aggregate with all other such events, could have a Material Adverse Effect; or

(vi) require a consent, license, permit, notice, application, qualification, waiver or other action of any kind, authorization, order or approval of, or filing or registration with, any governmental commission, board, regulatory, or administrative agencies or authorities or other regulatory body.

This representation is quite useful. It enables the buyer to address each adverse consequence of the transaction before the deal is closed. For example, many agreements provide for their termination in the event that there is a change of control of the company or a subsidiary, as the case may be. Advance notice of the number and nature of these agreements gives the buyer the opportunity to put replacement contracts in place. In addition, the disclosure of certain consents may prompt the buyer to condition its obligation to close upon the success of the seller in obtaining such consents.

The buyer should give careful consideration to the amount of the dollar thresholds, as items beneath the threshold will not be disclosed and may result in dollar-for-dollar liability to the surviving corporation.

Section 4.30. Unlawful Payments.   Neither the Company nor any Subsidiary, nor to the best of the Company's knowledge any officer or director of the Company nor any officer or director of any Subsidiary, nor any employee, agent or representative, of the Company or any Subsidiary has made, directly or indirectly, with respect to the business of the Company or such Subsidiary, any illegal political contributions, payments from corporate funds not recorded on the books and records of the Company or such Subsidiary, payments from corporate funds that were falsely recorded on the books and records of the Company or such Subsidiary, payments from corporate funds to governmental officials in their individual capacities for the purpose of affecting their action or the action of the government they represent to obtain favorable treatment in securing business or licenses or to obtain special concessions or illegal payments from corporate funds to obtain or retain business.

The purpose of this representation is to identify whether the company or any subsidiary has made any payments that violate laws, such as the Foreign Corrupt Practices Act, or any payments that are not accurately reflected on the company's or subsidiaries' books and records. In addition, disclosure of these payments might reveal the tenuous nature of certain aspects of the businesses of the company or its subsidiaries, or the necessity for continuing such payments in order to obtain favorable treatment.

Section 4.31. Brokers and Finders.   Neither the Seller, Company or any Subsidiary nor any stockholder, officer, director or agent of the Seller, the Company or any Subsidiary has incurred on behalf of Seller, the Company or any Subsidiary any liability to any broker, finder or agent for any brokerage fees, finders' fees or commissions with respect to the transactions contemplated by this Agreement, except to [name of broker or finder]. Such fees and commissions will be paid by Seller.

This representation protects the buyer against obligations of the company or any subsidiary to pay certain fees in connection with the acquisition. Buyer and seller may agree to share some of these fees, but the buyer certainly doesn't want to be obligated to pay any fees of which it is not aware or that are not included in its calculation of the purchase price. These liabilities can be incurred even though no formal written agreement has been executed.

Section 4.32. Absence of Certain Changes or Events.   Except as reflected in Section 4.32 of the Disclosure Statement or as specifically set forth herein, since the date of the Most Recent Balance Sheet neither Company nor any Subsidiary has

(i) conducted its business other than in the ordinary course of business;

(ii) issued or sold, or contracted to sell, any of its stock, notes, bonds or other securities, or any option to purchase the same, or entered into any agreement with respect thereto;

(iii) amended its certificate of incorporation or bylaws;

(iv) had or made any capital expenditures or commitments for the acquisition or construction of any property, plant or equipment in excess of _____Dollars ($_____) individually and _____Dollars ($ _____) in the aggregate;

(v) entered into any transaction inconsistent in any material respect with the past practices of its business or has conducted its business in any manner materially inconsistent with its past practices;

(vi) incurred (A) any damage, destruction or similar loss in an aggregate amount exceeding _____Dollars ($_____) and which is covered by insurance or (B) any damage, destruction or loss in an aggregate amount exceeding _____Dollars ($ _____) and which is not covered by insurance;

(vii) suffered any loss or, to the best knowledge of the Seller, Company and the Subsidiaries, any prospective loss, of any dealer, customer or supplier or altered any contractual arrangement with any dealer or supplier, the loss or alteration of which would (or would, when added to all other such losses or alterations) have a Material Adverse Effect;

(viii) incurred any material liability or obligation (absolute or contingent) or made any material expenditure, other than such as may have been incurred or made in the ordinary course of business and other than capital expenditures described in clause (iv) of this subsection;

(ix) suffered any material adverse change in the business, operations, earnings, properties, liabilities, prospects, assets or financial condition or otherwise of the Company or any Subsidiary and no event which would have Material Adverse Effect has occurred;

(x) declared, set aside or paid any dividend or other distribution (whether in cash, shares, property or any combination thereof) in respect of the capital stock of the Company or any Subsidiary;

(xi) redeemed, repurchased, or otherwise acquired any of its capital stock or securities convertible into or exchangeable for its capital stock or entered into any agreement to do so;

(xii) except as reflected on the Most Recent Balance Sheet and covered by an adequate reserve therefor, made any sale of accounts receivable or any accrual of liabilities not in the ordinary course of business or written off any notes or accounts receivable or portions thereof as uncollectible;

(xiii) purchased or disposed of, or contracted to purchase or dispose of, or granted or received an option to purchase or sell, any properties or assets having a value greater than _____Dollars ($ _____) for any single asset, or greater than _____Dollars ($ _____) in the aggregate;

(xiv) except for normal annual increases or increases resulting from the application of existing formulas under existing plans, agreements or policies relating to employee compensation, made any increase in the rate of compensation payable or to become payable to the Company's or any Subsidiary's officers or employees or any increase in the amounts paid or payable to such officers or employees under any bonus, insurance, pension or other benefit plan, or any arrangements therefor made for or with any of said officers or employees;

(xv) adopted, or amended, any collective bargaining, bonus, profit-sharing, compensation, stock option, pension, retirement, deferred compensation or other plan, agreement, trust, fund or arrangement for the benefit of employees;

(xvi) made any change in any material accounting principle, material accounting procedure or material accounting practice, if any, followed by the Company or any Subsidiary or in the method of applying such principle, procedure or practice [except as required by a change in generally accepted accounting principles in the country of domicile];

(xvii) made any provision for markdowns or shrinkage with respect to inventories other than in the ordinary course of business and consistent with past practices or any write-down of the value of inventory by the Company or any Subsidiary of more than _____Dollars ($ _____) in the aggregate;

(xviii) discharged any lien or paid any obligation or liability (whether absolute, accrued, contingent or otherwise) other than current liabilities shown on the Most Recent Balance Sheet, and current liabilities incurred thereafter;

(xix) mortgaged, pledged or subjected to any lien, except liens specifically excepted from the provisions of Section 4.17 hereof, any properties or assets, real, personal or mixed, tangible or intangible, of Company or any Subsidiary;

(xx) experienced any material shortage of raw materials or supplies;

(xxi) made any gifts or sold, transferred or exchanged any property for less than the fair value thereof; or

(xxii) made or entered into any agreement or understanding to do any of the foregoing.

In order to bring down the financial condition of the company and its subsidiaries from the date of the most recent balance sheet, the buyer should have the seller represent the lack of certain events since such date. Because there are no financial statements covering the period between the date of the most recent balance sheet and the closing date, it is important for the buyer to understand the operation of the business during this period. In addition, the buyer should require the seller to covenant that it will not breach this representation on or prior to the closing date (see Section 6.1). Included in Section 4.32 are representations regarding matters which, although not specifically related to the financial statements, provide vital information about the ongoing business of the company. For example, the representation requires the disclosure of any material shortage of raw materials or supplies. A buyer must, of course, tailor this representation to the business of its company.

Section 4.33. Accuracy of Information Furnished. No representation or warranty by the Seller or Company contained in this Agreement, the Disclosure Statement or in respect of the exhibits, schedules, lists or other documents delivered to Buyer by the Seller and referred to herein, and no statement contained in any certificate furnished or to be furnished by or on behalf of the Seller or Company pursuant hereto, or in connection with the transactions contemplated hereby, contains, or will contain as of the date such representation or warranty is made or such certificate is or will be furnished, any untrue statement of a material fact, or omits, or will omit to state as of the date such representation or warranty is made or such certificate is or will be furnished, any material fact which is necessary to make the statements contained herein or therein not misleading. To the best knowledge of the Seller, the Company and the Subsidiaries, there is no fact which could have a Material Adverse Effect on the Company or any Subsidiary which the Seller has not prior to or on the date hereof disclosed to Buyer in writing.

The buyer will request this representation to provide assurance that the information upon which the buyer has based its evaluation of the company and its subsidiaries is accurate and complete. This representation is typically referred to as a "10b-5 representation" because the language closely parallels Rule 10b-5 promulgated by the Securities and Exchange Commission (SEC).

Like the representation made in Section 4.6 with respect to undisclosed liabilities, the last sentence in this representation shifts to the seller the responsibility of providing any information of which the buyer should be aware. The seller, although typically reluctant to make this representation, may derive some comfort from the fact that it has already told the buyer everything it could possibly know about the company and the subsidiaries in the preceding representations.

Section 4.34. Reports Filed with the Securities and Exchange Commission. Buyer has been furnished with accurate and complete copies of each annual report on Form 10-K that Company has filed with the Securities and Exchange Commission, all other reports or documents, including all amendments and supplements thereto, required to be filed by the Seller pursuant to Section 13(a) or 15(d) of the Securities Exchange Act since the filing of the most recent annual report on Form 10-K and its most recent annual report to its stockholders. Such reports do not contain any material false statements or any misstatements of any material fact and do not omit to state any fact necessary to make the statements set forth therein not misleading in any material respect.

This representation is applicable only to companies that are publicly traded corporations required to file reports with the SEC. The buyer must assure itself that the company has discharged its obligations to file reports with the SEC, and that the statements contained in the company's filings are true and are not misleading. Failure to obtain this representation may expose the buyer to significant postclosing liabilities, as the company may be the object of stockholders' suits or SEC enforcement actions.

Section 4.35. Investment Purpose. The Seller's acquisition of the [describe securities of Buyer to be purchased by Seller] is made for its own account for investment purposes only and not with a view to the resale or distribution thereof. The Seller agrees that it will not sell, assign or otherwise transfer or pledge the [describe securities of Buyer to be purchased by Seller] or any interest therein except in compliance with the transfer restrictions set forth on such securities.

When the seller has agreed to accept securities of the buyer in partial payment of the purchase price for the acquisition, the buyer should require certain investment representations from the seller. The representations of the seller are intended to provide the basis for characterizing the sale of securities to the seller as a private placement, thereby exempting the securities from registration under the Securities Act of 1933 and applicable state securities laws. However, this representation is not meant to satisfy all the requirements for exemption under the securities laws, especially in cases where there are more than a handful of persons receiving these securities.

Section 4.36. Dealership and Franchises.

(i) Section 4.36(i) of the Disclosure Statement contains a list of (a) those franchisees or dealers who or which, as of the date of this Agreement, were authorized by the Seller to operate stores under the name "_____," or other similar name associating such franchisee or dealer with the Seller (the "Franchisees"), (b) those Franchisees whose relationship with the Seller, the Company or any Subsidiary has been terminated within one year prior to the date hereof and (c) those persons who have become Franchisees within one year prior to the date hereof. Such list is true, correct and complete and includes the expiration date of each existing Franchise Agreement. The Seller has given Buyer an opportunity to review true and correct copies of each of the agreements between it, the Company or any Subsidiary and each Franchisee. Except as stated in Section 4.36(i) of the Disclosure Statement, each agreement between the Seller, the Company or any Subsidiary and each Franchisee (A) has been duly and validly authorized, executed and delivered by, and is the valid and binding obligation of, such Franchisee, enforceable against such Franchisee in accordance with its terms, except as may be limited by applicable bankruptcy, reorganization, insolvency, moratorium or other similar laws or by legal or equitable principles relating to or limiting creditors' rights generally, and (B) does not violate any law or regulation applicable thereto, and (C) does not conflict with the provisions of any other agreement.

(ii) Except as set forth in Section 4.36(ii) of the Disclosure Statement, there is not, under any agreement between the Seller, the Company or any Subsidiary and any Franchisee, any existing default or event which with notice or lapse of time, or both, would constitute an event of default and which has or would be reasonably likely to have a Material Adverse Effect. The execution and delivery of this Agreement and the performance of the transactions contemplated hereby will not result in any event of default under any agreement between the Seller, the Company or any Subsidiary and any Franchisee.

(iii) Except as set forth in Section 4.36(iii) of the Disclosure Statement, each Franchisee was offered his, her or its franchise in accordance with all applicable laws and regulations, including, without limitation, the regulations of the Federal Trade Commission, and any state and/or local agencies regulating the sale of franchised businesses. The Seller has not offered any person or entity a franchise since [insert a date 18 months prior to date of Agreement].

Where the company has entered into franchise or distributorship arrangements in the conduct of its business, the buyer will want to obtain specific disclosures about the terms of these arrangements. This representation is designed to require the seller to disclose the health of its contractual relations with its franchisees and distributors. A statement certifying compliance with Federal Trade Commission (FTC) regulations is important, as the company may be liable for any failure to comply with FTC disclosure requirements.

ARTICLE V: REPRESENTATIONS AND WARRANTIES OF THE BUYER

The Buyer represents and warrants to the Seller and the Company as follows:

Section 5.1. Organization. The Buyer is a corporation duly organized, validly existing and in good standing under the laws of the jurisdiction of its incorporation. The Buyer has delivered to the Seller true and correct copies of its Certificate of Incorporation and Bylaws.

Section 5.2. Authorization. The execution, delivery and performance of this Agreement and any instruments or agreements contemplated herein to be executed, delivered and performed by the Buyer (including without limitation, [list important agreements to be executed by Buyer on or before Closing]) (the "Buyer's Related Instruments"), and the consummation of the transactions contemplated hereby and thereby, have been duly adopted and approved by the Board of Directors and the stockholders, of the Buyer. The Buyer has all requisite power and authority to execute, deliver and perform this Agreement and the Buyer's Related Instruments and to consummate the transactions contemplated hereby and in the Buyer's Related Instruments. This Agreement has been and as of the Closing Date, each of the Buyer's Related Instruments will be, duly and validly authorized, executed and delivered by the Buyer. This Agreement is and the Buyer's Related Agreements are or will be, as of the Closing Date, the valid and binding obligation of the Buyer, enforceable against the Buyer in accordance with their respective terms.

Section 5.3. Noncontravention; Consents. Except as set forth in Section 5.3 of the Disclosure Statement, the execution and delivery of this Agreement and the Related Instruments and the consummation of any of the transactions contemplated hereby and thereby by the Buyer do not and will not:
  (i) violate any provisions of the Buyer's certificate of incorporation or bylaws;
  (ii) violate, or result with the passage of time in the violation of, any provision of, or result in the acceleration of or entitle any party to accelerate (whether after the giving of notice or lapse of time or both) any obligation under, or result in the creation or imposition of any lien, charge, pledge, security interest or other encumbrance upon any of the properties of the Buyer pursuant to any provision of, any mortgage, lien, lease, agreement, permit, indenture, license, instrument, law, order, arbitration award, judgment or decree to which the Buyer is a party or by which it or any of its properties are bound, the effect of all of which violations, accelerations, creations and impositions would result, in the aggregate, in subjecting the Buyer to liabilities in excess of _____ Dollars ($_____);
  (iii) violate any law, order, judgment or decree to which the Buyer is subject;
  (iv) violate or conflict with any other restriction of any kind or character to which the Buyer is subject, or by which any of their assets may be bound, the effect of all of which violations or conflicts would result, in the aggregate, in subjecting the Buyer to aggregate liabilities in excess of _____ Dollars ($_____); or
  (v) require any consent, license, permit, notice, application, qualification, waiver or other action of any kind, authorization, order or approval of, or filing or registration with, any governmental commission, board, regulatory, or administrative agencies or authorities or other regulatory body.

Section 5.4. Litigation. There is no action, suit, proceeding or investigation pending, or, to the best of the Buyer's knowledge, threatened, against or related to the Buyer or its respective properties or business which would be reasonably likely to adversely affect or restrict the Buyer's ability to consummate the transactions contemplated hereby or in the Related Instruments; and there is no reasonable basis known to the Buyer for any such action that may result in such effect and is probable of assertion.

Section 5.5. Brokers and Finders.   Neither the Buyer nor any stockholder, officer, director or agent of the Buyer has incurred on behalf of the Buyer any liability to any broker, finder or agent for any brokerage fees, finders' fees or commissions with respect to the transactions contemplated by this Agreement, except to [name of broker or finder], whose fees will be paid by the Buyer.

Section 5.6. Business.   The Buyer has not engaged in any activities other than those incident to its organization or as contemplated by the terms of this Agreement.

Section 5.7. Accuracy of Information Furnished.   No representation or warranty by the Buyer contained in this Agreement, the Disclosure Statement or in respect of the exhibits, schedules, lists or other documents delivered to the Seller by the Buyer and referred to herein, and no statement contained in any certificate furnished or to be furnished by or on behalf of the Buyer pursuant hereto, or in connection with the transactions contemplated hereby, contains, or will contain as of the date such representation or warranty is made or such certificate is or will be furnished, any untrue statement of a material fact, or omits, or will omit to state as of the date such representation or warranty is made or such certificate is or will be furnished, any material fact which is necessary to make the statements contained herein or therein not misleading.

The representations and warranties of the buyer generally parallel the representations made by the seller and candidate company in Article IV. However, there is less need on the part of the buyer to make comprehensive representations and warranties, as required of the seller, because it is the businesses and assets of the seller that are being purchased.

In some instances, the buyer may accomplish its acquisition of the company by using a shell company as the acquirer. If properly structured, this strategy may permit the parties to avoid filing a premerger notification under the Hart-Scott-Rodino Antitrust Improvements Act of 1974. The representation made in Section 5.6 above regarding the scope of the business of the buyer is useful to the seller in that it assures the seller that there should be few contractual constraints on the shell company to consummate the acquisition.

When the buyer is not a shell company, it may be appropriate for the seller to include additional representations about the buyer. For example, a statement assuring the current appropriateness of the buyer's financial statements, stating that there have been no material changes or events since the last statements issued, might assure the seller of the buyer's ability to consummate the transaction.

ARTICLE VI: COVENANTS OF SELLER AND COMPANY

Section 6.1. Conduct of Business.   Except as set forth in Section 6.1 of the Disclosure Statement or required to consummate the transactions contemplated hereby, from and after the execution and delivery of this Agreement and until the Closing Date, the Seller shall cause the Company and each of the Subsidiaries (a) to use its best efforts to preserve the respective present business organizations of the Company and the Subsidiaries substantially intact; (b) to maintain in effect all foreign, federal, state and local approvals, permits, licenses, qualifications and authorizations which are required to carry on their respective businesses as now being conducted;

(c) to use their best efforts to maintain their respective relationships with and preserve the goodwill of, employees, agents, distributors, franchisees, licensees, customers, suppliers and others having business dealings with them; and (d) without the prior written consent of the Buyer, to take any action which would result in a breach of any of the representations set forth in Section 4.32 hereof.

The "conduct of business" covenant is used by a buyer to ensure that the seller will not do, or cause to be done, anything that would (1) alter the business being purchased, (2) diminish the value of such business to the buyer, or (3) create for the buyer an unanticipated liability or problem with respect to the business it is acquiring. This is important because the buyer has presumably negotiated an acceptable purchase price for the company based on the operations and performance of the business as it presently exists. If the seller were to allow necessary permits or licenses, or business relationships with distributors, employees, or franchisees to lapse, the value of the business could be diminished. If not restricted by such a covenant, the seller could render the buyer's valuation meaningless by taking some action outside of the ordinary course of business that impairs the financial position of the company or the value of the company to the buyer. One issue that often arises is how to define the actions that are in the ordinary course of business. Since most agreements fail to include a definition of this phrase, the buyer should acquaint itself with applicable case law in order to be aware of its usage in the jurisdiction governing the acquisition agreement.

Section 6.2. Preclosing Activities.   Prior to the Closing Date, the Seller shall cause the Company, with the cooperation of the Buyer where appropriate, and the Company shall and shall cause each Subsidiary to use their best efforts to obtain any consent, authorization or approval of, or exemption by, any governmental authority or agency or other third party, including without limitation, their landlords and lenders and those persons (other than the Company or a Subsidiary) who are parties to the agreements described in Section 4.29 of the Disclosure Statement required to be obtained or made by them in connection with the transactions contemplated by this Agreement and the Related Instruments or the taking of any action in connection with the consummation thereof, including without limitation, any consent, authorization or approval necessary to waive any default under any of the agreements described in Section 4.29 of the Disclosure Statement.

Once the buyer is made aware of the various consents necessary to consummate the acquisition by means of the seller's disclosure in Section 4.29, the buyer typically will attempt to require the seller to use its best efforts to obtain such consents. The seller, who has an interest in getting the deal done, should agree to accommodate the buyer, but only to the extent it is reasonable for the seller to do so under the circumstances. It should make clear that "best efforts" do not extend to spending money.

Section 6.3. Proposals; Disclosure.   Prior to the Closing Date, the Company and the Seller (i) will not, directly or indirectly, whether through any of their officers, employees, representatives or otherwise, solicit or encourage any written inquiries or proposals for the acquisition of stock, or all or substantially all of the assets or the business or any portion thereof of the Company or any Subsidiary and (ii) will promptly advise the Buyer orally and in writing of any inquiry or proposal for the acquisition of any stock, or all or substantially all of the assets or business or any portion thereof of the Company or any Subsidiary occurring on or after the date hereof.

This covenant is designed (1) to prevent the seller from shopping for a better deal during the period between signing of the acquisition agreement and the closing date, and (2) to keep the buyer apprised of any unsolicited inquiries. From the buyer's point of view, the seller has made a commitment to sell to the buyer and should be concentrating all its efforts toward a closing with the buyer rather than continuing to court other would-be suitors. In addition, the acquisition agreement represents a binding contract, and the buyer has made a commitment to purchase provided that all conditions to closing are satisfied. The buyer should have the benefit of having made such a commitment as well as the risk of a deterioration in the company's business in the ordinary course of events. One benefit of ownership is the opportunity to sell at a profit. The *Pennzoil v. Texaco* case has highly publicized the fact that this benefit belongs to a potential buyer once a contractual commitment between the seller and buyer has been put in place.

Section 6.4. Additional Financial Statements.   Prior to the Closing Date, the Company shall furnish to the Buyer as soon as practicable but in no event later than _____ days after the close of each quarterly period or _____ days after the close of each monthly period (i) for each successive quarterly period ending after the date of the Most Recent Balance Sheet, an unaudited consolidated quarterly balance sheet and related statements of income, stockholders' equity and changes in financial position of the Company and its Subsidiaries and (ii) for each successive monthly period ending after the date of the Most Recent Balance Sheet, an unaudited consolidated monthly balance sheet and related monthly statements of income, stockholders' equity and changes in financial position of the Company and its Subsidiaries. Such financial statements shall be complete, accurate and correct and present fairly the financial condition of the Company and the Subsidiaries, both individually and taken as a whole, as of the end of each such quarterly or monthly period, as the case may be, and shall present fairly the results of operations for each of the quarterly or monthly periods then ended, in accordance with generally accepted accounting principles consistently applied except for the footnotes thereto, normal year-end adjustments consistent with past practices or as contemplated by this Agreement.

Section 6.5. Additional Summaries of Accounts Receivable.   Prior to the Closing Date, the Company will deliver to the Buyer, as soon as practicable but in no event later than _____ days after the close of the appropriate monthly period hereinafter referred to, for each successive monthly period after the date of the Most Recent Balance Sheet a true and correct summary of all accounts receivable of the Company and the Subsidiaries as at the end of each such monthly period.

Sections 6.4 and 6.5 permit the buyer to monitor the operations of the business after the execution of the acquisition agreement by reviewing monthly and quarterly financial statements furnished by the seller. This can be extremely important to the buyer, especially if the financial statements reveal a material adverse change in the business. In this event, the buyer would not be obligated to close, since a customary condition to its obligation to close is the absence of any material adverse changes in the business. For a further discussion of material adverse change, see Section 9.6 below.

Section 6.6. Investigation by Buyer.   The Seller and Company shall, and the Company shall cause its Subsidiaries to, afford to the officers and authorized representatives of the Buyer **free and full access**, during normal business hours and upon reasonable prior notice, to the offices, plants, properties, books and records of the Company and its Subsidiaries in order that the Buyer may have full opportunity to make such **investigations** of the business, operations, assets, properties and legal and financial condition of the Company and its Subsidiaries as the Buyer deems reasonably necessary or desirable and the officers of the Seller, the Company and its Subsidiaries shall furnish the Buyer with such additional financial and operating data and other information relating to the business operations, assets, properties and legal and financial condition of the Company and its Subsidiaries as the Buyer shall from time to time reasonably request. Prior to the Closing Date, or at all times if this Agreement shall be terminated, the Buyer shall, except as may be otherwise required by applicable law, hold confidential all information obtained pursuant to this Section 6.6 with respect to the Company and its Subsidiaries and, if this Agreement shall be terminated, shall return to the Company and its Subsidiaries all such information as shall be in documentary form and shall not use any information obtained pursuant to this Section 6.6 in any manner that would have a material adverse consequence to the Company or its Subsidiaries.

The representations, warranties and agreements of the Seller, the Company and its Subsidiaries set forth in this Agreement shall be effective regardless of any **investigation** that the Buyer has undertaken or failed to undertake.

The "investigation" covenant ensures that the seller will cooperate with the buyer by granting **access and logistical support** for the buyer's **due diligence** review of the candidate company and its subsidiaries. It is important for the buyer to include the last paragraph of this covenant. Otherwise, the seller may try to prevent the buyer from taking action against the seller in the event of a material breach of the seller's or company's representations. The seller could say that since the buyer discovered or could have discovered the breach during its investigation of the company and its subsidiaries, the seller should be relieved of any responsibility for such misrepresentations.

Section 6.7. Notification.   The Seller shall give prompt notice to the Buyer of (i) any notice of, or other communication received by the Seller, the Company or any Subsidiary subsequent to the date of this Agreement and prior to the Closing Date, relating to a default or event which with notice or lapse of time or both would become a default, or which would cause any warranty or representation of the Seller or the Company to be untrue or misleading in any material respect, under this Agreement, or any other material contract, agreement or instrument to which the Company or any Subsidiary is a party, by which it or any of its property is bound or to which it or any of its property is subject, (ii) any notice or other communication from any third party alleging that the consent of such third party is or may be required in connection with the transactions contemplated by this Agreement, (iii) any material adverse change in the business, operations, earnings, prospects, assets or financial condition of the Company or its Subsidiaries, or (iv) any information received by the Seller or Company prior to the Closing Date relating to the operations of the Buyer which, to the best knowledge of the Seller or Company, constitutes (or would be reasonably likely to constitute) or indicates (or would be reasonably likely to indicate) a breach of any representation, warranty or covenant made by the Buyer herein or in any other document relating to the transactions contemplated hereby.

The "notice" covenant places on the seller the onus of notifying the buyer of any potential material breaches of the seller's representations and warranties. Upon such notification, the buyer has the option of asserting a breach and abandoning the deal on the grounds that the conditions to closing are not met. However, a buyer does not have a right to walk from the deal if the breach can be cured by the seller prior to the closing.

Section 6.8. Access to Records.   After the Closing, the Buyer shall be entitled **to reasonable access to the business and tax records of the Seller relating to the Company and its Subsidiaries** for proper business purposes, including the preparation of tax returns. In connection with any such purpose, the Seller agrees to cooperate with the Buyer in the communication of information contained in such records and the handling of examinations, appeals and litigations.

This covenant may be important when many of the records of the candidate company and its subsidiaries are consolidated with those of the seller. It is impossible in such circumstances for the seller to turn over to the buyer such records, since they may also relate to other companies owned by the seller.

Section 6.9. Stockholders' Meeting.   The Company, acting through its Board of Directors shall, as soon as practicable and in accordance with its Articles of Incorporation and By-Laws and applicable law:

(1) prepare and distribute proxy materials (the "Proxy Statement") in compliance with applicable law for, and duly call, give notice of, convene and hold, a special meeting (the "Special Meeting") of its stockholders as soon as practicable after the date hereof but not later than [insert the date] for the purposes of considering and voting upon this Agreement in accordance with the [name of business code for Company's state of incorporation] Code;

(2) include in the Proxy Statement (as hereinafter defined) the recommendation of the Board that stockholders of the Company vote in favor of the approval and adoption of this Agreement; and

(3) use its best efforts (a) to obtain and furnish the information required to be included by it in the Proxy Statement, (b) to file a preliminary version of the Proxy Statement with the Securities and Exchange Commission ("SEC") not later than [insert number of days] after the receipt by the Company of its audited financial statement for the year ended [insert year], furnish copies thereof to the Buyer and, after consultation with the Buyer, respond promptly to any comments made by the SEC with respect to the Proxy Statement and any preliminary version thereof, (c) to cause the Proxy Statement to be mailed to its stockholders as early as practicable after the date hereof but no later than [insert number of days], and (d) to obtain the necessary approval of this Agreement by its stockholders. Notwithstanding any consultation with the Buyer in connection with the Proxy Statement, neither the Buyer nor any of its officers, directors, employees or affiliates shall incur any liability to the Company or its stockholders with respect thereto, except with respect to any information contained in the Proxy Statement which any of them has furnished, or confirmed the accuracy of, in writing to the Company.

(4) amend, supplement or revise the Proxy Statement as may from time to time be necessary in order to insure that the Proxy Statement does not contain any statement which, at the time and in the light of the circumstances under which it is made, is false or misleading with respect to any material fact, or omits to state any material fact necessary in order to make the statements therein not false or misleading. Prior to submitting any such amendment, supplement or revision of the Proxy Statement to the stockholders of the Company,

such amendment, supplement or revision shall be submitted to the Buyer for its approval. Notwithstanding such approval, neither the Buyer nor any of its officers, directors, employees or affiliates shall incur any liability to the Company or its stockholders with respect thereto, except with respect to any information contained in such amendment, supplement or revision which any of them has furnished, or confirmed the accuracy of, in writing to the Company.

In an acquisition of a company whose equity securities are publicly traded, it is essential that the company comply with all relevant regulations, especially those promulgated by the Securities and Exchange Commission (SEC) dealing with proxies and required stockholder meetings. Failure to comply with these regulations can expose the company to stockholder suits or regulatory enforcement actions. The buyer is also desirous of placing an affirmative obligation on the company to solicit proxies and to obtain stockholder approval.

In some circumstances, the buyer may require the seller to deliver a comfort letter from a qualified independent source confirming the financial information in the proxy statement. The purpose of this requirement is to reduce the potential for error in the financial information presented in the proxy statement and thereby reduce the chance that a stockholder may prevail in a suit against the surviving corporation.

Section 6.10. Dissenting Stockholders; Notice.   The Company will promptly advise the Buyer of each notice given or demand made by a dissenting Company stockholder pursuant to [cite relevant section of business law in state where Company is incorporated].

No buyer wants to close a transaction in which a large percentage of the candidate company's stockholders are seeking appraisal rights. If such stockholders were to be awarded a price per share in excess of the price paid by the buyer, it could expose the surviving corporation to an inordinate amount of liability. Therefore, as covered in Section 9.10 and the discussion that follows, in order for a buyer to exercise its right not to consummate the transaction pursuant to Section 9.10, it must be aware of any dissenting stockholders of the company.

ARTICLE VII: COVENANTS OF THE BUYER

Section 7.1. Notice.   The Buyer shall give prompt notice to the Seller of (i) any notice of, or other communication received by the Buyer subsequent to the date of this Agreement and prior to the Closing Date, relating to a default or event which with notice or lapse of time or both would become a default, or which would cause any warranty, or representation of the Buyer to be untrue or misleading in any material respect, under this Agreement, or any other material contract, agreement or instrument to which the Buyer is a party, by which it or any of its property is bound or to which it or any of its property is subject, (ii) any notice or other communication from any third party alleging that the consent of such third party is or may be required in connection with the transactions contemplated by this Agreement, or (iii) any information received by the Buyer prior to the Closing Date relating to the operations of the Seller, the Company or its Subsidiaries which, to the best knowledge of the Buyer, constitutes (or would constitute) or indicates (or would indicate) a breach of any representation, warranty or covenant made by the Seller or Company herein or in any other document relating to the transactions contemplated hereby.

Similar to the representations, the seller's covenants usually far outnumber the covenants of the buyer. Typically, a seller would at a minimum require a buyer to give the same "notice" that it is required to give. One useful device (which is advantageous to both buyer and seller) is the requirement that each notify the other in the event that the first party is aware of the other's breach of a particular representation, warranty, or covenant. The utility of this obligation, especially for the seller, is that neither side has a distinct advantage over the other postclosing by reason of a breach that was known about prior to the closing.

ARTICLE VIII: COVENANTS OF BUYER, COMPANY, AND SELLER

Section 8.1. Governmental Filings.   The Buyer, the Company and the Seller shall cooperate with each other in filing any necessary applications, reports or other documents with any federal or state agencies, authorities or bodies (domestic and foreign) having jurisdiction with respect to the Merger, and in seeking necessary consultation with and prompt favorable action by any such agencies, authorities or bodies. Without limiting the generality of the foregoing, the Buyer, the Company and the Seller shall as soon as practicable, and in any event within fifteen (15) days, after the date hereof, make the necessary filings under the Hart-Scott-Rodino Antitrust Improvements Act of 1976 (the "Hart–Scott–Rodino Act") and shall cooperate in attempting to secure early termination of the applicable waiting period.

This covenant requires the buyer, candidate company, and seller to work together in making any government filing or application. The buyer and the seller should use a general covenant of this type and then specify the particular filings that must be made (Hart-Scott-Rodino Act filings with respect to a merger, SEC filings, state government filings, and so on).

Section 8.2. Publicity.   The Buyer, the Company and the Seller will consult with each other before making any public announcements with respect to the Merger or the Related Instruments or the transactions contemplated hereby or thereby, and any public announcements shall be made only at such time and in such manner as the Seller and the Buyer shall mutually agree, except that either party shall be free to make such public announcements as it shall reasonably deem necessary to comply with foreign, federal or state laws.

The buyer and the seller must be aware of each other's plans with respect to publicity surrounding the acquisition of a company so as to be able to coordinate their efforts. It can be extremely harmful to the transaction or one of the parties to the transaction if there are conflicting reports or misleading statements. For example, conflicting reports in the press can disrupt management of the company or may even damage the ongoing business. More important, when one or both of the entities involved are public companies, liability can arise from premature press reports alleged to have been made to manipulate the market or mislead stockholders and investors. When possible, the buyer and seller should issue joint press releases or, at least, carefully review releases before they are distributed.

ARTICLE IX: CONDITIONS TO OBLIGATIONS OF THE BUYER

The obligations of the Buyer to consummate this Agreement, and the transactions to be consummated by the Buyer hereunder on the Closing Date, shall be subject to the satisfaction, prior to or concurrently with the Closing, of each of the conditions set forth in this Article IX; such conditions may be waived in writing in whole or in part by the Buyer to the extent permitted by applicable law.

Section 9.1. Compliance with Agreement.   The Seller and the Company shall have complied with and performed the terms, conditions, acts, undertakings, covenants and obligations required by this Agreement to be complied with and performed by each of them on or before the Closing Date; and the Buyer shall have received from the Seller at the Closing a certificate, dated the Closing Date and signed by the President or a Vice President of the Seller to such effect.

This condition gives the buyer the opportunity to abandon the acquisition if the seller or the company has failed to perform its obligations under the acquisition agreement. Although this condition is less critical than the bringdown of representations and warranties to the closing date that appears in Section 9.2, it provides the buyer a valuable "out" if the seller or the company has breached a covenant that is essential to the buyer's valuation of the company. For example, the duty of the company to endeavor to obtain all regulatory approvals necessary for the transaction would usually arise from a covenant made to the buyer in the acquisition agreement, as would the obligation of the company to conduct business only in the ordinary and usual course. Because failure to perform under these covenants may compromise the value of the company, the buyer must ensure its right to abandon the transaction in these circumstances.

The requirement for an officer's certificate is based upon the belief that prior to any officer's execution of such a certificate, the officer will **investigate** to ascertain its accuracy, and the certificate can be drafted to include a representation to that effect.

This condition can be drafted without a materiality standard. However, sellers typically demand that the materiality qualifier be incorporated. This position is a reasonable one given the broad language of both the condition itself and the covenants and other agreements to which it refers. Consequently, the buyer should be prepared to accept "performance in all material respects of the terms" of the agreement as adequate protection of its interests. A similar qualifier appears in the condition set forth in Section 9.2 below.

Section 9.2. Representations and Warranties True as of Closing Date.   All representations and warranties of the Seller and the Company set forth in this Agreement shall be true and correct in all material respects on and as of the Closing Date with the same force and effect as though such representations and warranties had been made on and as of the Closing Date and the Buyer shall have received from the Seller at the Closing a certificate, dated the Closing Date and signed by the President or a Vice President of the Seller to such effect.

A bringdown of the representations and warranties to the closing date is, from the buyer's perspective, insurance that the company it acquires is the company for which it bid and upon which it conducted **due diligence.**

Section 9.3. Third-Party Orders and Consents.

(i) The Seller and the Buyer shall have fully complied with the applicable provisions of the Hart–Scott–Rodino Act and any and all applicable waiting periods thereunder shall have expired, or an opinion, reasonably acceptable to the Buyer, that no such filing is required shall have been delivered to the Buyer.

(ii) All consents and approvals listed in Section 4.29 of the Disclosure Statement hereto shall have been obtained, and the Seller and the Buyer shall have been furnished with appropriate evidence, reasonably satisfactory to them and their respective counsel, of the granting of such consents and approvals.

This condition enables the buyer to abandon a transaction if all necessary consents are not obtained before closing. Failure to obtain the consent of the company's lenders, for example, may prejudice the pricing of the acquisition or its financeability because consummation of the transaction may entitle the lenders to accelerate their debts or impose a lien on the property of the company. Failure to obtain necessary government consent to an acquisition may preclude the buyer from operating the business of the company as previously operated.

The seller should attempt to limit this condition to government consents necessary in order to consummate the transactions contemplated by the acquisition agreement. The seller could reasonably maintain that any debt instruments that are accelerated by their terms should be refinanced by the buyer. If this limitation is accepted, the obligation of the buyer to close the deal should not be conditioned upon the consent of the holders of such debt. Clearly, the buyer and the seller must agree on exactly what consents must be obtained prior to the closing.

Section 9.4. Corporate Action.   The Buyer shall have received:

(i) a copy of the resolution or resolutions duly adopted by the Board of Directors of the Seller and the Company and by the stockholders of the Company authorizing the execution, delivery and performance of this Agreement and the Related Instruments by the Seller and the Company, and authorizing all other necessary or proper corporate action to enable the Seller and the Company to comply with the terms of this Agreement, certified in each case by the Secretary or an Assistant Secretary of the Seller or the Company as the case may be; and

(ii) a certificate of the Secretary or an Assistant Secretary of each of the Seller and the Company, dated the Closing Date, as to the incumbency and signatures of the officers of the Seller and the Company, respectively, executing this Agreement and the Related Instruments and any other documents in connection with the transactions contemplated by this Agreement or the Related Instruments.

A further protection for the buyer that the acquisition agreement and related documents are properly authorized and delivered is a review of the resolutions authorizing such documents.

Section 9.5. Opinion of the Seller's and Company's Counsel.   At the Closing, the Seller shall furnish the Buyer and the banks and/or other financial institutions providing financing for the Merger (the "Acquisition Lenders") with an opinion, dated the Closing Date, of [name of Seller's counsel], in form and substance satisfactory to the Buyer and its counsel and the Acquisition Lenders and counsel to the Acquisition Lenders, to the effect that:

(i) Company (a) is a corporation duly organized, validly existing and in good standing under the laws of its state of incorporation, (b) is duly qualified or licensed to transact business as a foreign corporation and is in good standing in each jurisdiction in which the properties owned or leased by it or the nature of the business conducted by it makes such qualification or licensing necessary, except in those jurisdictions where the failure to be so qualified or licensed and in good standing will not, individually or in the aggregate, have a Material Adverse Effect, and (c) has full power and authority to carry on its business as it is now being conducted and to own the properties and assets it now owns;

(ii) Company has full power and authority to execute, deliver and perform the Agreement and the Related Instruments and to consummate the transactions contemplated hereby and by the Related Instruments; and the execution, delivery and performance of the Agreement and the Related Instruments and the consummation of the transactions contemplated by the Agreement and the Related Instruments have been duly authorized by all requisite action on the part of the Company;

(iii) the Seller is a corporation duly organized, validly existing and in good standing under the laws of its state of incorporation and has full power and authority to execute, deliver and perform the Agreement and the Related Instruments and to consummate the transactions contemplated by the Agreement and the Related Instruments; and the execution, delivery and performance of the Agreement and the Related Instruments and the consummation of the transactions contemplated by the Agreement and the Related Instruments have been duly authorized by all requisite action on the part of the Seller;

(iv) each of the Subsidiaries (a) is a corporation duly organized, validly existing and in good standing under the laws of its jurisdiction of organization, (b) is duly qualified or licensed to transact business and is in good standing in each jurisdiction in which the properties owned or leased by it or the nature of the business conducted by it makes such qualification or licensing necessary, except in those jurisdictions where the failure to be so qualified or licensed and in good standing will not, individually or in the aggregate, have a Material Adverse Effect and (c) has full power and authority to carry on its business as it is now being conducted and to own the properties and assets it now owns;

(v) the authorized, issued and outstanding equity capital of the Company and each Subsidiary consists solely of (a) in the case of the Company, _____ shares of Common Stock, of which _____ shares are issued and outstanding and _____ shares of Preferred Stock, of which _____ shares are issued and outstanding and (b) in the case of each Subsidiary, as set forth in Section 4.3 of the Disclosure Statement (the "Subsidiary Stock"). All outstanding shares of the Company Common Stock and the Subsidiary Stock have been duly and validly authorized and issued and are fully paid, nonassessable and free of preemptive rights and based upon an examination of the organizational documents, minute books, stock registers and other similar records of the Company, all of such shares are owned of record and beneficially by (a) the Seller, in the case of the Company and (b) as set forth in Section 4.1 of the Disclosure Statement, in the case of each Subsidiary, in each case free and clear of all claims, liens, mortgages, charges, security interests, encumbrances and other restrictions or limitations of any kind whatsoever, and there are no outstanding options, warrants, calls, convertible securities or other rights relating to unissued shares of capital stock of Company or any Subsidiary;

(vi) the Agreement and the Related Instruments have been executed and delivered by each of the Seller and the Company and constitutes the legal, valid and binding obligations of each of the Seller and the Company, enforceable against each in accordance with their respective terms, except (a) as such enforcement may be subject to fraudulent conveyance, bankruptcy, insolvency, reorganization, moratorium or other similar laws now or hereafter in effect, or by legal or equitable principles, relating to or limiting creditors' rights generally and (b) that the remedy of specific performance and injunctive and other forms of equitable relief are subject to certain equitable defenses and to the discretion of the court before which any proceeding therefor may be brought;

(vii) neither the execution, delivery and performance of the Agreement or the Related Instruments by the Seller or the Company, nor the consummation of the transactions contemplated hereby or thereby will violate any provision of the Certificate of Incorporation or Bylaws of the Seller or the Company or of any of the Subsidiaries or, to the best knowledge of such counsel after **due inquiry**, will violate, conflict with, or constitute a default under, or cause the acceleration of maturity of any debt or obligation pursuant to, or result in the creation or imposition of any security interest, lien or other encumbrance upon any property or assets of the Company or any of the Subsidiaries under, any contract, commitment, agreement, trust, understanding, arrangement or restriction of any kind to which the Company or any of the Subsidiaries is a party or by which the Company or any of the Subsidiaries is bound or violate any statute or law, or any judgment, decree, order, regulation or rule of any court or governmental authority;

(viii) to the best knowledge of such counsel, none of the Company, the Seller nor any Subsidiary is engaged in or threatened with any legal action or other proceeding or has incurred or been charged with or is under investigation with respect to any violation of any law or administrative regulation which if adversely determined might, in such counsel's opinion, materially adversely affect or impair (a) the business or condition, financial or otherwise, of the Company or any of the Subsidiaries except as specifically disclosed in the Agreement or the Disclosure Statement or (b) the ability of the Company and/or the Seller to consummate the transactions contemplated by the Agreement or the Related Instruments;

(ix) no filing, declaration or registration with, or any permit, authorization, license, consent or approval of, any governmental or regulatory authority is required in connection with the execution, delivery and performance of the Agreement or the Related Instruments by the Seller and the Company or the consummation of the transactions contemplated by the Agreement or the Related Instruments, except as expressly disclosed in this Agreement, all of which have been duly and validly obtained;

(x) no facts have come to the attention of such counsel that cause such counsel to believe that any information provided to the Buyer in writing by or on behalf of the Seller or the Company contained any untrue statement of a material fact or omitted to state any material fact necessary to make the statements therein, in light of the circumstances under which they were made, not misleading, except that counsel may also state that it has not independently verified the accuracy, completeness or fairness of such information, and the limitations inherent in the examination made by it and the knowledge available to it are such that it is unable to assume, and does not assume, any responsibility for the accuracy, completeness or fairness of such information.

As to any matter contained in such opinion which involves the laws of a jurisdiction other than the United States or the State of [state in which such counsel is licensed to practice], such counsel may rely upon opinions of local counsel of established reputation reasonably satisfactory to the Buyer, which opinions shall expressly state that they may be relied upon by the Buyer and the Acquisition Lenders. Such counsel may also expressly rely as to matters of fact upon certificates furnished by appropriate officers of the Seller, the Company and any Subsidiary, or appropriate governmental officials.

Typically, the seller and the candidate company will require an opinion from the buyer's counsel (see Section 10.5) that mirrors many of the provisions included in the opinion given by seller's counsel. Although these opinions may be heavily negotiated by the counsel who must render them, they are useful for a variety of reasons. First, legal opinions serve as a **due diligence device** and force counsel to closely examine the important aspects of the transaction. Second, counsel's reluctance to deliver an opinion regarding a particular issue raises a red flag, permitting the parties to reexamine that aspect of the transaction. Third, the opinion gives the party to which it is addressed legal recourse against counsel delivering the opinion. In this regard, the buyer may be asked to accept the opinion of general counsel to the seller or company. The buyer should resist this request, since the buyer's recourse against the general counsel of the company may be tantamount to recourse against the surviving corporation. In contrast, outside counsel's opinion provides recourse against an independent source, one that may be more diligent in its efforts and less biased in its evaluation as a result of its potential liability and relative "distance" from seller's management.

> **Section 9.6. No Material Adverse Change.**   No material adverse change in the business, operations, earnings, prospects, assets or financial condition of the Company or any Subsidiary and no event which would have such an effect shall have occurred.

As discussed, a customary condition to the buyer's obligation to close the transaction is that the company has not suffered any adverse change prior to the closing. The seller should attempt to limit this condition to the company and its subsidiaries taken as a whole, since the buyer is not buying the company and its subsidiaries piecemeal. The seller should also focus on the phrase "business, operations, earnings, prospects, assets or financial condition" because, in some instances, the buyer may not have bargained for a certain earnings stream or the prospects of the company. Conversely, when the buyer has relied on projections, it should specifically include the projections in this condition as a yardstick for measuring the prospects of the company.

Exactly what constitutes a "material adverse change" is unclear, and varies from circumstance to circumstance. It is easy to identify an obvious one, such as the single-line company that has lost the only supplier of raw materials for the manufacture of its product. But the loss of a customer whose purchase of goods from the company constitutes 5 percent of the company's overall revenues is a less clear-cut situation. The usual vagueness of this condition gives the buyer the opportunity to get out of the deal, even in circumstances where the change is of uncertain harm to the company, because the seller is usually disinclined to bring suit on the basis that no material adverse change has occurred. Of course, the buyer must have some real basis for its belief that a material adverse change has occurred. Usually, the seller and buyer attempt to restructure the transaction in light of any material adverse change.

> **Section 9.7. Litigation.**   At the Closing, there shall be no effective injunction, writ or preliminary restraining order or any order of any nature issued by a court or governmental agency of competent jurisdiction restraining or prohibiting the consummation of the transactions provided for herein or any of them or limiting in any manner the Buyer's right to control the Company and the Subsidiaries or any aspect of their businesses or requiring the sale or other disposition of any of the operations of the Company or any Subsidiary or making the consummation of the Merger or the transactions contemplated by this Agreement and the Related Instruments unduly burdensome to the Company or any Subsidiary, and immediately prior to the Closing Date no proceeding or lawsuit shall have been commenced and be pending or be threatened by any governmental or regulatory agency or any other person with respect to the transactions contemplated by this Agreement or the Re-

lated Instruments which the Buyer, in good faith and with the advice of counsel, believes is likely to result in any of the foregoing or which seeks the payment of substantial damages by the Company, any Subsidiary or the Buyer.

This condition is usually triggered in circumstances in which the acquisition is either unfriendly and a potential suitor has brought suit to enjoin the consummation of the transaction contemplated by the acquisition agreement, or a government agency has attempted to enjoin the transaction because of antitrust or other government concerns.

Section 9.8. Financing.
    (i) The Buyer shall have received the financing proceeds pursuant to, and on substantially the same terms and conditions as those contained in, the commitment letter from [name of Acquisition Lender].
    (ii) The final documentation of such financing arrangements referred to in the commitment letter from [name of Acquisition Lender] shall in all respects be reasonably satisfactory in form and substance to the Buyer.

This version of a "financing out" is appropriate if the buyer has obtained financing commitments before signing the acquisition agreement. Another method, which is appropriate if the parties have agreed that the buyer must finance the transaction within a certain period of time, is to build in a provision enabling the parties to terminate the acquisition agreement if commitment letters are not obtained or the deal is not closed by a specific date.

Section 9.9. Title Insurance.   [Insert name of title company], or any other reputable title company reasonably satisfactory to the Buyer (the "Title Company") shall have issued owners', lessees' and mortgagees' title insurance policies (or unconditional commitments therefor) with respect to, and in the amount of the fair market value of, the real property and the leased real property listed in Section 4.15 of the Disclosure Statement and located in the United States, the United States territories and possessions and Canada, on the current edition of the A.L.T.A. Form B, Rev. 1970 (or Loan Policy Form, in the case of mortgagees' title insurance) insuring title, with all standard and general exceptions deleted or endorsed over so as to afford full "extended form coverage," except for the lien of taxes not yet due and payable, and with no further exceptions not reasonably satisfactory to the Buyer. It is hereby agreed that if, in order to delete, or endorse over, standard form or general exceptions so as to afford to owners, lessees or lenders "extended form coverage," the Title Company requires standard form seller's affidavits, the conditions set forth in this Section 9.10 shall be satisfied by an authorized officer of the Seller giving such affidavit. The Buyer shall have received unconditional title insurance commitments reflecting the foregoing matters at least ten (10) days prior to Closing.

This condition provides the buyer comfort that the real property owned or leased by the candidate company is free from defects in title and, consequently, may be used to secure acquisition financing. The seller may demand that this condition be effective only to the extent that acquisition lenders require title insurance. On the other hand, the buyer may strengthen the condition to make the existence of a title defect that compromises the business of the company a sufficient basis for abandoning the transaction. To the extent that title insurance is unavailable and the real property is an integral part of the business of the company, this condition gives the buyer the opportunity to renegotiate the price of the acquisition or to walk away from the deal.

> *Section 9.10. Dissenting Stockholders.*   Holders of not more than [insert percentage] of the Company's Common Stock shall have elected dissenter's rights as provided in Section [ ] of the [business code of Company's state of incorporation] Code, and the Company shall have taken all action with respect to the rights of dissenting stockholders required of it pursuant to such Code.

In an acquisition of a company with numerous stockholders, a buyer should attempt to limit its exposure to liability in the event that the stockholders of the company achieve a higher price (through a postclosing appraisal) for the value of their shares than that paid by the buyer. The seller should obviously negotiate a percentage high enough to prevent the buyer from abandoning the deal without good cause, and the buyer should be willing to accept some level of risk.

ARTICLE X: CONDITIONS TO OBLIGATIONS OF THE SELLER AND COMPANY

The obligations of the Seller and the Company to consummate this Agreement, and the transactions to be consummated by the Seller hereunder on the Closing Date, shall be subject to the satisfaction, with the Closing, of each of the conditions set forth in this Article X; which conditions may be waived in writing in whole or in part by the Seller to the extent permitted by applicable law.

Section 10.1. Compliance with Agreement.   The Buyer shall have complied with and performed in all material respects the terms, conditions, acts, undertakings, covenants and obligations required by this Agreement to be complied with and performed by it on or before the Closing Date; and the Seller shall have received from the Buyer at the Closing a certificate, dated the Closing Date and signed by the President or a Vice President of the Buyer to such effect.

Section 10.2. Representations and Warranties True as of Closing Date.   All representations and warranties of the Buyer set forth in this Agreement shall be true and correct in all material respects on and as of the Closing Date with the same force and effect as though such representations and warranties had been made on and as of the Closing Date and the Seller shall have received from the Buyer at the Closing a certificate, dated the Closing Date and signed by the President or a Vice President of the Buyer to such effect.

Section 10.3. Third-Party Orders and Consents.
   (i) The Seller and the Buyer shall have fully complied with the applicable provisions of the Hart–Scott–Rodino Act and any and all applicable waiting periods thereunder shall have expired, or an opinion, reasonably acceptable to the Seller, that no such filing is required shall have been delivered to the Seller.
   (ii) All consents and approvals listed in Section 4.29 of the Disclosure Statement shall have been obtained, and the Seller and the Buyer shall have been furnished with appropriate evidence, reasonably satisfactory to them and their respective counsel, of the granting of such consents and approvals, and such consents and approvals remain in full force and effect on the Closing Date.

Section 10.4. Corporate Action.   The Seller shall have received:

(i) a copy of the resolution or resolutions duly adopted by the Board of Directors of the Buyer and by the stockholders of the Buyer authorizing the execution, delivery and performance of this Agreement and the Related Instruments by the Buyer, and authorizing all other necessary or proper corporate action to enable the Buyer to comply with the terms of this Agreement and the Related Instruments, certified in each case by the Secretary or an Assistant Secretary of the Buyer; and

(ii) a certificate of the Secretary or an Assistant Secretary of the Buyer, dated the Closing Date, as to the incumbency and signatures of the officers of the Buyer executing this Agreement and the Related Instruments and any other documents in connection with the transactions contemplated by this Agreement and the Related Instruments.

Section 10.5. Opinion of the Buyer's Counsel.   At the Closing, the Buyer shall furnish the Seller with an opinion, dated the Closing Date, of [name of Buyer's outside counsel], in form and substance reasonably satisfactory to the Seller and its counsel, to the effect that:

(i) the Buyer is a corporation duly organized, validly existing and in good standing under the laws of the state of its incorporation;

(ii) the Buyer has the power and authority to execute, deliver and perform the Agreement and the Related Instruments and to consummate the transactions contemplated by the Agreement and the Related Instruments; and the execution, delivery and performance of the Agreement and the Related Instruments and the consummation of the transactions contemplated by the Agreement and the Related Instruments have been duly authorized by all requisite action on the part of the Buyer;

(iii) this Agreement and the Related Instruments have been executed and delivered by the Buyer and is the legal, valid and binding obligation of the Buyer, enforceable against the Buyer in accordance with their respective terms, except (a) as such enforcement may be subject to fraudulent conveyance, bankruptcy, insolvency, reorganization, moratorium or other similar laws now or hereafter in effect, or by legal or equitable principles, relating to or limiting creditors' rights and (b) that the remedy of specific performance and injunctive and other forms of equitable relief are subject to certain equitable defenses and to the discretion of the court before which any proceeding therefor may be brought;

(iv) neither the execution, delivery and performance of the Agreement and the Related Instruments by the Buyer, nor the consummation of the transactions contemplated by the Agreement and the Related Instruments will violate any provision of the Certificate of Incorporation or Bylaws of the Buyer, or to the best knowledge of such counsel, will violate, conflict with, or constitute a default under, or cause the acceleration of maturity of any debt or obligation pursuant to, or result in the creation or imposition of any security interest, lien or other encumbrance upon any property or assets of the Buyer, any contract, commitment, agreement, trust, understanding, arrangement or restriction of any kind to which the Buyer is a party or by which the Buyer is bound or violate any statute or law, or any judgment, decree, order, regulation or rule of any court or governmental authority;

(v) to the best knowledge of such counsel, the Buyer is not engaged in or threatened with any legal action or other proceeding nor has it incurred or been charged with, nor is it under investigation with respect to, any violation of any law or administrative regulation which if adversely determined might, in such counsel's opinion, materially adversely affect or impair the ability of the Buyer to consummate the transactions contemplated hereby;

(vi) no filing, declaration or registration with, or any permit, authorization, license, consent or approval of, any governmental or regulatory authority is required in connection with the execution, delivery and performance of the Agreement and the Related Instruments by the Buyer or the consummation of the transactions contemplated by the Agreement and the Related Instruments, except as expressly disclosed in the Agreement or the Disclosure Statement, all of which have been duly and validly obtained;

(vii) no facts have come to the attention of such counsel that cause such counsel to believe that any information provided to the Seller in writing by or on behalf of the Buyer contained any untrue statement of a material fact or omitted to state any material fact necessary to make the statements therein, in light of the circumstances under which they were made, not misleading, except that counsel may also state that it has not independently verified the accuracy, completeness or fairness of such information, and the limitations inherent in the examination made by it and the knowledge available to it are such that it is unable to assume, and does not assume, any responsibility for the accuracy, completeness or fairness of such information.

As to any matter contained in such opinion which involves the laws of a jurisdiction other than the United States or the State of [state in which Buyer's counsel is licensed to practice], Buyer's counsel may rely upon opinions of local counsel of established reputation reasonably satisfactory to the Seller, which opinions shall expressly state that they may be relied upon by the Seller. Such counsel may also expressly rely as to matters of fact upon certificates furnished by appropriate officers of the Buyer, or appropriate governmental officials.

Section 10.6. Litigation. At the Closing, there shall be no effective injunction, writ or preliminary restraining order or any order of any nature issued by a court or governmental agency of competent jurisdiction restraining or prohibiting the consummation of the transactions provided for herein or any of them or limiting in any manner the Buyer's right to control the Company and the Subsidiaries or any aspect of their businesses or requiring the sale or other disposition of any of the operations of the Company or any Subsidiary or making the consummation of the Merger or the transaction contemplated by this Agreement and the Related Instruments unduly burdensome to the Company or any Subsidiary, and immediately prior to the Closing Date no proceeding or lawsuit shall have been commenced and be pending or be threatened by any governmental or regulatory agency or any other person with respect to the transactions contemplated by this Agreement or the Related Instruments which the Buyer, in good faith and with the advice of counsel, believes is likely to result in any of the foregoing or which seeks the payment of substantial damages by the Company, any Subsidiary or the Buyer.

Sections 10.1 and 10.2 afford the seller the same right to abandon the transaction as the buyer has under Sections 9.1 and 9.2. However, since the buyer enters into fewer and less expansive representations and covenants than the seller, this right is typically less valuable to the seller than it is to the buyer.

Sections 10.3, 10.4, 10.5, and 10.6 are the seller's equivalent of the bringdown, consent, and corporate action legal opinions and litigation conditions given the buyer in Sections 9.3, 9.4, 9.5, and 9.7, respectively.

ARTICLE XI: TAX MATTERS

The following sections are typically included in an agreement for a transaction in which the company being sold is one of several companies owned by the seller and reported on a consolidated basis.

Section 11.1. Representations, Warranties, and Covenants.
Section 11.2. Payment of Tax Liabilities
Section 11.3. Indemnification
Section 11.5. Further Assurances and Assistance
Section 11.6. Audit Matters
Section 11.7. Certain Tax Claims for Which Seller May Be Liable

In situations in which the company is not a member of the seller's consolidated group, much of Article XI may be unnecessary, and the buyer should instead require a representation by the seller in Article IV as follows:

Tax Matters. For purposes of this Agreement "Taxes" or "Tax" means all net income, capital gains, gross income, gross receipts, sales, use, ad valorem, franchise, profits, license, withholding, payroll, employment, excise, severance, stamp, occupation, premium, property, or windfall profit taxes, customs duties, or other taxes, fees, assessments, or charges of any kind whatsoever, together with any interest and any penalties, additions to tax, or additional amounts imposed by any taxing authority ("Taxing Authority") upon the Company or the Subsidiary.

(i) Except as set forth in Section _____ of the Disclosure Statement, the Company and the Subsidiary have filed or will file when due all federal, foreign, state, and local tax returns, tax information returns, reports, and estimates for all years and periods (and portions thereof) ending on or before the Closing Date for which any such returns, reports or estimates were due. All such returns, reports and estimates were prepared in the manner required by applicable law, and all Taxes shown thereby to be payable have been paid when due.

(ii) Section _____ of the Disclosure Statement sets forth all jurisdictions in which the Company and the Subsidiaries have filed or will file income or franchise tax returns for each taxable period, or portion thereof, ending on or before the Closing Date.

(iii) The Company and the Subsidiaries each has withheld or will withhold amounts from its respective employees and has filed or will file all federal, foreign, state and local returns and reports with respect to employee income tax withholding and social security and unemployment Taxes for all periods (or portions thereof) ending on or before the Closing Date, in compliance with the provisions of the Internal Revenue Code, as amended and currently in effect (the "Code"), and other applicable federal, foreign, state and local laws.

(iv) The Company and the Subsidiaries each have paid, or provided a sufficient reserve on the Balance Sheet for the payment of, all federal, state, local and foreign Taxes with respect to all periods, or portions thereof, ending on or before _____. The amount of any net operating loss for federal income tax purposes shown on the Company's federal income tax returns has been accurately and properly determined in accordance with the Code and other applicable law without giving effect to the transactions contemplated hereby.

(v) The separate and consolidated federal income tax returns of the Company and its Subsidiaries, through the taxable year ended [insert date], have been examined by the United States Internal Revenue Service (the "IRS") or closed by applicable statute of limitations, and any deficiencies or assessments, including interest and penalties thereon, claimed or made as a result of such examinations in respect of the Company and any of its Subsidiaries.

(vi) Except as set forth in Section _____ of the Disclosure Statement there are no material claims or investigations by any Taxing Authority pending or, to the best knowledge of the Seller and the Company, threatened, against the Company or the Subsidiaries for any past due Taxes; and there has been no waiver of any applicable statute of limitations or extension of the time for the assessment of any Tax against the Company or the Subsidiaries, except as set forth in Section _____ of the Disclosure Statement.

(vii) Neither the Company nor any Subsidiary has made, signed or filed, nor will it make, sign or file any consent under Section 341(f) of the Code with respect to any taxable period ending on or before the Closing Date.

(viii) Except as set forth in Section _____ of the Disclosure Statement, no event has occurred or will occur on or prior to the Closing Date that would require indemnification by the Company or the Subsidiaries of any tax lessor under any agreements relating to tax leases executed under Section 168(f)(8) of the Internal Revenue Code as to assets of the Company or its Subsidiaries.

(ix) Neither the Company nor any Subsidiary has ever been, nor is the Company or any Subsidiary currently, a party to any agreement relating to the sharing of any liability for, or payment of, Taxes with any other person or entity.

Many nontax lawyers (not to mention managers) merely skim the tax section of an acquisition agreement, since they find it extremely esoteric. Although this may be unavoidable, the importance of tax provisions should not be minimized or overlooked. Article XI is used in connection with the acquisition of a company whose federal income tax returns are filed as part of the consolidated tax return of the seller. Although preclosing federal tax liabilities of the company will be automatically included in the seller's consolidated return, the company will itself have liability to various other taxing authorities for periods prior to the closing. Therefore, since the company will file a tax return after closing that covers a portion of the period prior to closing, the agreement should require the seller to pay any taxes for periods prior to the closing that may be due to various taxing authorities. This is logical, as the seller reaped the benefits of the company's income during this period. It is also necessary for the seller and the buyer to coordinate the filing of tax returns postclosing as well as the handling of tax refunds or credits.

When agreeing to indemnify the company for the company's tax liability covering periods prior to the closing, the seller should require its indemnity obligation to be reduced by the amount of any offsetting tax benefits realized by the company by reason of preclosing tax liability. This is at least theoretically a fair result, since the buyer should not be expected to get a windfall from the indemnity provisions. The principal, and fairly valid, argument against such a provision is that the actual determination of an offsetting tax benefit can be quite difficult in practice.

ARTICLE XII: SURVIVAL OF REPRESENTATIONS; INDEMNIFICATION

Section 12.1. Indemnification by Seller.   Notwithstanding any other provision of this Agreement and subject to the terms and conditions of this Article XII, the Seller hereby agrees to indemnify, defend and hold harmless the Buyer, any subsidiary or affiliate thereof (including the Company, the Surviving Corporation and the Subsidiaries) and their respective successors, if any, and their officers, directors and controlling persons (the "Buyer Group"), at any time after the Closing Date, from and against all demands, claims, actions or causes of action, assessments, losses, damages, liabilities, costs and expenses, including without limitation, interest, penalties and attorneys' fees and expenses, which were reasonably incurred by or imposed upon the Buyer Group or any member thereof, net of any insurance proceeds received by any member of the Buyer Group with respect thereto (all such amounts, net of insurance proceeds being hereafter referred to collectively as "Buyer Group Damages"), asserted against, resulting to, imposed upon or incurred by the Buyer Group or any member thereof, directly or indirectly, by reason of or resulting from any misrepresentation, breach of any warranty or nonperformance or breach of any covenant, obligation or agreement of the Seller or the Company or its Subsidiaries contained in or made pursuant to this Agreement, the Disclosure Statement, the Related Instruments or pursuant to any statement, certificate or other document furnished pursuant to this Agreement or the Related Instruments (collectively referred to as the "Indemnity Documents") or any facts or circumstances constituting such a breach. (A claim for indemnification under this Section 12.1 shall be referred to as the "Buyer Group Claims.")

Section 12.2. Indemnification by the Surviving Corporation. Notwithstanding any other provision of this Agreement and subject to the terms and conditions of this Article XII, the Surviving Corporation hereby agrees to indemnify, defend and hold harmless the Seller and their respective successors, if any, and their officers, directors and controlling persons (the "Seller Group"), at any time after the Closing Date, from and against all demands, claims, actions, or causes of action, assessments, losses, damages, liabilities, costs and expenses, including, without limitation, interest, penalties and attorneys' fees and expenses, which were reasonably incurred by or imposed upon the Seller Group or any member thereof, net of any insurance proceeds received by any member of the Seller Group with respect thereto (all such amounts, net of insurance proceeds being hereafter referred to collectively as "Seller Group Damages"), asserted against, resulting to, imposed upon or incurred by the Seller Group or any member thereof, directly or indirectly, by reason of or resulting from any misrepresentation, breach of any warranty, or nonperformance or breach of any covenant, obligation or agreement of the Buyer contained in or made pursuant to any Indemnity Document or any facts or circumstances constituting such a breach. (A claim for indemnification under this Section 12.2 shall be referred to as the "Seller Group Claims.")

The buyer group damages and seller group damages take into account any insurance proceeds that are received by the indemnified party in order to reduce the amount of damages that can be recovered by the indemnified party. Another item that arguably should offset the amount of damages that an indemnified party can claim is the amount of any tax benefits that the surviving corporation has enjoyed as a result of such damages. The difficulty of determining the exact amount of the tax benefit that directly resulted from the damages almost always causes the buyer and seller to overlook this potential windfall.

Section 12.3. Materiality. For purposes of determining whether an event described in Section 12.1 or 12.2 has occurred, any requirement in any representation, warranty, covenant or agreement contained in any Indemnity Document that an event or fact be material, meet a certain minimum dollar threshold or have a Material Adverse Effect, which is a condition to such event or fact constituting a misrepresentation or a breach of such warranty, covenant or agreement (a "Materiality Condition"), shall be ignored, if the aggregate

Buyer Group Damages or Seller Group Damages, as the case may be, resulting from all such breaches and misrepresentations (determined by ignoring all Materiality Conditions) exceeds the amount of the Basket (as defined in Section 12.5). Notwithstanding the foregoing, an event described in Section 12.1 or 12.2 (other than a claim for indemnification under Article XI) that would otherwise give rise to a claim for Buyer Group Damages or Seller Group Damages, as the case may be, shall not be deemed to have occurred unless the Buyer Group Damages or Seller Group Damages, as the case may be, resulting from the single misrepresentation or breach of warranty, covenant or agreement that constitute such event exceeds _____ Dollars, provided that for the purposes of this sentence, all claims for Buyer Group Damages or Seller Group Damages, as the case may be, arising out of the same facts or events causing any such breach shall be treated as a single claim.

Section 12.4. Survival of Indemnification.   The right to make a claim for indemnification under this Agreement shall survive the Closing Date for a period of twenty-four (24) months except that a claim for indemnification under (a) Section 4.4 of this Agreement or based upon any misrepresentation or breach of a warranty which was actually known to be untrue by the indemnifying party when made or asserted or to any willful breach of a covenant, shall continue to survive indefinitely, (b) Article XI shall continue to survive until the latest to occur of (i) the date twenty-four (24) months after the Closing Date, (ii) the expiration date of the statute of limitations applicable to any indemnified liability for Taxes, and extensions or waivers thereof and (iii) ninety (90) days after the final determination of any such Tax liability, including the final administrative and/or judicial determination thereof, and thereafter no party shall have a right to seek indemnification under this Agreement unless a notice of claim setting forth the facts upon which the claim for indemnification is based, and if possible, a reasonable estimate of the amount of the claim, is delivered to the indemnifying party prior to the expiration of the right to make a claim as provided in this Section 12.4. This Section 12.4 shall have no effect upon any other obligation of the parties hereto, whether to be performed before or after the Closing Date. It shall not be a condition to the indemnification with respect to such claim that the loss or liability upon which the claim would be based actually be realized or incurred prior to the date that the indemnifying party is no longer obligated to indemnify the indemnified party pursuant to this Article XII.

The length of time that the seller's indemnification obligations survive the closing date is often heavily negotiated, and its outcome is largely dependent upon the nature of the transaction and the strength of the parties' respective bargaining positions. The buyer should require the seller to indemnify the title to the securities to be purchased by it for an indefinite period of time. For indemnification relating to tax liability, the buyer should require the seller to indemnify the surviving corporation until the company can no longer suffer any loss. In some cases, the buyer may require the seller to indemnify certain items, such as an environmental or product liability concern, beyond the general indemnification period.

Section 12.5. Limitation on Claims and Damages.   (i) No amount shall be payable in indemnification under this Article XII, unless (a) in the case of the Seller, the aggregate amount of Buyer Group Damages in respect of which the Seller would be liable under this Article XII, or (b) in the case of the Surviving Corporation, the aggregate amount of Seller Group Damages in respect of which the Surviving Corporation would be liable under this Article XII, exceeds in the aggregate _____ Dollars ($ _____) (the "Basket"); provided, however, the Basket shall not apply to (a) any Buyer Group Claim or

Seller Group Claim, as the case may be, based upon any misrepresentation or breach of a warranty which was actually known to be untrue by the indemnifying party when made or asserted or to any willful breach of a covenant or (b) any claim for indemnity under Article XI. In the event that the Buyer Group Damages or Seller Group Damages exceeds the Basket, the indemnified party shall be entitled to seek indemnification for the full amount of the Buyer Group Damages or Seller Group Damages, as the case may be.

(ii) The maximum amount of Buyer Group Damages for which the Seller may be liable under this Article XII shall be an amount equal to _____ Dollars ($ _____).

(iii) A party shall not be liable for Buyer Group Damages or Seller Group Damages, as the case may be, under this Article XII resulting from an event relating to a misrepresentation, breach of any warranty or nonperformance or breach of any covenant by the indemnifying party if the indemnifying party can establish that the party seeking indemnification had actual knowledge on or before the Closing Date of such event.

(iv) In any case where an indemnified party recovers from third parties all or any part of any amount paid to it by an indemnifying party pursuant to this Article XII, such indemnified party shall promptly pay over to the indemnifying party the amount so recovered (after deducting therefrom the full amount of the expenses incurred by it in procuring such recovery and any additional amounts owed to the indemnified party by the indemnifying party under this Agreement), but not in excess of any amount previously so paid by the indemnifying party.

(v) The indemnified party shall be obligated to prosecute diligently and in good faith any claim for Buyer Group Damages or Seller Group Damages, as the case may be, with any applicable insurer prior to collecting or indemnification payment under this Article XII. However, an indemnified party shall be entitled to collect an indemnification payment under this Article XII if such indemnified party has not received reimbursement from an applicable insurer within one year after it has given such insurer written notice of its claim. In such event, the indemnified party shall assign to the indemnifying party its rights against such insurer.

(vi) Except in the case of fraud and other than as set forth in Article XI or Section 12.5(vii) hereof, the indemnification and terms thereof provided for in this Article XII shall be the exclusive remedy available to any indemnified party against any indemnifying party for any damages arising directly or indirectly from any misrepresentation, breach of any warranty or nonperformance or breach of any covenant, obligation or agreement pursuant to the Indemnity Documents.

(vii) Nothing in this Article XII or in Article XI shall be construed to limit the non-monetary equitable remedies of any party hereto in respect of any breach by any other party of any covenant or other agreement of such other party contained in or made pursuant to the Indemnity Documents required to be performed after the Closing Date.

The seller, who usually has the most at stake under the indemnification provisions, should require the surviving corporation to pursue collection from an insurance company for the redress of buyer group damages if the insurance policy arguably covers the buyer group damages. In addition, with respect to the covenants in Section 6.7 and Article VII, the seller should not be liable for any buyer group damages if the buyer was aware of the seller's misrepresentation or breach prior to the closing date.

A seller should always attempt to limit its exposure for indemnification. As a practical matter, the seller should not be liable for any amount in excess of the purchase price paid for the company. During negotiations of this ceiling, every argument conceivable is put on the table for consideration. However, its outcome, like that of any other highly controversial provision, rests with the party holding the trump card.

Section 12.6. Claims by Third Parties. The obligations and liabilities of an indemnifying party under any provision of this Agreement with respect to claims relating to third parties shall be subject to the following terms and conditions:

(i) Whenever any indemnified party shall have received notice that a Buyer Group Claim or a Seller Group Claim, as the case may be, has been asserted or threatened against such indemnified party, which, if valid, would subject the indemnifying party to an indemnity obligation under this Agreement, the indemnified party shall promptly notify the indemnifying party of such claim in the manner described in Section 12.4; provided, however, that the failure of the indemnified party to give timely notice hereunder shall not relieve the indemnifying party of its indemnification obligations under this Agreement unless, and only to the extent that, such failure caused the Buyer Group Damages or the Seller Group Damages, as the case may be, for which the indemnifying party is obligated to be greater than they would have been had the indemnified party given timely notice.

(ii) The indemnifying party or its designee will have the right, but not the obligation, to assume the defense of any claim described in Section 12.6(i); provided, however, if there is a reasonable probability that a Buyer Group Claim may materially and adversely affect the Surviving Corporation or any other member of the Buyer Group despite the indemnity of the Seller, the Surviving Corporation or such member of the Buyer Group shall have the right at its option to defend, at its own cost and expense, and to compromise or settle such Buyer Group Claim which compromise or settlement shall be made only with the written consent of the Seller, such consent not to be unreasonably withheld. If the indemnifying party fails to assume the defense of such claim within 15 days after receipt of notice of a claim pursuant to Section 12.6(i), the indemnified party against which such claim has been asserted will (upon delivering notice to such effect to the indemnifying party) have the right to undertake, at the indemnifying party's cost and expense, the defense, compromise or settlement of such claim on behalf of and for the account and risk of the indemnifying party, subject to the right of the indemnifying party to assume the defense of such claim at any time prior to settlement, compromise or final determination thereof and provided, however, that the indemnified party shall not enter into any such compromise or settlement without the written consent of the indemnifying party. In the event the indemnified party assumes defense of the claim, the indemnified party will keep the indemnifying party reasonably informed of the progress of any such defense, compromise or settlement. The indemnifying party shall not be liable for any settlement of any action effected without its consent, but if settled with the consent of the indemnifying party or if there be a final judgment beyond review or appeal, for the plaintiff in any such action, the indemnifying party agrees to indemnify and hold harmless an indemnified party from and against any loss or liability by reason of such settlement or judgment. Any party who does not undertake the defense of a claim may, at its own expense, retain such additional attorneys and other advisors as it shall deem necessary, which attorneys and advisors will be permitted by the party undertaking such defense, and its attorneys, to observe the defense of such claim.

(iii) Any member of the Buyer Group shall give the Seller at least thirty (30) days prior written notice before such member shall waive the provisions of any statute of limitations as such provisions may apply to the assessment of taxes payable by the Surviving Corporation or any Subsidiary for any taxable year or period (or portion thereof) ending on or prior to the Closing Date.

Acquirers should try to assert control, if appropriate, over any legal actions based on a claim subject to indemnification. If the indemnifying party refuses to acknowledge its obligation to indemnify a claim, then it should certainly have no right to control the proceeding. However, if the indemnifying party has accepted its obligation to indemnify for a claim, then the indemnifying party will probably want to control the proceeding. If the buyer is comfortable with the creditworthiness of the seller, this should not pose a serious threat to the buyer. There are, of course, circumstances in which the buyer may want to control the proceedings notwithstanding the creditworthiness of the seller. For example, if the surviving corporation is temporarily enjoined from conducting its business as a result of the action of a third party, the buyer may feel that the seller will not move quickly enough to resolve the matter.

In some cases, the buyer and seller may have a joint interest in the outcome of a certain proceeding. For example, the proceeding may involve numerous claims against the surviving corporation, only one of which relates to a buyer group claim. One approach that may appease both the seller and buyer in this circumstance is to let the party that has the most to lose control the proceeding.

Section 12.7. Indemnity for Taxes of Indemnified Party. Each party hereto further agrees that, with respect to payment or indemnity under this Article XII, such payment or indemnity shall include any amount necessary to hold the indemnified party harmless on an after-tax basis from all taxes required to be paid with respect to the receipt of such payment or indemnity under the laws of any Federal, state or local government or taxing authority in the United States, or under the laws of any foreign government or taxing authority or governmental subdivision of a foreign country.

When the indemnification payment is taxable to the indemnified party, it is common for the seller and buyer to negotiate the inclusion of a tax gross-up provision. One difficulty with this concept is that the indemnifying party may be grossing up the indemnified party for taxes that it would have been responsible for had no indemnity been necessary.

Section 12.8. Right of Offset. In the event the Seller should be required to pay monies to the Surviving Corporation pursuant to Section 12.1 or any other indemnification provision of this Agreement, the Surviving Corporation may offset the amount the Seller owes in indemnification against any outstanding principal balance of the [insert title of instrument under which the surviving corporation has continuing payment obligations].

In some deals, a seller may agree to accept, as part of the purchase price of the company, a note or other instrument that represents a payment obligation of the surviving corporation. In such a deal, the buyer may attempt to satisfy its right to indemnification by the seller by canceling a portion or all of such payment obligations. A creditworthy seller should resist this provision on several grounds. First, the surviving corporation should have a setoff right only after it has demonstrated, through a final determination from which no appeal can be taken, that the seller is obligated to indemnify the surviving corporation for the buyer group claim. Second, if the seller has sufficient resources, it should be able to choose whether it wants to forgive a portion of the payment obligation or simply pay cash. It is conceivable that the payment obligation may bear an interest rate well in excess of the prevailing market rate. A creditworthy seller should not lose this benefit through an offset provision.

ARTICLE XIII: NONCOMPETE

The Seller agrees that for the period of three years following the Closing Date (the "Noncompete Period"), the Seller shall not, without the prior written consent of the Buyer, either directly or indirectly, engage in business of the type presently conducted by the Company or any Subsidiary in the United States or any other jurisdiction in which the Company or any Subsidiary currently conducts business (the "Business"). The Seller may acquire any entity which, directly or indirectly, engages in the Business or any portion thereof (the "Acquired Entity"), if (i) the total assets and gross revenues attributable to or derived from such Business do not exceed [insert percentage] of the total assets and gross revenues of the Acquired Entity and its subsidiaries in the fiscal year immediately preceding the date of acquisition, or (ii) the Seller uses its reasonable efforts to divest itself of the Acquired Entity within a reasonable time (not to exceed six months), subject to receipt of all regulatory approvals. The Seller also agrees that, after the Closing Date, the Seller will not disclose or reveal to any person or an Acquired Entity any trade secret or other confidential or proprietary information relating to the Business, including, without limitation, any financial information relating to the Company or any Subsidiary, or any customer lists, unless readily ascertainable from public information, and the Seller confirms that after the Closing Date, such information will constitute the exclusive property of the Company and its Subsidiaries. During the Non-Compete Period, the Seller agrees not to, and to cause its affiliates not to, recruit, directly or indirectly, employees of the Company or any Subsidiary for employment with or as a consultant to the Seller or its affiliates. The Buyer and the Seller hereby agree that of the total cash consideration to be paid to the Seller at Closing, $_____ represents the consideration for the covenants of the Seller contained in this Article XIII.

Covenants not to compete can be difficult to enforce if not structured properly. The difficulty arises from a court's reluctance on public policy grounds to give force to a contractual provision restricting the ability of one of the parties to work freely in any way it chooses, even if the party being restricted has voluntarily agreed and has received consideration to be so bound. Courts have invalidated noncompetition provisions (1) that continue for too long a period of time, (2) that are too broad geographically, or (3) that are too indefinite or broad with respect to the restricted activity. Consequently, the buyer must ensure that its noncompetition clause is specific with respect to the term (typically one to five years), extends to a limited geographic area, and restricts a specific activity in the industry.

The seller may also desire to modify clause (ii) above, which requires the seller's divestiture of the acquired entity within a reasonable period of time by providing that the seller is only obligated to divest the acquired entity "at a price which is economically reasonable in light of the circumstances."

ARTICLE XIV: TERMINATION

Section 14.1. Termination for Failure to Close on Time.   This Agreement may be terminated upon two (2) days' written notice (i) by Buyer, on the one hand, or the Seller, on the other hand, at any time after [insert date], or (ii) by the mutual agreement of all parties at any time. In the event of such termination, this Agreement shall be abandoned without any liability or further obligation to any other party to this Agreement unless otherwise stated expressly herein. This Section 14.1 shall not apply in the event of the failure of the transactions contemplated by this Agreement to be consummated as a result of a breach by the Seller, Company or Buyer of a representation, warranty or covenant contained in this Agreement. In such event, the provisions of Section 14.2 hereof shall apply.

Section 14.2. Default; Remedies. This Section shall apply in the event that a party refuses to consummate the transactions contemplated by this Agreement or if any default under, or breach of any representation, warranty or covenant of, this Agreement on the part of a party (the "Defaulting Party") shall have occurred that results in the failure to consummate the transactions contemplated hereby. In such event, the non-Defaulting Party shall be entitled to seek and obtain specific performance pursuant to Section 14.3 or to seek and obtain money damages from the Defaulting Party plus its court costs and reasonable attorneys' fees in connection with the pursuit of its remedies hereunder.

Section 14.3. Specific Performance. In the event that any party shall fail or refuse to consummate the transactions contemplated by this Agreement or if any default under, or breach of, any representation, warranty or covenant of this Agreement on the part of any party (the "Defaulting Party") shall have occurred that results in the failure to consummate the transactions contemplated hereby, then in addition to the other remedies provided in this Article XIV, the non-Defaulting Party may seek to obtain an order of specific performance thereof against the Defaulting Party from a court of competent jurisdiction, provided that it files its request with such court within forty-five (45) days after it became aware of such failure, refusal, default or breach. In addition, the non-Defaulting Party shall be entitled to obtain from the Defaulting Party court costs and reasonable attorneys' fees incurred by it in enforcing its rights hereunder. As a condition to seeking specific performance hereunder, Buyer shall not be required to have tendered the [insert defined term for the total purchase price] but shall be ready, willing and able to do so.

The termination section provides a way to terminate and enforce the acquisition agreement. In some cases, a seller may want to modify this section to limit liability for a willful failure to perform. Obviously, there are situations in which the buyer may be disadvantaged by the inclusion of this modifier. Therefore, like other disputed provisions, the outcome rests on the balance of power between seller and buyer.

In an acquisition requiring regulatory approval, the buyer and seller should consider extending the term of the acquisition agreement in Section 14.1 for a certain period of time in case the approval process takes longer than anticipated.

The relief of specific performance afforded the nondefaulting party in Section 14.3 is extremely difficult to enforce in a court of law. If a court can ascertain the amount of monetary damages to award the nondefaulting party, it will not generally grant specific performance.

ARTICLE XV: MISCELLANEOUS

Article XV contains provisions that govern the interpretation of the agreement and the taking of actions thereunder. Although the bulk of these provisions are generally not negotiated by the parties to the agreement, several sections provide valuable rights to both buyer and seller and may be subject to closer scrutiny by the parties.

Section 15.1. Definitions.

Agreement. See Article I.

Buyer. See Article I.

Closing. See Article III.

Closing Date. See Article III.

Company Capital Stock. See Section 4.3(i).

Disclosure Statement. See Section 4.1.

Financial Statements. See Section 4.5(i).

GAAP. See Section 4.5(i).

Material Adverse Effect. See Section 4.1(i).

Merger. See Article I.

Most Recent Balance Sheet. See Section 4.5(i).

Persons. First used in Section 4.5(ii) but not defined.

Related Instruments. See Section 4.2.

SEC. Defined in paragraph describing Section 4.33.

Seller. See Article I.

Subsidiary. See Article I.

Company. See Article I.

Section 15.2. Payment of Expenses. Buyer shall pay its own expenses and the Seller and Company shall pay their own expenses incident to preparing for, entering into and carrying out this Agreement and the Related Instruments, except as otherwise provided in this Agreement and the Related Instruments.

Section 15.3. Modifications or Waivers to the Agreement. The parties may, by mutual written agreement, make any modification or amendment of this Agreement.

Section 15.4. Assignment. Neither the Buyer, Seller nor Company shall have the authority to assign its rights or obligations under this Agreement without the prior written consent of the other party, except that the Buyer may assign all or any portion of its respective rights hereunder without the prior written consent of the Seller or Company to an entity controlled by, controlling or under common control with it or to any Acquisition Lender, and the Seller, Company and the Buyer shall execute such documents as are necessary in order to effect such assignments.

Section 15.5. Burden and Benefit.

(i) This Agreement shall be binding upon and, to the extent permitted in this Agreement, shall inure to the benefit of, the parties hereto and their respective successors and assigns.

(ii) In the event of a default by the Seller or Company of any of its or their obligations hereunder, the sole and exclusive recourse and remedy of the Buyer shall be against the Seller or Company and its assets and under no circumstances shall any officer, director, stockholder or affiliate of the Seller or Company be liable in law or equity for any obligations of the Seller or Company hereunder.

(iii) In the event of a default by the Buyer of any of its obligations hereunder, the sole and exclusive recourse and remedy of the Seller or Company hereunder shall be against the Buyer and its assets, and under no circumstances shall any officer, director, stockholder or affiliate of the Buyer be liable in law or equity for any obligations of the Buyer hereunder.

(iv) It is the intent of the parties hereto that no third-party beneficiary rights be created or deemed to exist in favor of any person not a party to this Agreement, unless otherwise expressly agreed in writing by the parties.

The buyer and seller may seek to include a provision, often entitled "Burden and Benefit," limiting the rights of the seller in the event of a breach of the agreement to an action against the buyer and not against any officer, director, or controlling stockholder of the buyer. This provision, assuming the entity purchasing the company has elected to do so through a shell or thinly capitalized corporation, generally should insulate the acquiring entity from liability to the seller in the event that the deal goes sour.

Section 15.6. Brokers.

(i) Each of the Seller and Company represents and warrants to the Buyer that there are no brokers or finders entitled to any brokerage or finder's fee or other commission or fee based upon arrangements made by or on behalf of the Seller or Company in connection with this Agreement or any of the transactions contemplated hereby other than the fee due [insert name of any such entity].

(ii) The Buyer represents and warrants to the Seller and the Company that no broker or finder is entitled to any brokerage or finder's fee or other commission or fee based upon arrangements made by or on behalf of the Buyer in connection with this Agreement or any of the transactions contemplated hereby other than fees payable by it in connection with the financing of this transaction.

Section 15.7. Entire Agreement. This Agreement and the exhibits, lists and other documents referred to herein contain the entire agreement among the parties hereto with respect to the transactions contemplated hereby and supersede all prior agreements with respect thereto, whether written or oral.

Section 15.8. Governing Law. This Agreement shall be governed by and construed in accordance with the laws of the State of [insert name of state].

Section 15.9. Notices. Any notice, request, instruction or other document to be given hereunder by a party shall be in writing and delivered personally or by facsimile transmission, or by telex, or sent by registered or certified mail, postage prepaid, return receipt requested, addressed as follows:

If to the Seller: [insert name and address of Seller]
with a copy to: [insert name and address of Seller's counsel]
If to Company: [insert name and address of Company]
If to Buyer: [insert name and address of Buyer]
with a copy to: [insert name and address of Buyer's counsel]
If to the Surviving Corporation: [insert name and address of Company post-Closing]
with a copy to: [insert any other desired parties] or to such other persons or addresses as may be designated in writing by the party to receive such notice. If mailed as aforesaid, ten days after the date of mailing shall be the date notice shall be deemed to have been received.

Section 15.10. Counterparts.   This Agreement may be executed in two or more counterparts, each of which shall be an original, but all of which shall constitute but one agreement.

Section 15.11. Rights Cumulative.   All rights, powers and privileges conferred hereunder upon the parties, unless otherwise provided, shall be cumulative and shall not be restricted to those given by law. Failure to exercise any power given any party hereunder or to insist upon strict compliance by any other party shall not constitute a waiver of any party's right to demand exact compliance with the terms hereof.

Section 15.12. Severability of Provisions.   The parties agree that (i) the provisions of this Agreement shall be severable in the event that any of the provisions hereof are held by a court of competent jurisdiction to be invalid, void or otherwise unenforceable, (ii) such invalid, void or otherwise unenforceable provisions shall be automatically replaced by other provisions which are as similar as possible in terms to such invalid, void or otherwise unenforceable provisions but are valid and enforceable and (iii) the remaining provisions shall remain enforceable to the fullest extent permitted by law.

The provision entitled "Severability," while addressing a purely legal issue, may have great practical impact. The section provides that, in the event particular portions of the document are found invalid, void, or otherwise unenforceable by a court interpreting the agreement, the remaining provisions shall be considered severable from the invalid provisions and shall therefore remain enforceable. This result is of particular concern when the agreement contains ancillary agreements, such as a covenant by the seller not to compete with the buyer after the acquisition. The enforceability of the agreement should not depend on the enforceability of a noncompetition agreement, and the severability provision serves to accomplish this end.

Section 15.13. Further Assurance.   The Seller, the Company and the Buyer agree that at any time and from time to time after the Closing Date they will execute and deliver to any other party such further instruments or documents as may reasonably be required to give effect to the transactions contemplated hereunder.

Section 15.14. Confidential Information.   The Seller, the Company and the Buyer for themselves, their directors, officers, employees, agents, representatives and partners, if any, covenant with each other that they will use all information relating to any other party, the Company or any Subsidiary acquired by any of them pursuant to the provisions of this Agreement or in the course of negotiations with or examinations of any other party only in connection with the transactions contemplated hereby and shall cause all information obtained by them pursuant to this Agreement and such negotiations and examinations, which is not publicly available, to be treated as confidential except as may otherwise be required by law or as may be necessary or appropriate in connection with the enforcement of this Agreement or any instrument or document referred to herein or contemplated hereby. In the event of termination of this Agreement, each party will cause to be delivered to the other all documents, work papers and other material obtained by it from the others, whether so obtained by it from the others, whether so obtained before or after the execution of this Agreement, and each party agrees that it shall not itself use or disclose, directly or indirectly, any information so obtained, or otherwise obtained from the other hereunder or in connection therewith, and will have all such information kept confidential and will not use such information in any way which is detrimental to any other party, provided that

(i) any party may use and disclose any such information which has been disclosed publicly (other than by such party or any affiliate of such party in breach of its obligations under this Section 15.14) and (ii) to the extent that any party or any affiliate of a party may become legally compelled to disclose any such information if it shall have used its best efforts, and shall have afforded the other parties the opportunity, to obtain an appropriate protective order, or other satisfactory assurance of confidential treatment, for the information required to be disclosed.

The confidential information section typically requires each party to keep confidential all information obtained in the course of the transaction. Because the company has already been or will shortly thereafter be the object of an intensive **due diligence** review when the agreement is signed, the seller is initially more concerned with disclosure issues than the buyer. The seller may take the position that all materials provided to the buyer relating to the company should be returned or destroyed in the event the parties fail to close the transaction.

Section 15.15. Writings and Disclosures.   Except as otherwise provided or contemplated herein, each exhibit, schedule, writing or other disclosure described in this Agreement as having been delivered or to be delivered by one party to the other shall be identified by reference to the section of this Agreement to which it relates and shall be signed or initialed on the first page by an officer or legal counsel of the Seller and by an officer or legal counsel of the Buyer and unless so identified and signed or initialed, the party receiving the same shall not be chargeable with notice of its content.

LANDMARK DUE DILIGENCE CASES

Cases Alleging Negligence in an Acquisition or Stock Offering

Cases Alleging Fraud or Negligence in the Sale of a Business

Cases Involving M&A Agreements (Re Chapter 5)

Cases Alleging Violation of:

- Securities Laws (Re Chapter 6)
- Tax Laws and Accounting Regulations (Re Chapter 7)
- Antitrust and Trade Laws (Re Chapter 8)
- Intellectual Property Laws (Re Chapter 9)
- Consumer Protection Laws (Re Chapter 10)
- Environmental Laws (Re Chapter 11)
- Health, Safety, and Labor Laws (Re Chapter 12)

CASES ALLEGING NEGLIGENCE IN AN ACQUISITION OR STOCK OFFERING

Ernst & Ernst v. Hochfelder, 425 U.S. 185 (1975).

Hochfelder was a customer of First Securities Company. The president of the company, Nay, convinced Hochfelder to invest funds in escrow accounts that would yield a high rate of return. Nay asked Hochfelder to write out checks in Nay's name. When Nay committed suicide, Hochfelder learned that there were no escrow accounts—not even phony ones. Nay's suicide note itself described First Securities as bankrupt, and the escrow accounts as "spurious."

Hochfelder filed suit in district court for damages against Ernst & Ernst under Section 10(b) of the Securities Exchange Act of 1934, charging that Ernst & Ernst had aided and abetted Nay by failing to conduct proper audits. The district court dismissed the case on the grounds that Ernst & Ernst's accounting procedures conformed to those in general use. The U.S. Court of Appeals reversed this decision, holding Ernst & Ernst liable for a breach of fiduciary duty of inquiry and disclosure under common law and statutory law.

The U.S. Supreme Court disagreed. It held that mere negligence was not a "manipulative device," and therefore not a violation of Section 10(b), and that good faith was indeed a valid defense. Furthermore, the Court held that a private right of action is not possible under Section 10(b) or Rule 10b-5, unless there is an intent to deceive, manipulate, or defraud (*scienter*).

Escott v. BarChris Construction Corp. 283 F. Supp. 643 (S.D.N.Y. 1968).

When BarChris Construction, a bowling alley builder, went bankrupt, bondholders accused its directors and officers of violating Section 11 by making material misstatements and omissions in their registration statement. The bondholders sued the auditors, the underwriters, and all those who had signed the statement—namely, the company's directors (including five officers) and the company's controller.

The court found the auditing firm liable for not following generally accepted accounting principles. It also found the underwriters liable for failing to prevent the material misstatements. The court asked, "Is it sufficient to ask questions, to obtain answers which, if true, would be thought satisfactory, and let it go at that, without seeking to ascertain from the records whether the answers, in fact, are true and accurate?" Its answer: "The purpose of Section 11 is to protect investors. To that end, the underwriters are made responsible for the truth of the prospectus. If they may escape that responsibility by taking at face value representations made to them by management, then including the underwriters among those liable under Section 11 affords the investors no additional protection."

Citing Section 11, the court found that there were misstatements and omissions in both the expert and nonexpert portions of the registration statement. It held the inside directors and financial officers responsible for the expert portions, declaring: "There is nothing to show that they made any investigation of anything which they may not have known about or understood. They have not proved their due diligence defenses." Furthermore, the court held the outside directors liable for the nonexpert portions. Directors showed different degrees of diligence, none high enough. One director, Coleman, who had been a partner with the company's investor banker, had previously checked with the company's lenders and Dun & Bradstreet, had read extensive documents, and had interviewed the underwriter. Once he became a director, though, he began to rely on others, including a junior associate from the company's outside law firm. "When it came to verification," said the court, "he relied upon his counsel to do it for him. Since counsel failed to do it, Coleman is bound by that failure."

Feit v. Leasco Data Processing Corp., 332 F. Supp. 544 (E.D.N.Y. 1971).

In 1968, Leasco Data Processing Equipment Corporation began negotiations to acquire Reliance Insurance Company. Leasco was particularly attracted to Reliance's "surplus surplus," the portion of surplus beyond what is required by law to maintain the integrity of an insurance operation. Because insurance companies at that time were not permitted to engaged in noninsurance business, the surplus surplus (as a highly liquid asset) had to be separated from the insurance operation. Leasco intended to form a parent holding company and to transfer the surplus surplus to it.

After some initial disagreements between the two managements, Leasco obtained 90 percent of Reliance in a tender offer. None of the various prospectuses (a supplement was issued each time the tender exchange period was extended) made any mention of the Reliance surplus surplus, an amount estimated by experts to have been between $100 and $125 million. Feit, a Reliance stockholder, brought a lawsuit to recover damages. The lawsuit centered on (1) the materiality of the surplus surplus question to the Leasco prospectus sent to holders of Reliance stock, and (2) the accountability of Leasco's directors for the decision to include no mention of the surplus surplus in the prospectuses.

The defendants contended that they were unable to get a good estimate of Reliance's surplus surplus because of poor relations with Reliance's management. They further argued that, in any case, an estimate of the surplus surplus in the prospectuses would have only made Reliance shareholders more eager to tender, since Leasco was known to be aggressive in employing liquid assets. Finally, they asserted, this kind of information could have violated SEC standards for prospectuses and turned this one into a "selling document."

The court rendered a decision in favor of the plaintiff Feit, according him monetary damages pursuant to Section 11 of the Securities Act of 1933. Relying on the due diligence portions of *Escott v. BarChris* (1968), the court held that the director defendants "failed to fulfill their duty of reasonable investigation . . . . and had no reasonable grounds to believe that an omission of an estimate of surplus surplus was not materially misleading." This case showed, said one expert, that officers and inside directors "are highly unlikely ever to sustain a due diligence defense."[1]

Hanson Trust PLC v. SCM Corp., 774 F.2d 47 (2d Cir. 1985).

Hanson Trust PLC tendered a $60 per share offer for any and all shares of SCM Corp. The offer was followed by a counteroffer by the SCM board and their white knight, Merrill Lynch Capital Markets. Hanson then increased its offer to $72 per share, contingent upon SCM's agreement not to enter into a lockup agreement. The SCM Merrill counteroffer was revised to $74 along with a lockup option for an SCM "crown jewel." Hanson terminated its offer as a direct result of the lockup option. (A lockup option is an agreement that says the option holder, Company A, will acquire all or part of Company B, and that Company A will realize an economic gain if another company buys Company B or a specified part of Company B.)

The question before the court was whether SCM's board of directors could be protected under the business judgment rule when they approved of the lockup option. The business judgment rule is a judicial doctrine under which informed decisions by directors are effectively insulated from second-guessing by the courts. The U.S. Court of Appeals for the Second Circuit denied protection under the business judgment rule on the grounds SCM directors had a "paucity of information" and the swiftness of their decision making strongly suggested a breach of the duty of care.

Laven v. Flanagan, 695 F. Supp. 800 (D.N.J. 1989).

This case is one of several cases finding that "what constitutes a reasonable investigation is measured largely by the common practices in the industry: i.e., one looks at the standards that have evolved among lawyers, accountants, and investment bankers generally in doing due diligence."[2]

The director's activities in this case were a far cry from the passive and total reliance on company management that defeated the due diligence defense in *Escott v. BarChris Construction Corp.* As such, the court found that the directors had made a reasonable effort to seek verification of the truth of the registration statement.

Software Toolworks Sec. Lit., 50 F.3d 615 (9th Cir. 1994).

The court stated that suspicious facts or transactions require inquiry, and offered a list of "red flags" that should raise suspicion in a reasonable person.[3] The court awarded a summary judgment to the underwriter after the underwriter provided extensive records showing its due diligence investigations.[4]

Liability under Sections 11 and 12(2) properly may fall on the underwriters of a public offering. Underwriters, however, may absolve themselves from liability by establishing a "due diligence" defense. Under Section 11, underwriters must prove that they "had, after reasonable investigation, reasonable ground to believe and did believe . . . that the statements therein were true and that there was no omission to state a material fact required to be stated therein or necessary to make the statements therein not misleading." Similarly, under Section 12(2), underwriters must show that they "did not know, and in the exercise of reasonable care, could not have known, of [the] untruth or omission."

Smith v. Van Gorkom, Del. Supr., 488 A.2d 858 (1985).

Shareholders brought a class action against the board of directors of Trans-Union Corporation alleging that the board was grossly negligent in its duty of care to the shareholders for recommending that the shareholders approve a merger agreement at $55 per share. Although the price per share was well above current market values, shareholders alleged that it was inadequate. The Delaware Court of Chancery granted the directors summary judgment and the shareholders appealed. The Delaware Supreme Court indicated that it would closely scrutinize the process by which the board's decision was made.

Historically, courts would generally not interfere with the good faith business decision of a corporate board; however, this case eroded that principle and the court embarked down a road of increasing judicial scrutiny of business decisions. The court struck down the long-accepted practice of affording corporate directors the almost ironclad presumption that, in making business decisions, the directors acted on an informed basis. The court held that the determination of whether the business judgment of a board of directors is informed turns on whether directors have essentially followed certain procedures to inform themselves prior to making business decisions. The court went on to say that, under the business judgment rule, there is no protection for directors who have made uninformed judgments.

CASES ALLEGING FRAUD OR NEGLIGENCE IN THE SALE OF A BUSINESS

Credit Managers Ass'n of Southern Cal. v. Federal Co., 629 F. Supp. 175 (C.D. Cal. 1985).

In 1980 Crescent Food Co., a cheese importation and distribution entity wholly owned by Federal Company, entered into a management-led leveraged buyout. The stock purchase price was over $1.4 million. Crescent received an additional loan from new management of $189,000, as well as approximately $10 million from General Electric Credit Corp. Crescent's debt service increased significantly because of the buyout. Finding itself with insufficient cash to continue operations, Crescent eventually shut down and executed an assignment of its assets for the benefit of creditors. The plaintiff brought action against Federal, alleging that the buyout was a fraudulent conveyance.

The question before the court was whether the transaction was a fraudulent conveyance. The U.S. District Court in California held that the law does not require that companies be sufficiently well capitalized to withstand any and all setbacks to their business; it requires only that the companies not be left with unreasonably small capital at the time of conveyance.

In Re Healthco International, Inc., Securities Litigation, 208 B.R. 288 (Bankr. D. Mass.1997).

In the spring of 1990 Healthco was involved in a struggle for corporate control with Gemini Partners L.P. In June 1990, Gemini, a minority shareholder of Healthco, alleging that the price of Healthco's stock was undervalued, began a proxy contest to remove the incumbent board. In September 1990 Healthco entered into a merger agreement with HMD Acquisition (an acquisition vehicle of Hicks Muse) subject to several conditions, including shareholder approval, realization of projected earnings, and the securing of financing. In January 1991 Healthco issued a proxy statement projecting unspecified losses, causing Gemini to withdraw its bid, leaving HMD as the sole bidder. HMD acquired Healthco for $15 per share—$4.25 per share less than Gemini's highest offer.

In March 1991, the new Healthco board, which included directors who were Healthco stockholders, experienced operating problems. Shareholders brought suit against Healthco, alleging material misstatement in the proxy statement. The question before that court was whether the projections of unspecified losses constituted fraud under Rule 10b-5 of the U.S. federal securities laws. Finding in favor of the defendants, the District Court held that "optimistic, vague projections of future success which prove to be ill-founded" do not by themselves trigger Rule 10b-5 liability. This liability is triggered when such overly optimistic projections "imply certainty" or rely on "statements of facts which prove to be erroneous."

In June 1993, Healthco filed for relief under Chapter 11 of the U.S. Bankruptcy Code. Then, in September of that year, the case was converted to Chapter 7 and the company was liquidated, causing severe losses to the company's creditors.

In June 1995, the bankruptcy trustee for the creditors began legal action (independent of the previous securities lawsuit) in U.S. Bankruptcy Court against virtually all the participants in the company—65 defendants in all, including the company's directors, who were accused of violating their duty of loyalty. The plaintiffs alleged that the directors' ownership of stock in Healthco rendered them "interested" in its sale. The directors, citing legal precedent and documenting their decision-making process, argued that they had fulfilled their duties of loyalty and care. They asked the Bankruptcy Court for a summary judgment dismissal, but the court refused, holding that the directors were indeed "interested" parties by law.

Two years later, the case came to trial again in U.S. District Court in Worcester, Massachusetts, where the court declined to adopt the Bankruptcy Court's ruling, and ordered a jury trial. The directors repeated their defense, this time bringing in an expert witness on behalf of the directors, Dr. Robert Stobaugh, emeritus professor at Harvard Business School. He testified that Healthco directors had met generally accepted practice with respect to both their duty of loyalty and their duty of care. After a seven-week trial, the jury returned a verdict in favor of all the defendants on all the claims in the bankruptcy case.

Humana v. Forsyth, USS 97-303, 1999.

In this case, the plaintiffs sued Humana, a hospital system, and several hospitals that Humana had sold to Columbia-HCA Healthcare Corp. in 1993.

Apparently, in conducting its due diligence study of the Humana-owned hospitals, Columbia had not discovered that some of the hospitals had failed to pass on an insurance discount they were getting for certain customers. The class action suit against Humana and against the acquired hospitals (now owned by Columbia-HCA) alleged that the absence of the discount was an attempt to defraud the customers. The plaintiffs sued Humana and Columbia under a federal statute called the Racketeer Influenced and Corrupt Organizations Act (RICO), a criminal law that exacts triple damages from defendants who are found guilty.

The RICO case went all the way to the Supreme Court, which had to decide whether the plaintiffs had standing to sue under this federal law. A trial court had said no, because the federal law allows more severe penalties than the applicable state law (Nevada). But the Appeals Court in San Francisco reversed the decision, saying that this difference was not great enough to matter. The Supreme Court upheld this view. Justice Ruth Bader Ginsburg, writing for the Court, said, "RICO's private right of action and treble-damages provision appears to complement Nevada's statutory and common law claims for relief."[5]

Kupetz v. Wolf, 845 F.2d 842 (9th Cir. 1989).

In July 1989 the owners of Wolf & Vine decided to sell their company to David Adashek. Adeshek formed Little Red Riding Hood to purchase Wolf & Vine from its owners with financing from Continental Illinois National Bank. Little Red Riding Hood then merged into Wolf & Vine. Subsequently Wolf & Vine could not meet its debt obligations and filed for Chapter 11 protection and later changed its petition to Chapter 7.

The bankruptcy trustee filed a complaint alleging that the original sale of Wolf & Vine to Little Red Riding Hood was a fraudulent conveyance. The previous owners sought summary judgment based on the argument that the business was sold in good faith for fair consideration. The U.S. District Court granted the summary judgment and the trustee appealed to the Ninth Circuit Court of Appeals.

The question before the court was whether the sale was a "fraudulent conveyance" within the meaning of the bankruptcy statute of California's fraudulent conveyance law. The existing creditors had the opportunity to gain the knowledge of Wolf & Vine's financial status and its heavy debt structure prior to extending credit to it. Creditors easily could have asked for financial information before extending credit. Moreover, the transaction was well publicized within the industry. To ask Wolf to underwrite the creditors' losses, due partially at least to their failure to inquire adequately, would not be just. Therefore, because no evidence was presented of actual intent to defraud creditors and the claims of existing creditors arose after the sale, the petition was denied.

U.S. v. Gleneagles Inv. Co., 565 F. Supp. 556 (M.D. Pa. 1983), 571 F. Supp. 935 (1983), 584 F. Supp. 671 (1984), aff'd sub nom. United States v. Tabor Court Realty Corp., 803 F.2d 1288 (3d Cir. 1986).

This case had been the subject of two earlier opinions by the U.S. District Court for the Middle District of Pennsylvania. In the first opinion, the court concluded that certain mortgages granted by Institutional Investors Trust (IIT) were fraudulent conveyances within the meaning of 354, 355, 356, and 357 of the Pennsylvania Uniform Fraudulent Conveyance Act, 39 Pa. Stat. 351, et seq. (United States v. Gleneagles Inv. Co., Inc., hereinafter Gleneagles I). In the second opinion, the court focused on Gleneagles' subsidiary, Pagnotti Enterprises, which purchased the IIT mortgages and caused the assignment thereof to its subsidiary, McClelland Realty. The court concluded that the subsidiary was not a purchaser of the IIT mortgages for fair consideration without knowledge that they were fraudulent conveyances (United States v. Gleneagles Inv. Co., Inc., hereinafter Gleneagles II). The court also concluded in

Gleneagles II that the Lackawanna County tax sales of the lands of Raymond Colliery in 1976 and 1980 and the consequent tax deed were void and ineffective to transfer title to the purchasers at those tax sales.

The United States had sought the third action to set aside as fraudulent conveyances mortgages held by IIT on the lands of Raymond Colliery and to foreclose on tax liens against Raymond Colliery and its parent, Great American Coal Company, free and clear of the IIT mortgages. Those mortgages were delivered by Raymond Colliery on November 26, 1973, to IIT and assigned by IIT to defendant McClelland Realty. The U.S. District Court for M.D. Pennsylvania made three points in its decision. First, it held that one (1) payment of $6.1 million would not place creditors of the mortgagor in the same or similar position that they held prior to the fraudulent transaction. Second, it stated that settlement monies paid to the mortgagor's creditors by former shareholders of the mortgagor could not be deducted from recovery to which creditors were entitled from mortgage assignee. Third, it stated that assigned mortgages were not entitled to protection under the Fraudulent Conveyances Act.

CASES INVOLVING M&A AGREEMENTS (RE CHAPTER 5)

Texaco Inc. v. Pennzoil Co., 729 S.W.2d 768 (Tex. App. 1987)

In December 1983 Pennzoil announced a tender offer for 16 million shares of Getty Oil common stock at $100 per share. Subsequently, Pennzoil met with Getty Oil representatives to discuss the tender offer and possible sale of Getty Oil to Pennzoil. Then, over a period of several days, the following occurred:

- On January 2, 1984, as a result of the meetings, Pennzoil and Getty Oil representatives signed a memorandum of agreement for the sale of Getty Oil to Pennzoil, subject to approval by the board of directors of Getty Oil.
- On January 3 Pennzoil revised its offer to $110 per share, plus a $3 stub. Getty Oil's board of directors rejected the offer but made a counterproposal for a $5 stub. Pennzoil agreed and a memorandum of agreement was executed.
- On January 4 both parties issued a press release.
- On January 5 Texaco contacted Getty Oil representatives to inquire about a possible sale to Texaco for $125 per share.
- On January 6 Getty Oil's board of directors voted to withdraw its Pennzoil offer and accept Texaco's offer. Texaco purchased Getty Oil stock and Pennzoil brought an action for tortious interference.

The question before the court was whether Pennzoil and Getty Oil had a binding agreement absent a definitive purchase agreement. On approval, the Court of Appeals for Texas, citing the language in the prospective stock buyer's draft and the term "agreement in principle" in the press release, found that there was a binding agreement.

Judgement was not rendered because Texaco won in a competitive tender offer situation. Rather, it was rendered pursuant to the jury's finding that Texaco had tortiously interfered with a binding agreement. A judgment based upon such a finding will not deter the "invitation of contests for corporate control throughout the country;" however, it should deter tortious interference with a binding agreement between parties.

Revlon Inc. v. McAndrews & Forbes Holdings, Inc., Del. Supr., 506 A.2d 173 (1986).

In June 1985 Pantry Pride approached Revlon to propose a friendly acquisition. Revlon declined the offer. In August 1985 Revlon's board recommended that shareholders reject the offer. Revlon then initiated certain defensive tactics. It sought other bidders. Pantry Pride raised its bid again. Revlon negotiated a deal with Forstmann Little, which included a lockup provision. Revlon also provided Forstmann additional financial information that it did not provide to Pantry Pride.

Eventually, an increased bid from Pantry Pride prompted an increased bid from Forstmann Little. The new bid was conditioned upon, among other things, the receipt by Forstmann Little of a lockup option to purchase two Revlon divisions at a price substantially lower than the lowest estimate of value established by Revlon's investment banker. It included a "no shop" provision that prevented Revlon from considering bids from any third party. The board immediately accepted the Forstmann Little offer even though Pantry Pride had increased its bid.

The questions before the court were (1) whether the lockup agreements were permitted under Delaware law and (2) whether the Revlon board acted prudently. The Delaware Supreme Court held the following:

- Lockups and related agreements are permitted under Delaware law where their adoption is untainted by director interest or other breaches of fiduciary duties.
- Actions taken by directors in this case did not meet that standard.
- Concern for various corporate constituencies is proper when addressing a takeover threat.
- Proper concern for multiple constituencies is limited by the requirement that there be some rationally related benefits accruing to the stockholders.
- There were no such benefits in this case.
- When sale of a company becomes inevitable, the duty of a board of directors changes from preservation of the corporate entity to maximization of the company's value at a sale for the stockholders' benefit. (This has come to be called the Revlon Doctrine.)
- The board's actions are not protected by the business judgment rule.

CASES ALLEGING VIOLATION OF SECURITIES LAWS (RE CHAPTER 6)

Basic, Inc. v. Levinson, 485 U.S. 224 (1988).

The plaintiff was a group of shareholders who sold stock in Basic, Inc., prior to formal announcement of a merger that caused Basic stock to rise. Basic spokespersons had denied that the merger was under consideration. The stockholders brought an action under Rule 10b-5 alleging material misrepresentation.

The question before the court was whether the public statements denying merger talks constituted material misrepresentation. The U.S. Supreme Court ruled that it is not proper to deny that a company is engaged in merger talks when, in fact, it is so engaged. In handing down its ruling, the Supreme Court rejected the "bright line" test for materiality offered in an earlier Sixth Circuit Court of Appeals decision. Materiality must be decided on a case-by-case basis, opined the High Court.

The standard for determining materiality is basically whether the reasonable investor's decision to vote would have been affected had he or she known the true facts. Materiality in the merger context depends on a balancing of the *probability* that a transaction will be consummated, and the *significance* of its potential impact on the company itself.

In this instance, negotiations were material—even though the talks had not yet resulted in any agreement on the price and structure of the transaction. The Supreme Court said that the appropriate response to an inquiry about undisclosed merger talks is either "no comment" or disclosure that the talks are taking place.

Koppers Co., Inc., v. American Express Co., 689 F. Supp. 1371 (W.D. Pa. 1988).

Koppers Co., Inc., brought an action against American Express, Shearson Lehman Brothers, and others seeking to enjoin the parties' hostile tender offer based upon Kopper's allegations that the tender offer violated federal securities laws (more specifically, certain disclosure requirements). American Express and the other defendants requested a preliminary injunction ordering Koppers to correct allegedly misleading statements regarding the tender offer.

The U.S. District Court for the Western District of Pennsylvania went to great lengths in the opinion to state that the case was difficult, the facts were intricate and complicated, and the law was unclear. The court stated that it would not hesitate to enjoin a tender offer until compliance with securities laws could be determined. Citing the purpose and intent of Congress in enacting the various securities laws and regulations, the court also concluded that "it is more prudent to err on the side of disclosure than obfuscation."

But the court also noted that the Williams Act (of 1968, regarding tender offers) does not require that a tender offeror disclose all information that it possesses about itself or the target company. Rather, it is required to disclose only those material objective factual matters that a reasonable stockholder would consider important in deciding whether to tender shares.

CTS Corp. v. Dynamics Corp. of America, 481 U.S. 69. (This case basically overturned Edgar v. MITE Corp.,[6] opening up the floodgates for state antitakeover statutes.)

Dynamics Corp. of America announced a tender offer for CTS Corp., an Indiana corporation. Six days prior the tender offer, the State of Indiana revised its business corporation law to include a provision affecting control via acquisition. The revised law allowed Indiana corporations to condition acquisition of control of the business on the approval of the majority of the preexisting disinterested shareholders. Dynamics brought suit to enjoin the enforcement of this statute, citing *Edgar v. MITE.*

The question before the court was whether the Indiana Act was preempted by the federal securities laws as amended by the Williams Act or by the commerce clause of the U.S. Constitution. The U.S. Supreme Court, approving the legality of the statute, held that the Indiana Act would be preempted by the federal securities laws only if it frustrated the purposes of those laws. In effectively overturning *MITE,* the *CTS* case allowed states to reenact, with some changes, the antitakeover laws that *MITE* had struck down.

Edelman v. Fruehauf Corp., 798 F.2d 882 (6th Cir. 1986).

In February 1986 the Edelman Group began acquiring Fruehauf stock on the open market. Edelman attempted a friendly acquisition, which Fruehauf's board of directors rejected. Subsequently, members of Fruehauf's management negotiated a two-tier leveraged buyout along with Merrill Lynch. A special committee of Fruehauf's outside directors approved the management-led buyout. Edelman sought a preliminary injunction restraining Fruehauf from completing the buyout.

The question before the court was whether the outside directors breached their fiduciary duty to the company. The Sixth Circuit Court of Appeals held that Fruehauf's board of directors, in using corporate funds to finance the buyer, did not act in good faith to negotiate the best deal for shareholders and thus breached their fiduciary duty to the shareholders. Moreover, the court stated that once it becomes apparent that a takeover target will be acquired by new owners, it becomes the duty of the directors to see that the shareholders obtain the best possible price.

Gollust v. Mendell, 498 U.S. 1023 (1991).

Mendell filed a § 16(b) (insider trading) complaint against a collection of limited partnerships, general partnerships, individual partners, and corporations alleging that these entities, acting as one, were liable for § 16(b) violations with regard to trading activities of Viacom stock. Six months after the complaint was filed, Viacom was acquired by another company and Mendell exchanged his Viacom stock for the new stock. The question before the court was whether a § 16(b) action can be pursued by any party other than an issuer or holder of a security.

The U.S. Supreme Court held that it was not necessary for a plaintiff to continue to hold stock of the issuer in order to maintain a § 16(b) action where the plaintiff has a financial stake in the parent corporation of the issuer. A shareholder whose shares in an issuer are converted by a business restructuring into shares of a newly formed parent corporation that owns all of the stock of the issuer does not lose standing to maintain a previously instituted § 16(b) suit. However, the Court also stated that the plaintiff who seeks to recover insider profits must own a security of the issuer whose stock is traded by the § 16(b) defendant.

Litton Industries, Inc. v. Lehman Brothers Kuhn Loeb Inc., 967 F.2d 742 (2nd Cir. 1992).

In 1982 Litton Industries, Inc., decided to expand its business through an acquisition. Litton retained Lehman Brothers to assist in its search for a suitable target. After Litton had decided upon Itek Corporation as its target, Litton acted upon Lehman Brothers' acquisition strategy.

Information regarding Litton's plans to acquire Itek was passed from Ira Sokolow, a member of the Lehman Brothers team working on the acquisition, to Dennis Levine, who began purchasing large blocks of Itek stock through offshore banks. Litton brought an action against Lehman Brothers, Sokolow, Levine, and the offshore banks, alleging that if they had not engaged in insider trading, Litton could have acquired Itek at a lower purchase price.

The question before the court was whether the insider trading, aside from its illegality, caused Litton harm with respect to its merger with Itek. More specifically, was the purchase price artificially inflated as a result of the insider trading? To recover, Litton must establish three "links:" (1) the trader appellees purchased stock on the basis of misappropriated information; (2) this trading inflated the market price of Itek stock; and (3) the Itek Board of Directors would have accepted a lower offer from Litton, if not for the artificially inflated market price of Itek stock. The Second Circuit Court of Appeals found that there was a genuine issue of material fact concerning whether Litton would have acquired Itek at a lower price absent the insider trading, and remanded the case back to the district court.

Martin Marietta Corp. v. Bendix Corp., 549 F. Supp. 623 (D.C. Md. 1982).

In August 1982 the Bendix Corp. announced a tender offer for approximately 45 percent of Martin Marietta Corp.'s common stock. On August 30, 1982, as a direct response to Bendix's tender offer, Martin Marietta announced its tender offer for approximately 51 percent of Bendix's common stock. In September 1982 United Technologies Corp. jumped into the fray and announced its tender offer for approximately 51 percent of Bendix's common stock. All three tender offers were considered hostile.

All three corporations brought actions in federal court to enjoin each other's tender offers. Each alleged that the tender offer in question was a violation of the antitrust laws. Martin Marietta sought a preliminary injunction against the Bendix tender offer on the grounds that Bendix made misrepresentations and omissions in its disclosures of material in violation of the Williams Act.

The question before the court was whether Bendix's disclosures violated the Williams Act. The U.S. District Court said they did not, counseling the parties to bear in mind the oft-quoted words of Judge Henry Friendly:

> Probably there will no more be a perfect tender offer than a perfect trial. Congress intended to assure basic honesty and fair dealing, not to impose an unrealistic requirement of laboratory conditions that might make the new statute a potent tool for incumbent management to protect its own interests against the desires and welfare of the stockholders. It would be as serious an infringement of these regulations to overstate the definiteness of the plans as to understate them.

Paramount Communications Inc. v. QVC Network Inc., Del. Supr., 637 A.2d 34.

On September 12, 1993, the board of Paramount Communications Inc. announced a proposed merger with Viacom Inc. Viacom was offering $69.14 per share in cash for controlling interests, with the remainder of the purchase price to be paid in stock. On September 27 Paramount directors rebuffed a comparably structured $80 per share bid from QVC Network Inc., saying they would not talk unless QVC could show evidence of financing. On November 15 Paramount directors refused a revised $90 per share offer on the grounds that it was too conditional.

Meanwhile, Paramount and Viacom continued to plan their merger. As Viacom's offer rose to the $85 per share level, Paramount granted Viacom an option to buy Paramount stock and promised to pay a termination fee in the event that Paramount rejected Viacom as a bidder. Paramount also made plans to redeem a shareholder rights ("poison pill") plan.

QVC sued Paramount and Viacom in the Chancery Court of Delaware, seeking to prevent these actions. The court upheld the termination fee, which it found a "fair liquidated amount to cover Viacom's expenses," but it handed QVC a victory on the other two points. The Chancery Court decision was upheld by the Delaware Supreme Court in a December 9 order, followed by a formal opinion on February 4, 1994.

In its opinion, the Delaware Supreme Court, concurring with the Chancery Court, stated repeatedly that directors in a "sale or change of control" must seek to obtain "the best value reasonably available to the stockholders." In cases that do not involve a sale or change of control, however, the court recognized "the prerogative of a board of directors to resist a third party's acquisition proposal or offer." (The *Paramount* decision spurred Paramount directors to set forth bidding rules in a contest to be decided by shareholders by a certain date. Viacom offered shareholders $105 per share, with certain protections against loss in share value. QVC offered $107 per share, but without such protections. The market chose Viacom, and the rest is history.)

When change of control is not at issue, the court gives great deference to the substance of the directors' decision and will not invalidate the decision, will not examine its reasonableness, and will not substitute its views for those of the board if latter's decision can be attributed to any rational business purpose. In sale or change of control situation, directors have burden of proving that they are adequately informed and acted reasonably.

Virginia Bankshares, Inc. v. Sandberg, 501 U.S. 1083 (1991).

This case occurred as part of a proposed "freeze-out" merger, in which First American Bank of Virginia (Bank) would be merged into petitioner Virginia Bankshares, Inc. (VBI), a wholly owned subsidiary of petitioner First American Bankshares, Inc. (FABI). The Bank's executive committee and board approved a price of $42 a share for the minority stockholders, who would lose their interests in the Bank after the merger. Virginia law required only that the merger proposal be submitted to a vote at a shareholders' meeting, preceded by a circulation of an informational statement to the shareholders. Nonetheless, Bank directors solicited proxies for voting on the proposal.

This solicitation urged the proposal's adoption and stated that the plan had been approved because of its opportunity for the minority shareholders to receive a "high" value for their stock. Respondent Sandberg did not tender her proxy and filed suit in District Court after the merger was approved. She sought damages from petitioners for, among other reasons, soliciting proxies by means of materially false or misleading statements in violation of Section 14(a) of the Securities Exchange Act of 1934 and the Securities and Exchange Commission's Rule 14a-9.

Among other things, Sandberg alleged that the directors believed they had no alternative but to recommend the merger if they wished to remain on the board. At trial, she obtained a jury instruction, based on language in *Mills v. Electric Auto-Lite Co.*, 396 U.S. 375, 385, that she could prevail without showing her own reliance on the alleged misstatements, so long as they were material and the proxy solicitation was an "essential link" in the merger process. Sandberg was awarded an amount equal to the difference between the offered price and her stock's true value. The remaining respondents prevailed in a separate action raising similar claims.

The Court of Appeals affirmed, holding that certain statements in the proxy solicitation, including the one regarding the stock's value, were materially misleading, and that respondents could maintain the action even though their votes had not been needed to effectuate the merger.

The U.S. Supreme Court ruled that the misstatements were material, but that if the solicitation of proxies was done purely for public relations purposes, the solicitation would not be an "essential link" in the merger process, and the misstatements would, thus, not be actionable.

Treadway Companies, Inc. v. Care Corp., 638 F.2d 357 (2d Cir. 1980).

In 1978 Care Corp. started acquiring shares of stock in Treadway Co., leading Treadway to believe that Care was mounting a hostile takeover. In response to this action, Treadway put certain officers of Care on its board. Then, without fully informing the Care representatives, the Treadway board sought other merger candidates and struck a deal with Fair Lanes. Care filed an action alleging violations of Section 13(d) of the 1934 Securities Exchange Act, breach of fiduciary duties, and misuse of confidential information.

The question before the U.S. District Court for the Southern District of New York was whether the directors had acted improperly in their actions arising out of a struggle for control of their company. The District Court entered a judgment in favor of Care Corp., two of its directors, and another individual. The U.S. Court of Appeals for the Second Circuit held that a director does not breach his or her fiduciary duty merely by supporting an effort or promoting a change of management. Moreover, a director does not owe his or her fiduciary duty directly to shareholders with respect to shares of stock they own and has no obligation to afford other shareholders an opportunity to participate in sale of stock.

Time Incorporated v. Paramount Communications Inc., 517 A.2d 1140 (Del. 1990).

In July 1989 the Delaware Chancery Court ruled that Time Inc. should be allowed to proceed with its planned $14 billion acquisition of Warner Communications, Inc., despite protest from would-be hostile acquirer Paramount, alleging violation of various securities laws. In a landmark 79-page decision affirmed later by the Delaware Supreme Court, Chancellor William T. Allen declared that "corporation law does not operate on the theory that directors, in exercising their powers to manage the firm, are obligated to follow the wishes of a majority of shares. In fact, directors, not shareholders, are charged with the duty to manage the firm."

This decision was widely considered to be an affirmation of the so-called business judgment rule, a judicial doctrine that protects decisions of directors, in their exercise of discretion based on informed judgment, from second-guessing by plaintiffs and judges. On the other hand, several legal commentators noted at the time of the decision that it did not necessarily cover instances of a sale or change of control, as in the classic case of *Revlon* (1985).

Sure enough, in a 1994 case involving Paramount and QVC, the court drew this change-of-control distinction, denying the protections of the business judgment rule to Paramount directors because the transaction they were considering did involve a change of control. (See *QVC Network Inc. v. Paramount Inc., Viacom Inc., et al.* (Del.1994), above.)

CASES ALLEGING VIOLATION OF TAX LAWS AND ACCOUNTING REGULATIONS (RE CHAPTER 7)

Indopco, Inc. v. C.I.R., 503 U.S. 79 (1992).

In 1977 Indopco, formerly named National Starch and Chemical Corporation, and Unilever United States, Inc., entered into a "reverse subsidiary cash merger" specifically designed to be a tax-free transaction for National Starch's largest shareholders.

In its 1978 federal income tax return, National Starch claimed a deduction for the approximately $2.3 million in investment banking fees it paid to Morgan Stanley & Co. as ordinary and necessary expenses under Section 162(a) of the U.S. Tax Code. The Internal Revenue Service disallowed the deduction and National Starch sought a redetermination, including the $490,000 legal fees it paid its attorney as well.

The question before the court was whether National Starch could deduct its expenses as ordinary and necessary business expenses.

The U.S. Tax Court and the Third Circuit Court of Appeals denied the deduction, saying that the expenses did not "create or enhance . . . a separate or distinct additional asset." The U.S. Supreme Court granted certiorari and held that investment banking, legal, and other costs incurred by the acquired corporation were not deductible as ordinary and necessary business expenses, but instead should be capitalized as long-term benefits to the corporation.

Newark Morning Ledger Co. v. United States, 507 U.S. 546 (1993).

In 1976 the Herald company purchased substantially all the outstanding shares of Booth Newspapers, Inc. The Herald Company, which was succeeded by the Newark Morning Ledger, claimed depreciation in the amount of $67.8 million, which represented the depreciable value of the future income stream from the newspaper's current subscribers.

The question before the U.S. Supreme Court was whether an intangible asset such as a subscriber list can be depreciated. The District Court entered a judgment in favor of Newark Morning Ledger Co. and the Court of Appeals for the Third Circuit reversed. The Supreme Court reversed the Court of Appeals, stating that an asset is depreciable if it is capable of being valued and if the asset's value diminishes over time. The Court concluded that if a taxpayer can prove that a particular asset can be valued, and that the asset has a limited useful life, the taxpayer may depreciate the asset's value over its useful life regardless of how much the asset appears to reflect the expectancy of continued patronage.[7]

CASES ALLEGING VIOLATION OF ANTITRUST AND TRADE LAWS (RE CHAPTER 8)

Olin Corporation v. Federal Trade Commission, 986 F.2d. 1295 (9th Cir. 1993).

In 1985 the Olin corporation entered into an agreement with the FMC corporation to purchase FMC's swimming pool chemicals business. Since the late 1970s Olin had been experiencing considerable difficulties in the manufacture of certain swimming pool sanitizing chemicals. The FMC assets that Olin was purchasing included the manufacturing plant for sanitizers.

The Federal Trade Commission challenged the acquisition on the grounds that it would violate federal antitrust laws. The FTC ordered Olin to divest itself of the assets it had acquired from FMC. An administrative law judge agreed with the commission and concluded that the acquisition would likely result in a substantial lessening of competition in the sanitizers' marketplace. Olin appealed the FTC's divestiture order.

The issue before the Court of Appeals for the Ninth Circuit was whether the FTC had the right to order Olin to divest itself of assets acquired through a merger and whether the acquisition would likely result in substantial lessening of competition. The Court of Appeals affirmed the FTC's ruling that Olin's acquisition of the assets would result in a substantial lessening of competition in the relevant markets. As such, the deal would violate Section 7 of the Clayton Act, 15 U.S.C. 18, and Section 5 of the Federal Trade Commission Act (FTC Act), 15 U.S.C. 45. The court went on to state that the FTC acted within its proper authority in ordering Olin to divest itself of the assets.

United States v. Philadelphia National Bank et al., 374 U.S. 321(1963).

In November 1960 the Philadelphia National Bank and the Girard Trust Corn Exchange Bank were the second and third largest commercial banks in the city of Philadelphia. The boards of directors for the two banks approved a merger of Girard into Philadelphia. The U.S. Department of Justice enjoined the merger, alleging that the consolidation violated the Sherman Antitrust Act and the Clayton Act. The U.S. District Court for the Eastern District of Pennsylvania ruled in favor of the banks, and the United States appealed.

The question before the Supreme Court was whether a merger that created anticompetitiveness and a monopoly violated the Clayton Act.

The Supreme Court rejected the banks' arguments that the merger did not violate the antitrust laws if it promoted the social good. A merger that substantially lessens competition is not saved from violation of the Clayton Act because, "on some ultimate reckoning of social or economic debits and credits, it may be deemed beneficial." The Court also stated that growth by internal expansion is "socially preferable to growth by acquisition."

CASES ALLEGING VIOLATION OF INTELLECTUAL PROPERTY LAWS (RE CHAPTER 9)

Electro Optical Industries v. White, 1999 Cal. App. LEXIS 1042 (Nov. 30, 1999).[8]

The plaintiff, Electro Optical Industries (EOI), supplied infrared testing devices to the military and to defense contractors. A key employee—Stephen White—abruptly left after 15 years to join Santa Fe Barbara Infrared, Inc. (SBIR), one of EOI's direct competitors. EOI asked the trial court for a preliminary injunction precluding White from participating in sales or development of infrared testing devices at SBIR. EOI argued that White knew trade secrets and, if permitted to work for SBIR, would inevitably use them. The trial court denied preliminary junction and EOI appealed.

In a California Appeals Court decision, the court adopted the doctrine of "inevitable disclosure," but said that instances must be decided on the basis of fact, and that the facts in this case favored the defendant. The court acknowledged that White possessed knowledge of certain EIO information. Some of the information was technical—namely, existing and future product designs, production methods, materials and process, and the status of patent applications. The court agreed that this information was a trade secret, but it stated that (1) White lacked the training to pass on the information, and (2) SBIR did not need the information. Some of the information was nontechnical, such as customer lists, sales prices, production costs, marketing plans, and sales strategies. But the court said these did not constitute trade secrets. As for customer preferences and specifications, the court said that this information was not a trade secret or, if it were, it would belong to the customer.

Feltner v. Columbia Pictures Television, Inc., 523 U.S. 340 (1998).

Respondent Columbia Pictures Television, Inc., terminated agreements licensing several television series to three television stations owned by petitioner Feltner after the stations' royalty payments became delinquent. When the stations continued to broadcast the programs, Columbia sued Feltner and others for, among other actions, copyright infringement. Columbia won partial summary judgment as to liability on its copyright infringement claims and then exercised the option afforded by Section 504(c) of the Copyright Act (Act) to recover statutory damages in lieu of actual damages. The District Court denied Feltner's request for a jury trial, and awarded Columbia statutory damages following a bench trial. The Ninth Circuit affirmed, holding that neither Section 504(c) nor the Seventh Amendment provide a right to a jury trial on statutory damages.

The Supreme Court reversed this decision. It held that there is no statutory right to a jury trial when a copyright owner elects to recover statutory damages. However, the Seventh Amendment of the Constitution provides a right to a jury trial on all issues pertinent to an award of statutory damages. Further, the Seventh Amendment applies to both common-law causes of action and to statutory actions.

The Court found close 18th-century analogues to Section 504(c) statutory damages actions. Before the adoption of the Seventh Amendment, the common law and statutes in England and this country granted copyright owners causes of action for infringement. More important, copyright suits for monetary damages were tried in courts of law, and thus before juries. There is no evidence that the first federal copyright law, the Copyright Act of 1790, changed this practice; and damages actions under the Copyright Act of 1831 were consistently tried before juries. The Court was unpersuaded by Columbia's contention that, despite this undisputed historical evidence, statutory damages are clearly equitable in nature.

Finally, the Court found that the right to a jury trial includes the right to have a jury determine the *amount* of statutory damages, if any, awarded to the copyright owner.

State Street Bank & Trust Co. v. Signature Financial Group, Inc., 149 F.3d 1368 (Fed. Cir. 1998).

The Federal Circuit reaffirmed the patentability of computer software and business processes, so long as these types of inventions meet other patent statutory requirements such as being new, useful, and nonobvious.

This case also showed that patentability does not turn on whether the claimed method does "business" instead of something else, but on whether the method, viewed as a whole, meets the requirements of patentability as set for in Sections 102, 103, and 112 of the Patent Act.

Niton Corp. v. Radiation Monitoring Devices, Inc., 27 F. Supp. 2d 102 (D. Mass. 1998).

In this case the court enjoined a certain use of metatags as a trademark infringement. Metatags are a hidden code detected by search engines looking for Web sites on a particular topic. The issue in question was using metatags in a way that could make Web searchers believe, incorrectly, that the defendant and the plaintiff, or their Web sites, are related.

Publications International, Ltd. v. Landoll, Inc., 164 F.3d 337 (7th Cir. 1998).

The court found that certain attributes of books—large pages and print, wipe-off covers, and gilt-edged pages—were aesthetically functional and not protectable as "trade dress." This weakened the protection of trade dress and boosted the doctrine of aesthetic functionality.

The term "trade dress" refers to the appearance of a product when that appearance is used to identify the producer. To function as an indentifier, the appearance must be distinctive by reason of the shape or color or texture or other visible or otherwise palpable feature of the product or its packaging. If it isn't distinctive, it won't be associated in the mind of the consumer with a specific producer. If it is distinctive, and if as a result it comes to identify the producer, the danger arises that the duplication of this appearance, this "trade dress," by a competing seller will confuse the consumer regarding the origin of the product; the consumer may think that it is the product of the producer whose trade dress was copied. Trade dress thus serves the same function as trademark, and is treated the same way by the Lanham Act and the cases interpreting it.

Pfaff v. Wells Electronics. Inc., 525 U.S. 55 (1998).

In this case, the Supreme Court resolved longstanding confusion about the "on-sale bar," which prevents patenting an invention that was "in public use or on sale in this country more than one year prior to the date of the application." The Supreme Court concluded that the on-sale bar applies when two conditions are satisfied: (1) the product must be the subject of a commercial offer for sale; and (2) the invention must be "ready for patenting," by being reduced to practice or the subject of a disclosure (i.e., a drawing) from which a person skilled in the art could practice the invention.

Qualitex Co. v. Jacobson Products Co., Inc. , 514 U.S. 159 (1995).

For years Qualitex Company had colored the dry-cleaning press pads it manufactured with a special shade of green gold. After respondent Jacobson Products (a Qualitex rival) began to use a similar shade on its own press pads, Qualitex registered its color as a trademark and added a trademark infringement count to the suit it had previously filed, challenging Jacobson's use of the green gold color. Qualitex won in the District Court, but the Ninth Circuit set aside the judgment on the infringement claim because, in its view, the Lanham Trademark Act of 1946 does not permit registration of color alone as a trademark.

The Supreme Court ruled unanimously that the Lanham Act permits the registration of a trademark that consists, purely and simply, of a color. The Court held that:

> Color alone can meet the basic legal requirements for use as a trademark is demonstrated both by the language of the Lanham Act, which describes the universe of things that can qualify as a trademark in the broadest of terms, 15 U.S.C.§1127, and by the underlying principles of trademark law, including the requirements that the mark "identify and distinguish [the seller's] goods . . . from those manufactured or sold by others and to indicate [their] source," *ibid.*, and that it not be "functional," see, e.g., *Inwood Laboratories, Inc. v. Ives Laboratories, Inc.*, 456 U.S. 844, 850, n. 10. The District Court's findings (accepted by the Ninth Circuit and here undisputed) show that Qualitex's green gold color has met these requirements. It acts as a symbol. Because customers identify the color as Qualitex's, it has developed secondary meaning, and thereby identifies the press pads' source. Also, the color serves no other function. (Although it is important to use *some* color on press pads to avoid noticeable stains, the Court found no competitive need in the industry for the green gold color, since other colors are equally usable.) Accordingly, unless there is some special reason that convincingly militates against the use of color alone as a trademark, trademark law protects Qualitex's use of its green gold color.

CASES ALLEGING VIOLATION OF CONSUMER PROTECTION LAWS (RE CHAPTER 10)

Geier v. American Honda Motor Company, Inc., USS 98-1811, 2000.

In 1992, Alexis Geier, driving a 1987 Honda Accord, collided with a tree and was seriously injured. The car was equipped with manual shoulder and lap belts, which Geier had buckled up at the time. The car was not equipped with airbags or other passive restraint devices. Geier and her parents sued the car's manufacturer, American Honda Motor Company, Inc., and its affiliates, under District of Columbia tort law, claiming, among other things, that American Honda had designed its car negligently and defectively because it lacked a driver's side airbag. The District Court dismissed the lawsuit, noting that the Federal Motor Vehicle Safety Standard gave car manufacturers a choice as to whether to install airbags. The court concluded that the National Traffic and Motor Vehicle Safety Act of 1966 preempted petitioners' lawsuit because it sought to establish an airbag requirement. The Court of Appeals affirmed.

The Supreme Court held: A common-law "no airbag" action conflicts with the Federal Motor Vehicle Safety Standard and is, therefore, preempted. The state tort law favored by petitioners stood as an "obstacle" to the accomplishment of the Federal Motor Vehicle Safety Standard's objective of developing a mix of alternative passive restraint devices for safety-related reasons.

Honda Motor Company Co., Ltd., et al. v. Oberg, 512 U.S. 415 (1994).

After finding petitioner Honda Motor Co., Ltd., liable for injuries that respondent Oberg received while driving a three-wheeled all-terrain vehicle manufactured and sold by Honda, an Oregon jury awarded Oberg $5 million in punitive damages, more than five times the amount of his compensatory damages award. In affirming, both the State Court of Appeals and the State Supreme Court rejected Honda's argument that the punitive damages award violated due process

Citing precedent, the U.S. Supreme Court reversed the lower courts' decisions, holding that Oregon's denial of review of the size of punitive damages awards violated the Fourteenth Amendment's due process clause. The Court held the following:

> (a) The Constitution imposes a substantive limit on the size of punitive damages awards . . . The opinions in these cases (case names and cites deleted) strongly emphasized the importance of the procedural component of the Due Process Clause, and suggest that the analysis here should focus on Oregon's departure from traditional procedures.
>
> (b) Judicial review of the size of punitive damages awards was a safeguard against excessive awards under the common law, and in modern practice in the federal courts and every State, except Oregon, judges review the size of such awards.
>
> (c) There is a dramatic difference between judicial review under the common law and the scope of review available in Oregon. Oregon law has provided no procedure for reducing or setting aside a punitive damages award where the only basis for relief is the *amount* awarded. No Oregon court for more than half a century has inferred passion or prejudice from the size of a damages award, and no court in more than a decade has even hinted that it might possess the power to do so. If courts had such power, the State Supreme Court would have mentioned it in responding to Honda's arguments in this very case. The review that is provided ensures only that there is evidence to support *some* punitive damages, not that the evidence supports the amount actually awarded, thus leaving the possibility that a guilty defendant may be unjustly punished.

(d) The court said that in the past it has found violation of due process where a party has been deprived of a well established common law protection against arbitrary and inaccurate adjudication. Punitive damages pose an acute danger of arbitrary deprivation of property, since jury instructions typically leave the jury with wide discretion in choosing amounts and since evidence of a defendant's net worth creates the potential that juries will use their verdicts to express biases against big businesses. Oregon has removed one of the few procedural safeguards that the common law provided against that danger without providing any substitute procedure and without any indication that the danger has in any way subsided over time.

(e) The safeguards that Oberg claims Oregon has provided—the limitation of punitive damages to the amount specified in the complaint, the clear and convincing standard of proof, preverdict determination of maximum allowable punitive damages, and detailed jury instructions—do not adequately safeguard against arbitrary awards. Nor does the fact that a jury's arbitrary decision to acquit a defendant charged with a crime is unreviewable offer a historic basis for such discretion in civil cases. The Due Process Clause says nothing about arbitrary grants of freedom, but its whole purpose is to prevent arbitrary deprivations of liberty or property.

Saratoga Fishing Co. v. J. M. Martinac & Co., et al., 520 U.S. 875 (1997).

This a complex case involving many parties and many issues. One issue was the liability of a manufacturer for a product that has been resold. The Supreme Court said that a series of resales should not progressively immunize a manufacturer from liability for foreseeable physical damage that would otherwise fall upon it. Such immunization could occur since the end user does not contract directly with the manufacturer, and it is more difficult for such a consumer to obtain the appropriate warranty on used products. Although nothing prevents a reseller from offering a warranty, said the Court, this does not often occur.

The ordinary rules of a manufacturer's tort liability should not be supplanted merely because the user/reseller may in theory incur an overlapping contract liability.

CASES ALLEGING VIOLATION OF ENVIRONMENTAL LAWS (RE CHAPTER 11)

Delaware County Redevelopment Authority v. McLaren/Hart, E.D. Pa. No. 97-3315, 1998 WL 181817 (April 16, 1998).

A redevelopment authority that purchased property in Pennsylvania relied on a consultant's report filed with the Resolution Trust Corporation (RTC). After purchasing the property, the redevelopment authority entered into a contract to sell the property. Prior to closing, the buyer and seller realized that the cost of the asbestos abatement at the site would be substantially higher than that anticipated based on the consultant's report. The redevelopment authority sued the consultant, with partial success. The court recognized the validity of the development authority's claim (as a third-party beneficiary) for breach of contract, but dismissed the plaintiff's claims for negligence and lost profits.

Grand Street Artists v. General Electric Co., D.N.J. 19 F. Supp. 2d 242 (August 25, 1998) and 28 F. Supp. 2d 291 (December 21, 1998).

In August 1998, the U.S. District Court denied summary judgment to an environmental consultant who had provided consulting services to a prior operator of the site in connection with its closure of operations. The closure of operations was required to be conducted under the oversight of the New Jersey Department of Environmental Protection pursuant to state law. As part of that process, the consultant's report was filed with the state. The current owner reviewed the filed report in conducting its preacquisition due diligence.

The report failed to mention the site's prior history in manufacturing involving mercury. After closing, the purchaser, a partnership of artists, learned that the building's interior was heavily contaminated with mercury and would be unsuitable for its intended use as residential condominiums. The court held that by participating in the process that resulted in it's report being filed with the state, thereby making it available to the public, the consultant could have foreseen that future purchasers would rely on it.

In December 1998, the court denied summary judgment to the individual property owners, who had acquired units in the condominium from the partnership in which they were partners. The court ruled that the individuals were not innocent purchasers under the Superfund law and therefore were strictly liable for cleanup. Even though the partnership acquired title to the property before the mercury contamination was discovered, the individual unit owners knew of contamination when they acquired their units. The court held that the relevant date for determining innocent purchaser status was the acquisition of units by the individual owners, not the acquisition of the entire property by the partnership.

Marsh v. New Jersey Department of Environmental Protection, New Jersey Supreme Court, 703 A.2d 927 (1997).

The New Jersey Department of Environmental Protection sued Marsh, a landowner, for leaking underground storage tanks on a property that Marsh had acquired. Counsel for Marsh established that she did not know of the leaking underground storage tanks when she purchased the property, and noted that the law's provisions relating to due diligence were enacted after the purchase. The court held that the due diligence provisions were an element of a defense to liability, rather than a duty imposed by law, and that therefore the timing was not relevant to the disposition of this case. The N.J. Supreme Court's ruling overturned an Appellate Division decision that allowed reimbursement from the state's Spill Compensation Fund. Marsh had to pay the cleanup costs herself.

CASES ALLEGING VIOLATION OF HEALTH, SAFETY, AND LABOR LAWS (RE CHAPTER 12)

Accardi v. Control Data, 836 F.2d 126 (2d Cir. 1987).
    The plaintiffs were former employees of International Business Machines (IBM) who worked for the BTSI division. In accord with the Employee Retirement Income Security Act of 1974 (ERISA), they received certain benefits. When IBM sold a predecessor of BTSI to Control Data Corporation (CDC), they entered into a "benefits agreement" under which CDC agreed to continue making benefits payments to the former employees of the division. On June 30, 1985, CDC sold BTSI to Automatic Data Processing (ADP) and the benefits payments stopped. The former BTSI employees requested continuation of their benefits.
    The question before the court was whether the plaintiffs were entitled to continued overall benefits under the IBM/CDC benefits agreement, and whether the denial of the plaintiff's request for continued benefits was arbitrary and capricious. The U.S. Court of Appeals for the Second Circuit stated that the plaintiffs were no longer eligible employees according to the terms of the benefits agreement. The court ruled that denial of continued benefits was not arbitrary and capricious.

Adcock v. Firestone Tire & Rubber Co., 822 F.2d 623 (6th Cir. 1987).
    The plaintiffs were nonunion salaried employees of Bridgestone Tire and Rubber Co. On January 1, 1983, Firestone Tire & Rubber Co. sold its Lavergne plant to Bridgestone for $55 million. The 75-page sales agreement included an "employee termination pay plan" stating that Firestone would not terminate the employment of any employee prior to the sale. It also stated that if Bridgestone reduced its workforce, any employee who lost his or her job would receive termination pay. At the time of the suit, Bridgestone had not reduced its workforce, so the plaintiffs remained employed. Nonetheless, they sought to receive termination pay.
    The question before the court was whether Firestone's interpretation of the termination pay plan was arbitrary and capricious. The U.S. Court of Appeals for the Sixth Circuit stated that Bridgestone's application of the termination pay plan was consistent with a fair reading of the plan, and that Firestone's interpretation and application of the termination pay plan was not arbitrary and capricious.
    Because separation policy described in the manager's manual of original employer and accepted by successor *did not address issue of severance benefits* in context of sale of division, but rather, discussed only voluntary resignation, mutual agreement resignation, and dismissal, and under former employer's separation policy, pay-

ment of severance benefits was *discretionary* and available only in cases of mutually agreed resignation or dismissal for substandard performance.

Blau v. Del Monte Corp., 748 F.2d 1348 (9th Cir. 1984).

In 1966 Del Monte Corp. purchased Granny Good, which became a wholly owned subsidiary of Del Monte. The employees of Granny Good became eligible for coverage under various Del Monte pension and benefit plans. In December 1980 Del Monte sold Granny Good to a group of investors. The new owners kept all but four employees. The four severed employees sued Del Monte for their severance benefits.

The question before the court was whether the denial of the severance benefits violated ERISA and whether the denial was arbitrary and capricious. The Ninth Circuit Court of Appeals held that the actions by Del Monte were arbitrary and capricious, violated ERISA, and that ERISA preempted employees' state common-law theories of breach of contract.

Blessit v. Retirement Plan for Employees of Dixie Engine Co., 817 F.2d 1528 (11th Cir. 1987) rec'd in part and rem'd 836 F.2d 1571 (11th Cir. 1988), vacated 848 F.2d 1164 (11th Cir. 1988).

The plaintiffs were employees of Dixie Engine Co. when it established an ERISA plan in 1972. Dixie Engine Co. was sold in 1982 and the ERISA plan was terminated. Employees brought action against their employer for violation of ERISA, claiming that upon termination of a defined benefits plan they were entitled to receive the full, unreduced pension benefits they would have received had they continued to work until normal retirement age.

The question before the court was whether ERISA requires the defined benefits plan to pay an employee the full, unreduced benefits the employee would have received had he or she continued to work until normal retirement age. The U.S. Court of Appeals for the Eleventh Circuit held that when a plan terminates, ERISA does not require that employees receive full benefits, only the benefits provided for under the plan (i.e., the benefits calculated on the basis of their actual years of service as of the termination date).

Fall River Dyeing and Finish Corp. v. NLRB, 482 U.S. 27, (1987).

In 1952 Sterlingwale began operating a textile dyeing plant; the plant continued to run for the next 30 years. For nearly its entire existence, the production and maintenance personnel of Sterlingwale were members of a union. Sterlingwale, along with the entire textile dyeing industry, began to suffer adverse economic conditions in late 1979. In February 1982 Sterlingwale laid off its employees and made an assignment for the benefit of its creditors.

In the fall of 1982 a former officer of Sterlingwale, together with the president of a creditor, formed an entity called Fall River Dyeing and Finish Corp. that purchased the assets of Sterlingwale from the auctioneer. Over time, the entity employed many former employees of Sterlingwale. The union requested that the entity recognize it as the bargaining agent for the employees, and the entity refused. The union then filed unfair labor practice charges with the National Labor Relations Board.

The question before the court was whether a successor employer is obligated to bargain with a union representing its predecessor's employees. The U.S. Supreme Court held that the successor employer's obligation to bargain with the union representing its predecessor's employees is contingent not only upon certification of the union but also on whether a majority of its employees were employed by its predecessor.

B.E. Tilley v. Mead Corp., 927 F.2d 756 (4th Cir. 1991).

The plaintiffs were employees of Lynchburg Foundry Company prior to its buyout by Mead Corporation. The employees then fell under the Mead retirement plan, which provided for early retirement benefits commencing at age 55. Subsequently, Mead sold off the foundry and terminated the plan. The plaintiffs received a sum of money equal to their portion of the present value of the plan reduced by 5 percent for each year the participant was under the age of 65. Plaintiffs sued Mead in Virginia state court, alleging that Mead's failure to pay the present value of the unreduced early retirement benefits violated ERISA. Mead removed the case to the Federal District Court for the Western District of Virginia, where the court granted Mead summary disposition, holding that the plaintiffs were not entitled to the unreduced early retirement benefits. The Court of Appeals for the Fourth Circuit reversed the District Court, and the Supreme Court reversed the Appellate Court and remanded the case back to the Court of Appeals.

The Court of Appeals held that, under the terms of ERISA, unreduced early retirement benefits that employees would have been eligible for upon reaching age 62 were "contingent liabilities" that had to be satisfied prior to reversion of the plan's surplus assets to the employer upon termination of the plan. They were not "accrued benefits" that employees had a vested right to receive in full upon plan termination.

ENDNOTES

1. Joseph McLaughlin of Brown & Wood LLP, op. cit. (Chapter 1, note 20).
2. Ibid. Other cases named by McLaughlin in this vein are *In re International Rectifier Securities Litigation* [1997 Tr. Binder] Fed. Sec. L. Rep. (CCH) par. 99, 469

(C.D. Cal. 1997); *Monroe v. Hughes*, 31 F.3d 772 (9th Cir. 1994); and *Weinberger v. Jackson* [1990–91 Tr. Binder] Fed. Sec. L. Rep. (CCH) par. 95, 693.

3. For a list of financial statement red flags, see Appendix 2A in Chapter 2.

4. Similar cases exonerating underwriters include *Weinberger v. Jackson* [1990–91] Fed. Sec. L. Rep. (CCH) par. 95, 693 at 98, 255 (D.D. Cal. 1990); *In re Worlds of Wonder Sec. Litig.*, 814 F. Supp. 850 (N.D. Cal. 1993), affd. in part, rev'd in part, 35 F.3d 1407 (9th Cir. 1994), cert. denied, 116 S. Ct. 185 (1995); *Phillips v. Kidder, Peabody & Co.*, 933 F. Supp. 303 (S.D.N.Y. 1996); *In re International Rectifier Sec. Litig.* [1997] Fed. Sec. L. Rep. (CCH) par. 99, 469 at 97, 135 (C.D. Cal. Mar. 31, 1997); and *Picard Chemical Inc. Profit Sharing Plan v. Perrigo Co.* 1998 U.S. Dist. LEXIS 11783 (W.D. Mich. June 15, 1998). The citations in this list were provided by William F. Alderman and John Kanberg, Orrick, Herrington, and Sutcliffe LLP, San Francisco, who served as counsel to the defendants in Software Toolworks (writing a friend-of-the-court brief for the Securities Industry Association), as well as *Worlds of Wonder*.

5. "High Court Rules That Health Insurers Can Be Sued for Fraud Under RICO," *The Wall Street Journal*, January 21, 1999, p. B8.

6. *Edgar v. MITE Corp.*, 457 U.S. 624 (1982). This case, now superseded by *CTS Corp. v. Dynamics Corp. of America*, struck down state antitakeover laws.

7. This case is consistent with later tax law.

8. This summary is adapted from a December 10, 1999, client letter from Fried, Frank, Harris, Shriver & Jacobson, entitled "One California Court Succumbs to the Inevitable: *EOI v. White* and the Doctrine of 'Inevitable Disclosure' of Trade Secrets by Departing Employees." The authors, Harvey J. Saferstein and three other attorneys in the Los Angeles office of the firm, note that "given the controversial nature of the doctrine, and California's historic policy favoring the employee's ability to compete . . . the EOI decision is likely to generate much discussion, debate, and further judicial scrutiny."

THE FEDERAL CIRCUIT COURTS

The Federal District Courts are divided into 11 regional circuits, as well as the United States Court of Appeals for the Federal Circuit. Each regional circuit has several district courts, and each district court has a bankruptcy court as well as a U.S. attorney and a U.S. marshal.

1st Circuit
Maine District
Massachusetts District
New Hampshire District
Rhode Island District
Puerto Rico District

2nd Circuit
Connecticut District
New York Eastern District
New York Northern District
New York Southern District
New York Western District
Vermont District

3rd Circuit
Delaware District
New Jersey District
Pennsylvania Eastern District
Pennsylvania Middle District
Pennsylvania Western District
Virgin Islands District

4th Circuit
Maryland District
North Carolina Eastern District
North Carolina Middle District
North Carolina Western District
South Carolina District
Virginia Eastern District
Virginia Western District
West Virginia Northern District
West Virginia Southern District

5th Circuit
Louisiana Eastern District
Louisiana Middle District
Mississippi Southern District
Texas Eastern District
Texas Northern District
Texas Southern District
Texas Western District

6th Circuit
Kentucky Eastern District
Kentucky Western District
Michigan Eastern District
Michigan Western District
Ohio Northern District
Ohio Southern District
Tennessee Eastern District
Tennessee Middle District
Tennessee Western District

7th Circuit
Illinois Central District
Illinois Northern District
Illinois Southern District
Indiana Northern District
Indiana Southern District
Wisconsin Eastern District
Wisconsin Western District

8th Circuit
Arkansas Eastern District
Arkansas Western District
Iowa Northern District
Iowa Southern District
Minnesota District
Missouri Eastern District
Missouri Western District
Nebraska District
North Dakota District
South Dakota District

9th Circuit
Alaska District
Arizona District
California Central District
California Eastern District
California Northern District
California Southern District
Guam District

Hawaii District
Idaho District
Montana District
Nevada District
Northern Mariana Islands District
Oregon District
Washington Eastern District
Washington Western District

10th Circuit
Colorado District
Kansas District
New Mexico District
Oklahoma Eastern District
Oklahoma Northern District
Oklahoma Western District
Utah District
Wyoming District

11th Circuit
Alabama Middle District
Alabama Northern District
Alabama Southern District
Florida Middle District
Florida Northern District
Florida Southern District
Georgia Middle District
Georgia Northern District
Georgia Southern District

12th Circuit
U.S. Court of Appeals for the Federal
   Circuit

INDEX

Alexandra Reed Lajoux is editor-in-chief, *Director's Monthly*, National Association of Corporate Directors, Washington, D.C., and senior consultant, E-Know, Inc., Herndon, Virginia. Dr. Lajoux is the author of *The Art of M&A Integration* and coauthor of *The Art of M&A: A Merger/Acquisition/Buyout Guide* and *The Art of M&A Financing and Refinancing*, all published by McGraw-Hill. Her work has appeared in *International Business, Los Angeles Times, M&A Today, Mergers & Acquisitions, Trustee*, and numerous other publications. The former editor of *Mergers & Acquisitions*, Dr. Lajoux has two decades of experience speaking and writing about M&A. A graduate of Bennington College, she holds an M.B.A. from Loyola College and a Ph.D. in Comparative Literature from Princeton University. A trustee of the Association of Princeton Graduate Alumni, she is listed in *Who's Who in American Women* (Marquis, 2000–2001).

Charles M. Elson is the Edgar S. Woolard, Jr. Professor of Corporate Governance and Director of the Center for Corporate Governance at the University of Delaware. He is "Of Counsel" to the Tampa law firm of Holland & Knight, LLP, and presently on leave from Stetson University College of Law where he has served as a professor since 1990. His fields of expertise include corporations, securities regulation, and corporate governance. He is a graduate of Harvard College and the University of Virginia Law School, and has served as a law clerk to judges of the United States Court of Appeals for the Fourth and Eleventh Circuits. He has been a Visiting Professor at the University of Illinois College of Law, the Cornell Law School, and University of Maryland School of Law. Professor Elson is a Salvatori Fellow at the Heritage Foundation in Washington, D.C., and a member of the American Law Institute. Professor Elson has written extensively on the subject of boards of directors and, he has served on five of the National Association of Corporate Directors' Blue Ribbon Commissions on various governance issues, and was a member of NACD's Best Practices Council on Coping with Fraud and Other Illegal Activity. He presently serves on NACD's Advisory Council. Additionally, Professor Elson served as an adviser and consultant to Towers Perrin, a director of Circon Corporation, and is presently a member of the Board of Directors of Sunbeam Corporation, Nuevo Energy Company, and the Investor Responsibility Research Center in Washington, D.C.